PATERNOSTER BIBLICAL MONOGRAPHS

# The Triumph of Grace in Deuteronomy

## Faithless Israel, Faithful Yahweh in Deuteronomy

PATERNOSTER BIBLICAL MONOGRAPHS

*A full listing of all titles in this series appears at the close of this book*

PATERNOSTER BIBLICAL MONOGRAPHS

# The Triumph of Grace in Deuteronomy

## Faithless Israel, Faithful Yahweh in Deuteronomy

Paul A. Barker

Foreword by Gordon J. Wenham

PATERNOSTER PRESS

First published 2004 by Paternoster Press

Paternoster Press is an imprint of Paternoster Publishing,
P.O. Box 300, Carlisle, Cumbria, CA3 0QS, U.K.
and
P.O. Box 1047, Waynesboro, GA 30830-2047, U.S.A.

10 09 08 07 06 05 04   7 6 5 4 3 2 1



**British Library Cataloguing in Publication Data**
A catalogue record for this book is available from the British Library

**ISBN 1-84227-226-8**

Typeset by Andrew Malone and printed and bound
in Great Britain by Nottingham Alpha Graphics

# Series Preface

One of the major objectives of Paternoster is to serve biblical scholarship by providing a channel for the publication of theses and other monographs of high quality at affordable prices. Paternoster stands within the broad evangelical tradition of Christianity. Our authors would describe themselves as Christians who recognise the authority of the Bible, maintain the centrality of the gospel message and assent to the classical credal statements of Christian belief. There is diversity within this constituency; advances in scholarship are possible only if there is freedom for frank debate on controversial issues and for the publication of new and sometimes provocative proposals. What is offered in this series is the best of writing by committed Christians who are concerned to develop well-founded biblical scholarship in a spirit of loyalty to the historic faith.

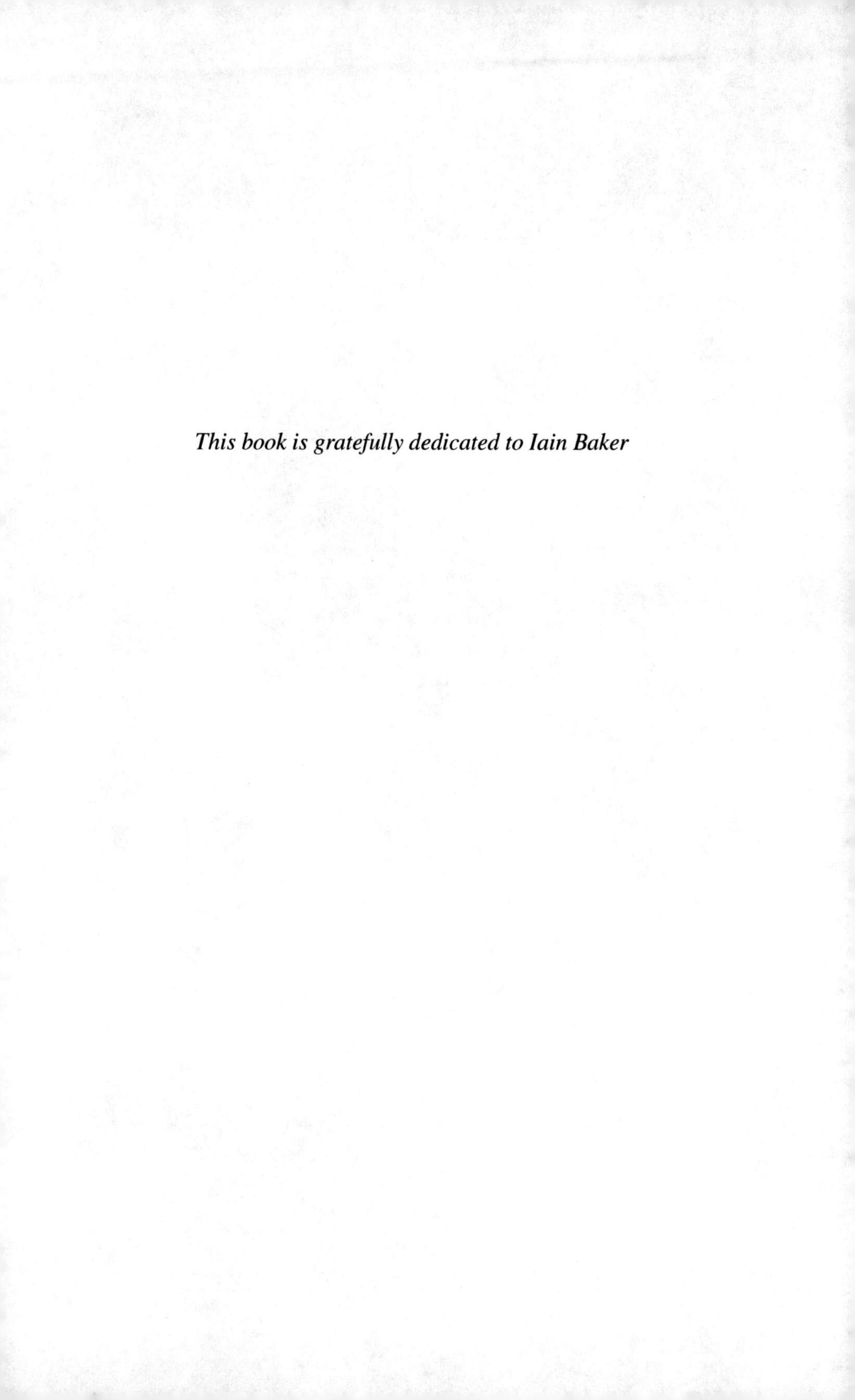

*This book is gratefully dedicated to Iain Baker*

# Contents

**Foreword** .......... xiii

**Preface** .......... xv

**Abbreviations** .......... xvii

**Introduction** .......... 1

**Chapter 1:**
**Faithless Israel, Faithful Yahweh in Deuteronomy 1–3** .......... 7
History of Interpretation .......... 7
Deuteronomy 1–3 as Introduction to Deuteronomy .......... 12
Faithless Israel in Deuteronomy 1 .......... 17
*Structure and Speeches* .......... 17
*Unholy War and Anti-Exodus* .......... 22
*Moses' Exclusion* .......... 23
*Paradigmatic Sin* .......... 24
*Good and Evil* .......... 29
Faithful Yahweh in Deuteronomy 1 .......... 30
*Yahweh's Promise* .......... 30
*Yahweh's Command* .......... 34
*Faithfulness and Faithlessness* .......... 34
Faithful Yahweh in Deuteronomy 2:1–3:20 .......... 36
*Structure of Deuteronomy 2:1–3:11* .......... 37
*Sihon and Og: Divine Initiative* .......... 41
*Transjordanian Land* .......... 43
*Edom, Moab, Ammon* .......... 44
*The Priority of Yahweh's Faithfulness* .......... 47
Moses in 3:21–29 .......... 48
*3:21–22* .......... 48
*3:23–25* .......... 49
*3:26–29* .......... 50
Conclusion .......... 51

**Chapter 2:**
**Faithless Israel, Faithful Yahweh in Deuteronomy 8–10 ................55**
Introduction........................................................................................55
Deuteronomy 8....................................................................................57
*Structure* ........................................................................................58
*Wilderness Test*...............................................................................64
*Israel's Heart and Knowledge*..........................................................68
*Observing the Commandments and Memory*...................................71
*Allusions to the Spies Incident*........................................................73
*Faithful Yahweh*...............................................................................73
*The Final Warning (8:19–20)*..........................................................76
*Conclusion* ......................................................................................77
Deuteronomy 9:1–6 ............................................................................78
*Introduction* ....................................................................................78
*Theology* ........................................................................................79
*Allusions to the Spies Incident*........................................................82
*Significance*.....................................................................................83
Deuteronomy 9:7–24 ..........................................................................84
*Structure* ........................................................................................85
*Israel's Sin* .......................................................................................86
*Allusions to the Spies Incident*........................................................91
*Significance*.....................................................................................92
Deuteronomy 9:25–10:11 ...................................................................93
*Moses' Intercessory Prayer (9:25–29)*.............................................94
*The Answer to the Prayer (10:1–11)* ...............................................98
Deuteronomy 10:12–22 ....................................................................101
*Structure* ......................................................................................102
*Theology* ......................................................................................103
Conclusion ........................................................................................106

**Chapter 3:**
**Faithless Israel, Faithful Yahweh in Deuteronomy 29–30 ............107**
Introduction to 28:69–30:20 ............................................................108
*Survey of Approaches* ...................................................................108
*28:69: Superscript or Subscript?*...................................................110
*Horeb and Moab*............................................................................112
Deuteronomy 29:1–8 ........................................................................117
*Structure* ......................................................................................117
*Responsibility for Knowledge* ......................................................119

*A Heart to Know* ........ 121
*Eyes to See* ........ 123
*Heart and Eyes* ........ 125
*Ears to Hear* ........ 126
*Conclusion* ........ 129
Deuteronomy 29:9–28 ........ 131
*29:9–14* ........ 131
*29:15–20* ........ 133
*29:21–27* ........ 137
*29:28* ........ 139
*Conclusion* ........ 140
Deuteronomy 30:1–10 ........ 140
*Structure* ........ 141
*The Priority of Yahweh* ........ 144
*The Heart* ........ 157
*The Patriarchal Promises* ........ 168
*Grace and Law* ........ 175
*The Frame of the Law* ........ 178
*Conclusion* ........ 181
Deuteronomy 30:11–14 ........ 182
*The Relationship of 30:11–14 to 30:1–10* ........ 182
*The Grounds for Israel's Capacity to Obey* ........ 187
*Deuteronomy 30:11–14 in Romans 10* ........ 194
*Conclusion* ........ 198
Deuteronomy 30:15–20 ........ 198
*Introduction* ........ 198
*Israel's Choice* ........ 200
*Absence of Israel's Reponse* ........ 202
*The Source of Life* ........ 206
*The Context of 30:15–20* ........ 209
*Conclusion* ........ 214

**Conclusion** ........ **217**

**Bibliography** ........ **223**

**Author Index** ........ **253**

**Scripture Index** ........ **259**

# Foreword

Hope is an elusive commodity. Is there a sure basis for it? On what does the Bible base its hope for the future? Ask these questions to an ordinary Bible reader and doubtless you would be given a variety of answers, but many would surely say that hope rests on the promises of God.

But is that true of the Old Testament? Do not the books of the law such as Deuteronomy insist that Israel's future depends on her obedience to the law? If the people break the covenant and disregard the law, they will be punished by drought, disease, defeat and exile. On the other hand if they keep it, they will be blessed by good harvests, health, prosperity and peace. Thus their future is essentially in their own hands: their action will determine their prospects.

Paul Barker in this important and well-researched book tackles these vital issues for the understanding of the Bible. Deuteronomy, many scholars contend, believes that Israel's future depends on her obedience and that Israel has the ability freely to choose whether to obey or not. Barker opposes this view. His argument is that Deuteronomy's hope rests not on Israel's potential fidelity to the law, but on God's proven fidelity to the promises he made to Abraham.

Deuteronomy reviews Israel's past behaviour and concludes that Israel's propensity to sin is congenital. When the spies brought back evidence of the goodness of the land, the people refused to move ahead because they doubted God's power to bring them into the land. Similarly the making and worship of the golden calf, so soon after they had witnessed God's saving power in the exodus and had been given the Ten Commandments demonstrate their natural bent away from God and obedience to his law.

The final chapters of the book look into the future and again envisage the likelihood of Israel sinning. Indeed they predict that the nation will end up exiled outside the land of promise. But that does not mean they have forfeited their special status as the chosen people. God's promises still hold, so if they repent, they will again enjoy his blessing. But how can they repent if they are so wont to sin? Deuteronomy's answer is: 'your God will circumcise your heart…so that you will love the LORD your God with all your heart and with all your soul, that you may live.' It is God's activity that is Israel's ultimate hope. He will fulfil his promise to the patriarchs by making their descendants willing and capable of keeping the law and so enjoying his promises.

This then is a most important discussion for anyone trying to understand the theology of Scripture and to preach it in a Christian context. But it is also a most thorough work that interacts with all the significant recent discussions of Deuteronomy in a very judicious way. I wholeheartedly recommend it.

Professor Gordon J. Wenham
*University of Gloucestershire*

# Preface

I am delighted that finally this thesis is being published. It was completed in 1995 under the title of 'Faithless Israel, Faithful Yahweh in Deuteronomy'. This book is a largely unchanged version of it, although I have accepted the suggestion of Professor Don Carson for the new title. I am grateful to Robin Parry, Commissioning Editor of Paternoster Press, for his encouragement and assistance in this process; to Andrew Malone for his hard work in preparing the text for publication; and to Ian Weickhardt for willingly compiling the indexes.

The Book of Deuteronomy remains a great love for me and since the completion of this thesis, I am thankful to God for the opportunities to teach and preach it afforded to me by Ridley College, Melbourne and Holy Trinity Doncaster, both of which I count a joy and privilege to serve.

This thesis was completed under the supervision of Professor Gordon Wenham at what was then the Cheltenham and Gloucester College of Higher Education and I am honoured that he has agreed to write the foreword to this book. His careful and thoughtful supervision challenged me and sharpened my thinking at many points. In addition, his warm encouragement and fellowship helped me persevere and complete my PhD. I am also very grateful for the stimulating responses of Professor John Barton, of Oxford University, my external supervisor, to this work. I also record my gratitude for the generous assistance of the library staff at the college. My study was greatly enhanced by the mutual support and interaction with my fellow post-graduate students and other lecturers in the Religious Studies Department.

It is appropriate to record my thanks for generous financial support from various sources that enabled me to study in England for three years: the Cheltenham and Gloucester College of Higher Education, the Archbishop of Melbourne, the Anglican Evangelical Trust of Melbourne, the Panahpur Trust, SPCK, and the Rector and Churchwardens of Cheltenham Parish Church.

I am especially grateful for the prayers, friendship and encouragement of many people, in England and Australia, during my three years of study, not least to the staff and congregation of St Matthew's Cheltenham who endured several sermons on Deuteronomy. In particular I am grateful to God for the close friendship begun in those years with Iain Baker who would pray with me each week for this work. This book is dedicated to him.

Paul Barker
*March 2004*

# Abbreviations

| | |
|---|---|
| AB | Anchor Bible |
| *ABD* | *Anchor Bible Dictionary* (ed. D.N. Freedman; Doubleday) |
| *AJSL* | *American Journal of Semitic Languages and Literature* |
| AnBib | Analecta Biblica |
| AOAT | Alter Orient und Altes Testament |
| ASOR | American Schools of Oriental Research |
| *AsTJ* | *Asbury Theological Jounrnal* |
| ATANT | Abhandlungen zur Theologie des Alten und Neuen Testaments |
| *ATJ* | *Ashland Theological Journal* |
| AUS | American University Studies |
| *AUSS* | *Andrews University Seminary Studies* |
| AV | Authorised Version (King James Version) |
| *BASOR* | *Bulletin of the American Schools of Oriental Research* |
| BBB | Bonner biblische Beiträge |
| BBC | Broadman Bible Commentary |
| *BBR* | *Bulletin for Biblical Research* |
| *BCPE* | *Bulletin du Centre protestant d'études* |
| BDB | *Hebrew and English Lexicon of the Old Testament* (ed. F. Brown, S.R. Driver, C.A. Briggs) |
| BEATAJ | Beiträge zur Erforschung des Alten Testaments und des Antiken Judentums |
| BETһL | Bibliotheca ephemeridum theologicarum lovaniensium |
| *BI* | *Biblical Interpretation* |
| BIBALCE | Berkeley Institute of Biblical Archaeology and Literature Collected Essays |
| *BibBh* | *Bible Bhashyam* |
| *BibLeb* | *Bibel und Leben* |
| *BibRes* | *Biblical Research: Journal of the Chicago Society of Biblical Research* |
| *BibRev* | *Bible Review* |
| *BibSac* | *Bibliotheca Sacra* |

| | |
|---|---|
| BJS | Brown Judaic Studies |
| *BN* | *Biblische Notizen* |
| BNTC | Black's New Testament Commentaries |
| BSC | Bible Students Commentary |
| BST | Bible Speaks Today Commentary |
| *BTB* | *Biblical Theology Bulletin* |
| *BTFT* | *Bijdragen Tijdschrift vor Filosophie en Theologie* |
| BWANT | Beiträge zur Wissenschaft vom Alten und Neuen Testament |
| *BZ* | *Biblische Zeitschrift* |
| BZAW | Beihefte zur Zeitschrift für die alttestamentliche Wissenschaft |
| CBC | Cambridge Bible Commentary |
| *CBQ* | *Catholic Biblical Quarterly* |
| CBSC | Cambridge Bible for Schools and Colleges |
| *ConsJud* | *Conservative Judaism* |
| ContBot | Coniectanea Biblica Old Testament Series |
| *CTJ* | *Calvin Theological Journal* |
| *CTM* | *Concordia Theological Monthly* |
| *CTQ* | *Concordia Theological Quarterly* |
| CUP | Cambridge University Press |
| *Das Deut* | *Das Deuteronomium: Entstehung, Gestalt und Botschaft* (BEThL 68; ed. N. Lohfink; Leuven University Press) |
| DNEB | Die Neue Echter Bibel |
| *DP* | *Deutsches Pfarrerblatt* |
| DSB | Daily Study Bible |
| *EBC* | *Expositor's Bible Commentary* |
| *EglT* | *Église et Théologie* |
| *EJT* | *European Journal of Theology* |
| *EThL* | *Ephemerides theologicae lovanienses* |
| *EvT* | *Evangelische Theologie* |
| FS | Festschrift |
| *FZPhTh* | *Freiburger Zeitschrift für Philosophie und Theologie* |
| *GKC* | *Gesenius' Hebrew Grammar* |
| GTA | Göttinger theologische Arbeiten |
| *GTJ* | *Grace Theological Journal* |
| *HAR* | *Hebrew Annual Review* |
| HAT | Handbuch zum Alten Testament |
| HBS | Herders biblische Studien |
| HKAT | Handkommentar zum Alten Testament |
| HSM | Harvard Semitic Monographs |
| *HTR* | *Harvard Theological Review* |
| *HTS* | *Hervormde Teologiese Studies* |
| *HUCA* | *Hebrew Union College Annual* |
| HUP | Harvard University Press |
| *IB* | *The Interpreter's Bible* (ed. G.A. Buttrick; Abingdon Press) |

| | |
|---|---|
| *IBS* | *Irish Biblical Studies* |
| IBT | Interpreting Biblical Texts |
| ICC | International Critical Commentary |
| *IDB* | *Interpreter's Dictionary of the Bible* (ed. G.A. Buttrick; Abingdon Press) |
| *IEJ* | *Israel Exploration Journal* |
| *Int* | *Interpretation* |
| ITC | International Theological Commentary |
| *ITQ* | *Irish Theological Quarterly* |
| *JAC* | *Jahrbuch für Antike und Christentum* |
| *JAOS* | *Journal of the American Oriental Society* |
| *JBL* | *Journal of Biblical Literature* |
| JBLMS | Journal of Biblical Literature Monograph Series |
| *JBTh* | *Jahrbuch für Biblische Theologie* |
| *JETS* | *Journal of the Evangelical Theological Society* |
| *JJS* | *Journal of Jewish Studies* |
| *JNES* | *Journal of Northeast Semitic Languages* |
| *JNSL* | *Journal of Norhwest Semitic Languages* |
| *JPOS* | *Journal of the Palestine Oriental Society* |
| *JPT* | *Journal of Pentecostal Theology* |
| JSNTSup | Journal for the Study of the New Testament Supplement Series |
| *JSOT* | *Journal for the Study of the Old Testament* |
| JSOTSup | Journal for the Study of the Old Testament Supplement Series |
| *JSS* | *Journal of Semitic Studies* |
| KAT | Kommentar zum Alten Testament |
| KB | *Lexicon in Veteris Testamenti libros* (ed. L. Koehler, W. Baumgartner) |
| KHAT | Kurzer Hand-Commentar zum Alten Testament |
| LBC | The Layman's Bible Commentary |
| NAC | New American Commentary |
| *NBC* | *New Bible Commentary: 21st Century Edition* (ed. D.A. Carson; R.T. France, J.A. Motyer, G.J. Wenham; IVP) |
| NCBC | New Century Bible Commentary |
| *NGTT* | *Nederuitse gereformeerde teologiese tydskrif* |
| NICNT | New International Commentary on the New Testament |
| NICOT | New International Commentary on the Old Testament |
| NIV | New International Version |
| *NTS* | *New Testament Studies* |
| *NTSup* | *Supplements to Novum Testamentum* |
| *NZSThR* | *Neue Zeitschrift für Systematische Theologie und Religionsphilosophie* |
| OBT | Overtures to Biblical Theology |
| *OTE* | *Old Testament Essays* |

| | |
|---|---|
| OTG | Old Testament Guide |
| OTL | Old Testament Library |
| OTM | Old Testament Message |
| *OTS* | *Oudtestamentliche Studiën* |
| OUP | Oxford University Press |
| PEF | Palestine Exploration Fund |
| *PEQ* | *Palestine Exploration Quarterly* |
| PFES | Publications of the Finnish Exegetical Society |
| *PIBA* | *Proceedings of the Irish Biblical Association* |
| POS | Pretoria Oriental Series |
| PTMS | Pittsburgh Theological Monograph Series |
| *PTSB* | *Princeton Theological Seminary Bulletin* |
| *RB* | *Revue Biblique* |
| RBC | Religious Book Club |
| *RestQ* | *Restoration Quarterly* |
| *RevExp* | *Review and Expositor* |
| *RSR* | *Recherches de science religieuse* |
| RSV | Revised Standard Version |
| *RTP* | *Revue de Théologie et de Philosophie* |
| *RTR* | *Reformed Theological Review* |
| *RUO* | *Revue de l'Université d'Ottowa* |
| SBAB | Stuttgarter Biblische Aufsatzbände |
| SBLDS | Society for Biblical Literature Dissertation Series |
| *SBLSPS* | *Society of Biblical Literature Seminar Paper Series* |
| SBS | Stuttgarter Bibelstudien |
| SBT | Studies in Biblical Theology |
| SBTS | Sources for Biblical and Theological Study |
| *SJT* | *Scottish Journal of Theology* |
| SOTBT | Studies in Old Testament Biblical Theology |
| SSLL | Studies in Semitic Languages and Linguistics |
| SSN | Studia Semitica Neerlandica |
| *Studies* | *Studies in Deuteronomy: In Honour of C.J. Labuschagne on the Occasion of His 65th Birthday* (VTSup 53; ed. F. García Martínez, A. Hilhorst, J.T.A.G.M. van Ruiten, A.S. van der Woude; E.J. Brill) |
| *SWJT* | *Southwestern Journal of Theology* |
| TBC | Torch Bible Commentary |
| TCC | The Communicator's Commentary |
| *TDNT* | *Theological Dictionary of the New Testament* (ed. G. Friedrich; trans. G.W. Bromiley; Eerdmans) |
| *TDOT* | *Theological Dictionary of the Old Testament* (ed. G.J. Botterweck, H. Ringgren, H.-J. Fabry; trans. J.T. Willis, G.W. Bromiley, D.E. Green; Eerdmans) |

| | |
|---|---|
| *THAT* | *Theologisches Handwörterbuch zum Alten Testament* (ed. E. Jenni, C. Westermann; Chr. Kaiser Verlag) |
| *ThPh* | *Theologie und Philosophie* |
| *TJ* | *Trinity Journal* |
| *TLZ* | *Theologische Literaturzeitung* |
| TNTC | Tyndale New Testament Commentaries |
| TOTC | Tyndale Old Testament Commentaries |
| *TR* | *Theologische Rundschau* |
| *TS* | *Theological Studies* |
| TSF | Theological Students' Fellowship |
| *TWAT* | *Theologisches Wörterbuch zum Alten Testament* (ed. G.J. Botterweck, H. Ringgren; Eerdmans) |
| *TynBull* | *Tyndale Bulletin* |
| *TZ* | *Theologische Zeitschrift* |
| UCOP | University of Cambridge Oriental Publications |
| *UF* | *Ugarit Forschungen* |
| *VT* | *Vetus Testamentum* |
| VTSup | Supplements to Vetus Testamentum |
| WBC | Word Biblical Commentary |
| WCB | World Christian Books |
| *WTJ* | *Westminster Theological Journal* |
| *ZAW* | *Zeitschrift für die alttestamentliche Wissenschaft* |
| ZB | Zürcher Bibelkommentare |
| *ZTK* | *Zeitschrift für Theologie und Kirche* |

# Introduction

Deuteronomy is sometimes described as an idealistic book, portraying Israel as it should be to the Israel that is.[1] It sets out a pattern for a utopian paradise which is premised on the complete, and expected, obedience of Israel. So Hoppe claims,

> Judah's future is absolutely dependent upon her obedience to traditional moral and religious obligations which are found in the collection of law which comprise (sic) the book's core.... obedience is the key to Israel's future.[2]

Similarly von Rad suggests that, "In the view of the Deuteronomic preacher, it is perfectly possible to fulfil the commandments, indeed, they are easy to fulfil."[3] Such a description is simplistic, even misguided. Deuteronomy's portrayal and expectation of Israel reflect more subtlety than this. This study will argue that Deuteronomy expects Israel to fail and that optimism is grounded in Yahweh, not Israel. If Israel were the only factor to consider, the book would be totally pessimistic. Indeed Deuteronomy exists only because Israel failed.[4]

The expectation of Israel's failure in Deuteronomy is concentrated towards the end of the book. Thus, for example, the curses far outweigh the space accorded the blessings in chapters 27 and 28, fourteen verses for the latter, sixty-six for the former. In addition, passages such as 31:16–17, 27–29 and 32:1–43 are quite gloomy.[5] This pessimism towards the end suggests the real direction of the book. Yet there is also expectation of Israel's failure early in Deuteronomy. This is explicit in 4:25–28, a passage which forms a frame, with 29:15–27, around the law, suggesting that the law should be read in the light of Israel's expected failure.

This study, concerned with Israel's failure is limited to three sections of Deuteronomy. These are the three major accounts of Israel failing: the

1 So Mayes (1979) 56–57. Also Holladay (1985) 326; Nicholson (1991) 191.

2 Hoppe (1985) 109–110.

3 Von Rad (1965) 393.

4 Rennes, 193.

5 Alexander (1995) 182.

retelling of the spies incident (1:19–46), the retelling of the golden calf incident (9:1–10:11), and the future prediction of failure and exile in 29:15–27.[6] Each of these is significant within Deuteronomy, though the negative assessment of Israel is often overlooked.

Israel's expected failure is, however, only one side of the coin. We are also concerned with the resolution of failure in each of these three incidents. None of them is purely negative. Each expresses hope beyond failure. Significantly, in each case, this hope is grounded, not in any change or repentance of Israel, nor in the general grace or mercy of Yahweh, but specifically in his faithfulness to the promises to Abraham. In the spies incident, future hope is based on Yahweh's commitment to the land promise, demonstrated in the renewed commands to the next generation in chapters 2 and 3. The apostasy at Horeb is resolved through Moses' intercession, appealing to the promises made to the patriarchs and demonstrated in the replacement of the tablets and renewed commands of chapter 10. Likewise the future curses and exile will not be the end. The promise of restoration in chapter 30 is grounded in those same promises. The significance of the Abrahamic covenant in these three sections is not always noticed, in particular in 30:1–10.[7] We shall argue that these promises permeate 30:1–10, as well as being significant in chapters 1–3 and, less contentiously, central in the resolution of the golden calf incident.

Thus this study aims to investigate the theological relationship between Israel's failure and Yahweh's faithfulness in each of these three episodes and their contexts. So chapter 1 considers Deuteronomy 1–3, the spies incident and its subsequent resolution. Chapter 2 considers the golden calf incident in the wider context of chapters 8–10. Finally chapter 3 considers the future failure expressed in chapter 29 and its resolution in chapter 30. We do not offer a complete exegesis of each section but concentrate on the features of the text which contribute to the portrayal of Israel in its response to Yahweh, whether faithful or not, and the motivation and grounds for hope beyond each account of failure. We shall pursue the issue of the priority of divine initiative and its relationship with human responsibility.

Given our argument that Deuteronomy expects Israel to fail, one may regard this selection of passages as biased. After all, each centres on Israel's failure. Yet past failures, which are discussed in the first two passages, need not presuppose future failure.[8] Indeed we have omitted discussion of the final chapters of the book (31–34) because they more obviously support our case. The accounts of Israel's failure focus the issue of the relationship

---

6 This is a fuller account than in 4:25–28.

7 For example, Braulik (1989) 331; (1994e) 111.

8 For example, Vermeylen (1985b) 13; Lohfink (1994a) 229, argue that the past generation is characterised by sin and the present generation by innocence. See further our discussion in chapter 1.

between pessimism and optimism most clearly. It is here that the juxtaposition with hope is sharpest. In addition, the past history of Israel establishes Deuteronomy's perspective about Israel's character. Our selection includes both history and parenesis but omits consideration of the legal corpus of Deuteronomy (chapters 12–26). We have also included the passage which most strongly seems to be against our thesis, namely 30:11–14, a passage read, almost without exception, as stressing Israel's inherent ability. Furthermore the passages chosen are highly significant within Deuteronomy. Chapters 1–3 begin the book, setting its tone and outlook in many respects. Chapters 8–10, within the parenesis of 5–11, function as a prelude to the laws of 12–26 and cast a shadow of pessimism over the hearer-reader's expectation regarding Israel's future capability. Chapters 29–30 end the main body of Deuteronomy. Indeed 30:15–20 can be regarded as the rhetorical climax of the book's exhortation.[9] Thus each of these three accounts is strategic for understanding the book as a whole. Nor is our selection of passages confined to any one layer or redaction. Both within each section, and across all three, most of the commonly accepted redactional stages are represented.

It is our contention that the fullest appreciation of the theology of Deuteronomy can be gained only through a synchronic reading of the book. McCarthy says,

> the essential meaning of a text grows out of its structure as a present (synchronic) whole, not out of its diachronic aspect, its history in terms of its antecedent parts and their adaptation to form the present whole.[10]

Such a reading takes seriously the theological nuances and juxtapositions of what other critics assume to be separate redactional layers. Too often, it seems, such critical approaches belittle the subtlety and richness of a biblical text by presupposing a single, univocal point of view at every step. The text can too easily be regarded as a compilation of simple, yet opposing, points. Paradox is ignored, subsumed under the category of contradiction. Yet, as Moberly insists, when dealing with the things of God, one can hardly but expect paradox, nuance, subtlety and multi-facetedness.[11] Our fundamental concern in this study is theology. Yet, a danger of reading a text synchronically is that of reading into it too much theologically. Moberly argues, that it is better to err on the side of too much than too little.[12] We agree, especially as we consider this a corrective to the majority of critical, diachronic approaches in current Old Testament study

9 Selman, 15, "now they must give their own Yes or No to the covenant".

10 McCarthy (1974) 99.

11 For a defence of a synchronic, final-form reading of a text, see Moberly (1983) 15–43. Also Lenchak, 40–41; Rendtorff (1993a) 25–30; (1993b) 34–53, especially 49–53.

12 Moberly (1983) 39–40.

which all too often are largely unconcerned with theology. Another reason for a synchronic reading is that it avoids redactional speculation. What we have, in the case of Deuteronomy, is a book of thirty-four chapters. No matter what the scholarly consensus is concerning the origins of Deuteronomy, any Urdt or redaction is ultimately hypothesis and speculation. Though in a minority in this approach, we are in fact on firmer ground than those who assume various sources, forms and redactions.[13]

Our concern to take seriously the final form of the text also means a concern to relate the optimism and pessimism of the book theologically. Many scholars attempt to solve the tension between hope and despair by distinguishing different redactions of Deuteronomy (and DtrH). Noth's thesis of a unified and pessimistic DtrH has largely given way to theories of double, triple, and multiple redactions which reflect concerns to identify strands of doom and hope. Many consider that pre-exilic hope gave way to exilic despair and, in turn, to later or post-exilic hope. As we shall discuss, these concerns impinge on the interpretation of Deuteronomy. However, though such approaches are beneficial in identifying various emphases and nuances, often they fall short of integrating these theologically. That is what we seek to do here. We shall argue that the pessimism attached to Israel is fundamental to Deuteronomy and that generally optimism is grounded not in Israel but in Yahweh's faithfulness to his promises. Yet at times Deuteronomy appears to regard positively Israel's own ability to obey, such as 30:11–14. We will argue that this is a misreading of this passage. Israel's ability is established through Yahweh's grace and faithfulness to the patriarchal promises. This is the heart of our thesis. Though a discussion of the law lies beyond the scope of this study, we do have cause to discuss the place of law and exhortation in Deuteronomy. Exhortation to keep the law need not presuppose Israel's ability to do so. Rather, in the context of the climactic exhortation of 30:15–20, we argue that law and exhortation function to expose Israel's need for grace, presupposing, in fact, its inability to keep it.

Unlike the first two incidents, that of chapters 29 and 30 is set in the future. Most commentators regard this as an artificial exilic or post-exilic construction. Regardless of the literary history of these chapters, such a reading can deprive the text of its rhetorical force and impact. Our concern is to take seriously the future nature of chapters 29 and 30 and not dismiss them as merely *vaticinia ex eventu*.[14] The common theological structure and appeal to the Abrahamic promises in each of the three accounts supports this reading. Israel's past experience of resolution of failure on two important occasions on the basis of the Abrahamic promises provides a

---

13 See Licht, 146.

14 See Zimmerli (1971) 72–82, who in responding to Schmid, attempts to take the future aspect of Deuteronomy and DtrH more seriously.

paradigm for hope in future failure, expressed in chapters 29 and 30. There is no reason therefore for not taking seriously the future aspect of chapters 29 and 30.[15]

The similar theological relationships in each of these accounts of Israel's failure sheds light on the relation between the Horeb, Moab and Abrahamic covenants. We shall argue that Moab is a renewal of Horeb, not a replacement for it. Both have the same theological structure. Both await further acts of Yahweh's grace. Nor is Horeb replaced by the patriarchal promises, as some argue, but rather Horeb, like Moab, is grounded in the Abrahamic promises. It is sometimes argued that early or Deuteronomic understandings of covenant were concentrated on Sinai-Horeb and understood the covenant to be a contract of obligation which could be broken. The emphasis on an eternal covenant and Abrahamic promise is regarded as late, perhaps priestly.[16] It is our contention that Deuteronomy has a theology which encompasses and integrates both Horeb and Abraham, law and promise. We shall argue that law derives from promise and that promise, and hence grace, is the basic ingredient of the relationship between Yahweh and Israel. Thus, "YHWH's fidelity extends further than Israel's apostasy, not only by a single act of grace, but basically".[17]

A consequence of our approach is that we shall treat Deuteronomy canonically. In practice this will mean that we understand Deuteronomy to presuppose Genesis to Numbers and to pave the way for Joshua to 2 Kings. The former is important for reading chapters 1–3 and 8–10 as the content of those chapters concerns events recorded elsewhere in the Pentateuch. Deuteronomy seems to be intended to be read presupposing a knowledge of the rest of the Pentateuch. For example, it presupposes that the promises made to Abraham are known to its readers. Similarly, the reading of these chapters of Deuteronomy will be illuminated by knowledge of their relation to previous accounts of the same events. Both omissions and changes of emphasis contribute to Deuteronomy's meaning.[18] Further, we will argue that Deuteronomy 30 is ambiguous about Israel's response to God. This open-endedness may well be deliberate, encouraging the reader to keep reading into Joshua and beyond. Some of the unresolved issues and implications of Deuteronomy 29 and 30 find further clarification in subsequent books.

---

15 Peckham (1985) 30–31, 42, suggests that the frame of Deuteronomy (1–3, 31–34) relates past failures to future defections in the land. Thus 1–3 is an analogue for 31–34, and that the failures reported are paradigmatic.

16 For example, Lohfink (1991b) 21; Clements (1967) 65–68.

17 Braulik (1994e) 110.

18 On the dangers of silence, allusion and assumed knowledge, see Moberly (1983) 32–33.

Deuteronomy 1–3, 8–10, 29–30, hold together pessimism and optimism, failure and hope. This does not reflect a straightforward alternative between obedience and disobedience.[19] More often than not, it seems, Deuteronomy is understood to represent a simple equation of reward for obedience and punishment for disobedience.[20] However it is our argument that the alternatives which Deuteronomy poses are either Israel, exercising its own strength and effort, with failure the inevitable result, or Yahweh and his enduring grace and faithfulness.[21] The key is not whether Israel will obey, because it cannot, but whether Israel will trust in itself or Yahweh and his grace. Each of the three accounts of Israel's failure demonstrates that Israel's hope is to be grounded in Yahweh's grace and not in its own obedience. The latter is not a viable option. The tension between the faithlessness of Israel and the faithfulness of Yahweh is not irreconcilable.[22] Ultimately the parenesis is theocentric, not anthropocentric. Deuteronomy is a call to trust in Yahweh, to choose grace and to choose Yahweh. In many ways Deuteronomy foreshadows the grace-law debate of St Paul. We find in Deuteronomy an expression of what he said in Romans 3:3–4: "Will their lack of faith nullify God's faithfulness? Not at all!"

---

19 Compare Fretheim, 21–22, who argues for Joshua–Kings, that the first commandment is the key to this history and that the relationship between Yahweh and Israel is "much too personally oriented, has too much flexibility in it, for contractual language to do it justice".

20 For example, Tunyogi, 385, suggests that Deuteronomy is like Mesopotamian religions, and unlike the rest of the Old Testament, in that it has no theology of Israel's failure and God's enduring forgiveness.

21 Compare Fretheim, 23, "From the divine side, the focus is on promise; from the human side the focus is...on faith and trust in God alone."

22 Similarly Fretheim, 26–27.

## CHAPTER 1

# Faithless Israel, Faithful Yahweh in Deuteronomy 1–3

We begin our study by looking at chapters 1–3. Our concern is firstly to see how they portray Israel, concentrating on aspects of its obedience and disobedience, faith and unbelief. Secondly we are concerned with the place and role of Yahweh in this picture. After a brief survey of approaches to these chapters, we shall consider the function and purpose of Deuteronomy 1–3 within the book. This will give some indication about how to read these chapters. Then we shall look at their theology, concentrating on Israel's faithlessness and Yahweh's faithfulness and the theological relationship between the two.

### History of Interpretation

The tension in Deuteronomy between failure and hope, pessimism and optimism, disobedience and obedience has been mainly resolved in recent years by isolating different redactional stages. This has inevitably resulted in dealing with Deuteronomy in the wider context of the Deuteronomistic History (DtrH). We shall now briefly survey the major views insofar as they deal with the tensions and purpose of Deuteronomy 1–3.

All modern approaches to Deuteronomy 1–3 begin with Noth.[1] He expounded the influential view that Deuteronomy 1–3 was not written as the introduction to Deuteronomy but rather to DtrH.[2] This was a unity which, though using isolated units as sources, was the first coherent history of Israel. Since 31:9–13 refers to "this law", all the Deuteronomic lawcode belongs to DtrH.[3] However, since 1:1–4:43 has nothing to do with the

---

1 Noth (1981). His *Überlieferungsgeschichtliche Studien* appeared in 1943. On Noth, see Preuß (1982) 77; A.F. Campbell (1994) 31–62; Römer, 178–212, especially 180–181; Boorer, 14–17; Lohfink (1993) 44; Mayes (1983) 4–6.

2 Not every scholar has followed Noth's thesis about DtrH. Preuß (1982) 77, mentions Fohrer who argues that Deuteronomy 1–3 serves to integrate Deuteronomy into the Pentateuch.

3 Noth (1981) 13.

Deuteronomic law, the first three chapters must be the introduction to DtrH and not the law.[4] Noth considered that the history of chapters 1–3

> does not seem intended to illustrate various admonitions and warnings, as, at times, in Deut. 5–11, but rather is obviously narrated out of interest in the reported events themselves.[5]

The chapters serve the purpose of explaining later history. For example 1:19–46 is to explain why entry into the land was from the east and not the south, as well as laying the groundwork for Caleb in Joshua 14.[6] Chapters 1–3 are fashioned as a speech of Moses, linking it to the proclamation of the Deuteronomic law in subsequent chapters.[7] Noth supposed that DtrH was basically a unity whose author was exilic, responding to and explaining the crisis of the loss of land. The main thrust of DtrH was pessimistic.[8]

A major weakness of Noth's view is his concentration on unmitigated doom in DtrH.[9] He more or less dismisses the tensions which we are seeking to resolve. So von Rad considered that he did not take enough account of the optimistic side of DtrH's outlook, especially the promises to David. In response, von Rad highlights the function of God's word which brings both judgment and hope. He argued that hope, not doom, was in fact central to DtrH and that the promises to David will ultimately prevail. The tension between the two in DtrH derives from a combination of, respectively, Davidic and Mosaic traditions.[10] Von Rad's argument, though brief and not fully worked out, has much to commend it. It is a serious attempt to

---

4 Noth (1981) 13–14. Thus the history of Deuteronomy 1–3 is resumed in 31:1. See Preuß (1982) 84. Compare Dillmann, 228–230.

5 Noth (1981) 14. Also Mayes (1979) 35; (1981a) 44. Clements (1989) 36, says the purpose of the historical survey is to give the law a unique historical setting. Seitz, 29, rejects this separation of law and history in 1–3.

6 Noth (1981) 14–15.

7 Noth (1981) 15. It does seem strange that 1–3 is given a form to tie it in with the Deuteronomic law yet Noth fails to see any other connection to that law. Noth (1981) 33, regarded chapter 4 as a bridge to the law. Also Dillmann, 229. The issue of whether the Deuteronomic law, with or without the Ten Commandments, was in the original DtrH is a contested issue. See Römer, 192–194, 197–199. Preuß (1982) 75–77, and Mayes (1983) 22–24, argue for the originality of the law in DtrH. Contrast Levenson (1975) 203–233. On the relationship between the Ten Commandments and the rest of the lawcode, see Kaufman, 105–158, who argued that the laws of 12:1–25:16 follow roughly the order of the Ten Commandments. Also Preuß (1982) 111–112; Braulik (1991b). Contrast Rofé (1988) 265–288; Westbrook. On chapters 5–11 as an exposition of the first commandment, see Lohfink (1963a) 154–157; Walton (1987) 213–225. Compare Kaufman, 110–111, 122.

8 Noth (181) 79, 89. Also Veijola (1988) 253. See Römer, 180–181, for the possibility of redactions within Noth's own work.

9 For example, Noth (1981) 89.

10 Von Rad (1953b) 74–91. Also Myers (1961) 16–18. See Fretheim, 19; Lohfink (1993) 46, for reviews of von Rad.

resolve the tension theologically. For our purposes however, it does not apply to Deuteronomy where the Davidic covenant is not mentioned. Nonetheless, as a model, it will be useful for our own approach.

Noth's one-sided approach gave rise to two main derivatives of his hypothesis which argue for multiple redactions of DtrH in order to resolve the tensions of hope and doom. Perhaps the most common English-speaking view is Cross's double Deuteronomistic redaction, the first pre-exilic, the second exilic.[11] Cross builds on both von Rad and Wolff. The latter had noticed the theme of hope is based on repentance, the call to שׁוב to Yahweh, and so suggested a double redaction of DtrH, where the theme of hope derives from the latter, exilic redaction.[12] In contrast, Cross argues that a Josianic edition (Dtr1) is basically optimistic, setting the agenda for the reform of Josiah who is portrayed as one of the greatest Davidic kings.[13] Then an exilic redaction (Dtr2) brings the history up to date, introducing the sub-theme of judgment and destruction.[14] Cross's thesis has been substantially supported, and provided with further support, by Nelson, among others.[15]

In contrast to the above, the major German derivative of Noth is that of Smend. His school is characterised by a generally later, usually exilic, dating of the original DtrH. Smend first suggested a nomistic redaction (DtrN) of DtrH, in Joshua and Judges at least, the focus of his essay.[16] This was developed by others of the Göttingen school into a three-layered theory with an intermediate prophetic redaction (DtrP), a development Smend accepted.[17] These redactions are primarily attempts to resolve tensions between different perceptions of conquest and law.[18]

---

11 Cross (1973) 274–289.

12 Wolff (1982) 83–100. Cross, 277–278; Fretheim, 19–20, critique Wolff, noting the lack of emphasis on Davidic promise. Compare Zimmerli (1971) 83–84; Brueggemann (1968).

13 Cross, 278–285, 287. 2 Kings 23:25–27 is a crucial text for Cross.

14 Cross, 285–289. It is unclear, in Cross, to which redaction Deuteronomy 1–3 belongs.

15 Nelson (1981). Also Friedman, 167–192; Nicholson (1970) 71–76; Ackroyd (1968) 78–83; Levenson (1975) 218–221. For a summary of Cross, see A.F. Campbell (1994) 44–47; Römer, 188–189; Collier, 224–225; McConville (1992) 67–71; Boorer, 18. For an alternative view, see Peckham (1985); Moenikes, 333–348. On Peckham, see Boorer, 22–23.

16 Smend (1971) 494–509. Compare Mayes (1981a) 36–54, who "attempts a rapprochement between the Smend and Cross schools of interpretation". So Römer, 189. See also A.F. Campbell (1994) 50; Lohfink (1993) 47.

17 Smend (1978) 122–123. See A.F. Campbell (1994) 47–49; McConville (1993b) 83–85; Boorer, 18–19; Begg (1985) 248. Compare the nine-layered redaction of Stahl (1983) 74–75, and Römer's response, 210.

18 See Smend (1978) 114–115, 118–119.

Lohfink also attempts to resolve tensions redactionally.[19] His first redaction, DtrL (= *Landoberungserzählung*), is primarily concerned with land, military and conquest themes. Like Cross's first stage, this derives from the Josianic expansion of territory.[20] The third stage is more pessimistic and is linked to the reasons for the ruin of Israel and the exile.[21] The next layer, DtrN (*Nomist*), has an exilic background. Its message is that if Israel keeps the law, it will take back the land.[22] The final layer, DtrÜ (*Überarbeiter*), provides the last version of Deuteronomy 7–9 to show Israel's fundamental disobedience, as well as including 30:1–10. It is this reviser who, Lohfink suggests, is the same as Wolff's second hand and, therefore, Cross's Dtr2.[23]

A number of scholars have sought to resolve tensions within DtrH and Deuteronomy by isolating redactions according to whether the address is singular or plural.[24] There is no consensus about whether the singular preceded the plural or vice versa, nor the dating of these redactions. Perhaps the most influential of these is Minette de Tillesse who argued that the primitive form of Deuteronomy was in the second-person singular and was later supplemented by a second-person plural layer (Noth's DtrH). He attempts to show that the number change in Deuteronomy is also associated with theological tensions, including attitudes to exile and judgment.[25]

With regard to Deuteronomy 1–3, opinion is thus divided about whether the chapters are Josianic or exilic or some combination of these. The strength of redactional analyses is that they identify tensions, difficulties and varieties of emphasis in the text. In the case of DtrH, and in part Deuteronomy 1–3, these concern the law, land conquest, optimism and

---

19 Lohfink (1981) 87–100; (1993) 44–61. See Boorer, 19–21. One of Lohfink's main arguments concerns the variations in sense which he identifies for יָרַשׁ. Lohfink (1983) 21–30; (1990) 368–396. For a rejection of this argument, see Veijola (1988) 253.

20 Lohfink (1987) 92–96.

21 Lohfink (1981) 96–97. He does not label this redactional stage.

22 Lohfink (1981) 98–99. This corresponds largely to Smend's DtrN. Veijola (1988) 253–255, argues that DtrN links Deuteronomy 1–3 with the Deuteronomic law by chapter 4, incorporating the law into the already existing DtrH. Deuteronomy 1:1–5 also comes from DtrN.

23 Lohfink (1981) 99–100. Köckert, 496–519, adopts by and large this analysis. See Römer, 190.

24 Some scholars regard the *Numeruswechsel* as stylistic. For example, Lohfink (1963a) 239–258; (1989) 39–52; Mayes (1981b) 28–30; Lenchak, 13–15.

25 Minette de Tillesse, 29–87. See also Smend (1978) 72; Begg (1979) 116–124; Römer, 184–185; Seitz, 13–17. Others who follow similar approaches include Mitchell, 61–109; Plöger, 1–59; Mittmann, 1–115, 164–184; Cazelles (1967) 207–219; Veijola (1988) 250–251. Compare Preuß (1982) 78–79, 83; Nelson, 90–91; Nielsen, 23–24; García López (1978) 6–8, 37–47; De Regt (1988) 63–65.

pessimism. The weakness of redactional analyses is that they fail to explain the text as an integrated unity. In particular, redactional approaches are often dependent on reconstructed history where the future of the text is dismissed as *vaticinia ex eventu*.

One attempt to read the text as a unity is the literary approach of Polzin. He concentrates on the differences between reporting and reported speech and argues that there is a distinction between the narrator and Moses. Though the narrator has only a background role, and the content of his words is trivial, Polzin claims that the narrator breaks Moses' speech significantly, thus limiting Moses' authority and showing himself to be the Moses of his generation. The shift between past and present is a rhetorical device to manipulate the audience's response.[26] Polzin sees a tension between these two voices. One downplays the uniqueness of Moses and Israel, and highlights retributive justice, judgment and despair. The other stresses the uniqueness of Moses and Israel and highlights hope and grace. These two voices transcend the distinction between the narrator and Moses.[27] In our opinion, Polzin makes too much of the distinction between the narrator and Moses, especially since by his own admission the major textual tensions apply to both.[28] More importantly, his approach does not deal satisfactorily with the interplay between the voices he identifies. They are always regarded as at odds with each other. He regards the "basic evaluative stance" of the book as that which promotes the retributive justice of God. This voice, he says, neutralises the subordinate voice which highlights grace, election and mercy. In the end, grace and mercy are "swallowed up" by the voice of retributive justice.[29] Polzin makes no attempt to reconcile the two theologically.[30] Thus his approach, despite its attempt to read the text as a unity, fails to resolve its tensions. It virtually dismisses one of the voices.

There is little or no methodological consensus on approaches to Deuteronomy 1–3.[31] Theologically, none of the above approaches successfully

---

26 Polzin (1981) 204–208; (1987) 93–99.

27 Polzin (1980) 36–41. For example, 1:37; 3:26; 4:21–22, diminish Moses; 2:5, 9, 19 diminish Israel; 2:21–22 diminish both Moses and Israel.

28 Veijola (1988) 249–250, says, "One can't get rid of the impression that we are dealing here with a very strange narrator who expresses his main concerns in this kind of marginal, ethnographic and geographic parenthesis". Similarly Perlitt (1985) 153.

29 Polzin (1980) 53–54, 66–67. He says, 42–43, "the bracketing of utterances of mercy and grace with neutralizing statements of a retributive nature is a consistent pattern in the Book of Deuteronomy".

30 For example, he maintains that "the distinction between the covenant with the fathers and the covenant at Horeb is absolutely basic to the ideological tension within the book". Polzin (1980) 54. Compare 68.

31 See Perlitt (1985) 149–163.

resolves the tensions of the text, many of which may have existed from the beginning.[32] We are not satisfied with this impasse. The need remains to investigate the theology of these chapters with respect to their expectation of Israel's willingness and ability to keep the covenant, the future hope for Israel and the theological relationship to Yahweh's grace and faithfulness. Our concern is to read the final form of Deuteronomy allowing more interplay between these tensions. We believe that theologically they are reconcilable.

The redactional approaches mentioned above indicate an uncertainty about the purpose of Deuteronomy 1–3. Do these chapters simply introduce the Deuteronomistic History? In this case, we may expect a concern with historiography, the recorded events themselves. Or can Deuteronomy 1–3 be legitimately considered as an introduction to Deuteronomy itself? In this case, we may expect a concern with the law and parenesis. If the latter is the case, then the theology of Deuteronomy 1–3 will be significant for how we read the rest of Deuteronomy. We turn then to a consideration of Deuteronomy 1–3 as an introduction to to the book.

## Deuteronomy 1–3 as Introduction to Deuteronomy

It is our conviction that Deuteronomy 1–3 is to be read as the introduction to the rest of Deuteronomy rather than directly DtrH. This issue is important in order to clarify the purpose of Deuteronomy 1–3. A clear understanding of the purpose of these chapters will contribute to an appreciation of its theology. It will also indicate the significance of our findings for the rest of the book. There are a number of grounds for reading chapters 1–3 as the introduction to Deuteronomy. Not least is that a synchronic reading of Deuteronomy will naturally read these chapters in such a way. However there are further indications that this is how chapters 1–3 are to be read.

One of these is the model of ancient treaties. The application of ancient treaty structures as a model for Deuteronomy's structure indicates that chapters 1–3 are an essential part of the book. An integral element of most ancient treaties, especially the Hittite treaties, is the historical prologue.[33] This would correspond to Deuteronomy 1–3[4].[34] In this context it is important to note that in ancient treaties, the historical prologue can carry a sense of admonition. So Weinfeld comments, "As in the Hittite treaty, the author employs a description bearing a general admonitory character".[35]

32 Perlitt (1985) 154–155; Mittmann, 164–184.

33 Weinfeld (1972) 66–67.

34 For example, Kline (1963); Wenham (1970); Craigie (1976).

35 Weinfeld (1972) 70–71. He, 69–74, gives evidence from ANE treaties showing parallels to Deuteronomy 1:19–46, noting descriptions of land borders and that the

Another indication that chapters 1–3 are to be read as the introduction to Deuteronomy is that the style of chapters 1–3 fits that of chapters 4–30 which are also in the form of speeches of Moses.[36] Significantly Deuteronomy is mostly a speech, unlike the subsequent books of DtrH, and this speech form in chapters 1–3 should be taken seriously. This indicates to us that we are to read chapters 1–3 primarily as an introduction to the following chapters and less as an introduction to the history of chapters 31–34, Joshua and following.

Furthermore, regardless of its compositional history, the opening paragraph (1:1–5) is intended as an introduction to the whole of Deuteronomy in its final form.[37] One of its functions is to tie together history and law. Christensen finds in 1:1–6a a concentric structure as follows:[38]

A These words (הַדְּבָרִים) Moses spoke (דִּבֶּר)
  B Place: In the vicinity of the Jordan
    C Time: It is eleven days from Horeb to Kadesh
      D Moses spoke what Yahweh commanded (דִּבֶּר)
    C' Time: After he had smitten the Amorite kings
  B' Place: In the vicinity of the Jordan
A' Moses expounded this torah which Yahweh spoke (דִּבֶּר)

The significance of this structure is that the beginning of Deuteronomy heralds the law. The reader-hearer is directed to the words spoken. Moses' words are identified with Yahweh's words and are identified with torah

---

prologues usually end with the grant of land. They also often included mention of vassals' rebelliousness. Compare Baltzer, 12; McCarthy (1981) 59. McConville (1984) 3–4, notes that history and parenesis are combined in ancient treaties.

36 Mayes (1983) 24, argues that the style of 1–3 is influenced by the law being a speech of Moses. It seems to us more reasonable to have expected a history writer to have kept his historical sections consistent and altered the incorporated law. Mayes fails to explain why the first person style breaks down after chapter 30.

37 So Watts, 191; D. Schneider, 29; Dillmann, 231; König, 60; McConville (1984) 3. 1:1 combines with the last verse of the book, 34:12, to envelope Deuteronomy with the expression "all Israel". See Driver, 1; Craigie (1976) 89.

38 Christensen (1991) 6. Christensen (1992) 197–202, omits v3a because it is from P. Lohfink's chiasm, (1962) 32, ends with v5b, not v6a. The strength of this is that vv1–5 are a distinct unit as v6 begins Yahweh's speech. The strength of Christensen's version is the inclusion of דִּבֶּר in v6a to balance v1. Merrill, 61, rejects Christensen's version on treaty grounds. Mayes (1979) 113, rejects Lohfink's version. Carpenter, 78, suggests a chiasm similar to Lohfink. On v3 as P, see von Rad (1966e) 36; Buis and Leclerq, 32; Nielsen, 20. For a detailed redaction-critical analysis, see Mittmann, 8–17.

(v5b).[39] There is also movement within these verses from Moses' words, to Moses speaking Yahweh's words, to Yahweh's words (v6).[40] Thus God's words are in focus from the beginning. The torah is set in time and place, in terms which suppose knowledge of Exodus and Numbers.[41] Further, torah comprises both law and history.[42] Indeed the history begins looking back to Horeb rather than to the exodus, showing a concern to focus history on the law.[43] We should not therefore set a rigid division between history and law, chapters 1–3 and 4–30, as Noth and others do. Such a division is artificial.

This tying together of law and history in the opening paragraph indicates that the concerns of chapters 1–3 belong with the preached law which follows. Perlitt remarks, "Es gibt hier kaum ein theologisches Motiv ohne Bezug zum Kern des Dtn."[44] Indeed the concerns of chapters 1–3 are not simply historiographical.[45] Rather, through its own selective narration, and a variety of rhetorical devices which we shall note in our analysis below, chapters 1–3 urge the current generation to faithful obedience. In chapters 1–3 this is only implicit but becomes explicit in chapters 4–30. There is no fundamental division between the two sections. They serve the same purpose.[46] "The historical prologue was not written as a simple narrative, but as a discourse of Moses with a purpose."[47] Thus the history is intimately connected to the parenesis, contra Noth. It is not totally inaccurate to call these chapters preaching, especially since their form is that of a speech.[48] We should note that elsewhere in Deuteronomy, notably in chapters 8–10, history and exhortation are explicitly intertwined. This should at least alert us to the fact that history is not incompatible with exhortation.

---

39 On the referents of דְּבָרִים in Deuteronomy (though there is no mention of 1:1), see Braulik (1970) 45–49; Merrill, 61–62. See also Seitz, 27–29. Compare Mittmann, 13–15.

40 Christensen (1992) 200; Miller (1990) 24; (1987) 246.

41 On the various identifications and difficulties with these place names see Mayes (1979) 113–115; Gemser (1952) 349–355; G.I. Davies (1979) 87–101; (1990a) 163–175. The places and times are transitional, notes Miller (1990) 22, showing that Deuteronomy is intended to be read after Numbers. Also D. Schneider, 30. Buis and Leclerq, 31, argue that 1:1–5 is a conclusion to Numbers.

42 Braulik (1986) 22. Also D. Schneider, 29. Kallai (1995) 188–197, argues that 1:1–5 is an integrated and purposeful construction to both the historical prologue and the law.

43 Braulik (1986) 23.

44 Perlitt (1985) 158.

45 Seitz, 29.

46 Rennes, 14; McConville and Millar, 30; Rose (1994) 478.

47 McKenzie, 95.

48 Though Preuß (1982) 83, rejects such a view. See further, McConville and Millar, 16–32, for a fuller discussion on the nature and function of these chapters.

Furthermore, the purpose and character of Deuteronomy 1–3 is clarified by a comparison with parallel accounts in Exodus and Numbers. Most scholars acknowledge, and we accept, that there is some dependence of Deuteronomy on at least the JE sections of Exodus and Numbers.[49] The hearer-reader is expected to know these parallel accounts.[50] In our opinion, there is also evidence which suggests dependence of Deuteronomy on the P sections of Numbers. Whether this is explained by dating P before Deuteronomy 1–3 or by supposing an essential unity to the Numbers account does not matter for this discussion.[51] Certainly a canonical reading will presuppose all of Exodus and Numbers. The opening paragraph (1:1–5) also asks the reader to do this.[52] This is not the place for a thorough discussion of the relationship between these books. However, we suggest that Deuteronomy does not slavishly follow Exodus and Numbers, and that where they differ, Deuteronomy expresses its own theological points and emphases.[53] This shall be our supposition in our analysis of Deuteronomy 1–3 below.

We regard Deuteronomy 1–30 as the main body of Deuteronomy. The parenesis comes to a climax at the end of chapter 30 with the command to choose life. Chapters 31–34 can then be regarded as a series of appendices or a postscript.[54] This is not to downplay the relevance of these chapters for the book. If chapter 30 forms an inclusio with chapter 4 around the preached law, as is commonly observed, then 31–34 does the same with 1–

---

49 There is debate about whether this dependence is literary (So Clements (1989) 15–16; Driver, xiv–xix, 10; Buis and Leclerq, 33) or whether it derives from common tradition (So Cairns, 32; Smend (1978) 71). See further Jacobs, 346–353. For an alternative view that Numbers is dependent on, or post-dates, Deuteronomy, see Coats, 177–190; Rose (1981); Van Seters (1994).

50 For example, Deuteronomy 1:36 does not explain why Caleb is exempt from punishment. Compare Numbers 14:24. See Braulik (1986) 25; Weinfeld (1991) 150; Driver, 26; Kalland, 29; Mayes (1979) 127. Compare Rose (1981) 264–270. Also see our discussion below on 1:28.

51 For example, on the spies incident, Wenham (1981) 126, notes Deuteronomy's dependence on P in 1:23 (Numbers 13:2), 1:36, 38 (Numbers 14:6, 30, 38), 1:39 (Numbers 14:3, 31). He leaves open the possibility of P pre-dating Deuteronomy though he advocates a basic unity to Numbers 13, 14. Similarly Milgrom (1976) 9–13; Weinfeld (1991) 25–37. See Olson (1985) 25–28, 132, for a critique of Wenham.

52 Miller (1990) 22; Mayes (1979) 115. Miller argues that the transitional time and place references in 1:1–5 indicate this.

53 For example, Cairns, 32, "Traditional material which does not serve (the Deuteronomist's) emphases, or that may have weakened their cogency is by-passed." Similarly Mittmann, 57; Perlitt (1985) 163; Lohfink (1960) 105–110; McKenzie, 95.

54 See further our discussion on 30:15–20.

3.[55] The link between the two hardly needs discussion when we remember that Noth, and others, argued that 1–3, 31–34 form a basically continuous narrative. The themes of Moses' denial and death and the succession of leadership from Moses to Joshua are evident in both.[56]

Yet so too is the theme of the oath to the patriarchs which occurs in 1:6–8 and 34:4. The promise to Abraham is the frame for the whole book.[57] The emphasis on the Abrahamic covenant sets the law and divine commands into a context of promise. The frequent references to Yahweh's promise to the patriarchs are generally, though not exclusively, found in the introductory and concluding sections of the book, chapters 1–11, 29–34.[58] Thus Horeb, and the covenant of Moab, are regarded as arising out of and being the means of fulfilment of the patriarchal promises.[59] The commands of 1–3 are a product of the promises. This theological relationship between promise and law is established in chapters 1–3, as we shall note below, and thus provides the grid through which the law should be read.

The tension we seek to resolve beween Israel's faithlessness and Yahweh's faithfulness is established as early as the first paragraph. Israel's failure lies close at hand in 1:1–5. The list of places and the eleven days-fortieth year contrast in vv2, 3a is a clear allusion to Israel's failure. Indeed the whole time orientation is determined by Israel's failure.[60] This is balanced with v4 where Yahweh is the subject, an acknowledgement that success is attributed to Yahweh rather than Israel.[61] Thus this introductory paragraph sounds the themes of Israel's failure, Yahweh's success, and the key role of Yahweh's words.

---

55 Olson (1994) 159. Compare Kessler, 44–49, who argues that strictly, inclusio is verbal, often of a single word, and occurs at the extremity of a literary unit.

56 Lohfink (1994b) 234–247.

57 It seems that Deuteronomy deliberately frames the law with statements of Yahweh's faithfulness in a succession of layers. Chapters 1–3 and 31–34 are the outer layer. Chapters 4 and 30 also form a frame for the law which places it within the context of Yahweh's faithfulness to the patriarchal promises. Also McConville (1984) 33–36, 119–121, on links between chapters 12 and 26. See also Craigie (1976) 320; Niehaus, 6–7.

58 D. Schneider, 31. See 1:8, 35; 4:31; 6:18, 23; 7:8, 12, 13; 8:1, 18; 9:5; 10:11; 11:9, 21; 13:18; 19:8; 26:3, 15; 28:11; 29:12; 30:20; 31:7, 20, 21, 23. He omits 34:4.

59 Phillips (1973) 14; Craigie (1976) 94; Hagelia, 46; Cairns, 33. Compare Clements (1968) 39–40, who states that the patriarchal covenant is subordinate to Horeb in Deuteronomy, despite its prominence in the introductory sections. See further below on 30:1–10.

60 Kline (1963) 51; G.I. Davies (1979) 88; Ridderbos, 52; Thompson, 82; Merrill, 64. McConville and Millar, 24, suggest that the geographical aside in v2 "is to bring the national failure at Kadesh Barnea to the forefront of the listener's or reader's mind, in contrast to the response demanded of Israel at Horeb".

61 McConville (1994) 202. See further our analysis of Deuteronomy 2–3 below.

In summary, Deuteronomy 1–3 is integral for the book. Its style as speech, even implicit preaching, links it to chapters 4–30. Its content links it to chapters 31–34 with which it frames the book. As the opening to Deuteronomy it raises the key issues of our investigation and even sets the agenda for the book.

## Faithless Israel in Deuteronomy 1

We turn now to explore the theology of Deuteronomy 1. Our concern is to understand the relationship, even tension, between the faithlessness of Israel and the faithfulness of Yahweh. We shall deal with each of these in turn, firstly, Israel's faithlessness, then the portrayal of Yahweh's faithfulness. Our discussion above about the purpose of Deuteronomy 1–3 suggests that this chapter is rich in theology. It is not simply a presentation of history. Serving as an introduction, it establishes the theological perspective, and indeed hortatory style, for the rest of Deuteronomy.[62]

The structure and emphases of chapter 1 show a deliberate portrayal of Israel as sinful and culpable without excuse. The selectivity of the account, in comparison to that of Numbers 13–14, brings to the fore the author's major themes.[63] In particular the account of the spies' actual reconnoitre is heavily abridged, showing the focus in Deuteronomy to be on their report and not their journey.

### *Structure and Speeches*

In order to investigate the portrayal of the faithlessness of Israel, we shall firstly consider the structure of the chapter, noting in particular the concentric structure of the speeches. In our opinion, structural patterns can highlight theological emphases and nuances.

Various attempts at demonstrating structure in Deuteronomy 1 have been made. Perhaps the most systematised is that of Christensen who argues that the structure of 1:19–2:1 is concentric centred on 1:29–31.[64] His structure fails to convince on various grounds, not least because Moses' speech in 1:29–31 parallels his earlier speech in 1:21.[65]

---

62 Miller (1990) 19.

63 McKenzie, 97; Mittmann, 57–58.

64 Christensen (1985a) 138–139. For further discussion of his method, see (1985b) 179–189, especially 181–183; (1986) 61–68. He also, (1975a) 137–138; (1991) 1, argues that all of Deuteronomy 1–3 is concentric. Carpenter, 79, proposes a chiastic structure for 1:6–46, centred on vv26–28. He argues that there is a movement from positive to negative in the chapter, highlighting Israel's unbelief. As with Christensen, many of Carpenter's pairs are not clear parallels.

65 His division of vv25–28 and 32–36 into three parts is artificial. His second mention of the spies in v28 is in fact the people speaking, allegedly quoting the spies. Like-

A more helpful observation is that the reported speech in chapter 1 follows a concentric pattern. The main cycle is as follows:

| | | |
|---|---|---|
| 1:6–8 | A | Yahweh |
| 1:20–21 | B | Moses |
| 1:22 | C | people |
| 1:25 | D | spies |
| 1:27–28 | C' | people |
| 1:29–31 | B' | Moses |
| 1:35–36 | A' | Yahweh[66] |

The weakness of this structure is the omission of vv9–18.[67] Despite this, however, this concentric structure of chapter 1, indicated by the speeches, is significant. Firstly, its concentricity matches Israel's lack of movement which is caused by its unbelief. In Deuteronomy 1, Israel ends up where it begins the spies incident, namely at Kadesh (1:19, 46).[68]

Secondly, this structure acknowledges the importance of the speeches in chapter 1. Each speech is its own scene; there is no dialogue.[69] This structure also separates the key players and clarifies their position. In particular, it aligns Yahweh, Moses and the spies in their outlook.[70] So Moses' speeches, the second (1:29–31) building on the first (1:20–21), are full of encouragement and exhortation, like Yahweh's first speech (1:6–8) and building on it.[71] Next, the spies' report is glowingly positive, adding to Moses' speech of 1:20–21. Yahweh aligns himself with the spies (v25) when he also describes the land as 'good' (v35).[72] His second speech is

wise in v36, the exception of Caleb is part of Yahweh's speech and not Moses' report.

66 Lohfink (1960) 122; Braulik (1986) 25. A second cycle is A - 37–40 Yahweh; B - 41 people; A' - 42 Yahweh. Thompson, 84, and Watts (1970) 194, also note the speech chiasmus in 1:6–46 and 1:20–30 respectively. See also Mayes (1979) 129; Lundbom (1975) 61.

67 Noted by Lohfink (1960) 123, though see his comments.

68 Though in v19 Israel does move from Horeb to Kadesh.

69 Lohfink (1960) 120–121. The speeches, he says, are "Trumpf" in Deuteronomy 1. Also Preuß (1982) 80. Compare Numbers where Caleb and Joshua also have a role and Moses' prayer (14:13–19) is replaced by a sermon. See Weinfeld (1991) 147–149; Mayes (1979) 130–131; Rose (1981) 289; Cairns, 35.

70 Preuß (1982) 81.

71 Lohfink (1960) 122; Mayes (1979) 128; Buis and Leclerq, 37. Compare 1:21 and 1:6–8. See Skweres, 25–27; Weinfeld (1991) 142–143; Miller (1990) 31; Craigie (1976) 100; Driver, 21; Steuernagel, 5. On the lack of distinction between Moses' speech and Yahweh's speech in Deuteronomy generally, see Lenchak, 11.

72 This description is typical of Deuteronomy. See 3:25; 4:21, 22; 6:18; 8:10; 9:6; 11:17. Compare Numbers 14:23. See Weinfeld (1991) 149; Driver, 26; Plöger, 87–90; Van Seters (1994) 376.

introduced by 1:34 which uses the verb שׁבע, linking back to 1:8, another indication of concentricity.[73] Also, Moses' two speeches link the spies and Yahweh through common vocabulary. So לְפָנֵינוּ in v22, referring to the spies, parallels לִפְנֵיכֶם in vv30, 33, referring to Yahweh. Both the spies and Yahweh are involved in spying or searching the land (חָפַר, v22; תּוּר, v33). Also דֶּרֶךְ occurs in v22, regarding the spies, and vv31, 33 (twice) regarding Yahweh.[74] Pitted against all three are the people. Their first speech, 1:22, contrasts with Yahweh's first speech (1:6–8), and their second speech, 1:27–28, changes phrases of it. These show a shift from hesitation to refusal.[75] Correspondingly, Yahweh's exhortation and promise in 1:6–8 changes into a statement of judgment in 1:35–36.[76]

Thirdly, the concentric structure of the speeches in chapter 1 has as its kernel the spies' report in v25.[77] In Deuteronomy, the despatch of the spies and their reconnaisance are quickly passed over.[78] The focus is on the spies' report. This report highlights the people's rebellion. In Deuteronomy, the report is unequivocal in its endorsement of the land.[79] Standing at the centre of the concentric structure of speeches, this throws the people's refusal into a damning light. Verse 26 begins with the strong contrast, וְלֹא אֲבִיתֶם. Deuteronomy thus creates a tension between the spies' speech, with its unqualified report of the good land, and the people's fear and unbelief.[80] This is further heightened by a comparison with the parallel account in Numbers. There, the spies' report is equivocal as it includes the description of the giant inhabitants. In Deuteronomy there is no such qualification. Thus the people's reluctance to enter, expressed in v28, has no foundation in the spies' report. It is made to appear groundless in Deuteronomy.[81] The

73 McConville (1994) 203; Van Seters (1994) 376.

74 Rose (1981) 275. Burden, 135, suggests that the frequency of דֶּרֶךְ in 1:19–46 shows the importance of obedience here. Also Munchenberg, 26.

75 Rose (1994) 488, argues that there is a deliberate development from Israel's hesitation (v22) to *Nicht-Wollen* (v26) to *Nicht-Glauben* (v32) to presumption (v43), the last of which is similar to Genesis 3:5.

76 Lohfink (1960) 122. Following Daube, Lohfink, 127, argues that 1:35 legally revokes 1:8.

77 Compare P's account which, McEvenue (1971) 114–115, argues, centres on the people's reaction to the spies' report. Deuteronomy sharpens the people's culpability.

78 Von Rad (1966e) 40.

79 On this report of the land, see Plöger, 88–89.

80 Preuß (1982) 80; Braulik (1986) 25; Mayes (1979) 127; Ridderbos, 60. Likewise McEvenue (1971) 115.

81 Rose (1994) 480. The spies' report in v25 concerns the land, with no mention of cities. However the charge to the spies in v22 mentions both. The people's complaint mentions cities only. Mittmann, 35–36, concludes that the end of v22 originally belonged with vv28–30. Yet that would make an incoherent narrative.

contentious issue is how to understand the people's accusation against the spies in v28. If the ambivalent spies' report in Numbers is presupposed, then at one level, the people's response is fair. However the lack of fear in the spies' report in Deuteronomy raises the question about the grounds for the people's fear. Their words place the blame on the spies. Yet within Deuteronomy there is, deliberately we might argue, no supportive evidence. Thus at another level, the hearer-reader is expected to know the Numbers background and notice the change in Deuteronomy that the spies' report is totally positive. This would make the people's response all the more blameworthy and portray them in the worst possible light.[82] Thus in Deuteronomy, the blame rests finally on the people, and not the spies. Cairns concludes,

> In Numbers the scouts' report is a mixture of positive and negative factors, so that the people's fear is to some degree 'understandable'. In Deuteronomy, however, the basic report is positive.... The effect is to place responsibility for the people's attitude to Yahweh squarely on the people themselves.[83]

The linking of the speeches of Yahweh, Moses and the spies, in opposition to the people, further contributes to the portrayal of the culpability of the people. Thus the repeated encouragement of Moses in 1:29–31, corresponding to the encouragement of Joshua and Caleb in Numbers 14:7–9, expands on 1:21, and appeals to the promises of Yahweh, thus further underscoring the gravity of Israel's rebellion and making its reaction even more culpable.[84] In addition, the repetition of words in this section highlights Israel's sin. For example, the "seeing" motif demonstrates the contrast between fear and faith. In v19, Moses notes that רְאִיתֶם the wilderness. In v21, the exhortation begins רְאֵה. In v30 the promise is that God will fight for you, לְעֵינֵיכֶם. In v31, Moses notes that רָאִיתָ how God provided in the wilderness. Thus the seeing motif binds together the two speeches of Moses. Significantly Israel's statement of fear concludes, in v28, with רָאִינוּ the Anakim there. Where Israel should have seen Yahweh and his acts, they saw only Anakim. Where seeing should have inspired faith, they saw and were afraid.[85]

---

82 Boorer, 385–386, 389. She largely follows Lohfink and Mayes on this point. Compare Van Seters (1994) 375.

83 Cairns, 35. Also Braulik (1986) 25; McKenzie, 97, "The people appear again here as responsible agents of decision...". D. Schneider, 40, says that Moses is drawing attention to Israel's 'incomprehensible' unbelief.

84 Watts (1970) 195. Christensen (1991) 29, regards vv21, 31 as a constructional pair forming a singular frame around the plural vv22–30.

85 Miller (1990) 35, 204, that in 1:19–46, "seeing is not necessarily believing". The relationship between seeing and believing is important in Deuteronomy. See below on 29:3. Craigie (1976) 102, notes that the facts are the same for the spies and

The people have heard Moses' encouragement in vv20–21, the spies' positive report in v25, which endorses Moses' previous words, further encouragement by Moses in vv29–31, and the accusation of v32 in sharp relief with the statement of God's gracious providence in v33.[86] All this has the effect of isolating Israel in its fear and rebellion, showing it to be without excuse in its sin.[87] In v32, the people's unbelief is directed against God and not Moses, as in Numbers 14:2.[88] Verse 32 is important. After the effusive encouragement of vv29–31, v32 is simple, stark and to the point. Unbelief is serious.[89] The request of the people to send spies in v22, immediately following the exhortation not to fear, is thus an expression of reluctance to discharge God's will.[90] In the concentric scheme, it is the counterpart of the people's explicit refusal in vv27–28. In Numbers the initiative for sending spies lay with Yahweh. Significantly here it is from the people.[91] Thus the reworking of the spies incident from Numbers spotlights the previous generation's serious failure.[92] Further, the linking of the spies' mission with Yahweh's own activity in Moses' two speeches, as mentioned above, also implies that the spies' mission, according to Deuteronomy, was in error from the beginning.[93]

---

Moses as for the people. Yet their responses differed markedly. Also Mayes (1979) 128; Driver, 24; Weinfeld (1991) 148; Thompson, 84.

86 The accusation against the people of their refusal to trust (אמן hiphil) is direct to the people in Deuteronomy but in Numbers 14:11 it is expressed by Yahweh to Moses. See Mann, 483–484, on the importance of this motif. Also Blenkinsopp (1968) 104.

87 Braulik (1986) 26–27; Preuß (1982) 81.

88 Braulik (1986) 25. Also v43.

89 D. Schneider, 42. The continuous sense of the participle highlights the strength of rebellion. See Driver, 25; Mayes (1979) 131; Cairns, 36. Buis and Leclerq, 39, suggest the absence of Moses' prayer (compare Numbers) underlines the seriousness of sin.

90 Luther, 21; Lohfink (1960) 112–113; Braulik (1986) 26; McKenzie, 97; Weinfeld (1991) 144; Steuernagel, 5; McConville (1994) 202; Mittmann, 58; Burden, 110–113. Lohfink, 112, notes that the request to send the spies has been put between the two speeches of encouragement from Moses, making this request a distinctive contrast. Bertholet, 5, considers v26 to be the first sign of the people's obstinacy.

91 Dillmann, 237; Mittmann, 58; Preuß (1982) 80; Blair (1964) 19. Weinfeld (1991) 145, says, "The author of Deuteronomy could not ascribe to Moses a mission with the underlying aim of verifying the promise made by the Lord. The promised land is a *good* one…and there can be no doubt about it." On the portrayal in Numbers, and its JE and P sources, see Mayes (1979) 127–128. On reconciling the two accounts, see Driver, 22; Craigie (1976) 101; Merrill, 73; Kalland, 25.

92 Weinfeld (1991) 144; McConville and Millar, 20.

93 Burden, 113. He suggests that 1:8, 21 show that Yahweh has already scouted out the land. Thus the request to send spies in v22 is to be viewed negatively. Similarly Rose (1994) 479. Munchenberg, 24, suggests the syntax of v22 indicates Israel's lack of faith.

Israel's failure is thus not merely a failure of obedience, but also a failure of faith.[94] Its grumbling in vv26–28 challenges the motivations and integrity of Yahweh as expressed in the words of Moses and the spies.[95] It is important to see that the issue of obedience-disobedience turns on the character of Yahweh. The people claimed that Yahweh hated them and was intending to destroy them (vv27–28).[96] This false understanding about Yahweh lies at the heart of Israel's sin. That is why these chapters are ultimately theocentric.

In summary, the speeches, and their concentric structure, draw attention to Israel's culpability, showing it to be groundless and serious. The people are isolated against Yahweh, Moses and the spies. We turn now to other factors contributing to the overall portrayal of Israel's faithlessness.

### *Unholy War and Anti-Exodus*

The description of Israel's faithlessness is further heightened by the inverted allusions to Holy War and the exodus which in fact portray an Unholy War and an Anti-Exodus.[97] For example, in v28, the expression, הֵמַסּוּ אֶת־לְבָבֵנוּ, is from the language of Holy War.[98] However now it is Israel who is afraid whereas in the language of Holy War, Israel's enemies will be afraid. Moses' encouragement thus functions like the priest's words in war.[99] The language of Holy War pervades the chapter. For example, it is found in Yahweh's first speech (vv6–8), in the encouragement of vv20–21 where Yahweh is the decisive actor, likewise in v25b, in the use of אָמַן (hiphil) in v32, which also occurs in Holy War texts such as Exodus 14:31 and Isaiah 7, in v35b, which is a further reference to 9:1–6, and in vv39–46 which is a parody of Holy War.[100]

---

94 McConville (1993b) 133; Nielsen, 36; Carpenter, 80.

95 J.G. Janzen (1987b) 293. Compare Deuteronomy 9. On lack of faith, see Luther, 22; McConville (1994) 202.

96 On the hatred of the LORD, see Mayes (1979) 129; Merrill, 75, and on the irony created by 9:28b, see Cairns, 36; D. Schneider, 41.

97 This is the thesis of Lohfink (1960), extended by Moran (1963a) 333–342, to cover 2:14–16.

98 Lohfink (1960) 110–111; Weinfeld (1972) 344; D. Schneider, 41. See for example, Joshua 2:11; 5:1; and Deuteronomy 20:8. Also Thompson, 88; Mayes (1979) 129; Merrill, 77. This is not to deny Holy War terminology in Numbers. For example 14:9, 39–45. We should also note that Israel's failure is a failure of the heart (לֵבָב), the first occurrence of this important word in Deuteronomy, and one we shall discuss in chapters 2 and 3 below.

99 See 20:3. Lohfink (1960) 111; Christensen (1991) 30; Weinfeld (1972) 45.

100 Lohfink (1960) 112–114. See Moran (1963a) 333–339, for further references in Deuteronomy 1–3.

This final paragraph (1:39–46) shows that after all the encouragement and rebuke, Israel still acts presumptuously. A lack of hearing in v43, despite all the speeches of encouragement they have heard, leads to Israel's rebellion. This accusation against Israel is the culmination of the episode.[101] Their humiliating defeat is an eloquent and sufficient statement of judgment, for Yahweh is noticeably silent (v45). Though hardly necessary, this final act underlines Israel's total stubbornness.[102] It is clear that any future for Israel does not lie in its repentance or ability to change. Its repentance in v41 was superficial. Its remorse in v45 falls on deaf ears. The futility is seen in that the chapter ends at Kadesh. Israel is back where it was in v19b.[103]

The background of the exodus is also significant. Moses' words of encouragement in vv29–31 are a mini-creed with the exodus as its paradigm. Yet, as v32 makes clear, this creed is not believed by Israel. Verse 33 alludes to Exodus 13:21, the beginning of the exodus story, and v32, אָמַן (hiphil), refers to Exodus 14:31, the end of the exodus story.[104] The contrast is that in Exodus 14:31, the people believed; here they do not.[105] Thus the spies incident is portrayed in terms both of an Unholy War and an Anti-Exodus. The result of this is to show the utter reprehensibility and horror of Israel's sin. It is a complete perversion of how Israel is meant to be.

### *Moses' Exclusion*

The depth of Israel's sin is seen in Moses' own exclusion from the land which is attributed to בִּגְלַלְכֶם (v37). There is no allusion to Moses' own sin, though it is mentioned in Numbers 20:10–12.[106] While it may be possible to presuppose the account of Moses' own sin, silence about the matter keeps the spotlight on Israel's sin. Thus the blame seems here to be

---

101 Perlitt (1990b) 106–107; Rose (1994) 486–488.

102 Kalland, 28. As in Numbers 14:44, the verb עָלָה in vv41, 43 each time suggests presumption and arrogant foolhardiness. Likewise זוד in v43. See Weinfeld (1991) 151–152.

103 Braulik (1986) 26.

104 Lohfink (1960) 119. Compare also Exodus 14:13 and Deuteronomy 1:29. See Braulik (1986) 27. See further Moran (1963a) 339–342. Compare Preuß (1982) 80.

105 Thompson, 88; Weinfeld (1991) 147; Mayes (1979) 130; Braulik (1986) 27; Buis and Leclerq, 39.

106 Luther, 21–22, says "because of you" suggests the sending of the spies is regarded as a sin of Moses, so v23. Also Rose (1994) 479, 485. See Lohfink (1960) 112–113; Mann, 485. Moses' own sin is mentioned in Deuteronomy 32:51–52, often attributed to P. So Miller (1987) 253.

put on the people.[107] Lohfink has suggested that the reader is intended to identify with Moses in these chapters and that their intention is to provide consolation to innocent exiles. However the similarity of position between the previous sinful generation at Kadesh and Moses' audience at Moab shows that the hearer-reader is to identify with the people.[108] That Moses is prevented from entering the land shows that the ramifications of Israel's sin are great indeed. The impending death of Moses, addressed in 1:37–38 and 3:23–28, heightens the sense of doom for the reader. The future will be without Moses, the leader, law-giver and intercessor. If Moses fails to reach the land, one must doubt whether the next generation has any chance either.

### *Paradigmatic Sin*

One of the most important ways in which Israel's past faithlessness is portrayed is as a paradigm for the current and future generations. The importance of this will be seen in each of the three sections we are dealing with, 1–3, 8–10 and 29–30. It is important because this portrayal has clear implications for Israel beyond the past generation.

Of all the incidents of wilderness rebellion which Moses could have recounted, the spies incident is singled out and highlighted.[109] Why? We can only surmise an answer. The selection is certainly not to downplay Israel's rebelliousness. In many respects, by concentrating on just one incident, Israel's rebelliousness is put in a sharper focus.[110] Yet the singling out of the spies incident is surely not inappropriate given that Israel, addressed by Moses, is theologically in the same place as then, on the verge of entering the promised land. As at Kadesh, so at the Plains of Moab,

---

107 Ridderbos, 62; Kalland, 27; Mann, 486; though see Merrill, 82; Driver, 26. The suffering of Moses, the innocent one, need not imply vicarious suffering, contra von Rad (1960) 15–17; Cairns, 38; Kline (1963) 54; Phillips (1973) 19; D. Schneider, 42; Miller (1990) 42; (1987) 251–254; Lohfink (1994a) 231–232; Buis and Leclerq, 41; Munchenberg, 27. Vicarious suffering is "in the place of" and not the same thing as "because of". See Mann, 486; Burden, 113–114. Nielsen, 53, suggests that Moses' punishment is a model of the suffering servant of Isaiah 53. 1:37–38 are proleptic, foreshadowing chapters 31 and 34. On prolepsis in Deuteronomy, see Peckham (1985) 46. See Daube (1947) 25–39, on Moses' viewing the land as representing legal transference of ownership. He also discusses various possibilities of traditions about Moses' innocence and sin.

108 As Mann, 487–488, rightly argues. Compare Lohfink (1994a) 45–53.

109 Though see 9:7–24 for further incidents. The spies incident is important in Numbers, contra McConville and Millar, 20–21, but has a new significance in Deuteronomy. On the significance of the spies incident in Numbers, see Olson (1985) 138–144.

110 McKenzie, 95, "The motif of rebelliousness is found in the story of the scouts, and apparently he thought that this was a sufficient exposition of the idea."

Israel is on the border. The geographical border of the promised land is also the border of decision. Further, the spies incident throws all of the patriarchal promises into doubt. It is an extremely serious rebellion, rivalled only by the golden calf incident.[111] The dilemma of the whole of Deuteronomy is what decision Israel will make.[112] Will it choose life or not? Thus it seems highly significant that at the outset of the book, this story is retold. The covenant in the plains of Moab is a second chance; Moab is a second Kadesh.[113] Therefore the account of the spies is not told for the sake of a history lesson. It is told to encourage Israel to choose correctly. This is parenetic narrative, to bring Israel to the point of decision.

The placing of this account of Israel's failure at the beginning of Deuteronomy is strategic for it creates an initial sense of pessimism in the book.[114] Israel's sin and guilt are painted in as dark a way as possible. Despite every encouragement, Israel seems incapable of faithful obedience. As McConville says,

> At the outset the book anticipates...the people's inability to receive from God in faith and their corresponding tendency to trust their own perception of situations.... (1:26–46) has a special significance in the book because of its prominent position....[115]

The failure at Kadesh is Deuteronomy's, and DtrH's, "original sin", a paradigm (perhaps) for the future.[116] This failure casts a shadow over the book. Can the new generation be any different? Is this failure paradigmatic or not?

One indication that this failure is paradigmatic is that in Deuteronomy there is an actualisation of the past for the present. This feature identifies

---

111 Olson (1985) 144–145. See chapter 2 for a discussion of the golden calf incident.

112 Compare Olson (1985) 140, "The question of Numbers is this: what will be the fate of the new generation who did not see the Exodus and Sinai and who did not participate in the rebellion of the golden calf or the spy story? Will they also fail or will they be the recipients of the promise and enter the promised land?"

113 McConville and Millar, 23.

114 Indeed the Kadesh incident is featured as early as 1:2. See our discussion on 1:1–5 above.

115 McConville (1993b) 133.

116 Lohfink (1960) 118; Braulik (1986) 25; Buis and Leclerq, 39; Rose (1994) 477. Perlitt (1990b) 106–107, argues that Israel's failure at Kadesh is paradigmatic in that Israel still fails, at the time of writing Deuteronomy, even though there is a fluctuation between faith and unbelief. Tunyogi, 388, suggests that the representation of the wilderness generation as a failure and evil was to explain Israel's later disobedience in the land. Thus the fathers became "negative archetypes". Also Sailhamer (1987) 307–315; (1991) 241.

the current generation with its parents.[117] There are a number of illustrations of this in chapter 1. For example, v26 says וְלֹא אֲבִיתֶם לַעֲלֹת, linking the two generations, implying, perhaps, that the second generation is also expected to fail.[118] Similarly the expression "before your eyes" in v30 indicates that the current generation is identical with the one which left Egypt.[119] Also the first person plurals in chapters 1–3 draw in the current generation as if they were the previous one.[120] Possibly Deuteronomy reflects a corporate personality for Israel where there is a fundamental unity between all generations.[121] Deurloo argues that this generational link is demonstrated through the menorah-form of vv34–40. Central is Moses, flanked by Caleb, representing the old generation, and Joshua, the leader of the new. In turn, they are flanked by the ban imposed on the old generation and the permission to enter given to the new. The new generation "can recognise themselves in the little children and the sons who on account of their age cannot yet bear responsibility".[122] This argument however is weak. It is perhaps better to regard both Caleb and Joshua as witnesses linking both generations rather than Caleb belonging to the former and Joshua to the latter.[123] Deurloo further argues that Moses' denial in v37 is because of the past generation (בִּגְלַלְכֶם) but his refused request in 3:26 is because of the current generation (לְמַעַנְכֶם), the two verses thus conflating the generations. Again this point is unconvincing.[124]

Generational conflation is a feature of Deuteronomy designed to existentialise the decision facing the hearer-reader, but also giving the suggestion that the new generation is no different from its predecessor. This conflation is sometimes regarded as cultic whereby the present generation effectively participates in the same event as its predecessor because the content and context of the cultic event remain the same.[125] Though a cultic background may be possible, it is not certain. Narrative is just as, if not more, likely to

---

117 Von Rad (1965) 394. Also Whybray, 96. Also McConville and Millar, 42–43, on the importance of "today" in Deuteronomy; van Goudoever (1985) 145–148; Deurloo, 42–46.

118 Ridderbos, 60; Childs (1979) 215.

119 Weinfeld (1991) 148. Also Dillmann, 239. McConville and Millar, 31–32, suggest 1:7, 9, 18 all serve to link generations together.

120 Cairns, 32.

121 Plöger, 81.

122 Deurloo, 38–39. The menorah form is advocated by Labuschagne (1987) 130, on the grounds of logotechnical analysis.

123 See further Deurloo, 43.

124 Deurloo, 39.

125 Brueggemann (1961) 252–260. Also Childs (1979) 219; Murphy, 28. See chapter 3 on the supposition of a cultic background in Deuteronomy.

give rise to the cult than *vice versa*.[126] The current generation, in hearing preaching of past events is identified in those events and in some respects is regarded as being eyewitnesses of them.[127]

> The Moab-generation is supposed to identify with the Horeb-generation, with regard to the guilt of their seeing without perceiving and hearing without listening.[128]

This feature of generational conflation is pessimistic in nature. It contributes to the foreshadowing of doom in Deuteronomy 1–3, as Noth understood it, as DtrH moves inexorably toward exile. Thus it may be significant that Deuteronomy 1–3 omits Moses' intercession which occurs in the parallel in Numbers 14:13–19.[129] Lohfink further says,

> Ist der erste im großen Geschichtswerk erzählte Vorgang ein dunkles Gegen-Stück dazu, dann deutet dies noch Dunkleres für die Zukunft an. Schon im ersten Akt der zu erzählenden Geschichte erweist sich das Volk als unfähig, das heilige Grundbild seines Glaubens nachzuvollziehen.[130]

Yet these chapters are not all gloom and doom. For example, in the account of the spies in Numbers, the rebellion of Israel threatens its very survival. Yahweh pledges to Moses that he will destroy Israel and begin again with Moses (14:12). Moses' subsequent intercession succeeds in softening the punishment so that only the adult generation is excluded from entering the land.[131] None of this dilemma is repeated in Deuteronomy. The exclusion of the adult generation is simply announced (v35). Deuteronomy's account concentrates on Israel's condition of unbelief rather than the punishment. By avoiding discussion of the initial threat of punishment, and merely stating that punishment is restricted to the one generation, Deuteronomy places the Kadesh episode on an existential level.[132] That generation

---

126 Moberly (1983) 127–131. Though his argument concerns Exodus 32–34, this statement is just as applicable here.

127 Amsler, 15. Geller, 122, 128–129, discusses the relationship between 'hearing' and 'seeing' in Deuteronomy 4. He argues for a "covenantal primacy of hearing". Likewise Brueggemann (1961) 174–176; B. Smith, 20; Rennes, 233; Kittel, 218; Lenchak, 16–19. Horst, 548, writes, "Revelation is especially to the ear of man".

128 Deurloo, 43.

129 Lohfink (1960) 117–118; von Rad (1966e) 41. However compare Moses' intercession in Deuteronomy 9:26–29. Perhaps its omission in chapter 1 is for other reasons. Compare Van Seters (1994) 381.

130 Lohfink (1960) 120.

131 Though the concession to the next generation, 14:26–38, is usually regarded as P. See Jacobs, 351.

132 In both Numbers and Deuteronomy, Yahweh is active in instigating punishment. Compare Koch, 57–87; Jacobs, 64–65. See Gammie (1972) 5.

is gone; now another one is in its place. Will it abrogate its responsibility as its predecessor did or not?[133]

The conflation of generations in Deuteronomy is not absolute.[134] A distinction is made between the generations which suggests new possibilities and hope.[135] This tension between generational conflation and distinction is a theological one and should not be eased through literary or redactional solutions. The key is how the new generation relates to the old, a tension which runs through the whole book.[136] Though the distinction does suggest the possibility of hope, this must not be taken too far. It is overstating the point to argue that the first generation is defined by sin whereas the next is defined by obedience or that the first generation is guilty but its children are innocent.[137] Though the first generation is described as evil (v35), which is without parallel in Numbers,[138] the second generation is not innocent or spotless but under scrutiny. No firm decision has been made about it; its future is unresolved.[139]

New hope is also suggested by the relationship between 1:19–46 and the law of firstfruits in chapter 26, the climax of the legal corpus. Both passages refer to Numbers 13 and contain the theme of the goodness of the land. These two passages frame the laws. In the former, Israel rejects the land. The latter anticipates enjoyment of the land. The pessimism of 1:19–46 gives way to the optimism of chapter 26, a suggestion of new possibilities and new hope.[140]

Thus even in the account of the spies there is a suggestion of optimism in the face of pessimism. These twin threads run throughout not only chapters 1–3 but the whole book.

---

133 McKenzie, 97, suggests that what was a threat to the survival of Israel in Numbers is merely a postponement of the possession of the land in Deuteronomy. This ties in with his very positive view of chapters 1–3, almost the opposite of Noth. See McKenzie, 101.

134 McConville and Millar, 32–69, 124, argue that conflation is more apparent in 4–11 than in 1–3.

135 Jacobs, 354, notes the *waw*-adversative in 1:39, "but as for...", contrasting the two generations. Compare 2:14–16.

136 Childs (1979) 215.

137 Respectively Lohfink (1994a) 229 and Vermeylen (1985b) 13. See also Tunyogi, 390. This distinction of guilt and innocence is the basis for Vermeylen's postulation of a third Deuteronomistic redaction in 560BC. Rennes, 227, suggests that the Jordan is the frontier between disobedience and obedience.

138 Driver, 25; Weinfeld (1991) 149.

139 See Olson (1985) 151; Alexander (1995) 158. They consider the portrayal of the second generation in Numbers to be clearly positive, in contrast to Deuteronomy.

140 McConville (1984) 120–121.

## *Good and Evil*

Another expression which occurs in Deuteronomy but not in Numbers is בְּנֵיכֶם אֲשֶׁר לֹא־יָדְעוּ הַיּוֹם טוֹב וָרָע in v39.[141] This expression also contributes to Deuteronomy's portrayal of Israel. Most obviously it simply means children who, according to Numbers 14:29, are under twenty years old.[142] In Deuteronomy, the two generations are distinguished by knowledge of good and evil.[143] Lack of trust distinguishes those excluded from the land from those allowed to enter. Jacobs argues that the Deuteronomist has given particular content to this expression.[144] He argues that "good and evil" are defined in Deuteronomy by action responding to the commandments, basing his argument on 6:18; 12:28 and 30:15–19. As in 30:15–19, where good and evil parallel life and death, and the choice turns on the commandments, the adults in Deuteronomy 1 "chose" evil by disobeying the commandment and thus received death.[145] Thus Jacobs suggests that the expression in v39 foreshadows the choice placed before the people in 30:15–20 and that the covenant in Moab is the "coming of age" of the second generation.[146] His argument, though not totally convincing, nonetheless fits in with the observations we have made above. The connection between v39 and 30:15–20, the rhetorical climax of the book, poses the key question: What will this generation choose? Will it make the wrong choice,

---

141 Wenham (1981) 126, suggests that 1:39 presupposes Numbers 14:3, 31. Compare Skweres, 195–197. Both 1:39 and Numbers 14:31 begin in the same way, וְטַפְּכֶם אֲשֶׁר אֲמַרְתֶּם לָבַז יִהְיֶה.

142 Compare Cairns, 38, "two years old and under".

143 Jacobs, 353. The expression can refer to legal responsibility or be a cliché for "of age". See Clark, 267, 274. Rose (1994) 484, notes the play on good land and evil generation in 1:35. He also, 486, notes that the offer of land to the next generation, so defined in Deuteronomy, emphasises grace and not merit.

144 Jacobs, 354–355; Clark, 267. This is indicated by the insertion of הַיּוֹם into the cliché. Jacobs, 360, suggests that Dtr used the expression as a double entendre, using a well-known cliché but with his own content. It is unclear whether any allusion to Genesis 2 and 3 is intended or possible. The expression in 1:39 is the closest anywhere to Genesis 2:17 (Clark, 274; Dillmann, 240). One cannot fail to notice that as Adam and Eve failed and lost their right to their place with God, so did the earlier generation. Rose (1994) 477, 481, 486, 488, traces a number of motifs from Genesis 2, 3. Brueggemann (1982b) 33, suggests that the "motifs of Deut. 6:20–24 are strikingly parallel to those of Gen. 2:15–17: 'good/preserve/alive'". He also, 37, suggests "a playful connection between the *earth* of Genesis 1 and the *land* in Deuteronomy". Also see Plöger, 90. Carpenter, 80–81, suggests that the spies incident left Israel out of the land, in a similar way in which Adam and Eve were expelled from the land.

145 Jacobs, 356–360. He notes that נָתַן לִפְנֵי occurs in 1:21 and 30:19. See Lohfink (1960) 125–126, on this expression. Merrill, 75, notes that תַּמְרוּ אֶת־פִּי יְהוָה, in 1:26, expresses violation of specific commandments. Also Driver, 22.

146 Jacobs, 360–364. He argues this is part of the book's redactional scheme.

like its predecessor? Or will it choose life? Though Deuteronomy 1 is pessimistic, failure is not a foregone conclusion.

In summary, the portrayal of Israel in Deuteronomy 1 highlights a faithless people, despite repeated encouragement from Moses, the spies and Yahweh. Its faithlessness is both serious and without excuse. Not only so, it is also paradigmatic for future generations. Thus the current generation is identified in the sinfulness of its predecessor. However, there remain some small suggestions of hope. The generational conflation is not total. Some possibility exists that the new generation will be different. The question is thus raised, will this new generation respond correctly? Though the indications suggest a negative answer, nonetheless the question remains open. We turn now to consider the other side of the equation, the faithfulness of Yahweh in Deuteronomy 1.

## Faithful Yahweh in Deuteronomy 1

The previous section concentrated on the faithlessness of Israel portrayed in Deuteronomy 1. Even in that discussion we noted some possibilities of hope. We now look further at the optimistic strand in chapter 1 by examining the faithfulness of Yahweh which, in its juxtaposition with Israel's faithlessness, is highlighted.[147]

### *Yahweh's Promise*

The spies incident is set in the context of the faithfulness of Yahweh to his covenant promises to Abraham. This is first established in vv6–8, verses which are programmatic for the next three chapters.[148] As in 1:8, Yahweh's first speech, 1:35, Yahweh's second speech, also refers to the oath to the patriarchs. Thus the outer elements of the concentric speech structure both refer to the patriarchal promises. 1:6–8 begins with an emphasis on "Yahweh our God" which stands at the beginning of the sentence.[149] The reference in v8 to a sworn oath emphasises Yahweh's faithfulness and commitment. This is stronger than just a promise.[150] There is much debate,

---

147 Kline (1963) 53. McKenzie, 98, considers the antithesis between Yahweh's fidelity and Israel's infidelity to be one of the major themes of DtrH.

148 Preuß (1982) 79; McConville and Millar, 25; McComiskey, 70; Minette de Tillesse, 83. There are eighteen explicit references to the patriarchal promise of land, fifteen of which also speak of giving it. Miller (1990) 45. Compare J.G. Janzen (1987a) 291. Burden, 135–136, says, "The fulfillment of the promises and fidelity to the covenant are the primary motivating forces in God's actions". McKenzie, 96, calls 1:6–8 a theological correction of Numbers 11:11–15.

149 Miller (1990) 95. Compare Kalland, 20.

150 Driver, 14, gives a comprehensive list of references in JE to the oath to the patriarchs and to the promise, without oath specified. Mittmann, 23–24, regards 1:8

and no consensus, about the oath tradition given the scarcity of the word "oath" in such a context in Genesis. The three references in Genesis to such an oath, 24:7; 26:3; 50:24, are often regarded as secondary or Deuteronomic, in contrast to the Sinai covenant.[151] However the sense of oath, if not the vocabulary, exists in Genesis 15:18; 17:8 and need not be regarded as especially late, for the promise of land to Abraham is connected to the oaths to Isaac and Jacob, possibly in JE. Thus Deuteronomy's *Rückverweise* to the patriarchal oath in Genesis are legitimate.[152] So quite possibly Deuteronomy 1:8 alludes to Genesis 15:18, even though oath is not explicit there.[153] Some argue that Deuteronomy knows only a land promise to the patriarchs.[154] However, though land is certainly the main promise in Deuteronomy, those of descendants, increase and blessing to other nations also occur.[155]

The appeal of Deuteronomy to the patriarchal promises has been contested by Römer. Following a suggestion by Van Seters that the patriarchal tradition is post-Deuteronomy, Römer argued that "'the fathers' in Deuteronomy refers not to the patriarchs but to the ancestors of Israel in Egypt or at the exodus".[156] According to this view, the seven explicit references in Deuteronomy to Abraham, Isaac and Jacob, the first of which is in 1:8, are late redactions.[157] Lohfink has criticised Römer's thesis and argued that

---

as a general appeal to a range of Genesis references. Also Hagelia, 166–167; Steuernagel, 3; D. Schneider, 31. Oath, נִשְׁבַּע, plus either אֶרֶץ or אֲדָמָה, occur in 1:8, 35; 6:10, 18, 23; 7:13; 8:1; 9:5; 10:11; 11:9, 21; 19:8; 26:3, 15; 28:11; 30:20; 31:7, 23. See Plöger, 63–65; Skweres, 87–110.

151 See Plöger, 63–79. Similarly Bertholet, 4; Anbar (1982) 49–50, who considers that in a later version, covenant and oath were combined in a "strange hybrid phrase" in 4:31; 7:12; 8:18.

152 Skweres, 87–110. Compare Lohfink (1991b) 30; Kutsch, 103–115

153 Steuernagel, 3, says that though oath is not explicit in Genesis, it is implied in 15:18 to which Deuteronomy 1:8 alludes. He attributes Genesis 22:16; 26:3 to the Deuteronomist. Compare Alexander (1995) 51–56. Genesis 22 is the key passage in his analysis.

154 So von Rad (1966b) 80, "Deuteronomy understands the oath to the early patriarchs only as a promise of the land". Likewise Clements (1967) 65; Plöger, 66, 68, 78.

155 Kutsch, 107, says that "fast ausnahmslos" Deuteronomy has in mind the land promise. Clines, 58–59, acknowledges the elements of progeny and relationship. Thompson, 85, notes the twin promises of land and seed. Diepold, 79; Skweres, 87, note the promise of increase and relationship. Also Rennes, 190. Braulik (1994a) 13, notes that the promise to Abram regarding other nations in Genesis 12:2–3 is alluded to in Deuteronomy 4:7–8, 31. Von Waldow, 497, argues that the promises of land and greatness go together. Reference to the forefathers in Deuteronomy is not restricted to the promise of land. See 7:8, 12; 8:18; 13:18; 29:12.

156 Römer, 205; Van Seters (1972b) 451–452.

157 Römer, 206–207. See Preuß (1993) 243–244.

> the first mention of the fathers in Deut. 1.8 explicitly identifies them as Abraham, Isaac and Jacob and gives the key for understanding all further occurrences of אָבֹת.[158]

The seven explicit references to the patriarchs are one of many groups of seven in Deuteronomy. Whether or not they are original or late in the book, there is recognition that they are strategically placed in Deuteronomy.[159] Römer himself concedes that "Deut. 1.8 leads the reader to identify the fathers with the patriarchs" anyway.[160] The argument that the fathers are identified with the exodus generation breaks down in some places. For example, in 1:35 the two are explicitly distinct.[161] For our synchronic reading, the issue is perhaps not important. Deuteronomy intends that the references to the fathers are to be undersood as references to the patriarchs.

The perfect tense of נָתַן in v8 underlines the certainty of fulfilment of the land aspect of the patriarchal promise.[162] The borders of the territory described in v7 are perhaps more extensive than ever realised in Israel's history. Yet again they allude to a patriarchal passage, Genesis 15:18.[163] With respect to the conquest of the land, the promise undergirds any action Israel is called to take.[164] Further, the promise extends to the descendants, לְזַרְעָם, emphasising its perpetuity.[165] Perhaps herein lies already a statement of the extent of Yahweh's grace, that it will endure no matter what. Another implication of this opening emphasis on the patriarchal promise is that Horeb and Moab are set within that covenant. They are part of the fulfilment of patriarchal promise.[166]

---

158 Lohfink in Römer, 207. Also Diepold, 77–79; Veijola (1995) 153. Preuß (1993) 245, argues that Lohfink is too synchronic in his approach.

159 Braulik (1991a) 47. The others are 1:8; 6:10; 9:5; 29:12; 30:20; 34:4. Preuß (1993) 243, notes that Römer himself argues that these verses are strategically placed through the Pentateuch and not only in Deuteronomy.

160 Römer, 207.

161 Skweres, 101–110, lists other examples.

162 Weinfeld (1991) 134, that the perfect is a declarative present; as a legal conveyance, von Rad (1966e) 39 (contra Plöger, 62–63); as an already stated resolution or promise, König, 67; as 'promise to give', Whybray, 53.

163 Christensen (1991) 12; Miller (1990) 25; Hagelia, 167–169; Merrill, 68; Kalland, 22; D. Schneider, 31; Dillmann, 235; Steuernagel, 3; Craigie (1976) 96; Thompson, 85; Driver, 14; Mayes (1979) 120; Kline (1963) 52; Braulik (1986) 23; Mittmann, 23; Rose (1994) 375. Compare Exodus 23:31; Deuteronomy 11:24; Joshua 1:4. See Mittmann, 18–24. On the depiction of borders in ancient grant documents, see Weinfeld (1972) 78. On the relationship of this description and Eden, see Ottoson, 177–188. On Genesis 15:18 as Deuteronomic, see Anbar (1982) 51–52. On these boundaries and their relation to the Davidic kingdom and Josiah's expansionary policy, see Diepold, 31–41.

164 Miller (1990) 45.

165 Driver, 14. Weinfeld (1972) 181, regards this as P language.

166 Phillips (1973) 14.

This emphasis on the patriarchal promise continues in the next section, vv9–18, often regarded as an interruption in the context of chapter 1.[167] However the introduction to this section explains its presence: v10 is a statement of fulfilment of another aspect of patriarchal promise, descendants, כְּכוֹכְבֵי הַשָּׁמַיִם לָרֹב deliberately echoing Genesis 15:5.[168] It is the first time that this promise is said to have been fulfilled.[169] Thus unlike Numbers 11:11–15, the appointment of officials yields praise (v11), not complaint, for Yahweh is faithful.[170] Verse 11 also expresses continuity of covenant relationship from one generation to another.[171] This promise-fulfilment context is absent in the Exodus and Numbers accounts. The account of the appointment, vv12–18, therefore demonstrates concretely the reality of fulfilment.[172] These officials are thus a good thing, and not a challenge to Moses or an indication of decline in leadership and authority.[173] This is also the conclusion of Brueggemann whose argument is that the expression בָּעֵת הַהִוא in vv9, 16, 18, refers to a time which acknowledges the graciousness of Yahweh. This expression occurs clustered in three groups relating to three actions of Moses. These are the appointment of officals (1:9–18), the conquest of Transjordan (3:12, 18, 21, 23), and Moses' intercession (9:20; 10:1, 8). Each of these, he says, highlights Yahweh's

---

167 Veijola (1988) 252. Weinfeld (1991) 139, comments that these verses interrupt the command in v8 and its fulfilment in v19. He also, 137, noted Loewenstamm, 99, that "at that time" introduces a digression.

168 Brown, 34; Dillmann, 236; Craigie (1976) 96; McConville (1994) 202; Kalland, 24; Bertholet, 4. Burden, 109, "The covenant promises, then, stand at the heart of the motive for choosing the leaders". See also Hagelia, 57–59; Clines, 59. Compare Anbar (1982) 39–55. Skweres, 173–175, argues that 1:10 refers to a number of verses in Genesis (12:2f; 13:16; 15:5; 17:2–6; 22:17; 26:3f, 24; 28:14; 35:11; 46:3). See also Hagelia, 57.

169 Contrast Rose (1994) 472. See also Genesis 22:17; 26:4; Exodus 32:13, each time with כְּכוֹכְבֵי הַשָּׁמַיִם and the verb רבה. Compare 1:10 with 10:22; 28:62. Steuernagel, 3; Dillmann, 236; König, 67; Ridderbos, 57; Kline (1963) 53, all link vv10–11 to Genesis 12:2. On the hyperbolic language of this expression, see Eybers, 44–45.

170 Kline (1963) 53; Burden, 109; Mayes (1979) 119.

171 Driver, 16; Craigie (1976) 97; Maxwell, 36. Compare Mittmann, 31. Mayes (1979) 121, says that v11 explicitly links v10 to the patriarchal promise. Contrast Skweres, 173–175, who argues that 1:11 could refer back to Exodus 23:25–29 or Numbers 23:10 because it is a promise to Israel and not the patriarchs.

172 Braulik (1986) 24; Burden, 109.

173 So Mayes (1979) 119; Burden, 109, on the grounds that in Deuteronomy the people, not Moses, choose the officials. Both regard this as part of the overall picture of Israel's rebellion in this chapter. Similarly McConville and Millar, 25–26. Millar, 232, says the appointments have "disastrous effects" which vv19–46 show.

grace.[174] Thus the purpose of vv9–18 is encouragement. The fulfilment of progeny suggests the future fulfilment of land.[175] 1:9–18 is an appeal to the character of Yahweh as a faithful God.

That Yahweh is faithful is a vital truth in Deuteronomy. It is the major motivation for the future behaviour of the people both in entering the land and in their subsequent residence there. The past acts of Yahweh, so often appealed to in Deuteronomy, are not recalled simply to bear witness to Yahweh's power but they attest to his faithfulness to his promises.[176] The people fear that Yahweh will not be faithful. Such fear Deuteronomy seeks to dispel.[177]

### *Yahweh's Command*

Related to Yahweh's promise is his command, also an important feature in Deuteronomy 1. Though chapter 1 is predominantly about Israel's failure, and Israel returns to Kadesh at the end of the chapter, nonetheless Israel does move from Horeb to Kadesh. This movement, described in v19, is at Yahweh's command (v7) which is itself part of the fulfilment of promise.[178] This feature recurs in chapters 2 and 3. Everything which Israel does successfully is initiated, commanded and directed by Yahweh.[179] This is in contrast to Numbers where the movement of Israel, though guided by Yahweh, is mediated through his cloud. Deuteronomy instead stresses the commandment.[180] The importance of these divine commands in 1–3 militates against Noth and Mayes who fail to see any exhortation or warning in them. The frequency and importance of the divine commands to the first generations serve to draw in the reader under God's ongoing commands.[181]

### *Faithfulness and Faithlessness*

In order to complete the picture of the faithfulness of Yahweh in chapter 1, we need to see how this interacts with Israel's faithlessness. What we find is that in spite of its serious sin, there is hope for Israel, grounded in Yahweh's faithfulness to the Abrahamic promises. Israel's sin is expressed in v32 with אמן (hiphil), the same as in Genesis 15:6, possibly suggesting

174 Brueggemann (1961) 246–249. The expression also occurs in 2:34; 3:4, 8; 4:14; 5:5.

175 Clifford, 16.

176 Boissonard and Vouga, 9.

177 Boissonard and Vouga, 14.

178 McConville (1994) 202.

179 Weinfeld (1991) 131; Braulik (1986) 22. See below on Deuteronomy 2–3.

180 Clifford, 14–15; Kline (1963) 52. Compare Numbers 10:11–13.

181 McConville (1984) 3.

that its sin is related to the promises of Yahweh.[182] We have seen how the first speech, that of Yahweh in vv6–8, based on those promises is programmatic. Moses' first speech elaborates on this in v20 with a participle of נָתַן, suggesting imminence of fulfilment,[183] in combination with v21, the perfect of נָתַן, stressing certainty of fulfilment.[184] The spies' brief declaration, v25, endorses Yahweh's faithfulness by stressing the goodness of the land.[185] Thus at the centre of the chapter, in the midst of the account of great rebellion, is an unequivocal affirmation of Yahweh's promises and his faithfulness to them. This is continued in Moses' second speech, encouraging the people by appealing to Yahweh's faithfulness, power and fatherly provision. Even in the desert, the place of punishment, Yahweh was a tender father carrying his children all the way.[186] This is a poignant picture of undeserved care, faithfulness in the face of faithlessness.

Just as important is Yahweh's second speech, vv35–40, the counterpart to vv6–8. The significance of vv8, 35, which both mention patriarchal promise, is seen in that they belong to the frame of the concentric structure.[187] Though, in v35, Yahweh pronounces judgment against the first generation, his judgment is limited.[188] Caleb is rewarded for his wholehearted faithfulness.[189] Yet the future does not depend on Caleb nor on his faithfulness nor even on general future obedience. The promise is extended unconditionally to the next generation, children, whose lack of knowledge of good and evil (v39) shows that they themselves have no merit warranting this promise. Thus hope is based on the patriarchal promise, the language of

---

182 See Hagelia, 64–65, "This underlines emphatically the absurdity of the disbelief". This vocabulary, also in Numbers, shows the spies incident to be "the central example of disbelief in the Hebrew Bible", Hagelia, 68. This is in marked contrast to the belief of Abraham.

183 So Craigie (1976) 100, "is about to give" (participle of the immediate future); Kalland, 26; Joüon (1991) §121e; Cairns, 35. This participial expression is common in Deuteronomy. See Driver, 21.

184 Merrill, 72; Thompson, 87; Watts, 195, the repeated promise showing that Yahweh is irrevocably faithful to his word; Kalland, 26.

185 The brevity of the report compared to Numbers stresses the fruit of the land and, hence, Yahweh's faithfulness. Merrill, 74; Craigie (1976) 102.

186 This father metaphor occurs also in 8:5; 14:1; compare 2:7. See Weinfeld (1972) 368–369, for treaty parallels.

187 See above. On v35, see Skweres, 101–103.

188 קָצַף (v34) expresses strong anger in contexts where Yahweh is tempted to respond in kind and break the covenant (Merrill, 81). See 9:19 (qal); 9:7, 8, 22 (hiphil). The noun קֶצֶף occurs in 29:27 (Lisowsky, 1268). This root word occurs in each of the three accounts of Israel's failure, and nowhere else, in Deuteronomy. Rennes, 16, 230, notes that in Deuteronomy, only Israel or Moses is the object of Yahweh's anger, never the nations.

189 On comparison with Numbers, see Rose (1981) 288; Van Seters (1994) 378.

which is reflected in v39 (land, enter, give, possession).[190] As we have noted above, there is no threat to the survival of Israel in vv19–46 perhaps because, by comparison with Numbers, the "fidelity of Yahweh to his promises is thus stated with greater clarity".[191] Lohfink, following Daube, suggests that in v35, Yahweh legally withdraws the offer expressed in v8, but only for one generation. He immediately extends the offer to the next generation.[192] Lohfink sums up,

> Der Väterschwur Jahwes ist ein einseitiger Akt göttlicher Huld, eine göttliche Selbstverpflichtung, die durch keinerlei fehlenden Vertragswillen eines Partners vereitelt werden kann, die deshalb bei einer neuen Generation wieder neu wirksam wird.[193]

Thus Yahweh's faithfulness extends to an unfaithful people. His grace is greater than Israel's sin. There can be, and is, hope for the future, not based on any optimism about the behaviour of the next generation but hope grounded in Yahweh's faithfulness to his promises to Abraham. This, then, is a sure and confident hope.[194]

## Faithful Yahweh in Deuteronomy 2:1–3:20

It is sometimes said that whereas chapter 1 describes the disobedience and failure of Israel, chapters 2 and 3 are a counterpart describing its obedience and success.[195] Yet this is not a totally accurate representation. The emphasis in this section is on Yahweh, in particular his faithfulness and power. It is remarked that DtrH thinks of history theologically.[196] Indeed Deuteronomy 2–3 conceives of history both theologically and theocentrically. We turn firstly to the issue of structure in Deuteronomy 2–3 and its contribution toward an understanding of its theology.

---

190 Braulik (1986) 25; Skweres, 195–197.

191 McKenzie, 97.

192 Lohfink (1960) 124–127; Daube (1947) 25–55; Braulik (1986) 26. The onus was on the rebels who refused the offer, and therefore forfeited their right to the land.

193 Lohfink (1960) 127. See also Braulik (1986) 28. Likewise he argues that the failure of one treaty partner cannot render the oath invalid.

194 Compare Preuß (1982) 82.

195 Braulik (1986) 29; Perlitt (1985) 161, "Dem Scheitern dort (1:19–46) entspricht das Gelingen hier. Diese Gegensatz-Spannung exemplifiziert die dtr Predigt-Alternative Ungehorsam/Gehorsam." Similarly Millar, 232; Thompson, 90; Nielsen, 36.

196 For example, Lohfink (1994a) 228.

### *Structure of Deuteronomy 2:1–3:11*

Christensen detects concentric structures for 2:2–25 and 2:26–3:11. His structure for 2:2–25 is as follows:[197]

| | |
|---|---|
| 2:2–4a | a - Summons to Turn North (for battle) |
| 2:4b–6 | b - Summons: Not Contend with "Children of Esau" |
| 2:7 | c - A Look Backwards – the Exodus |
| 2:8–9a | d - Travel Notice and Summons Not to Fight Moab |
| 2:9b–11 | e - Emim dispossessed by "Children of Lot" |
| 2:12 | e' - Horites dispossessed by "Children of Esau" |
| 2:13–15 | d' - Summons to Cross Zered and Travel Notice |
| 2:16–18 | c' - A Look Forwards – the Conquest |
| 2:19–23 | b' - Summons: Not Contend with "Children of Ammon" |
| 2:24–25 | a' - Summons to Cross Arnon (for battle) |

We find this unconvincing. Concentric structures usually highlight the central elements. It seems odd then that the centrepoint should be the archaeological note, 2:9b–12, commonly regarded as a late insertion and even irrelevant to the narrative. The focus in the narrative is on Israel and its relations with these three nations. The pre-history, though serving a purpose in the narrative, is secondary. Christensen is in fact inconsistent for he subsumes the second archaeological note, 2:20–23, under b', the summons not to contend with Ammon.[198] 2:24–25 properly belongs to the accounts of Sihon and Og. It is also inconsistent to divide 2:9.[199] 2:9 corresponds to 2:5, 19. The closeness of the parallels between the three should make us question why Christensen sees only 2:5, 19 paralleling each other. His attempt to link 2:8–9a and 13–15 (dd') is unconvincing.[200] In all, Christensen's structure does not fit these verses nor does it shed any light on their purpose.

His structure for 2:26–3:11 is as follows:[201]

197 Christensen (1985a) 138–139. This is modified slightly in Christensen (1991) 39, but this does not affect our critique.

198 The modification in his commentary does not rectify this.

199 This is not done in the modified structure in his commentary.

200 In his commentary, 2:9 is linked to 2:12. It is hard to see why. He also links 2:13–14 with 2:8, a better link, but 2:14–16 is made to parallel 2:7.

201 Christensen (1985a) 138–139. Compare Christensen (1991) 52, where a slight modification is made regarding b' (3:3–7) and a' (3:8–11). This does not affect our critique.

| | |
|---|---|
| 2:26–30 | a - Anecdote about Sihon: Refusal of Request |
| 2:31–36 | b - Conquest of Heshbon |
| | 1) The Defeat of Sihon |
| | 2) Sihon's Kingdom Devoted to Destruction *at that time* |
| 2:37–3:1 | c - Travel Notice: Turn towards Og |
| 3:2 | c' - Summons Not to Fear Og |
| 3:3–10 | b' - Conquest of Bashan |
| | 1) The Defeat of Og *at that time* |
| | 2) Og's Kingdom Devoted to Destruction |
| | 3) Summary: Transjordan Conquest *at that time* |
| 3:11 | a' - Anecdote about Og: Last of Rephaim |

Again this is unconvincing. Christensen himself notes that b' has three parts whereas b has just two.[202] Also the anecdotes aa' are quite different in content. c' balances 2:31. c has as its closest counterpart 2:26, 32. Perhaps it is even better to regard cc' together paralleling 2:24–25.[203] Indeed apart from the offering of terms of peace to Sihon (2:26–30) and the epithet about Og (3:11), the two accounts are very similarly structured.[204] In Christensen's opinion, 2:37–3:2 is the focus of these accounts, but this is odd. The key is the defeat of the two nations, demonstrating the power and faithfulness of Yahweh.[205] We must look elsewhere to find more helpful structural suggestions for these five encounters of Israel with other nations.

The contrast between chapter 1 and chapters 2–3 is marked.[206] In chapter 1, the failure of the people means they do not progress after their sin, for which a concentric structure is highly appropriate. From 2:2, the action proceeds towards its goal with a new rhythm of command and execution.[207] Lohfink sees this pattern occurring four times, namely 2:2–8, 9–13, 14–33, after which there is a delay (vv34–37) before the cycle resumes in 3:1–3.[208] The absence of a report of execution with respect to Ammon leads Lohfink into combining Ammon and Sihon in the one cycle. This is the major weakness in Lohfink's structure, especially as the account of Ammon is peaceful and that of Sihon is not. Given that there are five nations with whom Israel deals, it seems better to look for parallels between the five.

---

202 The parallels between bb' are the most convincing in this structure. On the many similarities, see Weinfeld (1991) 180; Driver, 46; Craigie (1976) 119; Mayes (1979) 143.

203 2:31 repeats 2:24 in a stronger way. See Driver, 44; König, 75.

204 D. Schneider, 52. See further below.

205 Craigie (1976) 119.

206 Lohfink (1960) 129–130, notes that the contrast is verbal, factual and structural. He lists a number of allusions in chapters 2–3 to chapter 1. Also Braulik (1986) 33.

207 Lohfink (1960) 128. Also Buis and Leclerq, 43.

208 Lohfink (1960) 128–129.

Miller identifies three parallels in the accounts of Edom, Moab, Ammon, Sihon and Og. These are journey markers, divine commands and reports of accomplishment. His table is as follows:[209]

| | Journey Marker | Divine Command | Report of Accomplishment |
|---|---|---|---|
| Edom | 2:1 | 2:3–7 | 2:8a |
| Moab | 2:8b | 2:9–13a | 2:13b |
| Ammon | 2:18 | 2:18–20 | |
| Sihon | 2:24 | 2:24–31 | 2:32–37 |
| Og | 3:1 | 3:2 | 3:3–11 |

The similarities between the accounts of Sihon and Og suggest that these are parallel panels.[210] Each conquest is at the explicit command of Yahweh. His command is associated with a corresponding promise.[211] This pattern highlights the divine control over the events.[212] The priority rests on Yahweh's control and action. His control is promised: רְאֵה נָתַתִּי בְיָדְךָ (2:24), אָחֵל תֵּת פַּחְדְּךָ (2:25), רְאֵה הַחִלֹּתִי תֵּת לְפָנֶיךָ (2:31), בְיָדְךָ נָתַתִּי אֹתוֹ (3:2). This promise is fulfilled: וַיִּתְּנֵהוּ יְהוָה אֱלֹהֵינוּ לְפָנֵינוּ (2:33), אֶת־הַכֹּל נָתַן יְהוָה אֱלֹהֵינוּ לְפָנֵינוּ (2:36), וַיִּתֵּן יְהוָה אֱלֹהֵינוּ בְּיָדֵנוּ (3:3). Yahweh's control over Sihon's heart is recorded in 2:30.[213]

A similar, but more elaborate, structure is suggested by Braulik and Sumner. They argue for five common elements for each of Israel's five encounters in chapters 2 and 3. These are Israel's movement, divine command to Moses, prehistory of settlement of territory, provisions for the journey, and departure and/or possession.[214] There are weaknesses with this structure. The first element, Israel's movement, is in the form of a divine

209 Miller (1990) 37. Again there is no report of accomplishment for Ammon.

210 Craigie (1976) 120. Parallel panels and palistrophe are not necessarily mutually exclusive. For example, McEvenue (1971) 75–78, argues that Genesis 9:12–17 comprises both. Similarly Genesis 17:9–14 (167–171), Genesis 17 as a whole (157–159), and Numbers 13–14 (113–115).

211 Thompson, 94; Luther, 40.

212 Miller (1990) 37. Compare Rose (1994) 391.

213 Weinfeld (1991) 176, suggests this emphasis on Yahweh's command, promise and control reflects the context of Holy War, derived from Exodus 15:14–16. See Mayes (1979) 140; Weinfeld (1972) 45. The hardening of Sihon's heart also indicates that this is Yahweh's war. See Christensen (1991) 53; Brown, 49. The completeness of victory, ascribed to Yahweh and not Israel's heroism, is a further reflection that this is Yahweh's war. See Thompson, 96–97; Craigie (1976) 116–117, 119; Weinfeld (1972) 167; Cairns, 44. The laws of חרם apply to this Holy War. See 2:34 and 3:6, 7, and comments by Christensen (1991) 55; Thompson, 98; Driver 45, 51; D. Schneider, 52; Kalland, 35; Weinfeld (1972) 167, 344; König, 75.

214 Braulik (1986) 29–30; Sumner, 218–222. Also Mayes (1979) 134.

command in the cases of Ammon and Sihon, but a report in the other cases.[215] The prehistory element is out of order for Edom and Moab (2:12, 10 respectively), lacking for Sihon, and comprises 3:11 for Og. Yet 3:11 does not quite fit the category of prehistory. The provision of food element only occurs in the cases of Edom and Sihon.[216] Sumner argues that the final element in the case of Ammon is in 2:24.[217] However this is a command, not an execution, and seems to apply to Sihon rather than Ammon. Thus the only consistent element is the divine command. Both Sumner and Braulik argue that geographically one would expect Sihon to precede Ammon. The current order is artificial, in order to group together the nations into two groups of peace and war.[218]

Despite the gaps in the approaches of Lohfink, Miller, Braulik and Sumner, there are sufficient indications that 2:2–3:11 is a series of parallel panels rather than two concentric structures. The structural contrast between chapter 1 and chapters 2 and 3 is important. In the former, the structure was concentric based on the speeches. In that chapter, there was no effective movement of Israel. However in chapters 2 and 3, Israel moves towards the land. So the structure changes. Five parallel panels for the five nations Israel encounters, each initiated by a command of Yahweh which is then executed, show a steady and successful movement towards the Plains of Moab.

Finally, we should note that the system of five journey markers mentioned above also has a parallel in 1:6–8, 19, though we are not convinced by the suggestion that the resulting seven references are from a first person travel narrative source.[219] Similarly, the tenfold occurrence of בָּעֵת הַהִוא is regarded as a unifying structural link.[220] Miller's other two components, the divine command and report of accomplishment, also occur in chapter 1. So 1:6–8 is completed in 1:19; 1:40 in 2:1, further stressing the initiative and control of God.[221]

215 Mayes (1979) 134.

216 Sumner, 220–221, argues that 2:29 and Judges 11:17 suggest that Moab was originally associated with the provision of food. He argues the same for Ammon from Deuteronomy 23:3 but that the Deuteronomist has deliberately omitted these two for theological reasons. He makes no mention of the absence of this element in the case of Og.

217 Sumner, 221.

218 Sumner, 217; Braulik (1986) 30.

219 Plöger, 5–25; Watts (1970) 191. Contrast Skweres, 80. Christensen (1985) 140; Mayes (1979) 117; Braulik (1986) 22, extend this to chapters 31–34.

220 Braulik (1986) 22.

221 Skweres, 15, 39–42, notes that 2:1 refers back to 1:40, which, with 1:41, refers further back to 1:19 which in turn refers back to 1:6–8. This chain is without parallel in Exodus and Numbers. Also Cazelles (1966) 98; Braulik (1986) 22, note that 1:6–8 is a command without parallel in Exodus. Thus the importance of the

These structural observations prepare us for comment on the theology of the chapters, concentrating on the faithlessness of Israel and the faithfulness of Yahweh. The parallel panels of chapters 2 and 3 reflect the direct motion of Israel under the command of Yahweh towards the land. Clearly the two are to be contrasted.

### *Sihon and Og: Divine Initiative*

We have noted that each of the five encounters with Edom, Moab, Ammon, Sihon and Og is initiated by a divine command, which is then explicitly executed, making it clear that everything which happens does so at God's command, a feature absent in Numbers. The divine command is also emphasised by the expression in 2:17: וַיְדַבֵּר יְהוָה אֵלַי לֵאמֹר. Six times, namely in 1:42; 2:2, 9, 31; 3:2, 26, a simpler expression, וַיֹּאמֶר יְהוָה אֵלַי, occurs. The odd one out is 2:17, the central one of the seven.[222] The effect of the change in 2:17 is to highlight the passing of the first generation and thus the beginning of a new era inaugurated by Yahweh's words. The frequency of these divine words highlights the control of Yahweh as well as rhetorically bringing the audience under Yahweh's word.[223]

The account of the victory over Sihon in Deuteronomy is strikingly different from its parallel in Numbers. Yahweh is the key actor in Deuteronomy; in Numbers 21:21–31 he is not even mentioned.[224] In Deuteronomy, victory is credited to Yahweh. This is made clear in the command to attack, where Yahweh promises נָתַתִּי בְיָדְךָ אֶת־סִיחֹן (2:24), augmented by אָחֵל תֵּת פַּחְדְּךָ וְיִרְאָתְךָ (v25). These notions are repeated in v31, הַחִלֹּתִי תֵּת לְפָנֶיךָ אֶת־סִיחֹן. Then the promise is fulfilled by a victory ascribed to Yahweh in v33, יִּתְּנֵהוּ יְהוָה אֱלֹהֵינוּ לְפָנֵינוּ. This is repeated in v36, אֶת־הַכֹּל נָתַן יְהוָה אֱלֹהֵינוּ לְפָנֵינוּ. 2:37 mentions Israel's obedience to Yahweh's command in not encroaching on Ammon's territory. Thus the account of Sihon is pervaded by an emphasis on Yahweh's faithfulness and

---

divine command is clear as early as 1:6–8. Similarly Weinfeld (1991) 131, "Moses takes the trouble to inform each time that the move was executed according to God's command." Also Miller (1990) 25.

222 Langlamet, 79–81, followed by Weinfeld (1991) 158. Weinfeld suggests these expressions are almost prophetic in character.

223 Clifford, 11, "only when Israel follows the word of the Lord mediated through Moses (or 'a prophet like Moses') can they possess the land." Lohfink (1995) argues that the statements כַּאֲשֶׁר עָשָׂה (or similar) in 1:30; 2:12, 20–22, 28f; 3:2, 6, 21, function typologically with respect to the inheritance of the land.

224 Van Seters (1972a) 184; Perlitt (1985) 161; McKenzie, 99. Moses is also not mentioned in Numbers 21:21–31. Coats, 184–187, explains the absence of God in the Numbers account as due to its perception that Sihon's land was not part of the promised land. See further below. Cairns, 44, suggests that in Numbers Israel is heroic; in Deuteronomy Yahweh's role is decisive.

power. He promises victory; his own power achieves that victory. Even Sihon's opposition to terms of peace in v30 is attributed to Yahweh, כִּי־הִקְשָׁה יְהוָה אֱלֹהֶיךָ אֶת־רוּחוֹ וְאִמֵּץ אֶת־לְבָבוֹ, showing this is Yahweh's war.[225] The same emphasis on divine control occurs in the account of Og which is modelled on the account of Sihon (3:2, 3).[226] Indeed, the victory over Sihon and Og is signalled as God's work as early as 1:4. Yet human responsibility is never denied. The people are commanded to fight and their obedience is recorded (2:34–36; 3:3–10). Despite Yahweh's action on Sihon's spirit and heart, his own responsibility and guilt are upheld.[227] Nonetheless, human responsibility comes under divine sovereignty. The two are not incompatible.[228]

The persuasive rhetoric of the Sihon and Og accounts is also seen in the deliberate and repeated allusions to 1:28, the people's statement of fear at Kadesh. Thus all the towns were taken (2:34; 3:4) and "not one town was too strong for us" (2:36), even though they were fortified with high walls (3:5). 3:8–10 repeats what has been said, a rhetorical device to convince the current generation of Yahweh's faithfulness and power.[229] Furthermore the defeated Og was himself a giant, descended from the Rephaim.[230] These verses ridicule Israel's fear of 1:28 and exhort the current generation to trust Yahweh.[231]

---

225 This explains theologically Numbers 21:23. See Craigie (1976) 116; Driver, 42. Compare Exodus 7:3; 10:27. Usually the language refers to the heart; here the spirit is also mentioned. Weinfeld (1991) 174, states that the defeat of Sihon in Numbers is virtually an accident because of Sihon's refusal to allow passage. Also Braulik (1986) 33.

226 In Deuteronomy, unlike the supposedly Deuteronomic Numbers 21:33–35, Og, like Sihon, is a king of the Amorites. See Bartlett (1970) 275.

227 Cunliffe-Jones, 38; Ridderbos, 72; Cairns, 45; Clifford, 23; McConville (1994) 204. Contrast Phillips (1973) 26, who regards Sihon as "a mere pawn in God's hands". Thompson, 95, says, "the demands of God, once rejected, become a hardening influence".

228 Braulik (1986) 23, "So sind Gesetz und Land von Anfang eng miteinander verbunden. Beides ist zwar in die Verantwortung des Volkes gelegt. Doch ist es Gott, der die Geschichte in Gang bringt. Er rüttelt Israel aus seiner Stagnation beim Offenbarungsberg auf. Das Volk muß eine Wendung vollziehen und ins verheißene Land wandern".

229 Dillmann, 246; Craigie (1976) 120, "the emphasis and repetition serve to hammer home to the listeners the truth of God's faithfulness".

230 The Rephaim were mentioned in 2:20–21 and explicitly linked there to the Anakim, the object of Israel's fear in 1:28.

231 McConville (1994) 204; Kalland, 35; Craigie (1976) 119; Maxwell, 71.

### *Transjordanian Land*

Deuteronomy's presentation of Yahweh's faithfulness involves its portrayal of the status of the territory of Sihon and Og in Transjordan. Unlike Numbers 34:1–12, where Transjordan is regarded as distinct from the promised land, Deuteronomy gives the impression that Transjordan was part of it.[232] So, in Deuteronomy, Moses' final view of the promised land includes Gilead in Transjordan (34:1–4). The command to defeat Sihon (2:24–25, 31) resembles commands in Joshua (2:9–11; 4:24; 5:1). Thus the defeat of Sihon marks the beginning of conquest and 2:25b is modelled on Exodus 15:14, 16.[233] The Arnon (2:24) is like the Jordan in Joshua, the boundary of the promised land.[234] The Holy War חֵרֶם functions in Transjordan (2:34; 3:10); it is not mentioned in Numbers.[235] The land of Sihon and Og conquered by Israel is more extensive in Deuteronomy.[236] Gad and Reuben's request for land east of the Jordan is not considered sinful as in Numbers 32:7–15 and the distribution of the land in 3:12–17, with the territorial details, seems to parallel land distribution in Joshua 13.[237] In 3:20, they are also promised rest there, an indication of a legitimate inheritance not found in Numbers.[238]

---

232 Weinfeld (1991) 172–177; (1985) 93; Diepold, 30–31, 60–62. Braulik (1986) 33, argues that since Moses is in charge, Transjordan is not part of the promised land. McKenzie, 99, regards the land of Sihon and Og as a bonus for Israel. Kline (1963) 56, suggests that the offer of peace to Sihon shows Transjordan was not part of the promised land. Also Craigie (1976) 116; Thompson, 94–95. D. Schneider, 51, suggests this offer of peace to Sihon may have reflected Israel's fear and avoidance of war. Also Buis and Leclerq, 47.

233 Weinfeld (1993) 69–70; Kallai (1982) 183; Coats, 181; von Rad (1966e) 43. On the resemblance with Exodus 15, see Mayes (1979) 140; Moran (1963a) 340; Weinfeld (1972) 45.

234 Weinfeld (1993) 70; Coats, 188; Christensen (1991) 42; Diepold, 62. The Wadi Zered is also important as the threefold עָבַר in 2:13–14 suggests, Deurloo, 38.

235 Weinfeld (1993) 70–71; Driver, 45; Kalland, 35. Compare Kline (1963) 56, who suggests that the חֵרֶם principle applies because Sihon was an Amorite (Genesis 15:16), rather than because the land was part of the promise.

236 Compare 3:10 with Numbers 32:42; 3:14 with 32:40–41; 3:16–17 with 21:24. See Bartlett (1970) 276; Merrill, 104; Weinfeld (1991) 173; Rose (1981) 308–313; Mayes (1979) 142.

237 Weinfeld (1991) 174; Thompson, 98; Cairns, 48. Weinfeld (1993) 73, notes that unlike Numbers, the land is given to Reuben and Gad unconditionally. Diepold, 178, says the distribution of land to these tribes in Deuteronomy deliberately prefigures that of the remaining tribes in Cisjordan.

238 Weinfeld (1993) 73; McKenzie, 100; Mayes (1979) 146. The expression also occurs in 12:10; 25:19 and frequently in Joshua. See Weinfeld (1972) 343; Roth, 5–14. On Deuteronomy's theology of rest, see Braulik (1994d) 87–98. Weinfeld (1993) 66, argues that the conception of this extensive Transjordan as part of the

However, the issue is not clear cut. Transjordan is not regarded as equal in status to Cisjordan.[239] There is a tension between two representations in Deuteronomy. The one includes Transjordan. The other marks the Jordan River as the major boundary, and the land west of it remains the focus of promise and anticipation.[240] The descriptions of the land which emphasise its fruitfulness and beauty and describe it as a "good" land exclusively refer to Cisjordan.[241] The representation of Transjordan in terms identical to Cisjordan serves, it seems to us, to undergird the faithfulness of Yahweh and encourage trust in him. The defeat of Sihon and Og is regarded as partial fulfilment of the patriarchal promise in order to give further encouragement for the imminent Cisjordanian conquest. This characterisation thus serves as an argument *pars pro toto*, "as the firstfruits, so the main harvest".[242] Thus Deuteronomy's way of describing Transjordan is rhetorical. It serves to highlight the faithfulness of Yahweh to his promise.

### *Edom, Moab, Ammon*

Divine control is also found in the peaceful encounters in chapter 2. In contrast to Numbers 20:14–21, any opposition threat, especially that of Edom, is toned down. Rather than being hostile, Edom is afraid.[243] Bartlett suggests that v5 acknowledges enmity but disapproves of it, stressing instead Edom's kinship as אֲחֵיכֶם בְּנֵי־עֵשָׂו, which is absent in Numbers.[244] This Deuteronomic emphasis could be explained theologically. It wants to stress the absolute control of Yahweh, that real opposition (Sihon and Og) is easily defeated and other nations are friendly and not a threat. This sovereignty of Yahweh strengthens the appeal to his faithfulness. The successes over Sihon and Og show that what Yahweh promised happens, just as we saw in chapter 1.[245] He is faithful to his promise. Even the aside

---

promise was fostered in the United Monarchy period. See Kaiser (1973) 138–142; Weinfeld (1991) 172–178.

239 Compare Weinfeld (1985) 93.

240 Diepold, 29–41. On the importance of the Jordan, see Diepold, 29, 57, who notes 2:29; 3:18, 25–27; 9:1; 11:31; 30:18; 31:3. Craigie (1976) 116, notes 2:29 suggests a lower view of Transjordan than Weinfeld argues. The Jordan is mentioned in chapters 1–3 in: 1:1, 5; 2:29; 3:8, 17, 20, 25, 27.

241 Compare Diepold, 85–87.

242 Cairns, 49.

243 Miller (1990) 37–38.

244 Bartlett (1989) 181–184, 194–200. He concludes that the positive attitude to Edom may suggest a religious connection, as in Judges 5:4. D. Schneider, 44, suggests that God effects blessing in concentric circles around the Abraham relationship. Hence the Edomites are "brothers", though not Moab or Ammon. See Cairns, 39; Weinfeld (1991) 166; Dillmann, 242.

245 Compare Braulik (1986) 31.

in vv14–16, which three times solemnly mentions the death of the previous generation, shows the fulfilment of Yahweh's oath recorded in 1:35. It is his hand (v15) which is instrumental, not human causes as in Numbers.[246] The description of that generation as "warriors", unlike in Numbers, plays down Israel's current might and directs attention to Yahweh's power.[247] Yahweh keeps his word. He can be trusted.

The theme of Yahweh's faithfulness is also found in the description of the land given by Yahweh to Edom, Moab and Ammon "as a possession", יְרֻשָּׁה, in 2:5, 9, 19 respectively, a word which does not occur in Numbers. Firstly, this statement is the basis for the prohibition against trespass and hostility by Israel. Secondly, Israel's possession is analogous to that of the other nations.[248] So in v12, יְרֻשָּׁה is applied to Israel in what looks like a later note.[249] The noun יְרֻשָּׁה occurs just seven times in Deuteronomy: 2:5, 9 (twice), 12, 19 (twice); 3:20.[250] The more usual noun for the land given to Israel is נַחֲלָה. In Deuteronomy, every occurrence of נַחֲלָה and the verb נָחַל, except one, refers to Israel, a tribe of Israel or an Israelite.[251] Thus, normally, נַחֲלָה is not used of other nations. Hence in 2:1–23, יְרֻשָּׁה is used for Edom, Moab and Ammon. Though there is a semantic distinction between the two words, nonetheless the implications of יְרֻשָּׁה in chapter 2 are much the same as for נַחֲלָה elsewhere.[252] That is, there is a sense of permanence, protection, even inviolability, attached to the land. Now the point being made in Deuteronomy 2 is not just about the prohibition against attacking Edom, Moab and Ammon. The description of Israel's land as יְרֻשָּׁה in v12 makes an important rhetorical point. In the same way that Yahweh has both given and protected the יְרֻשָּׁה of these three nations, so will he do the same for Israel. Thus the function of this section is to motivate and encourage the Israelites in their forthcoming conquest by

---

246 Weinfeld (1991) 163–164; Mayes (1979) 138; Braulik (1986) 32; Driver, 39; Clifford, 21; Dillmann, 244; Merrill, 95; Thompson, 93; D. Schneider, 44; Skweres, 68–69. Moran (1963a) 334, comments on the solemn style of vv14–16. The גַּם in v15 is emphatic, says Muraoka, 145.

247 Moran (1963a) 335–338. See also Weinfeld (1972) 45.

248 Sumner, 220.

249 The mention of Israel in v12 is usually regarded as an anachronism. Kalland, 32, suggests it refers to the territory already taken, namely that of Sihon and Og.

250 See Braulik (1991a) 40. He states, "Seine Belege bilden eine palindromische Struktur, in deren Zentrum Israels Inbesitznahme des Landes als seiner יְרֻשָּׁה steht".

251 The exception is 32:8 (נָחַל hiphil), though compare 32:9. De Menezes, 20, fails to notice 2:12, and thus wrongly concludes that יְרֻשָּׁה applies to non-Israelites and נַחֲלָה to Israel.

252 Lohfink (1990) 384, argues that there is a terminological distinction between the conquest under Moses, using יְרֻשָּׁה, and that under Joshua, using נַחֲלָה. Lohfink himself acknowledges there is no semantic distinction between יְרֻשָּׁה in 3:20 and נַחֲלָה. He says, 376, that in Deuteronomy 2, יְרֻשָּׁה is like a family נַחֲלָה.

appealing to the faithfulness of Yahweh.[253] Because the argument depends on the similarity between Israel's possession of land and that of these other nations, the same word must be used for both. As נַחֲלָה is not generally applied to other nations, יְרֻשָּׁה is used for both Israel and the other nations. In summary, the two points being made are the grounds for not attacking Edom, Moab and Ammon, as well as the rhetorical encouragement about Yahweh's faithfulness, made by the inclusion of Israel's land as יְרֻשָּׁה in v12.

The archaeological notes of 2:10–12, 20–23, so often dismissed as out of place and late inclusions,[254] in fact specifically contribute to the rhetorical and theological function of the surrounding verses, namely encouraging faith in Yahweh.[255] In 1:28, the people are afraid to enter the land for the inhabitants are stronger, taller and include Anakim. Now, for the next generation, these archaeological notes serve to dispel directly those same fears. Thus 2:10 mentions that the descendants of Esau drove out עַם גָּדוֹל וְרַב וָרָם כָּעֲנָקִים.[256] So in v10 the Anakim are deliberately mentioned as a foil to 1:28 and Israel's past failure.[257] The implication is obvious. If Yahweh defeated the Anakim for Esau, so can he surely do for Israel. The fears of Kadesh are groundless. Yahweh can indeed be trusted; he is faithful and able.[258] The same can also be said for vv20–23. Again the dispossessed people are described as עַם גָּדוֹל וְרַב וָרָם כָּעֲנָקִים (v21), again countering 1:28. Again the main purpose of this parenthesis is to instil faith and trust on the part of Israel.[259] The argument continues that Israel is to be compared with Edom, Moab and Ammon in that what Yahweh has

---

253 Maxwell, 62.

254 For example, Dillmann, 243; Mayes (1979) 139.

255 McConville and Millar, 28. Weinfeld (1972) 72, notes that in Hittite treaties, there is often mention of land given to others by the overlord. Compare Buis and Leclerq, 45. Christensen (1991) 41, argues that prosodic analysis suggests these notes are an essential part of the original. Similarly Labuschagne (1985) 113. Compare Weinfeld (1991) 161; Polzin (1987) 94; (1981) 206–208; Van Seters (1994) 384.

256 Compare 1:28 which has גָּדוֹל and רָם. A Samaritan text has רַב in place of רָם whilst the LXX has both, thus making the parallel with 2:10, 21 even more precise. Compare Numbers 13:31. See further, Weinfeld (1991) 142.

257 On the identity of the Anakim and links with the Rephaim, Emim, etc., see Driver, 36–38; Craigie (1976) 111; Weinfeld (1991) 156, 161–162. Compare also Numbers 13:33.

258 Clifford, 19; Dillmann, 243–244. There is perhaps a sense in which these archaeological notes embarrass Israel, ridiculing its former fear. See McConville and Millar, 28; D. Schneider, 46.

259 So also the description of Og's cities in 3:5, עָרִים בְּצֻרוֹת, recalls 1:28, עָרִים בְּצוּרֹת בַּשָּׁמָיִם. In 3:11, Og's size is stressed, showing that the Kadesh fear of giants is unfounded. See Sumner, 220. Could it even be that by saying that Og is the last survivor of the Rephaim that Israel's confidence is to be boosted further, for there will be no more giants on the West side of the Jordan?

promised to do for Israel, he has already done for them. He has the ability to keep his promises. He can be trusted to fulfil the same promise to Israel. Indeed within the broader context of the special relationship between Yahweh and Israel, the implication is that if Yahweh has driven out such giants before Edom and Ammon, how much more will he so do for his special people Israel.[260]

These asides then serve not only a rhetorical function but a theological one as well. They draw attention to Yahweh's power, universal sovereignty and faithfulness. The greatness of Yahweh's character is in fact heightened by the absence of any dismissive comment about the opposition. There is never a hint of denial of the size and strength of Israel's opposition. They are great, numerous and giants. But Yahweh is greater and more powerful. It is thus to these attributes that Israel is called to respond appropriately in faith. As we have noted, Israel's failure at Kadesh was a failure of faith (1:32). Deuteronomy 1–3 is a call to faith.[261]

### *The Priority of Yahweh's Faithfulness*

We have seen in our discussion of Yahweh's faithfulness two complementary appeals. In order to trust in Yahweh's promises, two things must hold. Yahweh must be regarded as both reliable and able. Reliability is addressed by appeals to past promises, showing that Yahweh has kept them. Ability is addressed by showing that Yahweh has the power to keep promises he has made. The latter is the precise issue addressed in 2:1–3:11. Reliability without ability is an insufficient ground for faith, and vice versa.

The significance of this argument is that the failure to see the theocentric nature of 2:1–3:11 and its appeal to Yahweh's sovereignty and faithfulness, results in regarding this section as a statement of Israel's ability to obey, in contrast to Israel's disobedience in chapter 1. This is too simplistic. An appreciation of the theocentricity allows us to see more carefully the real contrast. Though Israel does obey, the initiative and power for victory belong to Yahweh. Israel is to rely on Yahweh, not its own ability. Success is grounded in Yahweh and not Israel. This is also what we found in chapter 1. Hope beyond the spies incident lies in Yahweh and not Israel.

From another angle, we can consider the relationship between command and promise. Important though they are in 2:1–3:11, if Yahweh's commands stood alone, Israel's obedience would be the key for hope. A concentration on the command-execution schema in chapters 2 and 3 runs

---

260 D. Schneider, 50, "Wenn er nun schon anderen Völkern half, mit übermächtigen Gegnern fertig zu werden, um wieviel mehr wird er seinem auserwählten Volk gegen übermächtige Feinde helfen!"

261 On the relationship between faith in and obedience to the Mosaic law, see Sailhamer (1991) 241–261.

this risk. However, all the commands in chapters 1–3 derive from the programmatic 1:6–8 which sets the command into the context of the patriarchal promises. Yahweh commands in order to fulfil his promises. Thus the priority lies with Yahweh's faithfulness and not Israel's ability. It is important then to read chapters 2 and 3 as a clear expression of Yahweh's faithfulness to the Abrahamic promises.[262]

These, then, are the two options. Israel could attempt to act in its own strength, but such an option gives no hope, for Deuteronomy is pessimistic about Israel. Alternatively Israel can depend on Yahweh, his power and faithfulness to his promise. Therein lies a sure hope, even in the midst of Israel's failure, for Deuteronomy is optimistic about Yahweh. The strands of optimism and pessimism are not irreconcilable. Yahweh remains faithful whatever the situation. Israel's faithlessness does not contradict his faithfulness. It merely casts it in a clearer light.

## Moses in 3:21–29

The final paragraphs in chapter 3 continue the interplay between pessimism and optimism, Israel's failure and Yahweh's faithfulness. Many of the themes of chapter 1 return in 3:18–29, showing the enduring validity of Yahweh's promises for the new generation.[263]

### *3:21–22*

The sufficiency of Yahweh is highlighted in 3:21–22. Verse 21 stresses the activity of Yahweh, making explicit the parenetic character of all that precedes. What Yahweh has begun in the past, he will complete in the future. The syntax of v22 also reveals the pre-eminence of Yahweh's activity: "Yahweh your God, he will fight for you".[264] This expression also alludes to the encouragement of Moses in 1:30 which was given in the midst of Israel's rebellion thirty-eight years previously. The inference to be drawn is clear. Israel may have failed, but the promise of Yahweh still stands, even a generation later. It is an appeal again to his faithfulness. The imminent loss of their leader may well have been a cause for despair. Yet there is hope, not because of Joshua's capability, but because of Yahweh's

---

262 Minette de Tillesse, 83.

263 Braulik (1986) 37, lists a number of parallels. The emphasis on seeing "with your own eyes" (3:21) was also a feature of chapter 1. Also see McConville and Millar, 30; Weinfeld (1991) 189.

264 Muraoka, 70. There is also a striking contrast between the second and third persons. Compare 1:30 and the emphatic הוּא there (Driver, 24).

promise and faithfulness. The commissioning of Joshua (3:21–22, 28) focuses on Yahweh, not Joshua.[265]

### *3:23–25*

Moses' prayer in 3:23–25 is without parallel in Numbers. Moses is convinced of Yahweh's faithfulness in his prayer and makes it a point of praise (v24 "begun").[266] His prayer is full of expressions typical in Deuteronomy expressing faith in the God of the exodus.[267] The goodness of the land is stressed, טוֹב occurring twice in v25, as in 1:35 highlighting Israel's previous error.[268]

Moses' prayer begins אֲדֹנָי יְהוִה.[269] This personal expression also occurs in prayers of Abram (Genesis 15:2, 8), Moses (Deuteronomy 9:26), Joshua (Joshua 7:7), Gideon (Judges 6:22), Samson (Judges 16:28), David (2 Samuel 7:18–29, seven times) and Solomon (1 Kings 8:53).[270] Each of these occasions is significant in the context of the promises of Yahweh. In the prayers of Genesis, Deuteronomy, Joshua and Judges, the promises of Yahweh are under threat. In 2 Samuel, David is overawed by the promise. In 1 Kings, the appeal is to Yahweh's faithfulness to his covenant promise. It seems then, in Genesis–2 Kings, that the expression is reserved for important prayers within a covenantal promise context.[271] Therefore this address serves to highlight what we have already seen, that Moses' prayer stresses the faithfulness of Yahweh to his promises even when they are under threat, in this case through the people's sin and Moses' own imminent death.[272]

---

265 Kline (1963) 58; Maxwell, 79.

266 Bertholet, 13, who says, "Jahwe hat angefangen; warum sollte er nicht fortfahren?" On praise in prayers for help, see Miller (1994) 63–64.

267 For example, "strong hand", "what God is there…", "mighty works". See Weinfeld (1991) 190–191; (1972) 329; Maxwell, 80; Driver, 60.

268 Ridderbos, 79; Driver, 60.

269 Weinfeld (1991) 190–191.

270 The only instance in Genesis–2 Kings where the expression occurs outside a prayer is 1 Kings 2:26, referring to the ark of the Sovereign LORD. The expression is common elsewhere, most especially Ezekiel and Amos.

271 Hagelia, 30–31.

272 The closest prayer to this is that of David, both in address and the statement of praise and incomparability which follows. See Miller (1994) 63–64.

### *3:26–29*

Moses' request is turned down. As in 1:37, Yahweh's anger at Moses is strongly expressed.[273] This wrath of Yahweh "helps create a troubled atmosphere of foreboding at its beginning, and its intentional direction points to the final catastrophe".[274] As in 1:37, the blame is laid on Israel. The repetition of this denial, "because of you",[275] the second time after his prayer, leaves us in no doubt that Israel's failure was a serious matter. Moses' exclusion from the land sharpens the concern for Israel to reverse the decision made at Kadesh.[276] His imminent death hangs like a shadow over Deuteronomy, giving it the character of a "last will and testament".[277] Its announcement here, at the end of the historical prologue, and its realisation in chapter 34, frame all the law with a sense of impending doom.[278]

The mention of Beth Peor in 3:29, scene of great sin in Numbers 25:1–9, ends the chapter with tension.[279] Will the new generation be any better than its predecessor? There is absolutely no indication that it will. Indeed the new start described in chapters 2 and 3, after the failure of chapter 1, also culminates in the ominous refusal to heed Moses' prayer and his imminent death.[280] Yet there remains great hope, not in Israel, but Yahweh. The future is determined by the promises he made to Abraham, even in the face of Israel's failure. Braulik comments on vv23–28,

---

273 Here using the even stronger word יִתְעַבֵּר than the strong word הִתְאַנַּף in 1:37 and 4:21 (Driver, 60), connoting furious anger, and a pun on עָבַר at the end of v27. So Christensen (1991) 66. Also Cairns, 50; Mayes (1979) 147. The anger against the people in 1:34 is expressed by קָצַף.

274 McCarthy (1974) 106. He notes that mention of the wrath of Yahweh is common in the framework of Deuteronomy. He lists: 4:21; 6:15; 7:4; 9:8, 19, 20; 11:17; 29:19, 23, 26, 27; 31:17, omitting 1:37.

275 Here לְמַעַנְכֶם, whereas בִּגְלַלְכֶם in 1:37.

276 McConville and Millar, 30. Mann, 487–488, suggests that the death of Moses could not provide consolation for exiles but rather despair. That Moses suffers may seem unjust. Maybe that sense of injustice is intended to be an added spur for the next generation to trust and obey.

277 Mann, 483, 491.

278 Mittmann, 172; Lohfink (1994b) 234–247, note that the death of Moses (3:23–27; 34:1–8) is a concentric construction, along with mention of his successor (3:28; 31:1–2, 7). See further Olson (1994) 17, 27, 165, 170, 175, who suggests there is some ambivalence about Moses' death in Deuteronomy since it is also the avenue of life for the people (understanding his death almost vicariously). However this reads too much into Moses' death being "because of" the people. Similarly Miller (1988) 34–35.

279 McConville and Millar, 30–31. Whether anything should be made of the term "Beth Peor", rather than "Baal Peor" or "Peor" as in Numbers, is hard to tell. Deuteronomy avoids the name of any other god.

280 Mann, 491–492.

> Das in 1 entworfene Gottesbild, Jahwes Gnaden- und Gerechtigkeitsprinzip in seiner Treue gegenüber dem Väterschwur und in seiner Strafgerechtigkeit angesichts der Glaubensverweigerung, ist also endgültig.[281]

## Conclusion

Deuteronomy 1–3 deals explicitly with the faithlessness of Israel. Its sin in the spies incident is highlighted as being without excuse, totally culpable and in clear opposition to the spies, Moses and Yahweh. Moreover, the sin is seen to be paradigmatic, in particular in the technique of generational conflation. This indicates that the current, and future, generations share the same character as the past generation. This depiction creates a sense of pessimism in Deuteronomy 1–3. However the failure of Israel in the spies incident is resolved in these chapters. This resolution is not due to any repentance or change on the part of Israel, for there is none. Rather it is due to the grace of Yahweh, in particular expressed in the promises to the patriarchs. Deuteronomy 1–3 shows that Yahweh's faithfulness to the patriarchal promises is not annulled by Israel's faithlessness. It is this faithfulness to promise which provides the impetus for the successful journey and victory in chapters 2–3. Success belongs to Yahweh, not Israel. Thus in tension with the pessimism of Israel's faithlessness, but theologically compatible with it, is the overarching faithfulness of Yahweh to his promises.

Related to this we suggested that law is a subset of promise. That is, God's commands serve the fulfilment of his promises. By its position at the beginning of the book, this account of Israel's failure and Yahweh's faithfulness provides a filter for reading the rest of the book. That is, Deuteronomy 1–3 colours how we should read the law and parenesis. The extraordinarily demanding requirements, summed up in the Shema, are idealistic. In the light of Israel's inevitable failure, the idealism of the law exposes Israel's inability and its need to depend on Yahweh's grace. However failure is not the final story. Yahweh's faithfulness encompasses Israel's failure. The promises are greater than the law. The alternatives in Deuteronomy are not simply obedience and disobedience, nor grace and law.[282] They are Israel, and hence its sin and faithlessness, and Yahweh, his

281 Braulik (1986) 38.

282 Polzin (1980) 39, speaks in terms of grace and law, the former linked to Yahweh's mercy, the latter to his retributive justice. The term "law" has many senses. The problem is not with God's law but the inability of God's people to keep it. We are concerned not to set up an opposition between law and grace, which both come from God, for that could suppose an opposition within God. Grace and law are compatible, as our discussion on promise and command implies. Indeed grace demands obedience. See D. Schneider, 33–34. On Polzin, see McConville (1989) 32–33.

grace and faithfulness. In a sense then chapters 1–3 set the agenda for the rest of the book. As Israel received over and over the divine promise but refused to act, so the book "will echo and anticipate disobedience and unwillingness to live by promise and instruction."[283]

Optimism and pessimism, idealism and realism, are not fundamentally opposed strands or themes. They need not be explained as stemming from different redactions or historical circumstances. In the wilderness Israel had already experienced serious failure. It also knew that subsequent generations were no different from that exodus generation. Indeed if that generation could personally experience the glory of the miracles of the exodus and wilderness, and yet fail, one could hardly expect future generations to succeed. It did not need a long history of the nation in Canaan to develop a theology of Israel's basic inability to keep the covenant faithfully.[284] Yet also in the wilderness Israel had already experienced the grace of restoration. It did not need an exile in Babylon to develop a theology of Yahweh's grace and faithfulness to patriarchal promise. If both these themes had already been experienced together, then there is no reason why the theology of Deuteronomy cannot hold them together for the present and the future.

Thus we contest the redaction-critical presuppositions that for one particular audience either optimism or pessimism, but never both, is relevant. Jacobs, for example, identifies two themes in Deuteronomy 1–3, namely "loss of promise and faithfulness of Yahweh's word". However he can only hold them together via different redactional levels, namely the audience of the second generation and the exilic audience of DtrH. To the former, the message is a warning, a pessimistic threat of loss of land. To the latter, the message is a statement of hope and optimism.[285] We argue that for the second generation, the two can co-exist because of the uncertainty of their response to "אֵלֶּה הַדְּבָרִים". In any case, we would contest the title "loss of promise". The very point is that the promise stands, even if one generation (in 1:19–46) forfeits their opportunity to receive it.[286] So Schneider says,

> Es erhebt sich nun die Frage: Sollte der ständig im Blick stehende zukünftige (z.T. auch gegenwärtige) Abfall des Volkes den Schwur Gottes den

283 Miller (1990) 36.

284 Compare McKenzie, 97, who suggests that "there are hints in Deuteronomy that Israel because of its infidelity to the covenant never achieved the fullness of the promise of the land".

285 Jacobs, 349–350.

286 Compare Plöger, 53, "Es bedarf kaum noch einer Erklärung, was diese Deutung der Historie für die Generation bedeutete, die Dtr angeredet hat. Alles Unglück, Exil und Verlust des Landes ist Folge eures Ungehorsams gegen Jahwes Willen aus Glaubensschwäche.... Aber auch jetzt noch bleibt die Verheißung in Kraft für eine kommende Generation."

> Vätern und ihren Nachkommen die Treue zu halten, hinfällig machen? Das Deuteronomium sagt: Nein! Um des Schwures Gottes an die Väter willen, der nicht annulliert werden kann, gehören auch die Passagen über die endzeitliche Sammlung und Rückkehr Israels konstitutiv zum Aufriß dieses Buches hinzu und können nicht als spätere Zugaben abgetrennt werden.[287]

The themes of optimism and pessimism are integral to Deuteronomy for it is a book preaching for decision. Chapters 1–3 set the agenda for the book by raising the question: How will this, and every, generation choose? The implications are that Israel will fail. Yet Yahweh's grace will stand.

287 D. Schneider, 32.

## CHAPTER 2

# Faithless Israel, Faithful Yahweh in Deuteronomy 8–10

The second major account of Israel's failure in Deuteronomy is the report of the golden calf incident in chapter 9. As with Israel's failure in the spies incident in Deuteronomy 1, the resolution of failure into future hope after the golden calf incident is entirely due to Yahweh's grace and his faithfulness to the patriarchal promises. It is not grounded in any optimism about Israel's ability to keep the covenant. Though our primary concern in this chapter is with the golden calf incident (9:7–10:11), the broader context of 8:1–10:22 is important for understanding these themes.

As explained in the introduction, our rationale for moving from chapters 1–3 to 8–10 is the account of Israel's failure in the golden calf incident. The same themes of Israel's faithlessness and Yahweh's faithfulness occur in chapter 4 but these have a fuller parallel in chapters 29–30 which we discuss in detail in the next chapter. Within chapters 5–11, these themes find their clearest expression in chapters 8–10.

### Introduction

Deuteronomy 5–11 has occasioned much discussion regarding its form, structure, redaction, coherence and relationship to other parts of the book. There is no clear consensus about these chapters. Few scholars nowadays maintain the overall unity of chapters 5–11 though some argue for coherence based on covenantal traditions, whether liturgical or treaty documents. This covenantal background is then used to explain the contiguity of history, law and parenesis.[1]

Most commonly redactional layers are identified in chapters 5–11, adapting the redactional theories mentioned in the previous chapter. We

---

1 See Preuß (1982) 95–96; Tiffany, 25–28; von Rad (1953a) 53; Baltzer, 36–38. Also McCarthy (1981) 159–170. Compare Welch, 10. Tiffany, 28, notes that Deuteronomy 5–11 is the report of a speech, not a covenant treaty, and though covenantal themes and ideas influence the content of these chapters, covenant treaties do not govern its composition. Also Alexander (1995) 165–166.

shall briefly mention four studies which deal specifically with Deuteronomy 5–11. Peckham identifies a seventh-century Dtr1 and its exilic updating by Dtr2. The criteria for his distinction is in part theological. He argued that Dtr2 substituted the Decalogue for the covenant and the patriarchal promises for the gift of the land.[2] Vermeylen also reconstructs various historical redactions of Deuteronomy 5–11. He argues that at the beginning of the exile, the primitive introduction of Deuteronomy consisted of a continuous narrative paralleling that of Exodus 19–34. Because of the scandal of the fall of Jerusalem, there was no parenesis in the 575 plural redaction. The Deuteronomic code is presented as the fundamental law of the Decalogue. There is an accent on Yahweh's generosity. The fall of Jerusalem is attributed to Israel's rebellion. A more positive singular redaction, mainly parenetic, in 560 compares the exile to the forty years of the wilderness and thus offers new hope for the future and a possibility of return. The redaction of 525 is a plural appeal to obey and highlights Moses' role as mediator.[3] Vermeylen's approach is also an attempt to explain the juxtaposition of what he regards as tensions or contradictions in the text, especially that of pessimism and optimism with which we are concerned.

Typical of the most common current view of chapters 5–11 is that of García López.[4] He distinguishes sharply between parenetic and historical material, though each of the two types of material includes a variety of genres.[5] He argues that the parenetic material, which coincides generally with the singular address, is the base text of 5–11. The historical material, with plural exhortation, is regarded as later. Thus García López considers the *Numeruswechsel* as indicative of redactional stages associated with the distinction between narrative and parenesis.[6] Though his analysis is mainly motivated by form, theological considerations are also taken into account and tensions resolved through his redaction-critical solution.

García López's conclusions lie in direct contrast with the major analysis of Deuteronomy 5–11 by Lohfink. He argued that the narrative material preceded the parenesis.[7] Unlike García López, Lohfink regards the

---

2 Peckham (1983) 221, 227–228.

3 Vermeylen (1985a) 179–207.

4 García López (1977) 481–522; (1978) 5–49. See Vermeylen (1985a) 174; Preuß (1982) 95.

5 García López (1978) 47–48. Also Preuß (1982) 98.

6 The parenetic material is 6:4–9:7a; 10:12–11:25. See García López (1977) 481–522. The second half of his article, (1978) 5–49, deals with the historical material. However, note (1977) 518–519, on stylistic changes in blessings and curses. See further Seitz, 45–91; Peckham (1975) 4–5; Preuß (1982) 97–98. Preuß (1982) 93–95, reviews approaches based on the *Numeruswechsel*.

7 Vermeylen (1985a) 174–175, reviews the two approaches.

*Numeruswechsel* as primarily stylistic.[8] He prefers the term *Numerus-mischung* and suggests that "(d)en verschiedenen Gattungen 'Erzählung' und 'Paränese' entsprechen also verschiedene Typen der Numerus-mischung".[9] In parenesis, one expects number change but especially at its highpoint there is a rapid mixing of number to intensify the announcement of command and create a sense of urgency.[10] By distinction, narrative is more mathematical and generally refers to the nation in the plural. Where a narrator is conscious of mixing narrative and parenesis, then there is confusion in the usage of singular and plural.[11] Though we cannot be certain that Lohfink is right about the existence of a fomal delineation between narrative and parenesis *Gattungen* with corresponding stylistic distinctions, his argument is more persuasive than that of García López. Certainly the mixing of singular and plural does not seem to have bothered any redactor. Maybe less should be made of the *Numeruswechsel* than often is the case.[12] Despite Lohfink's attempts at a unified stylistic analysis, he also resolves tensions by delineating a seven- or eight-phase redactional history of Deuteronomy 5–11.[13]

In summary, as in chapters 1–3, theological tensions are usually resolved through diachronic solutions. Our concern is to see whether these tensions can be resolved synchronically. Further, as we argued in the previous chapter, there need not be a distinction between narrative and parenesis. As with the narrative of Deuteronomy 1–3, that of 8–10 is also aimed at eliciting a response of faithful obedience by its hearers-readers.

## Deuteronomy 8

We turn now to a consideration of chapter 8, concentrating on its portrayal of Israel and Israel's relationship to Yahweh. In particular chapter 8 compares and contrasts the past with the future.[14] We are concerned with the way Israel's past is understood and its bearing on future expectation.

8 Lohfink (1963a) 239–258.

9 Lohfink (1963a) 242.

10 Lohfink (1963a) 246–249. At the highpoint of parenesis, the unity of the people, expressed via the singular, is dissolved into the plurality of individuals being addressed.

11 Lohfink (1963a) 249–251; Mayes (1981b) 29.

12 Mayes (1981b) 30. Number change also occurs elsewhere in the Hebrew Bible and in ancient treaties.

13 The stages begin with ANE vassal treaties and Israel's own covenant treaty documents and cult. Within 8–10, the main author of 5–11 was responsible for 9:9–19, 21, 25–29; 10:1–5, 10–18, 20–22. A reviser was then responsible for 8:1–9:8, 22–24. The last three phases bound the chapters to 12–26 and incorporated various Levitical glosses and later additions. For a summary, see Lohfink (1963a) 289–291.

14 Rennes, 52.

Though Israel's past behaviour is not portrayed as bleakly as in chapter 9, nonetheless this chapter, like 1–3, gives little encouragement for Israel's future apart from the grace and faithfulness of Yahweh.

### *Structure*

Before dealing with the theology explicitly, we need to consider the structure of the chapter in order to gain a clearer picture of its purpose and theology. Numerous attempts at describing structural patterns in chapter 8 have been made. We shall survey some of these, noting their contributions to understanding chapter 8.

#### PALISTROPHES

Lohfink observed various words and terms which are repeated in Deuteronomy 8 in a way which suggests a palistrophic structure for the chapter.[15] So הַיּוֹם occurs in vv1, 19, as well as in the centre, v11.[16] In addition, he lists: אֲשֶׁר־נִשְׁבַּע לַאֲבֹתֵיכֶם (v1, compare v18), וְזָכַרְתָּ אֶת־ (vv2, 18), הֹלִיכֲךָ, אֲשֶׁר לֹא...יָדְעוּן אֲבֹתֶיךָ, וַיַּאֲכִלְךָ אֶת־הַמָּן, בַּמִּדְבָּר (vv2–3, compare vv15–16), אָכַל, שָׂבָע, טֹבִים/טֹבָה (vv10, 12). These observations certainly give much weight to the thesis for a concentric structure of chapter 8, even if the list is perhaps selective. Lohfink identified the following palistrophe:

| | | |
|---|---|---|
| A | 1 | Exhortation |
| B | 2–6 | Wilderness |
| C | 7–10 | Cultivated Land |
| D | 11 | Exhortation |
| C' | 12–13 | Cultivated Land |
| B' | 14–17 | Wilderness |
| A' | 18–20 | Exhortation[17] |

Braulik modified Lohfink's revision in two places. He divided v14 between B' and C', and included v18 in B', not A'.[18] The division of v14 is reasonable for the keyword שָׁכַח in v14 represents a transition between two sections.[19] However Braulik has not dealt satisfactorily with vv17–18.

15 Lohfink (1963a) 195.

16 He ignores its occurrence in v18.

17 Lohfink (1965) 76. Compare his earlier version, (1963a) 195, which was followed by Moran (1969) 266; Watts (1970) 223. It omitted vv5–7a, 10, 14a, 17–18. The revised version is followed by Clifford, 55. Craigie (1976) 184, rejects Lohfink's structure saying it "does not fit well with the natural punctuation of vv. 11–16 (17)".

18 Braulik (1986) 68. Compare Weinfeld (1991) 397.

19 Andersen, 137–138, notes that the second פֶּן clause of v12a has three branches in vv12a–14a which come together with שָׁכַח in v14b and that vv14c–16 are depend-

These verses are in the context of the land, not the wilderness, hence, perhaps, Lohfink's original difficulty in including them in his chiastic structure.[20] Verses 14b–16, concerning the wilderness, are embedded in verses dealing with the land in the future. It seems best to consider vv17, 18 as part of the final exhortation. Verse 18 in particular is exhortation, like vv19–20.[21] The matching vocabulary about the oath to the fathers in vv1, 18 also hints that v18, at least, should be part of A'. On this point, Lohfink's structure, rather than Braulik's is to be preferred. Regarding v17, the vocabulary it shares with v18 suggests they belong together, despite the fact that syntactically v17 is dependent on v12 whereas v18 resumes the sequence from v11a.[22] Thus we opt for the inclusion of v17 with v18 in A'.[23]

All the above palistrophes centre on v11. At one level this seems appropriate. The verse is definitely the turning point from protasis to apodosis of what is possibly the longest sentence in Biblical Hebrew, vv7–18.[24] In a sense the verses preceding v11 build up to it and those after v11 are dependent upon it. It is also clearly exhortation. A palistrophe centred here shows that the chapter is exhorting Israel to appropriate future behaviour in the land based on having learned lessons from the past in the wilderness. This highlights the fact that the chapter is not about the land and wilderness *per se*, but sets the two into a sphere of obedience-disobedience. Wilderness and land are contexts for covenant loyalty.

Having said this, the straightforward palistrophe of Lohfink, and those derived from him, is inadequate as a total explanation of the structure of the chapter. Lund argues that in a chiasm, identical ideas will often occur in the

---

ent on Yahweh in v14b. Similarly L'Hour (1967) 110, with vv11–17 the first Nachsatz and v18 the second. Compare Bertholet, 29; Steuernagel, 31; Rose (1994) 464.

20 See note 17 above.

21 Compare Jacobs, 242, who argues for a chiasm within vv1, 19b–20, the outer elements of the palistrophe. However the oath of v1 corresponds better to v18. He also notes, 240–241, that vv1, 19b–20 are a plural frame, contrasting with vv2–19a which is a unit complete in itself. He suggests, that 8:2 follows from 7:26. Also Preuß (1982) 101. Compare Westermann (1994) 54, 57.

22 Andersen (1974) 137.

23 Another variation on the structure of the chapter is that of Christensen (1991) 173. He has two middle sections, vv7–10, v11. He omits vv19–20 because they are separated by a paragraph marker and are a summary of all of 7:12–8:18. Verse 18 links to v1 with common vocabulary. Compare Andersen, 137–138, on separating vv17, 18. The question is whether chiastic structures are governed by syntax or not. Lund makes no mention of this. See also Carpenter, 79.

24 Mayes (1979) 191–192; Weinfeld (1991) 391; Lohfink (1965) 81–82; Braulik (1986) 70; Veijola (1995) 143. Compare Andersen, 137–138, who considers vv11–18 only.

centre and extremes but nowhere else.[25] However, the memory motif, which occurs in v11, also occurs in vv2, 14, 18, 19 (twice).[26] Nor are the occurrences of the significant words remember (vv2, 18) and "do not forget" (vv11, 19, compare 14) chiastic, though if the plural frame is excluded, then זָכַר in vv2, 18 functions chiastically with שָׁכַח in v11.[27] Also there is repeated vocabulary in v11 from vv1, 2, 6 (שָׁמַר plus מִצְוֹת) which is more significant than הַיּוֹם in vv1, 11, 19 noted above. This is also not limited to the centre and extremes. If שָׁמַר plus מִצְוֹת is as important as its fourfold repetition suggests, then its occurrence in v6 especially should not be passed over as Lohfink does. Furthermore the appeal to the past in vv14b–16 functions differently from the mention of the wilderness in vv2–5. In vv14b–16, the events of the past are in apposition to Yahweh in v14b, and this is part of a series dependent on פֶּן in v12.[28] Thus a straightforward palistrophe is in the end inadequate for Deuteronomy 8. Given the restricted vocabulary of Deuteronomy, possibly some chiastic patterns are even accidental.

An alternative palistrophic structure is the elaborate and complicated proposal of O'Connell.[29] The major point of discussion is the centre of the chapter. Apart from vv6–11, almost all O'Connell's structure fits into

---

25 Lund, 41.

26 Mayes (1979) 189; (1981b) 37, argues that in the early material of the chapter, vv7–11a, 12–14, 17–18a, 'forget' means an arrogant ascription to oneself of power belonging to Yahweh. In the later verses, vv1–6, 11b, 15–16, 18b–20, 'forget' concerns the commandments. Seitz, 79, argues that the motif of forgetfulness has three contexts. The latest, v19, refers to idolatry; the earliest, vv14, 17, is due to pride; the middle term, v11b, refers to the commandments. Compare Westermann (1994) 57; Nielsen, 109; Veijola (1995) 151, 155. Burden, 119–120, argues that the commandments are in order for Israel *not* to forget. On remembrance in Deuteronomy, see Blair (1961) 45.

27 Perlitt (1981) 406. Andersen, 137–138, notes that הִשָּׁמֶר in v11a is continued by וְזָכַרְתָּ in v18 and that everything in between is governed by two פֶּן clauses in apposition. This syntax highlights the command at the beginning of v11 and also that of v18.

28 Andersen, 137–138.

29 O'Connell (1990) 439–440. He rejects, 438, Lohfink's palistrophe on the grounds that there are significant gaps in his schema of keyword collocations. In its place he suggests a twelve-tiered asymmetrical concentric structure. There are a number of problems with it. O'Connell pairs "heart" in v14a with the same word in v5. Yet the word also occurs in vv2, 17. The occurrences in vv14a, 17 go together to frame vv14b–16. García López (1977) 485, 490, argues that vv17–18a are the syntactic continuation of v14a. Not all O'Connell's pairs have matching vocabulary. Their correspondence is due to common general subject matter, palistrophic position and rhetorical function.

Lohfink's palistrophe.[30] Rather than matching vv7–10 with vv12–14, leaving v11 central, O'Connell matches vv6 and 11, and 7a and 10, leaving vv7b–9 as his centre. Admittedly the link between vv6 and 11 is important, as we have already noted.[31] However, he dismisses the repetition of אָכַל, שָׂבַע, טֹבִים/טֹבָה in vv10, 12 which frame v11.[32] Instead, he argues that the repeated expression אֶרֶץ טוֹבָה in vv7a, 10 frames his centre, vv7b–9. Which of the two pairs is the most decisive for the overall structure? We prefer that of vv10, 12. The repetition of אֶרֶץ טוֹבָה in vv7a, 10 is part of a chiasm within the one section, rather than part of the palistrophic structure of the whole chapter. Verses 7–10 (Lohfink's C) are chiastically structured on the words "good land" (vv7, 10), "hills" (vv7, 9), "wheat" and "bread" (vv8, 9), and "olives" (v8). Thus the repeated "good land" forms an inclusio for vv7–10.[33] All in all, O'Connell's analysis fails to convince. The centrepoint of the chapter is v11, not vv7b–9.[34]

The argument about the centre of the chapter is important for our understanding of it. O'Connell's reading of the chapter is that vv5–9 say that Israel "must continue to obey YHWH in order to receive the blessings of the land".[35] The description of the land is thus the focus of the motivation for obedience.[36] However the key issue is the condition of Israel and how it will respond to blessings in the land, and not whether it will receive them.[37] The chapter is thus concerned about Israel's past behaviour in the wilderness as a model for its future response once in the land. It makes subtle suggestions about this, preparing the way for the clear statements in the following chapters.

---

30 O'Connell merely subdivides many of Lohfink's elements. Apart from vv6–11, the only differences are his treatment of v14, which fits Braulik's revision of Lohfink, and his division of v18 to match vv1bγ, 2a.

31 Though O'Connell (1990) 439, dismisses the similar expressions in vv1, 2. As suggested above, the repeated expression in vv1, 2, 6, 11 weakens the case for concentricity.

32 O'Connell (1990) 440. He notes the repetition but fails to explain why v12 matches v5.

33 Moran (1969) 266. Compare Plöger, 89. Also van Leeuwen (1984) 247.

34 Compare Christensen (1991) 173, who combines vv7–10 and v11 as joint central elements.

35 O'Connell (1990) 449. Compare Zimmerli (1971) 73, that 8:1 makes the actual entry and conquest conditional on obedience.

36 O'Connell (1990) 443–444. Compare Jacobs, 227, who considers that כִּי in v7 is causal and refers back to v6. Also L'Hour (1967) 110. Compare Lohfink (1963a) 189–190, 192, Tiffany, 170, Mayes (1979) 191; Weinfeld (1991) 386, 391, who read the כִּי as temporal.

37 O'Connell (1990) 450, rightly states that the rhetorical focus of the chapter is that Yahweh is Israel's sole provider.

One possibility regarding Israel's future response derives from the observation that the second half of the palistrophe does not merely repeat the first. There is a significant change in tone. The shift from positive motivation in v1 to negative threat in vv18–20 suggests a deliberate movement from positive to negative expectation in the chapter. The same can be said for vv7–10, which end in praise, by comparison with vv12–14a, or vv12–18, which end in forgetfulness and pride. The exhortation to obey which occurs four times in the first half of the palistrophe is absent in the second, possibly suggesting that the exhortation will remain unheeded. Likewise the wilderness functions in vv2–5 as educative for the current generation as well as the past (v5) but in the second half it merely leads to a statement of pride (v17). The humbling and testing is kept in the past. All of this suggests that not only does the palistrophe turn on v11 but v11 is the turning point from positive to negative.[38]

PARALLEL PANELS

We have argued that palistrophe, though helpful in many respects, does not adequately explain chapter 8. We need to look further for a solution. Simple parallel panels occur in chapter 8 as follows:[39]

| I | II | Content |
|---|---|---|
| 2 | 11 | Parenesis: remember, not forget |
| 3a | 12, 13 | Situation: hunger, plenty |
| 3b,4 | 14–16 | Purpose: know that, humble; lest, humble |
| 5,6 | 17–18 | Know: Yahweh disciplines, gives strength |
| 7–10 | 19–20 | Land, Exile |

There is some merit in this structure. The first panel suggests that the lessons of the wilderness have been learned and, applying them in the land in the future will result in appropriate praise. The second panel then suggests that the bountiful land is itself another test which, if failed, leads to loss of land and destruction. This panel presupposes that the lessons from the past have not been learned. Parallel panels indicate that the land is, like

38 On the centre of a chiasm, see Lund, 40–41. His first two "laws" are that the centre of a chiasm is its turning point and that often at the centre the thought changes and an antithetical idea is introduced. The change from positive to negative is discussed by O'Connell (1990) 448. On the pessimistic expectation of the chapter, see Westermann (1994) 60.

39 Jacobs, 228. He, 227, also finds a temporal progression in the chapter: In the desert (vv2–6); At the entrance to the land (vv7–10); In the Land (vv11–18); Threat of Exile (vv19–20).

the wilderness, also a test.[40] Further, the movement from positive to negative in the chapter also fits a parallel panel structure.[41]

An attempt to integrate palistrophe and parallel panels is that of van Leeuwen. His "Duplex Macro-structure of Deuteronomy 8" is as follows:[42]

| | | | | |
|---|---|---|---|---|
| I | (vv2–10) | | Admonition: Remember → praise God (v10) | |
| | | A | (vv2–5) | Desert/Past |
| | | B | (vv7–10) | Promised Land/Future |
| II | (vv11–17) | | Admonition: Don't forget not → praise self (v17) | |
| | | B' | (vv11–14a, 17) | Promised Land/Future |
| | | A' | (vv14b–16) | Desert/Past |
| I' | (v18) | | Admonition: Remember → prosperity | |
| II' | (vv19–20) | | Admonition: Don't forget not → death | |

Unfortunately, van Leeuwen, in criticising Lohfink's original structure, seems unaware of his later revision. The omission of vv1, 6 is another weakness.[43] Van Leeuwen's treatment of v17 rightly reflects that the verse is concerned with the land and not the wilderness (contra Lohfink), but his inclusion of it in B' destroys the chiasm. Rather, by noting that v17 belongs with v18, he could have included it as part of I'. Instead, he argued that the repeated vocabulary, כֹּחִי, עָשָׂה, הַחַיִל in v17, כֹּחַ לַעֲשׂוֹת חָיִל in v18, is an anadiplosis which "functions both to link the two sections and to delimit their respective conclusion and beginning".[44] He gives no reason for reading the repetition this way. It is equally justified to regard the repetition as binding the two verses together.[45]

In his comparison of A and A' (in particular vv2–3, 14b–16), van Leeuwen suggests there is a word play on מוֹצָא (v3) and הַמּוֹצִיא (vv14, 15) supported by the paronomasia of מִצְרַיִם (v14) and מִצּוּר in (v15).[46] Also the sevenfold repetition of 'land' in vv7–10 corresponds to the seven verbs

40 Jacobs, 227.

41 McCarthy (1981) 160–162, 167–168, regards chapter 8 as conforming to a pattern which has a declaration of duty at the beginning and a threat at the end.

42 Van Leeuwen (1984) 237–238.

43 Van Leeuwen (1984) 238–239, calls v1 an introductory frame element. Yet it is puzzling that it is omitted given that he notes that it forms a plural frame with vv19, 20, as well as paralleling the end of v18 in matched vocabulary. He says, 241–242, that the repetition of a keyword in v6 marks a transition between sections A and B.

44 Van Leeuwen (1984) 240.

45 He also suggests, 240, that the repetition between vv10, 12 mentioned above is also an anadiplosis which links B and B' around the pivotal v11. However in this case v11 intervenes between the repetition creating a chiasm. That is a different case to vv17–18.

46 Van Leeuwen (1984) 240. The pun is extended also by מְצַוְּךָ in vv1, 11 (241). Also Clifford, 56; Cazelles (1958) 49.

describing Yahweh's actions in vv14b–16.[47] These two sections both refer to water, in the former coming from the hills naturally, in the latter from rock miraculously.[48]

One further strength of his analysis is the observation of the parallel pairs 'remember/do not forget'. The sequence within the chapter is remember (v2), forget (v11), remember (v18), forget (v19).[49] The 'remember' motifs, which control panels I and I', have positive consequences; the 'do not forget' motifs which control panels II and II' have negative ones.[50] Thus the movement from positive to negative in the chapter is now seen to be tied to the memory motif. Forgetting Yahweh is identified with failure to keep his commandments (v11); remembering Yahweh is associated with obedience (vv2, 6). This expresses the "fundamental bipolar tendencies" of the covenant: blessing and life or curse and death.[51] Yet the two poles are not simply obedience and disobedience. There is a more subtle relationship inherent.

We have already commented that the wilderness and land are contexts for covenant loyalty. The repeated שָׁמַר plus מִצְוֹת makes this clear. Furthermore the links between the wilderness and the land, primarily through the word plays on מוֹצָא in v3, show that the source of life in both the wilderness and the good land is what proceeds from Yahweh's mouth.[52] Covenant obedience is grounded in this. Theologically the importance of this observation is that life is grounded in Yahweh, in particular his promises to the fathers (vv1, 18) and not an achievement of Israel's obedience. So remembrance confirms the covenant promises (v18). Van Leeuwen's is certainly the most helpful analysis of the structure of Deuteronomy 8.[53]

### *Wilderness Test*

We turn now to look at the theology of 8:2–6. These verses are significant in that they discuss the purpose of the wilderness as a test which Yahweh placed on Israel in order to know what was in its heart, whether it would keep his commands, and whether it would learn that life derives from what comes out of Yahweh's mouth. This section comes to the heart of the issue of the condition of Israel in Deuteronomy. These verses also provide

---

47 On the similar syntax of each, see van Leeuwen (1984) 246–247.

48 Van Leeuwen (1984) 240; García López (1977) 489.

49 Van Leeuwen (1984) 242, argues rightly that וְשָׁכַחְתָּ in v14 is not part of this sequence. Rather it is dependent on פֶּן in v12 and marks the transition between his B' and A'. See Andersen, 137–138, noted above in note 27.

50 Van Leeuwen (1984) 239.

51 Van Leeuwen (1984) 241.

52 Van Leeuwen (1984) 242.

53 Compare Olson (1994) 55; Roberge, 174.

background for 29:1–5, an important section which we shall discuss in the next chapter.

THE NATURE OF THE TEST

Firstly we shall consider the exact nature of the test before turning to consider its result. This section has three key verbs: וְזָכַרְתָּ (v2), וְיָדַעְתָּ (v5) and וְשָׁמַרְתָּ (v6). These verbs hold the section together in three parts, the second and third drawing consequences from the first.[54] The second and third parts also pick up key words from the first, notably לֵבָב (vv2, 5), שָׁמַר plus מִצְוֹת (vv2, 6), and הָלַךְ plus דֶּרֶךְ (vv2, 6). All these back references to v2 show the logic of the argument in this section. The pre-history, vv2–4, is formed with the conclusions of vv5, 6 in view. Further, the repetition of 'these forty years' in vv2, 4 forms an inclusio round the pre-history in vv2–4.[55] Mayes suggests that the structure of vv2–6 is similar to that of 4:35–40 and 7:7–11 with three sections: a call to remember the past, an appeal to know the implication, and a command to apply this to behaviour.[56]

The conception of the wilderness in these verses is distinctive. That period is not regarded as punitive, rebellious or idyllic, but educative.[57] The difficulties of the wilderness are passed over quickly; there is only a brief mention of hunger (v3). The description of the wilderness highlights the grace of Yahweh, nowhere more so than in v4 which is without parallel in the Pentateuch and is an astounding statement of God's grace.[58] The difficulties of the wilderness mentioned in vv15, 16 are also in a context where the stress is on the gracious leading and providence of Yahweh who is the emphasised subject of each clause there.[59] Nonetheless, יִסַּר in v5 is not simply instruction and teaching but also has a connotation of pain and privation, training by chastising and punishing.[60] This conception of the wilderness is different even from Deuteronomy 1–3 and 9.[61] It is important to note that the educative test comprises both the situations of hunger and miraculous provision of manna. Blessing is also educative. This is reflected

---

54 Lohfink (1963a) 190; (1965) 77.

55 Lohfink (1963a) 190; Weinfeld (1991) 385. Peckham (1983) 232, suggests the phrase comes from 2:7. Compare also 29:4.

56 Mayes (1979) 190; Lohfink (1963a) 125–131; Miller (1990) 115; Braulik (1986) 68.

57 Compare JE (punitive); Psalms 78; 106; Ezekiel 20 (rebellious); Jeremiah 2:2 and Hosea 9:10 (idyllic). See further Weinfeld (1972) 31; Blair (1964) 43; Cunliffe-Jones, 66–67; von Rad (1966e) 71; Buis and Leclerq, 85; Burden, 116–121; Nielsen, 105. Merrill, 186, compares this verse to Exodus 16:4; 20:20; Deuteronomy 8:16; 13:4. Burden, 117–118; Bertholet, 28, compare this passage with 1:31.

58 Lohfink (1965) 78. Compare 29:5; Nehemiah 9:21.

59 Lohfink (1965) 79; Braulik (1986) 72. Compare Rose (1981) 301–304.

60 Lohfink (1965) 79; Braulik (1986) 70; Weinfeld (1991) 390.

61 Weinfeld (1972) 31; Miller (1990) 115.

in the later verses of the chapter where the extraordinarily bountiful land is also a test.[62] This test has two purposes. Firstly, it is that Yahweh will learn something, namely the state of Israel's heart, which will be demonstrated through obedience (v2).[63] Secondly, it is that Israel will learn something, namely that one must live by what proceeds from Yahweh's mouth (v3) and that Yahweh is a disciplining father (v5). This could be described as a test about whether Israel would rely on God's grace or not.[64] So the wilderness period was a type of experiment "in dem die Wirklichkeit des Volkes und Gottes dem jeweils anderen Partner sichtbar werden soll" (לְמַעַן plus a form of יָדַע in vv2b, 3b).[65] So עָנָה (piel), a key verb in the chapter occurring three times (vv2, 3, 16), is to make the hearer-reader aware of divine dependence.[66]

THE RESULT OF THE TEST

Strikingly there is a degree of ambiguity about the result of the test. Miller says,

> We are never told whether God received an answer or what that answer might be. That ambiguity or unanswered question is not unimportant for comprehending the purpose of Deuteronomy.... For it is precisely the case in Deuteronomy that the issue of the whole book is to answer: Has Israel learned the lessons of the past and will it now, in a (later) situation of prosperity and abundance, remember who is the provider and live by that one's word? The matter is still open-ended and even more acute, for the richness of life on the land with beautiful houses...creates an even larger possibility that prosperous people will forget....[67]

It is our contention that these verses, and chapter 8 as a whole, are not neutral regarding the answer to the question about Israel's disposition. Firstly, at the heart of 8:2–6 is the reference to manna (v3a). This reference would have reminded the people not just of the manna itself, but also of their grumbling and murmuring in their hunger and thus their lack of trust in Yahweh as provider.[68] So the key illustration for the wilderness as a test is one in which Israel clearly failed. The same applies for vv14b–16 where the miraculous provision of water from the rock is mentioned. Again Deuteronomy provides a typically bare allusion to past well-known

---

62 Lohfink (1965) 80; D. Schneider, 108. Compare Bertholet, 28.

63 Bertholet, 28, asks "weiss er (Gott) das nicht schon?" Burden, 118, suggests that the subject of לָדַעַת is ambiguous and probably should be read as Israel.

64 Weinfeld (1991) 389, "God tests man to see whether he really puts his trust in him".

65 Lohfink (1963a) 191. Weinfeld (1991) 388, contrasts this passage with 6:16 where Israel tested Yahweh. See his general discussion, 346, on testing both by Israel and Yahweh. Also Millar, 241; Mayes (1979) 191; Braulik (1986) 69.

66 Clifford, 56. Also Cairns, 96; Braulik (1986) 69.

67 Miller (1990) 116–117.

68 D. Schneider, 112; Thompson, 135. See Exodus 16:3–4; Numbers 11:4–6; 21:5.

tradition. Its hearers-readers would be expected to know of the grumbling and murmuring of the people.[69]

Secondly, the expression פִּי־יְהוָה in v3 recalls 1:26, 43. There, Israel is described as defying the mouth of Yahweh.[70] Thus, as with the manna, the mention of the mouth of Yahweh in v3 also recalls Israel's rebellion.[71] These allusions suggest a negative outcome to the test.

Thirdly, the positive side of this test (v3b) is a statement of Yahweh's grace, not Israel's obedience: כִּי לֹא עַל־הַלֶּחֶם לְבַדּוֹ יִחְיֶה הָאָדָם כִּי עַל־כָּל־מוֹצָא פִי־יְהוָה יִחְיֶה הָאָדָם. This is "the central theological pronouncement" of these verses.[72] Its third person singular form and unusual subject, הָאָדָם, separate it from its surrounds and lift it up as a universally applicable statement.[73] Yet there is dispute about its sense. Some have taken v3b to contrast bread and manna, understanding living as physical life. Here, what comes out of the mouth of the LORD is his powerfully creative word. However in other places in the Old Testament, manna is identified with bread.[74] Furthermore, the rare combination of חָיָה plus עַל which occurs here, means more than merely "living on", but has a deeper sense of "existing or depending on", referring to what one's life ultimately rests upon.[75]

Others understand v3 to contrast the physical with the spiritual.[76] However the verse is not simply dismissive of the physical. Man lives on *both* bread and what comes out of Yahweh's mouth. The two are not mutually exclusive, though they lie in different planes.[77]

Often כָּל־מוֹצָא is limited to refer to Yahweh's commandments. In this case the sentence is then interpreted as a call to obedience.[78] However it is

---

69 Numbers 20:2–5. See Cairns, 98; Lohfink (1965) 78.

70 Weinfeld (1991) 151–152; Veijola (1995) 157.

71 Burden, 119.

72 Van Leeuwen (1985) 55. García López (1977) 508–509, suggests that 8:2–6 is a chiasm where the outer members, AA', are vv2a, 6b with common vocabulary דֶּרֶךְ; BB' are vv2b, 5–6a, with common vocabulary יָדַע, לֵבָב, שָׁמַר, מִצְוֹת; and the central element is v3b. He omits detailed mention of vv3a, 4. He also notes that the metre of 8:2–6 fits the chiasm, with 18 words in each of A+B and A'+B'. In fact he, 511, suggests 8:3b is the centre of chapters 6–11. See also Veijola (1995) 155.

73 Perlitt (1981) 411, 414. In Deuteronomy elsewhere only 4:28, 32; 32:8 (אָדָם without the article); 5:24; 20:19 (הָאָדָם with the article).

74 Perlitt (1981) 405–410. Also Weinfeld (1991) 389; Veijola (1995) 156.

75 Weinfeld (1991) 389; Perlitt (1981) 415–419. See Genesis 27:40; Ezekiel 33:19.

76 Perlitt (1981) 403–404, mentions Luther and von Rad in this connection. Driver, 107–108, "that by yielding inopportunely to physical necessity, higher spiritual needs may be neglected or frustrated". Also García López (1977) 508; Nielsen, 105.

77 Perlitt (1981) 419.

78 Watts (1970) 224; Miller (1990) 115–116; Bertholet, 28. Wolff (1974a) 76; Clifford, 56; García López (1977) 508–509; Jacobs, 237, note that מוֹצָא sounds

preferable to see a broader sense. Literally the expression is "everything", not every "word".[79] What comes out of Yahweh's mouth is the fulness of his word, not just his creative word but also his revelatory and salvific word.[80] Thus the issue is about relying on Yahweh, the giver of life in its fullest sense.[81] This also links in with v18 which is explained by v3: Israel is to rely on God's gracious provision.[82] This broader sense is also indicated by the wordplay, noted above, between מוֹצָא (v3) and הַמּוֹצִיא (vv14, 15), supported by the chiasm of the chapter. This wordplay "suggests that what comes from Yahweh's mouth is sovereign in the realm of history (exodus) and nature (water from the rock)". Manna is thus to be regarded as "*one* of the manifestations of the divine מוֹצָא". Another is water from the rock. So also the commandments.[83] The goal of the test lies beyond human obedience. It is a recognition of divine grace. This relates to the conception that the desert is a foil for grace, highlighted by the rebellion of Israel.[84] Important for a correct understanding of this issue is that there is no suggestion at all that Israel has learnt from this past failure. Nor is there any suggestion here that Israel at present or in the future has or will have any different disposition. The two options are these: disobedience and reliance on grace.

### *Israel's Heart and Knowledge*

Two important words in Deuteronomy which indicate something of the condition of Israel are לֵבָב and יָדַע. The word לֵבָב occurs in this chapter in vv2, 5, 14 and 17.[85] Verse 2 expresses the purpose of the wilderness test as

---

like מִצְוָה and thus alludes to the commandments. Also Veijola (1995) 157. Compare Driver, 107–108.

79 Jacobs, 236–237, comments that 'word' usually means 'commandments'. However דָּבָר does not even occur here. (Compare LXX, Vulgate, Aramaic Targum which all add 'word'. Similarly Matthew 4:4. See Willis (1973) 142.) He considers that 'to live by' denotes obedience to the commandments. Willis, 144–145, argues that 'mouth' is to be understood metaphorically and that it does not necessarily imply words or speech. Contrast Perlitt (1981) 420.

80 Perlitt (1981) 421; Keil and Delitzsch, 331; Rose (1994) 459. García López (1977) 509, argues that this verse shows the commandments are salvific and compares with 6:20–24.

81 For example, von Rad (1966e) 72; Mayes (1979) 191, link this verse with 30:15 and 32:47. See also Willis, 147–149; Cunliffe-Jones, 67; Weinfeld (1991) 389; Dillmann, 276. On the possible ANE background, see Brunner, 428–429. Such a background supports the broader reading of the sentence.

82 Perlitt (1981) 406–407.

83 Van Leeuwen (1985) 57. Similarly Lohfink (1965) 79.

84 Carroll (1977) 188.

85 Typically, Deuteronomy prefers לֵבָב (47 times) to לֵב (4:11; 28:65; 29:3, 18). Of the 51 occurrences, eight are in chapter 30 and four in each of 4, 8, 28 and 29.

לָדַעַת אֶת־אֲשֶׁר בִּלְבָבְךָ.[86] There is nothing in vv2–4 which suggests Israel's heart is acceptable. The exhortation וְיָדַעְתָּ עִם־לְבָבֶךָ in v5 is the first consequence to be drawn from the wilderness lesson.[87] The object of this knowledge is the fatherly discipline of Yahweh.[88] This exhortation addresses the current generation. The need for such an exhortation suggests that Israel's heart does not yet know what it should and, consequently, that the current generation is unchanged from Israel in the wilderness.

The exhortation וְיָדַעְתָּ עִם־לְבָבֶךָ, in v5, is its only occurrence in Deuteronomy, though וְיָדַעְתָּ occurs in 4:39; 7:9; 9:3, 6 and, in plural, in 11:2.[89] The verb יָדַע is important in Deuteronomy.[90] In each of the above verses, and in a few others, the knowledge required is not simply experience but rather a deep and correct acknowledgement of and response to Yahweh who stands behind the events experienced. This is knowledge which feeds appropriate action, as 8:6 shows.[91] It is useful to consider these verses and the object of knowledge expressed therein.

The verses expressing this deep knowledge are: 4:9, where the adults are to cause the children to know (יָדַע hiphil) what they have seen; 4:35, with object: כִּי יְהוָה הוּא הָאֱלֹהִים אֵין עוֹד מִלְּבַדּוֹ; 4:39, which begins וְיָדַעְתָּ הַיּוֹם וַהֲשֵׁבֹתָ אֶל־לְבָבֶךָ and has as its object כִּי יְהוָה הוּא הָאֱלֹהִים בַּשָּׁמַיִם מִמַּעַל וְעַל־הָאָרֶץ מִתָּחַת אֵין עוֹד; 7:9, where the object is כִּי־יְהוָה אֱלֹהֶיךָ הוּא הָאֱלֹהִים; 8:3, where the hiphil is used in referring to the purpose of the

There seems to be no semantic distinction between them. Lisowsky, 708–715; KB, 468–471, treat the two words as one; BDB, 523–525, though treating the two separately, has the same ten areas of definition for each. These include: inner being, heart, mind, will, seat of conscience, memory, moral character, the man himself, the seat of appetite, courage and emotions. Eichrodt (1967) 143–144, argues that "the element of responsibility" distinguishes לֵבָב from נֶפֶשׁ or רוּחַ. Cazelles (1951–52) 10, suggests that the three (sic) occurrences of לֵב in Deuternomy (he lists 4:11; 28:65 and 29:3) belong to a later redaction. Similarly Dhorme, 493. This fails to explain, however, the occurrences of לֵבָב which occur in passages also generally regarded as late. We will not distinguish between לֵב and לֵבָב but for convenience refer to לֵבָב.

86 Compare 13:4.

87 Lohfink (1965) 77. The second is in v6a with וְשָׁמַרְתָּ.

88 On father–son as a possible wisdom theme, see McCarthy (1981) 161; Weinfeld (1972) 316–317; Mayes (1979) 191. See also 1:31; 4:36. Compare Emerton, 147, 159.

89 Weinfeld (1972) 357. The idea of discipline also occurs in 4:36; 11:2. See Weinfeld (1972) 303; Dillmann, 276.

90 יָדַע occurs 46 times (43 qal; 1 niphal and 2 hiphil). Many of its occurrences need not concern us here. The verb יָדַע occurs in collocation with לֵבָב six times: 4:39; 8:2, 5; 13:4; 18:21; 29:3. The verb occurs in 8: 2, 3 (3 times), 5, 16.

91 Lohfink's structure of 8:2–6 binds vv5, 6 together. Compare Weinfeld (1991) 216.

manna in the wilderness;[92] 9:3, where the object is Yahweh going ahead in the conquest; 9:6, with the object a statement of Israel's unrighteousness; 11:2 (twice), in reference to knowing and seeing the discipline of Yahweh in both the exodus and the desert; and 29:3, which stands in parallel to 29:5, whose object is כִּי אֲנִי יְהוָה אֱלֹהֵיכֶם.

Miller, citing 4:35; 7:9; 8:5 and 9:3, says,

> All these texts make it clear that the people are to understand and acknowledge that the one they know as the Lord, who has acted powerfully, redemptively, and providentially in their history, is God and God alone.[93]

This point is well illustrated in 11:2–8. Here, the focus on the past events of the exodus and wilderness fits the focus of 8:2–6. The point is stressed in 11:2 that it is the current generation, not its children, which רָאוּ and יָדְעוּ these events. Here יָדַע obviously has the sense of "experience". However the verse begins with the exhortation וִידַעְתֶּם הַיּוֹם כִּי. The purpose of this exhortation (11:8) is the right response to Yahweh in obedience. Thus יָדַע, at the beginning of v2, has the deeper sense of right recognition of Yahweh.[94]

Another verse which illustrates this deeper sense attached to יָדַע is 4:9 where the verb occurs as a hiphil. The current generation is warned to be careful

פֶּן־תִּשְׁכַּח אֶת־הַדְּבָרִים אֲשֶׁר־רָאוּ עֵינֶיךָ וּפֶן־יָסוּרוּ מִלְּבָבְךָ כֹּל יְמֵי חַיֶּיךָ.

The things which this generation must not forget or let slip from their hearts, they must also הוֹדַעְתָּם their children. Clearly יָדַע here does not carry the sense of experience. Rather it suggests the deeper level of right response to Yahweh, as the context of 4:10 shows. This deeper sense is thus not dependent on having experienced the actions of God.

Israel should have gained from the wilderness test a deep knowledge of Yahweh as the God standing behind the events of their experience which would lead into obedient action (8:6). There is no indication that Israel gained such knowledge. Indeed the occurrences of לֵבָב in 8:14, 17 suggest otherwise. As knowing in the heart (v5) parallels remembering (v2), so forgetting and a proud heart (v14) are paralleled. Verses 14b–18 correspond to vv2–6 as proof schema (*Schema der Beweisführung*), but in direct contrast to v5, vv14, 17 reflect an arrogant heart.[95] The heart described in v17 fills out what is meant by a proud heart in v14.[96] Indeed v17 receives

---

92 The verb occurs also in this verse twice in qal referring to the manna which neither this generation nor its fathers knew. In this case there is almost a play on the two senses of יָדַע apparent, the qal meaning 'experience', the hiphil with the deeper sense.

93 Miller (1990) 205.

94 Tiffany, 91–92.

95 Braulik (1986) 72.

96 Christensen (1991) 177.

some emphasis in this chapter, coming at the end of this long sentence. Further, vv14b–16, a hymnic praise of Yahweh, not only interrupts the connection between vv14a, 17,[97] but also delays v17, suspending the climax of this sentence which was anticipated by v14a. All of this contrives to highlight the corrupt heart described in v17.[98] Further, vv17, 18 continue the sense of v3b, showing that Israel has failed the test.[99] If Israel had learned the lesson from the wilderness test, its heart would be right. That the warning of the second half of the chapter is required suggests the lesson is not learned. "For such is the heart of man that in the midst of gifts he can forget the giver, and in blessings he can sow the seed of curses".[100] This agrees with our basic contention that Deuteronomy presupposes corrupted human nature which is fundamentally unable to respond properly to God.[101] Apart from 8:17, the expression, וְאָמַרְתָּ בִּלְבָבֶךָ or similar, occurs in 7:17 and 9:4. Each of the three times is associated with wrong thinking. The sequence of these three binds the three chapters together and suggests a deep-seated corrupt heart rather than a transitory wrong thought.

### *Observing the Commandments and Memory*

The exhortation to observe the commandments (שָׁמַר plus מִצְוֹת) stands at the centre of the chapter (v11). Yet this is the fourth occurrence of the word pair in the chapter, the others being in vv1, 2, 6. The first verse functions as an opening general exhortation for the chapter, full of typical Deuteronomic expressions.[102] This exhortation, which largely repeats those of 5:29; 6:2, 17–19; 7:11–12, is given a fresh motive in chapter 8.[103] The first verse also gives the chapter its underlying presupposition of the grace and faithfulness of Yahweh to his promises.[104] In v2, observance of the commandments is the ideal result of the wilderness test. The repetition in v6 to the current generation suggests that the test has been failed. This is supported by the association of observance with both memory and the heart.

---

97 Weinfeld (1991) 395; Bertholet, 30.

98 Kline (1963) 70, argues that v17 is the focal point of the chapter.

99 Perlitt (1981) 407.

100 Moran (1969) 266. Also Kalland, 75.

101 Lohfink (1965) 77, 81, argues that the cultic 'today' of this preaching shows that the current generation is facing a test but that it is no different from the preceding generation.

102 See Weinfeld (1972) 307, 343, 345, 357; Driver, 106. The singular 'commandment' could denote the first of the ten commandments (Watts (1970) 223) or be a summary for all the law (Mayes (1979) 190; Thompson, 134). Weinfeld (1991) 388, follows Dillmann, 268, 384, in arguing that the singular refers to the basic demand for covenant loyalty.

103 Driver, 106; Dillmann, 276.

104 Braulik (1986) 67–68.

In v6, the call to observe the commandments is coupled with a call to fear. This may well recall 5:29, a statement of surprising pessimism about Israel's ability to keep on fearing Yahweh.[105] The notions of testing and fear are combined in the narrative of Abraham and the sacrifice of Isaac in Genesis 22, as well as in Exodus 20:20.[106] The latter reference may be more apposite. Israel's test has not, thus far, led to fear.[107]

Observance is tied to the memory motif by the verbal parallel between vv2a, 6a, supported by common vocabulary in the two verses.[108] The memory motif frequently recurs in chapters 4–11. Usually it has as its object the historical events of the exodus or wilderness.[109] In v2, it is the test in the wilderness which is to be remembered, not the events of the wilderness *per se*, since knowledge of them is presupposed. These calls to remember suggest Israel has an inherent tendency to forget. "The memory motif inevitably tends to promote a pessimistic view of the people of God".[110] Secondly, obedience is to come from the heart, as seen by the sequence of perfect verbs, וְיָדַעְתָּ (v5a) and וְשָׁמַרְתָּ (6a). Given our comments on the heart above, we again see a negative assessment implied about Israel.

The fourth occurrence of the exhortation to observe the commandments comes in v11. This begins the apodosis of vv7–17.[111] However the verse also functions in parallel with v6. Like it, v11 ties together memory and observance. Both vv6, 11 address the current generation, one for the present and one for the hypothetical future. The repetition of the exhortation suggests a lack of confidence about Israel's ability, or willingness, to keep the commands. Also, the intensity of the exhortation in v11a, הִשָּׁמֶר לְךָ,

---

105 Millar, 241, "Probably the most striking expression of a lack of confidence in Israel comes from the lips of Yahweh himself in 5:29."

106 Moberly (1992) 144.

107 On 'fear' in Deuteronomy, see Weinfeld (1972) 274, 332.

108 See p65 above; and Braulik (1986) 68–69; König, 105.

109 The verb זָכַר occurs fifteen times (contra Watts (1970) 223, who says sixteen!). With the exodus as object: 5:15; 7:18 (twice); 15:15; 16:3, 12; 24:18, 22; with wilderness events: 9:7; 24:9; 25:17; with other objects: 8:18; 32:7; in Moses' speech to God with patriarchs as object: 9:27. The verb שָׁכַח occurs twelve times. With exodus events: 6:12; 8:14; with Horeb and laws: 4:9, 23; 26:13 (compare 8:11); with wilderness events: 9:7; 25:19; with God: 8:11, 19; 32:18; other contexts: 4:31; 24:19. García López (1977) 500, suggests that the forget-remember motif is chiastic with the following elements: A - 6:12; B - 7:18; C - 8:14, 17; B' - 9:7a; A' - 9:7a. This chiasm is based on a primitive form of the chapters.

110 Millar, 240. Brueggemann (1977) 53–59; (1985) 21, says that the prosperity and satiety of the land dulls the memory.

111 Mayes (1979) 193; Braulik (1986) 70.

suggests that Israel is quite prone to forgetfulness and that obedience will not come easily.[112]

In summary, remembering, observing and a heart to know are linked together. The chapter is not just a simple appeal to these things. Its whole tenor betrays a sense that as Israel in the past has not passed the wilderness test, so will it fail in the future.

### *Allusions to the Spies Incident*

These thoughts are further supported by noticing that Israel's failure in the spies incident, and God's enduring grace and faithfulness, form a background to the thinking of this chapter. So the command of 8:1 takes up 1:8. The description of the land as אֶרֶץ טוֹבָה (8:7, 10) is the same as that seen by the spies but rejected by the wilderness generation (1:25, 35). In both, the land has brooks (נְחָלִים 1:24; 8:7). The promise that Israel will lack nothing in the land (8:9) compares with the statement that Israel lacked nothing (2:7) in the wilderness. The journey through the vast and dreadful desert (8:15) uses the same expression as in 1:19 and 2:7.[113] These allusions to Israel's past failure in the spies incident, give the chapter pessimistic undertones. There is no reason given why the hearer-reader should expect Israel to behave any differently now than it did in the past. However, this is not the full story. The chapter is not totally pessimistic. We turn now to the second half of the equation, Yahweh's faithfulness.

### *Faithful Yahweh*

As in chapters 1–3, hope is here grounded in Yahweh's grace and faithfulness to the patriarchal promise. References to the patriarchal promises occur in vv1, 18 explicitly, and implicitly through וּרְבִיתֶם in v1, and its threefold mention in v13.[114] A concern of the chapter is to link the God of the wilderness with the God of bounty.[115] Both are descriptions of the grace of Yahweh. As mentioned above, the troubles of the wilderness are passed over briefly. The focus is on Yahweh's outstanding provisions. L'Hour thus characterises chapter 8 as saying,

---

112 Craigie (1976) 187; Millar, 235. On the expression הִשָּׁמֶר לְךָ פֶּן־תִּשְׁכַּח, see Weinfeld (1972) 357.

113 Peckham (1983) 224–225; Driver, 110; Weinfeld (1972) 358; (1991) 394.

114 Peckham (1983) 232; Skweres, 101–110, 142. See further on this verb, p171 below. Also 1:10 (see previous chapter); 6:3; 7:13; 11:21; 13:18; 30:16. Compare Genesis 22:17; 26:4, 24. Braulik (1986) 67, states that chapter 8 takes up the grace theology of chapter 7.

115 D. Schneider, 105.

> daß alles Gnade ist, die gegenwärtige Mitarbeit ebensosehr wie die vergangenen Heilstaten, denn es handelt sich immer um die Erfüllung einer Verheißung.[116]

In the same way, the description of the land in vv7–10, 12–13 is striking. This hymnic "Song of the Good Land"[117] is in stark contrast to the desert in the preceding verses.[118] It is often noted that the fivefold description of the land in vv7–10, like that of 6:10–11,[119] reflects the Garden of Eden in Genesis 2, 3.[120] In particular water and fruitfulness are the marks of Edenic paradise and the characterisation of the land as both good and a gift may also suggest Eden. Both of these notions are prominent in Deuteronomy.[121] Nonetheless, despite the rhetorical style, the "description is somewhat utopian but has roots in reality".[122]

If this description is an allusion to the Garden of Eden, there may also be an allusion to the sin of Adam and Eve.[123] That is, by portraying the land in Edenic terms, it suggests the comparison between Israel and Adam and Eve. This could imply that Israel is no better than Adam and Eve.[124] Secondly, if the description is deliberately hyperbolic, what is its purpose? Possibly the description of the land in such exalted terms is a statement of faith in divine splendour.[125] Possibly this description serves to encourage the despairing Babylonian exiles.[126] Whatever the precise historical situation, the hyperbole emphasises God's grace and faithfulness. In v10 Israel praises Yahweh for the good land. This commendable behaviour is

116 L'Hour, 111.

117 Christensen (1991) 175. Similarly von Rad (1966e) 72; D. Schneider, 108; Lohfink (1965) 83.

118 Christensen (1991) 176; Clifford, 56.

119 Lohfink (1963a) 192; Braulik (1986) 70, say 8:7–10 is dependent on 6:10–15. Compare Weinfeld (1991) 397; D. Schneider, 108.

120 Olson (1994) 55; von Rad (1966e) 72; McConville and Millar, 63, 65; Braulik (1986) 71.

121 Berg (1988) 36–38. He refers to 33:13f, 16, 28, and the expression "flowing with milk and honey" in 6:3; 11:9; 26:9, 15; 27:3; 31:20.

122 Weinfeld (1991) 392. Cunliffe-Jones, 67, states that the fertility of Palestine was greater in ancient times than today. On hyperbole here, see Buis and Leclerq, 85; von Rad (1966e) 72; Driver, 108; König, 105; Weinfeld (1972) 172; Mayes (1979) 192; D. Schneider, 108.

123 Eden as paradise, without mention of Adam and Eve, is mentioned in Isaiah 51:3; Ezekiel 28:13–14. See also Ezekiel 36:35; Joel 2:3. On sin in Eden, see Ezekiel 28:15–17. Adam's sin is mentioned in Hosea 6:7 in terms of breaking the covenant. See also Carpenter, 80–81.

124 Possibly the concern for Israel's heart in Deuteronomy is an allusion to the corrupt heart in Genesis 6:5; 8:21. See further Moberly and Rendtorff, p82 below.

125 Zimmerli (1978) 65–69.

126 Berg, 36–38.

part of the protasis, not apodosis as in the RSV and NIV.[127] The point of the description is not praise. Praise is part of the description. Within the structure of vv7–10, attention remains on Yahweh, not the people. Praise, as part of that description, also directs attention to God's grace.

Thirdly, the contrast between the goodness of God's grace and the rebellion of the people in chapters 1–3 also exists in chapter 8. Thus the function of the description of the land is to heighten God's grace in the face of Israel's past rebellion. It is a call to rely on grace. This contrast is also evident in vv12–17 where the people's future rebellion is under the shadow of another statement of the bounty of the land (vv12–13) and a hymn of God's grace in the exodus and wilderness events (vv14b–16).[128] The rejection of Yahweh could not be made more serious, for the grace of God could hardly be expressed more clearly. None of the bounty of the land or the exodus or the wilderness provision is the accomplishment of Israel; all is of Yahweh, the gracious provider.

Verse 18, in correcting the people's wrong thinking of v17, places human achievement in the context of divine grace and anchors this grace in Yahweh's faithfulness to the patriarchal promises, unusually, here, called covenant.[129] These covenant promises still stand, and are applicable 'this day', and will only be fulfilled with the cultivated land.[130]

Another suggestion of the grace of Yahweh is the expression, in vv3, 16, about the manna "which your fathers have not known". Giles argues that this expression is significant in Deuteronomy 8. Everywhere else in Deuteronomy (and Jeremiah) where a similar expression is used, "this lack of knowledge (by the fathers) was a desirable quality".[131] Deuteronomy 8:3, 16 are the exceptions. A contrast is made between the knowledge of the fathers and that of the present generation.[132] Weinfeld argues that the reference to the fathers is to "stress whatever was exceptional in the event"

127 Mayes (1979) 192; Lohfink (1965) 81–82. Compare Ranck, 74.

128 On the hymnic participles in these verses, see von Rad (1966e) 73; Braulik (1986) 72; Weinfeld (1991) 397.

129 McEvenue (1971) 74; Weinfeld (1991) 395; Mayes (1979) 194, suggest this expression is typical of P. Anbar (1982) 49, suggests the collocation of "swear" and "covenant" is late Deuteronomistic. See also 4:31 and 7:12. On these , see Skweres, 137–151. On links with 4:37; 7:8 and 9:5, see Dillmann, 278; Driver, 110. See also Naylor, 138, 143. Compare Welch, 100.

130 Braulik (1986) 72; Weinfeld (1972) 175. Merrill, 187–188, argues against the MT here and prefers a ו before לְמַעַן, thus following LXX, Sam Pent, Qumran and NIV, reading the clause as a final or result clause and not a purpose clause. He appeals to Waltke and O'Connor, §38.3c. This means that wealth is not a prerequisite for a relationship with God.

131 Giles, 155.

132 Giles, 158–159. Compare Hoftijzer, 34–38, 125.

and highlight the miracle of the manna provision.[133] However more is intended by this. The reference to the lack of knowledge of the fathers highlights the privilege of this wilderness generation.[134] Stressing this privilege highlights Yahweh's grace.

### *The Final Warning (8:19–20)*

Chapter 8 concludes on a sombre note. Verses 19, 20 comprise the concluding element of the chapter, a plural frame complementing v1. Unlike v1, these verses represent a solemn warning of future curse.[135] Where the opening verse speaks of life, these speak of destruction. This underscores the movement from blessing to curse within chapter 8, which reflects the expectation of the chapter that Israel will fail, as its predecessors did. Verses 19 and 20 are particuarly severe in their warning.[136] The expressions used (הָלַךְ, עָבַד, הִשְׁתַּחֲוָה) have covenantal overtones, reminiscent of the first commandment.[137] The seriousness of the threat is indicated in the development from vv17–18 into a warning against idolatry, an issue not raised in chapter 8 but nonetheless of great importance in Deuteronomy. Thus these final verses link the chapter to the major themes of the book.[138]

The expression תִשְׁמְעוּן בְּקוֹל יְהוָה אֱלֹהֵיכֶם at the end of v20 is also important. As we shall show in our discussion on 29:3, the expression שָׁמַע בְּקוֹל, typically with Yahweh as the object, is important in Deuteronomy. It denotes not just hearing but obedience and acts as a summary statement of covenant requirement. The prepositional object especially conveys this sense.[139] In Deuteronomy, the expression usually occurs in conditional blessing or curse statements, as here.[140] Here it anticipates its recurrence in 9:23. Further, it possibly takes up 1:43, in which case this is another allusion to the background of the spies incident.[141] In addition, there may

---

133 Weinfeld (1972) 172.

134 Giles, 163.

135 Mayes (1979) 194, lists 4:26; 30:19; 32:46. Weinfeld (1991) 388, 395, notes that like 4:26 and 30:19, 8:19–20 is plural.

136 Note הַעִדֹתִי in v19, "call to witness". See Weinfeld (1991) 388; Merrill, 188.

137 Mayes (1979) 194; Merrill, 188; Craigie (1976) 189.

138 Von Rad (1966e) 73. On tying in to other parts of the book, see Christensen (1991) 177; Craigie (1976) 189–190; Weinfeld (1972) 309, 320, 321. On complementing 7:12ff, see Moran (1969) 266. The last clause of 8:20 repeats the opening one of 7:12.

139 So Braulik (1986) 73; (1978) 124–125. Brueggemann (1961) 201, says שָׁמַע can mean "to listen attentively with the intention of responding in obedience, so that the relation to Yahweh may be sustained".

140 Braulik (1986) 80. His exceptions are 9:23, 13:5. However 26:14, 17 are better described as hypothetical future statements.

141 Braulik (1986) 80, suggests that 8:20 alludes to 1:7f, 41, 42–43.

also be another allusion to the Garden of Eden. Berg regards the ideal of the Garden of Eden as being available for man "wenn er «auf die Stimme Jahwes» hören würde".[142] Certainly Adam is punished כִּי שָׁמַעְתָּ לְקוֹל אִשְׁתֶּךָ (Genesis 3:17; compare 3:8, 10). Finally the phrase, תִשְׁמְעוּן בְּקוֹל יְהוָה אֱלֹהֵיכֶם, is not an inappropriate end to a chapter which is concerned with what comes out of Yahweh's mouth.[143] As argued above, this is broader than the commandments, thus תִשְׁמְעוּן בְּקוֹל יְהוָה אֱלֹהֵיכֶם could have a broader sense than simply obedience. In the context of this chapter, it suggests paying attention to God's grace.

### *Conclusion*

Our discussion of chapter 8 has shown that Israel is regarded as having a propensity to sin. Its failure in the past colours the expectation for its future. Future hope, like the wilderness provisions, rests on grace. The enjoyment of the blessings of the land depends ultimately on Yahweh's grace and his faithfulness to the patriarchal covenant rather than on any optimism associated with Israel's disposition. Though the sense of Israel's inclination to sin is subtly conveyed in this chapter, it becomes blatant in the next. Nonetheless there is no theological inconsistency between the two. The options which Deuteronomy considers are Israel's disobedience and reliance on Yahweh's grace and faithfulness. They are both apparent here.

Chapter 8 introduces chapter 9.[144] Both share common vocabulary and themes. Both 8:20 and 9:1 use שָׁמַע, the warning of 8:19–20 underlining the importance of the command in 9:1.[145] In addition, both chapters draw lessons from the wilderness, the former self-sufficiency, the latter self-righteousness.[146] Chapters 7–9 are linked by the expression "to say in your heart" (אָמַר plus בְּ plus לֵבָב plus pronominal suffix) which occurs in 7:17; 8:17; 9:4. This series of exhortations against pride suggests that these chapters are to be read in sequence.[147] In addition בַּמִּדְבָּר occurs in 8:2; 9:7.[148] The memory motif, so important in chapter 8, recurs in 9:7.[149] 9:5 picks up the language of 8:18 (הָקִים) regarding the confirming of the covenant promises.[150]

---

142 Berg, 35.

143 Wolff (1974a) 76.

144 See Lohfink (1965) 86; Braulik (1986) 73; Preuß (1982) 102. Compare Ranck, 90. Tiffany, 293–295, argues that chapters 5–11 have a concentric structure.

145 Rose (1994) 465–466.

146 Miller (1990) 118; Thompson, 134. Compare Olson (1994) 53.

147 Weinfeld (1991) 406.

148 Lohfink (1963a) 205.

149 Peckham (1983) 225.

150 Weinfeld (1991) 407; Kutsch, 106–107; Rose (1994) 465, 468. See also Gammie (1972) 10–12, who argues that chapter 8 and 9:1–6 are linked theologically on the

Having noted these links with chapter 9, we turn to see how the themes of Israel's faithlessness and Yahweh's faithfulness are developed there.

## Deuteronomy 9:1–6

### *Introduction*

Chapter 9 in large part recounts the story of the golden calf incident. It is the second great account of Israel's failure in Deuteronomy. Whereas that of the spies in chapter 1 concerned the land, this concerns the law. Thus Israel's failure connects the two great themes in Deuteronomy. However the account of the golden calf incident is prefaced by 9:1–6 which is one of the clearest statements in Deuteronomy of our thesis of the priority of divine grace over Israel's obedience. This paragraph is the key for interpreting the rest of the chapter.

Redaction-critics identify a number of inconsistencies and doublets in chapter 9. These include the fivefold mention of forty days and nights, repeated mentions of the giving of the tables of law (9:10, 11), "at that time" (9:20; 10:1, 8), Aaron (9:20; 10:6–7), the threefold mention of Moses' intercession (9:18, 20, 26–29), inconsistency with Moses on the mountain (10:5, 10) and disjunction with Moses' prayer, its lack of relation to 9:22–24 and its answer not occurring until 10:10. Scholars seek to resolve these tensions by various suggestions: assumption that there is no problem, simple verse disorder, late insertions, removal from original context, an original layer, and supplements.[151] Even Lohfink, who explains most of the problems as stylistic devices, in part due to dependence on Exodus, considers 9:1–7, 22–24 as later than the bulk of the chapter.[152] Nevertheless, he recognises that 9:1–7 is the hermeneutic key for the following narrative.[153] For example, the allusion to the patriarchs in 9:27 is

---

issue of correcting wrong views of divine retribution. In particular, 8:2, 3, 18; 9:4–6.

151 Lohfink (1963a) 207–208. Seitz, 51–69; Peckham (1975) 8–10, suggest two strata. For a discussion of Seitz, see Peckham (1975) 3–5; Preuß (1982) 97–98; Boorer, 273–274. Compare Buis and Leclerq, 87–93; Van Seters (1994) 301–310. Preuß (1982) 102, mentions Dillmann and García López as two who suggest that 9:7–10:11 originally occurred before 1:5. Mayes (1979) 195–196, notes chronological disorder, for example, 9:25 is delayed after 9:18 and 9:13–14 could not have followed 9:12.

152 Lohfink (1963a) 200–218. See Boorer, 274–277; García López (1978) 6–8, 18–25. Almost invariably scholars distinguish between 9:1–6 and 9:7–10:11. So, for example, von Rad (1966e) 75; Craigie (1976) 194; García López (1977) 484–485; Merrill, 191; O'Connell (1992b) 492; Boorer, 272–280. Compare Mayes (1979) 194–196; Christensen (1991) 182–183.

153 Lohfink (1963a) 200.

grounded in 9:5 and the motif of stiff-neckedness, which extends to 10:16, is based on 9:6.[154] The theology of 9:1–6 undergirds the rest of the chapter.

Again we shall consider this chapter synchronically, attempting to find a theological resolution to the tensions between the faithlessness of Israel and the faithfulness of Yahweh.

## *Theology*

We turn to a consideration of the theology of 9:1–6, a section crucial for our thesis. The two key words of 9:1–6 are יָרַשׁ (vv1, 3, 4a, 4b, 5a, 5b, 6a) and צְדָקָה (vv4, 5, 6).[155] There is no obvious structural pattern to this section to elucidate its content,[156] though the sevenfold occurrence of יָרַשׁ alternates qal and hiphil forms reflecting a dialectic between grace and obligation. The centrepoint is v4b, where the hiphil shows that at the heart is Yahweh's grace.[157] There is also an allusion here to the patriarchal promises, especially to Genesis 15:7 which uses יָרַשׁ in a similar way.[158] This links the wickedness of the inhabitants in 9:4–6 with the sins of the Amorites in Genesis 15:16.[159] Unusually for Deuteronomy, 9:5 mentions the oath to the patriarchs but in a relative clause not dependent on land, even though the land is the general context.[160]

The chapter begins with an urgent call, שְׁמַע יִשְׂרָאֵל, arguably an allusion to the Shema of 6:4–5.[161] The repetition of this call to hear in 9:1 suggests that Israel's action in making the golden calf, which is the content of most

154 Seitz, 54.

155 Peckham (1983) 230, argues that Dtr2 changed the theology of possession of the land from dependence on obedience to dependence on the patriarchal promise. So 9:4–6 is Dtr2. Compare Lohfink (1990) 368–396; (1983) 14–33.

156 Lohfink's chiasm, (1963a) 201, fails to convince. It is:

| | | |
|---|---|---|
| I | 1ab, 2 | no typical words, future history |
| II | 3 | יָדַע |
| III | 4, 5 | Imperative in verse 4 |
| II | 6 | יָדַע |
| I | 7 | remember. |

See Tiffany's comments, 186.

157 Braulik (1991a) 38; (1989) 328. On the play on יָרַשׁ in qal and hiphil in 9:1, see Lohfink (1983) 18, 32.

158 Lohfink (1983) 22. Compare Skweres, 87–101, 143. He traces the *Rückverweis* back to Genesis 15:18. See our discussion on 1:8, pp30ff; Hagelia, 85.

159 Hagelia, 141. Lohfink (1963a) 204, notes that both 9:4–6 and Genesis 15:16 connect patriarchal promise, land possession and the guilt of the inhabitants.

160 Plöger, 64. The exceptions are 7:8, 12; 8:18; 28:9. On 9:5, see Skweres, 88–92, 143; Driver, 111; Weinfeld (1972) 350.

161 Merrill, 189; Mayes (1979) 196; McConville and Millar, 63, 66. Compare Ridderbos, 130, who states that 9:1 continues the narrative from 5:33. The same expression also occurs in 4:1 and 5:1.

of chapter 9, is being set in contrast to the fundamental demands of 6:5. In 6:4–5, it is clear that fulfilment of these demands can only be through a right heart. Chapter 8, where לֵבָב was a key word, shows that Israel's heart is corrupt. The same interest in Israel's heart now continues in 9:1–6 where לֵבָב occurs twice, in vv4, 5. The warning in v4a, אַל־תֹּאמַר בִּלְבָבְךָ, more or less repeats 7:17; 8:17, and further alerts the reader to expect Israel's failure. This is made explicit in v5 where entry to the land is not וּבְיֹשֶׁר לְבָבְךָ. Though not said explicitly, the suggestion again is that Israel's heart is not in fact upright. The closest explicit statement is made in v6, since stiff-neckedness is a matter of the heart, as 10:16 shows. These verses take then a further step in developing the theology of Israel's heart from chapter 8. Gradually an acknowledgement of Israel's inherently sinful heart is unfolding.

One of the difficulties of these verses is how to read v4b. The alternatives are, firstly, to read it as a continuation of the statement of Israel in v4a, though the change to second person at the end of v4b seems to militate against this. Secondly it could be read as Yahweh's response to v4a, though the repetition with v5b would then seem unnecessary. In this view, many consider consider v4b as a gloss.[162] It is preferable to read v4b as a continuation of Israel's words of v4a, despite the person change, understanding רִשְׁעָה and צְדָקָה in the two halves of the verse as legal terms interpreting each other.[163] Thus the argument of v4 is based on the conception that defeat in war reflects the judgment of God with victory corresponding to innocence before God.[164] These two statements of v4 are then answered point for point in v5, 5a corresponding to 4a, 5b to 4b.[165] The fallacy of Israel's thought is demonstrated in that the wickedness of the nations does not logically demand the innocence of Israel. Israel is not measured against the standard of its enemies but against those of Yahweh. In such a light, it cannot claim righteousness.[166]

Both vv3, 6 are calls to the right knowledge of God, similar to 8:5. As 8:17 countered 8:5, so these calls to right knowledge are pitted against 9:4.

---

162 Lohfink (1963a) 201, suggests that this is the consensus. So Bertholet, 30; Steuernagel, 32; Nielsen, 110. See further Braulik (1982) 148.

163 Lohfink (1963a) 202; Miller (1990) 120; Tiffany, 188; Braulik (1989) 329. Christensen (1991) 183, regards v4b as the central element of the paragraph. See García López (1977) 483.

164 Lohfink (1963a) 202; Peckham (1975) 16, refer to 25:1 for a contrast between רִשְׁעָה and צְדָקָה. Similarly Miller (1990) 120; Weinfeld (1991) 406. On the ANE background for the understanding of victory as vindication, see Lohfink (1963a) 202–204; Tiffany, 187; Braulik (1984) 9–10; (1982) 149. For a somewhat idiosyncratic view that these verses are cultic, see Gottwald, 304. Compare Braulik (1989) 329, who regards vv4–5 as cultic.

165 Lohfink (1963a) 201–203.

166 L'Hour, 111–112.

Again this knowledge is not just experience but a deep-seated trust in God's grace and faithfulness which will be demonstrated in obedience. Thus what we found in chapter 8 continues in chapter 9.[167]

Righteousness in Deuteronomy is not an act but an attitude and is measured vertically not horizontally.[168] The model of righteousness behind these verses is that of Abraham. This is conveyed by the mention of the patriarchal promises in v5b, a fuller statement than v3b. These promises alone determine Yahweh's acting for Israel. That is the real difference between Israel and the nations.[169] However Peckham suggests that Israel's righteousness is never explicitly denied. Despite its stiff-neckedness, Israel is not declared guilty but merely has no legal right to the land.[170] Yet the statement of Israel's stiff-neckedness is quite condemning. Israel is not righteous.[171] Thus 9:1–6 is one of the most explicit statements of Yahweh's grace and faithfulness in all of Deuteronomy.[172]

Sometimes the theology of righteousness found here is regarded as a corrective to that of 6:18–25 where, it is alleged, a works-righteousness is described.[173] However the offer of law in 6:18–25 was an act of redemption for a people already justified. So 6:18–25 is also not about works righteousness and should be read in the light of 9:4–6.[174] Both 6:25 and Genesis 15:6 agree that, "Was Gerechtigkeit ist, das bestimmt allein Jahwe, und von dieser Anerkenntnis lebt der Mensch".[175]

The statement כִּי עַם־קְשֵׁה־עֹרֶף אָתָּה in v6b is not a description of Israel's past, though subsequent verses give evidence from the past to support the contention. Rather, v6b stands emphatically at the end of the section as a definition of the present nature of the people: "Israel was and is

167 García López (1977) 502–503, sees a similar pattern in both 8:2–6 and 9:4–7 in that both have the verbs זָכַר, יָדַע and שָׁמַר. Both deal with undeserved grace grounded in the patriarchal promises. Also L'Hour, 111.

168 Braulik (1982) 149–150. Contrast Hagelia, 72–73.

169 Harper, 219; Ridderbos, 131; von Rad (1966e) 73; Olson (1994) 56; Braulik (1986) 75; (1982) 151; Goldingay (1987) 143; Watts (1970) 226. See 7:7–8. Braulik (1989) 330, understands the similarity of Israel to the nations to reflect the universality of sin, along the lines of Romans 3:9.

170 Peckham (1975) 16–18.

171 As noted in the previous chapter, comparing 1:32 and Genesis 15:6.

172 See Luther, 103.

173 Braulik (1989) 330, argues that DtrÜ in 9:4–6 corrects misunderstandings of DtrN in 6:18–25. Similarly Mayes (1979) 197; Cairns, 100; Weinfeld (1991) 406.

174 Braulik (1982) 137–140; Perlitt (1990a) 35–36; Roehrs, 596. Compare Preuß (1993) 232.

175 Perlitt (1990a) 35–36. Similarly García López (1977) 504–509. See also Perlitt (1982) 37. Tiffany, 145, 188–189, argues that in both places, righteousness is based on obedience. See also McConville (1993b) 153.

a stubborn people".[176] It is with this presupposition that the covenant is renewed at Moab. It does not anticipate a changed Israel exercising faithful obedience. So the renewal of the covenant is a further demonstration of the grace and faithfulness of Yahweh which is not annulled by Israel's failure. Stiff-neckedness suggests at least unwillingness to submit to the yoke of Yahweh's sovereignty.[177]

Moberly and, apparently independently, Rendtorff make some interesting suggestions about the characterisation of Israel as stiff-necked.[178] Addressing Exodus 32–34, they note that Israel is called stiff-necked in 32:9 and this is the basis of Yahweh's threat to destroy them after the making of the golden calf. Then, in his intercession, Moses acknowledges that Israel remains stiff-necked (34:9; compare Deuteronomy 9:27b). Yahweh's startling response in 34:10 is that he is making a covenant with Israel. Thus the renewal of the covenant with Israel is on the basis (כִּי) that it is sinful.[179] Israel's character remains explicitly unchanged. This is compared with the account of Noah, in particular Genesis 6:5; 8:21. There are a number of parallels regarding the people's sinfulness and the threat of destruction and its withdrawal. Only Genesis 6:8 and Exodus 33:12 mention "found favour in the sight of Yahweh" about an individual.[180] Both Noah's sacrifice and Moses' intercession are significant for Yahweh's mercy. These observations suggest that Israel's future is grounded in God's mercy. Its sinfulness is inherent.

### *Allusions to the Spies Incident*

The sense of Israel's failure is also brought out by allusions to the spies incident and its aftermath recounted in chapters 1–3.[181] In fact 9:2 clearly

176 Von Rad (1966e) 74. Also Goldingay (1987) 155; Watts (1970) 229, "When Israel heard these words centuries later, the people were reminded that they were still stubborn and rebellious". Similarly Miller (1990) 121; Braulik (1986) 75. Polzin (1980) 85–86, regards the Rahab account as an illustration of Israel's failure and a reflection on 9:4–6. See McConville (1993b) 96.

177 See Couroyer (1981) 216–225; Merrill, 190. Compare Nielsen, 121. On the occurrences of the expression in the Old Testament, see Kalland, 79; and in Exodus 32–34, see Moberly (1983) 183–185.

178 Moberly (1983) 89–93; Rendtorff (1989) 389–390.

179 Moberly (1983) 89–90, argues that כִּי here is, if not causative, emphatic concessive: "Although they are indeed a stiff-necked people, yet forgive…".

180 Moberly (1983) 92.

181 Similarities between 1:1–3:29 and 9:1–10:11 are often made. For example, Merrill, 189.

presupposes knowledge of Deuteronomy 1.[182] So the fortified cities and the Anakim in 9:1, 2 recall the failure of Israel to enter the land a generation before (compare 1:28).[183] This description of the opposition, even without the background of chapter 1, suggests the impossibility of Israel's task. Verses 1–2 emphasise Israel, אַתָּה occurring three times. By the thrice-mentioned גָּדֹל and the mention of Anakim they indicate its incapability.[184] Peckham says of 9:1–6,

> in composing his resounding call to conquer, DTR has used only those texts which allude to their rebellion, their terror, their refusal to go in and conquer the land. It seems grandiose, but is actually sarcastic.[185]

The juxtaposition of Israel's unfaithfulness with Yahweh's faithfulness in 1–3 also continues here. We note that אַתָּה עֹבֵר הַיּוֹם in 9:1 also occurred in 2:18.[186] In contrast to the threefold stress on Israel in 9:1, 2, the threefold mention of Yahweh by the pronoun הוּא in v3, "is peculiarly emphatic".[187] The contrast between Israel and Yahweh in 9:1–3 reflects the contrast expressed in chapter 1 through the speeches of Israel compared with those of Yahweh, Moses and the spies. In addition, three times is it mentioned in vv4, 5, and 6 that Yahweh will drive out the Canaanites.[188] The mention in v3 of the promise of Yahweh and his victory are possibly allusions to 1:21, 30.[189] As in 1:35; 3:25 and 8:10, the land is again called 'good' (9:6).

### *Significance*

9:1–6 indicates a constant awareness of Israel's failure. This, plus the greatness of the opposition "described in typical hyperbolic terms" serves "to enhance the prestige of Yahweh who was able to overcome even such foes as these".[190] Thus the "unbounded optimism" of the passage is entirely a result of confidence in Yahweh, for none is placed in Israel.[191] This is not to deny human responsibility. Whilst there is a "careful unity of divine and

---

182 Dillmann, 278; Driver, 111; Nielsen, 111. On the presupposition that the hearers-readers were familiar with source texts, Peckham (1975) 12, agrees with Lohfink (1960) against Plöger. See Lohfink's response to Plöger, (1968) 110–115.

183 Peckham (1975) 10–12; Lohfink (1963a) 205–206; Christensen (1991) 183; Craigie (1976) 192. Weinfeld (1991) 400, notes that the description also recalls 2:10, 21.

184 Merrill, 189. Compare Weinfeld (1972) 49.

185 Peckham (1975) 13. He, (1983) 221, 225, notes that the history of rebellion begins and ends (9:1–3, 23) with references to the spies' rebellion.

186 Driver, 111; Christensen (1991) 183; Craigie (1976) 192.

187 Keil and Delitzsch, 335. Also Peckham (1975) 10, 13; Miller (1990) 119; Craigie (1976) 193; García López (1977) 495.

188 Kalland, 78.

189 Driver, 111; Kalland, 78; Dillmann, 278; Peckham (1975) 14; (1983) 225.

190 Thompson, 137–138.

191 Thompson, 137; Buis and Leclerq, 87.

human action", the emphasis is on the effectiveness of God's power and grace.[192] What Israel does "it accomplishes out of the 'prevenient' and 'cooperative' grace of its God".[193] "The contrast is between the fidelity of Yahweh (9:25–29; 10:11) and the sin of Israel".[194] No hope is expressed that Israel will now obey.

This devastating description of Israel at first sight rests uneasily with the overwhelming exhortation in Deuteronomy for Israel to obey. All the commands, motivations, promises and appeals to Yahweh's grace, faithfulness and power fail to induce the heart to change. Israel remains stiff-necked and stubborn.[195] Its heart remains corrupt. This is one of Deuteronomy's most interesting dilemmas. How can a people unable to keep the covenant be commanded to do so? The placing of this account of Israel's failure before the law sharpens this dilemma.[196] The resolution to this dilemma, anticipated in 10:16, is explicitly resolved only in 30:6. Yahweh himself has to act on Israel's heart. Yet here in chapter 9, a theology of undeserved "justification" is anticipated.[197] In Galatians and Romans especially, "justification" derives from God's faithfulness to the patriarchal promises. The justified person is the one who relies on Yahweh's grace and promises.[198] That is entirely consistent with Deuteronomy 9:1–6. Israel's standing with Yahweh is ultimately dependent on his faithfulness to his promises.[199] Indeed the clarity of the exposition of Israel's helplessness, weakness and sinfulness anticipates Romans 5:6–8.[200]

## Deuteronomy 9:7–24

9:1–6 is the key to understanding 9:7–24, to which we now turn, again concentrating on its portrayal of the faithlessness of Israel. The resolution of this failure is dealt with in the next section, 9:25–10:11. Firstly, we shall briefly comment on its structure in order to aid in an understanding of its theology.

---

192 Miller (1990) 119; Craigie (1976) 193.

193 Braulik (1984) 9.

194 Peckham (1983) 233. Compare Polzin (1980) 54, that the Abrahamic promises are effectively neutralised in 9:4–5.

195 D. Schneider, 114.

196 McConville (1993b) 134. He goes on to say, 134–136, that the inevitability of the curses of chapter 28, in the light of 9:4–6, is unsurprising.

197 Roehrs, 595–599.

198 Braulik (1982) 152, "Wer dieses »Gericht« Gottes annimmt, wer sich also auf Gottes Gnadenhandeln hin verläßt, dem wird dieser durch das Gotteswort vermittelte »Glaube« zur Gnade der Rechtfertigung angerechnet". See Roehrs, 598.

199 Braulik (1984) 10.

200 On Deuteronomy and Romans, see Braulik (1982) 130, 146–147.

### *Structure*

Lohfink suggests that the fivefold mention of "forty days and forty nights" (9:9, 11, 18, 25; 10:10) plus the fourfold repetition of "fire" (9:10, 15, 21; 10:4) are structural markers yielding five episodes in this passage as follows:[201]

| | | |
|---|---|---|
| A | 9:9–10 | Making of the Covenant |
| B | 9:11–17 | Covenant Breach |
| C | 9:18–21 | Atonement Measures |
| D | 9:25–10:5 | Covenant Renewal |
| E | 10:10–11 | Consequences of Renewal for Moses |

Though Lohfink identifies key words, he fails to show how structurally they elucidate the passage. We suggest that the repetition of "forty" is rhetorical. As far as the people are concerned, the forty days and forty nights signifies failure. This parallels the forty years in the wilderness. Just as the seriousness of the failure at Horeb is marked by the repetition of "forty days and forty nights", so also the seriousness of the failure at Kadesh is marked by the forty years in the wilderness.[202]

Christensen's argument for a chiastic structure for 9:8–29 is weak.[203] He fails to show the significance of this for understanding the passage. He fails to see that 10:1–11 continues the section and picks up the key words "forty days and forty nights" and "tablets". The content of each of his sections does not provide a good match. He fails to consider the matching of 9:7, 22–24 through common vocabulary and themes which is widely recognised. The two decisive words in v7 both occur in vv22–24, namely קָצַף and מָרָה, and form an inclusio for the section.[204] 9:22–24 fills out what is expressed only in abstract form in v7.[205] O'Connell builds on this parallel, arguing that 9:7–24 was originally a concentric structure (ABA') but was extended by 9:25–10:11 (B') to form a parallel panel with 9:8b–21 (B).[206] We shall discuss below 9:25–10:11. Certainly the fact that 9:7–8a and 22–24, which share so much important vocabulary and are such small units suggests that

---

201 Lohfink (1963a) 214–216. Also Watts (1970) 227. Braulik (1986) 76, divides the final two episodes into three. Weinfeld (1991) 427, suggests the repetition of "forty" is also liturgical. The omitted verses Lohfink attributes to later levels of redaction. "Forty days and forty nights" occurs only twice in Exodus, namely 24:18; 34:28. אֵשׁ also occurs in 9:3. On devouring fire in a military context, see Miller (1965) 259–261.

202 Compare McConville and Millar, 66, who suggest that "forty" rhetorically suggests intimacy.

203 Christensen (1991) 189.

204 Weinfeld (1991) 407; Merrill, 191.

205 Lohfink (1963a) 200; Peckham (1975) 38–39.

206 O'Connell (1992b) 499.

these are a deliberate frame to 9:8b–21. They thus delimit the section 9:7–24.[207] In summary, 9:8b–21 retells the golden calf incident but its frame (9:7, 22–24) shows that the issue is broader than that.

## *Israel's Sin*

9:7–24 makes two points about Israel's faithlessness. Firstly it provides the evidence for the statement made at the end of v6 regarding Israel's stiff-neckedness. Secondly it addresses the seriousness of this sin.

### EVIDENCE

9:7–24 is not just concerned with the golden calf, though that is the main event recorded. The issue is the evidence for the persistence of Israel's rebelliousness. The frame sets the golden calf incident into a context of universal failure.[208] 9:22–24 is not a gloss or digression but indispensable to the argument of the chapter for without these verses the statement of v7 remains unproven since the single incident of Horeb hardly demonstrates continual rebellion. These verses complete the section of evidence for the statements of vv6, 7. This closing element of the frame shows that the golden calf was not an isolated event "but one that was part and parcel of a history of rebellions both before and after it took place".[209]

That the issue of 9:7–24 is Israel's sinfulness is seen in the delay of the content of Moses' prayer until vv25–29. The prayer is anticipated in v18, even perhaps in v14.[210] Yet this is not a case of repetition or verses out of place or even chronological confusion. Rather, the content of the prayer addresses a different issue, as we shall discuss below, and thus the detail of the intercession (9:26–29) is inappropriate here and is kept until this section is complete.[211] The allusion to this prayer in v18 then, does two things. Firstly, it demonstrates the seriousness of the sin in that prayer is necessary, thus fitting the theme of 9:7–24. Secondly it creates a sense of suspense for 9:25–29 which then gives the content of the prayer some emphasis. Similarly, the insertion of vv22–24 shifts the focus on the restoration of the people from v18 to vv25–29. Thus vv7–24 concentrate on the rebellion whereas what follows discusses its resolution.[212] Deuteronomy also omits Moses' first prayer, recorded in Exodus 32:11–14, though the language of

207 Compare the chiasm of Buis and Leclerq, 89.

208 Peckham (1975) 41; Mayes (1979) 197. 9:7 changes from singular to plural, which Weinfeld (1991) 407, suggests corresponds to the change from parenesis to history.

209 Merrill, 196. Compare Olson (1994) 128–129; Watts (1970) 229. Boorer, 291, argues that the frame is a later layer, which generalises Horeb.

210 So Phillips (1973) 70; Cairns, 104; Weinfeld (1991) 410. Compare Exodus 32:10.

211 Lohfink (1963a) 210–211. Compare Peckham (1975) 38, who says that vv22–24 are parenthetical.

212 Boorer, 293.

that prayer is incorporated into Deuteronomy 9:25–29.[213] It is suggested that 9:19 acknowledges that there was an earlier prayer, unrecorded in Deuteronomy, though this may refer back to Kadesh (1:34–39).[214] Again, we suggest the author of Deuteronomy 9 has been deliberate in his selection and arrangement of material to deal firstly with the issue of sinfulness and only then pass to its resolution (9:25–10:11). "(T)he narrative is not in strict chronological order but rather in an order that emphasizes the people's wrongdoing".[215]

SERIOUSNESS

The framing of the section with references to Yahweh's severe anger illustrates the seriousness of Israel's sin. By comparison with Exodus, Deuteronomy emphasises divine wrath. Words for the anger of Yahweh, and the destruction of Israel as a consequence of that anger, occur in vv7, 8, 14, 19, 20, 22 and 25, underlining the seriousness of Israel's sin.[216] This emphasis on divine anger is less obvious in Exodus. For example, Deuteronomy 9:14a, adds the threat of blotting out Israel's name to its parallel in Exodus 32:10a.[217] The mention of the mountain ablaze with fire in 9:15, possibly alluding to the heat of Yahweh's anger, is absent in Exodus.[218] Verse 19 especially uses strong and rare language for Moses' terror at God's red hot anger.[219] Also there is no account of Moses' own anger in Deuteronomy though it is mentioned in Exodus 32:19b. The addition of "crushing" in 9:21 to the instructions for the destruction of the golden calf possibly casts Israel's sin in a more serious light.[220] Begg suggests that the Exodus instructions, apart from being a definitive mode of eliminating all traces of the calf, represent an ordeal, to identify and punish the sinners and discover who was innocent.[221] However the intention of both Exodus 32:20 and Deuteronomy 9:21 is "to administer punishment

213 D. Schneider, 115. Compare Vermeylen (1985b) 4–5, that Exodus 32–34 is itself Deuteronomistic; Rose (1994) 507, that Exodus 32–34 is not a *Vorlage* here.

214 Cairns, 105. Contrast Weinfeld (1991) 411; Driver, 115.

215 Kalland, 80. See Kline (1963) 74–75; Weinfeld (1991) 411, for attempts to reconstruct the chronology. Compare Nielsen, 116.

216 Olson (1994) 57.

217 Driver, 114; Weinfeld (1972) 347; (1991) 410.

218 Merrill, 194. Compare Weinfeld (1991) 410. Compare Exodus 19:18.

219 Kalland, 81; Braulik (1986) 79. Kalland notes the combination of synonyms אַף and חֵמָה with a conjunction (also in 29:22, 27) intensifies the meaning.

220 Vermeylen (1985a) 188. This is countered by Exodus' instructions about drinking the ground up idol which are more direct than in Deuteronomy. Compare Braulik (1986) 80; Weinfeld (1991) 411; Van Seters (1994) 303–307.

221 Begg (1985) 208–233. He cites ANE parallels. Also Weinfeld (1972) 234; (1991) 413.

rather than determine guilt".[222] In contrast to Exodus, Mayes suggests that Deuteronomy's instructions show a presupposition of forgiveness and answered intercession, suggesting a playing down of the punishment notion.[223] That is perhaps too strong. The lack of forced drinking may be a statement of universal guilt. All Israel is guilty. No trial or ordeal is necessary.

The seriousness of the sin is indicated by its being a clear infringement of the first two commandments of the Decalogue.[224] Further, the double imperative of 9:7, זְכֹר אַל־תִּשְׁכַּח, adds weight to what follows.[225] The present generation, which was not at Horeb, is now identified with the one that was. This conflation of generations has the effect here of making the golden calf, perhaps Israel's most serious sin, a paradigm of Israel's life, one of its original sins.[226] This is the same as in chapter 1 where the spies incident was also portrayed as paradigmatic. So in 9:8, and also v16 which links back to v8, the current generation is accused of this sin.[227] The golden calf becomes, especially after the warning of 8:19–20, a fearful present event, symptomatic of Israel's continual disobedience.[228] The paradigmatic nature of this sin is also indicated by the observation that material from Numbers 14:1–25 has been used in Deuteronomy's report, even though this is from the context of the spies incident.[229]

> That material from other contexts is adapted to reinforce the 'golden calf' narrative confirms our earlier impression that this is, for the deuteronomic school, *the* sin par excellence.[230]

Deuteronomy supposes that Israel has a propensity to sin, based on its past record. Its history is not of occasional blemishes amidst an otherwise good record. Israel's sin is persistent and deep-seated.[231]

---

222 Moberly (1983) 199; Budd (1973) 12. They reject a similarity between this passage and Numbers 5. Contrast Vermeylen (1985b) 13.

223 Mayes (1979) 201. See Begg (1985) 242–243, and his reference to Hoffmann. Boorer, 217, 313, suggests that apart from weakening the punishment motif, Deuteronomy concentrates on the destruction of the "sin" itself.

224 Skweres, 52–53.

225 Thompson, 139; Kalland, 81. This continues the memory motif from chapter 8. See Craigie (1976) 194; Christensen (1991) 184.

226 Braulik (1986) 75; Vermeylen (1985b) 1, 7. Vermeylen suggests that the golden calf episode is modelled on Jeroboam's sin which is paradigmatic for future kings of Israel. Compare Rose (1994) 509, who notes that in Deuteronomy, the whole of Israel sins.

227 König, 107. See also 9:22–24.

228 D. Schneider, 114; Olson (1994) 56–57; Merrill, 191.

229 McEvenue (1971) 91. Also Boorer, 363–370.

230 Cairns, 104. More generally, see 101. Compare the more restrained view of Driver, 112. Mayes (1979) 199, links Numbers 14:12 with Deuteronomy 9:14.

231 Merrill, 191; Miller (1990) 122.

This propensity to sin is not quenched by the giving of the law. That the golden calf incident happened at Horeb *of all places* is stressed at the beginning of 9:8.[232] This does not augur well for future generations.[233] The place of theophany and law-giving is a place of great failure. The law does not solve the problem of sin.[234]

Deuteronomy's "free retelling" of Exodus, highlights its "juristisch-theologische" concerns and emphases.[235] A major example of this is Deuteronomy's use of words from the root חָטָא (qal verb in vv16, 18; noun in vv18, 21, 27). In Exodus 32, this root occurs in v21, about Aaron, and in vv30–34. None of these has a parallel in Deuteronomy 9. Yet wherever חָטָא occurs in Deuteronomy 9, the root does not occur in its Exodus parallel.[236] For Deuteronomy the crucial matter is Israel's sin, "of which the calf they had made is a symbol".[237] So in Exodus 32:19a, Moses sees the calf and people dancing; in the parallel in Deuteronomy 9:16a, he sees that the people have sinned.

> It is the sin which is crucial: it is mentioned first; it is preceded by וְהִנֵּה which is a linguistic indicator of factuality and sufficient evidence.[238]

The same applies in 9:18–20 which is "a reflection on sin".[239] The use of both verb and noun from חָטָא in v18 conflates vv16, 21. The two occur together only here in Deuteronomy.[240] That the issue of this section is broader than the golden calf and concerns the general sinfulness of Israel, which the golden calf typifies, is reflected in the addition of כָּל in v18.

> That is, he is talking about their sins in general, or their continual sinfulness. Therefore he proceeds (9:18b[b]) to describe their sinfulness as 'doing what is evil in the sight of Yahweh' and 'provoking him'.[241]

---

232 Mayes (1979) 198, suggests that the verse should be read this way. Also Keil and Delitzsch, 336; Niccacci, 69–71.

233 Christensen (1991) 189.

234 Millar, 242.

235 Lohfink (1963a) 215. Also Thompson, 139; Merrill, 191; Nielsen, 117. Compare Rose (1994) 507; Van Seters (1994) 301–310. Driver, 112, calls it a free reproduction based on JE. See Driver, 112; Boorer, 301–302, for a list of parallels with Exodus. Boorer, 272–325, more generally argues that Deuteronomy presupposes Exodus. See Buis and Leclerq, 89; Braulik (1986) 79. On Aaron's role in the golden calf, see Kaunfer 87–94; Lewy (1959) 318–322. Also Boorer, 245; Aberbach and Smolar, 129–140.

236 Lohfink (1963a) 212; Boorer, 310–311. On חָטָא, see Youngblood, 203.

237 Peckham (1975) 36. Similarly Merrill, 191.

238 Peckham (1975) 30. Compare Braulik (1986) 78.

239 Peckham (1975) 32.

240 Peckham (1975) 32–33.

241 Peckham (1975) 33. See also Weinfeld (1972) 339, 340. Note also the repetition of "stiff-necked" from 9:6.

The seriousness of Israel's sin is indicated by both the anger of Yahweh (vv18, 19) and the mention of fasting and prayer on the part of Moses (vv18, 19, 20). The seriousness of the sin is seen in that even Aaron stood under the wrath of Yahweh. It also prepares the hearer-reader for 10:6, 7.[242] These references to prayer in vv17–20 are framed by mentions of sin (vv16, 21).[243] As mentioned above, the content of the prayer is as yet unimportant. Furthermore 9:21, in comparison to its parallel in Exodus 32:20, like 9:16, emphasises the theological significance of the golden calf, that it is a "sinful thing". The Exodus parallels of both vv16, 21 do not mention sin.[244]

There are other indications of Deuteronomy's emphases in contrast to those of Exodus. Yahweh's statement in v13, though repeating almost verbatim Exodus 32:9, "broadens the horizon of the text" and makes the "general observation that the people are irreformable".[245] The verse serves to show the proof of the statement in v7. וְהִנֵּה is exclamatory: Israel is stiff-necked *indeed.*[246] Also, Deuteronomy, unlike Exodus, uses the expression "tables of the covenant" in vv9, 11, 15. Here, clearly, "covenant" refers to the Decalogue.[247] The rebelliousness of the people (vv12, 16) is also highlighted by the contrast with Moses' obedience in response to Yahweh.[248] So Moses' actions, in vv15–17, correspond to Yahweh's instructions in vv12–14.

The expression "day of assembly" which occurs in 9:10 and 10:4 links the exodus and current generations.[249] It is made clear that the people have heard the commandments and thus their rebellion is not an act of ignorance but one of culpability.[250]

The seriousness of Israel's sin is highlighted by the frame of vv7–24. Verses 22–24 list various places where Israel sinned but not in chronological order. This list has occasioned some discussion. Possibly the order indicates a progression from the smaller to the more serious forms of guilt.[251] The frame also juxtaposes Israel's sin with mention of divine grace. The account of Israel's sin is begun with a mention in v7 of leaving Egypt, attributed in 8:14 to Yahweh's grace, and the wilderness period, also

---

242 Keil and Delitzsch, 338.

243 Peckham (1975) 35. Rose (1994) 509, suggests the mention of a "calf" in v16 is derisory.

244 Lohfink (1963a) 212; Peckham (1975) 36; Weinfeld (1991) 411–412; König, 108.

245 Peckham (1975) 26, 28.

246 Kalland, 81.

247 Von Rad (1966e) 78; Weinfeld (1991) 408; Olson (1994) 7.

248 Boorer, 295.

249 See Cairns, 104, on this verse as cultic. Kalland, 81, notes the expression in 9:10 refers back to Exodus 19.

250 Maxwell, 163.

251 Keil and Delitzsch, 338–339. See also Christensen (1991) 191; Craigie (1976) 197; Kalland, 82; Braulik (1986) 80.

characterised in the previous chapter by Yahweh's gracious provision. Verse 8 begins וּבְחֹרֵב, setting Israel's sin in the context of Yahweh's grace, this time the theophany at Horeb. 9:7–24 concludes similarly, with mention of מִיּוֹם דַּעְתִּי אֶתְכֶם, referring to the covenantal relationship begun by Yahweh with Israel.[252]

The seriousness of the sin is dramatically portrayed by the breaking of the tablets "before your eyes" (9:17), a phrase which does not occur in Exodus. This act is not a spontaneous reaction due to Moses' anger, as in Exodus, but an intentional and legal act denoting the end of the covenant relationship, paralleled in ancient treaties.[253] It cannot be clearer that Israel has broken the covenant.

### *Allusions to the Spies Incident*

The portrayal of Israel's faithlessness in chapter 9 is much the same as that of the spies incident which we discussed in the previous chapter. There are a number of direct allusions to the spies incident in 9:7–24. Indeed the history of Israel's rebellion begins and ends with allusions to the spies incident. The wilderness is described as "this place" (v7, compare 1:31). The rebellion of Israel (מָרָה hiphil) in vv7b, 23, 24 alludes to 1:26, 43. Israel's not hearing in both 1:43 and 9:23 leads to rebellion.[254] Yahweh's rage in 9:7, 8, 22 (קָצַף hiphil) uses the same verb as in 1:34 (קָצַף qal; also 9:19).[255] שָׁלַח in 9:23 implies refusal as in 1:22, in that only the spies were ever 'sent'. 9:23a alludes to 1:21 and v23b to 1:26b, 32b.[256] Certainly an important reference to the spies incident is the link between 9:23, לֹא הֶאֱמַנְתֶּם לוֹ, and 1:32, אֵינְכֶם מַאֲמִינִם.[257] Cognates of this verb occur in a theological sense elsewhere in Deuteronomy only in 7:9; 32:4, 20 and references to faith are rare in the Old Testament in general.[258] In many ways 9:23 sums up the entire spies incident.

---

252 This assumes that the first person is Yahweh and not Moses. On יָדַע here denoting a covenantal relationship, see Naylor, 400–405; Huffmon, 35; Mayes (1979) 202. Huffmon follows the Samaritan reading, דַּעְתּוֹ, "from the day he knew you", referring to Yahweh. Similarly Merrill, 196. In parallel with 9:7–8, this is probably a reference to Horeb. See Cairns, 105; Ridderbos, 136.

253 Weinfeld (1991) 410; Braulik (1986) 78; Kline (1963) 74; Cairns, 104; Mayes (1979) 200; Van Seters (1994) 303.

254 Brueggemann (1961) 203.

255 Peckham (1983) 225.

256 Peckham (1975) 40; Mayes (1979) 202; Rose (1994) 511. Compare Nielsen, 31, that 9:23 and 1:32 have different connotations.

257 Dillmann, 281; Weinfeld (1991) 414.

258 D. Schneider, 116; J.G. Janzen (1987a) 292.

> In einen einzigen Vers 9,23 wird eine Erzählung des Unglaubens bei der Kundschaftersendung in Kadesch Barnea zusammengepreßt.[259]

Finally, insofar as the call to remember in 9:7 resumes the themes of 8:1–20, it is another (indirect) link to the spies incident.[260]

*Significance*

One of the significant points that this section makes is that from the beginning, the law, represented by Horeb, has been an occasion of sin.[261] This suggests a gloomy outlook for Israel. Just as Moab was seen in Deuteronomy 1–3 to be a second Kadesh, the place of failure with regard to the land, so Moab is also a second Horeb, the place of failure with regard to law.[262] There is no expectation that the current generation is any different from its predecessor. That the detailed laws are given soon after chapter 9 suggests these should be read in a context of failure. Also the warning of 8:19–20 is not just a transition from chapter 8 to 9 but sets the sin of the golden calf into context: Israel has broken the *Hauptgebot*. Nothing could be more serious. The warning of 8:20 that Israel will be destroyed because לֹא תִשְׁמְעוּן בְּקוֹל יְהוָה אֱלֹהֵיכֶם is picked up in 9:23. Here, rarely for Deuteronomy, not hearing Yahweh's voice is an absolute statement, not a warning or conditional statement.[263] Israel's past shows that they failed to heed what is warned in 8:20. Nor is it a matter of only the past generation failing, for 9:22–24 also accuses the current generation. The implication is that Israel remains rebellious.

Though the primary purpose of 9:7–24 is to demonstrate Israel's recalcitrance, there are hints of Yahweh's grace also. Apart from those mentioned above in the frame of the section, vv19b–20 show that Moses' intercession was heard. As we discussed in the previous chapter, the expression, בָּעֵת הַהִוא, which occurs in Deuteronomy mainly in three clusters, signifies Yahweh's grace. One of these clusters is 9:20; 10:1, 8, dealing with Moses' prayer and the renewal of the covenant after the golden calf incident.[264] In Deuteronomy, the expression, בָּעֵת הַהִוא, shows that the past event has ongoing consequences for today and that the events are decisive acts of

---

259 Lohfink (1963a) 210. Weinfeld (1991) 414, suggests 9:23 "looks like an epitome of the episode of the spies in Deut. 1:19b–32". Also Vervenne, 265–266. Boorer, 368–369, argues that 9:23 is a late summary of the spies incident modelled on the report in Numbers 13–14. Also Boorer, 398, that 9:23 is closely related to 1:19–2:1. See also Hagelia, 66–68.

260 Burden, 121.

261 Peckham (1975) 41.

262 On Horeb as a prologue to Moab, see Peckham (1983) 226.

263 Braulik (1986) 80. The exceptions are here and 13:5. He suggests the expression also alludes to 1:7, 41, 42.

264 Brueggemann (1961) 246–249. See p33 above.

Yahweh in Israel's life.[265] The point of this, then, is that Yahweh's grace can still be relied upon by the current hearers-readers.

The faithfulness of Yahweh becomes more significant in the next section, 9:25–10:11, to which we now turn.

## Deuteronomy 9:25–10:11

This passage contrasts the recalcitrance of Israel (9:7–24) with the fidelity of Yahweh.[266] From 9:25–10:11 the emphasis shifts from the former to the latter. This is achieved through three stages: the grounds of Moses' intercession (9:25–29), the answer to the prayer (10:1–11), and the renewed call to covenant fidelity (10:12–22). The resolution of Israel's failure is restricted to the golden calf incident. No broader context is explicitly given. However the resolution of this one incident implies that this is a paradigm of Yahweh's faithfulness generally. This is supported by noting that the theology of this resolution is the same as what we found in Deuteronomy 1–3.

That 9:25–10:11 is the resolution to 9:8b–21 is reflected in the repetition of key words.[267] These include "forty days and forty nights" (9:25; 10:10) and the threat to destroy (9:25; 10:10). The tablets are mentioned seven times in each section and "mountain" occurs five and four times respectively.[268] The purpose of this matching is to indicate that the reinstitution of the two stone tablets resolves the crisis of the golden calf and signifies the reinstatement and fulfilment of covenant relations between Israel and Yahweh.[269] We now address the content and theology of this section.

---

265 Brueggemann (1961) 251.

266 Peckham (1983) 234; Boorer, 293.

267 O'Connell (1992b) 493–495, suggests that 9:7–10:11 is structured in four sections: A - 9:7–8a; B - 9:8b–21; A' - 9:22–24 and B' - 9:25–10:7, 10–11. He argues for a complex structure within each section, calling the result "a compound inverse frame comprising two triadic frames". While he does identify important words, they do not occur in a fixed pattern. See O'Connell (1992b) 494–497; Lohfink (1963a) 200; Peckham (1975) 38–39.

268 O'Connell (1992b) 499–501. He also suggests that the central occurrences of "mountain" occur in the rhetorical apex of each.

269 O'Connell (1992b) 502–503, thinks that 9:25–10:11 is structurally redundant in order to elicit empathy with Yahweh's frustration with Israel. He, 492–493, argues that the retelling of the giving of the commandments, already reported in 4:11–13 and 5:2–23a, functions to rebuke Israel for its repeated failure. Perhaps this would be more obvious if the content of the Decalogue were also repeated.

### *Moses' Intercessory Prayer (9:25–29)*

The first section of the resolution to the golden calf incident is Moses' intercessory prayer. The delayed content of this prayer is finally reported in vv25–29, 25 resuming v18.[270] This delay has the effect of annexing the prayer, a common procedure in ancient texts.[271] Suspense is built up in the narrative culminating in this prayer, which initiates the resolution to Israel's failure. Indebted though Israel may be to Moses' intercession, the grounds of Israel's future lie in the patriarchal promises and Yahweh's faithfulness to them.[272] We would structure the prayer as follows:[273]

Address (26a)
    Request I: do not destroy (26a)
        Reason I: Yahweh's redeemed people (26b)
        Reason II: Patriarchs (27a)
    Request II: overlook sin (27b)
            Rhetorical argument about Yahweh's honour
                – his impotency (28a)
                – his hatred (28b)
        Reason I': Yahweh's redeemed people (29)

The address, אֲדֹנָי יְהוִה, occurs only here and 3:24, both times introducing prayer.[274] As argued in the previous chapters, this address indicates a context of the promises of Yahweh, mainly to Abraham though also to

---

270 Christensen (1991) 191; Weinfeld (1991) 414; Buis and Leclerq, 89; Dillmann, 281; Craigie (1976) 197. On the background to the prayer in Exodus 32 and Numbers 14, see Weinfeld (1991) 414–416; McEvenue (1971) 99; Peckham (1983) 234; Boorer, 366. O'Connell (1992b) 505–507, notes that 9:27–29 reverses the order of Exodus 32:11–13, part of Deuteronomy's rhetorical strategy of covenantal rebuke.

271 Daube (1947) 74–101; Weinfeld (1991) 414.

272 Driver, 116. On prophets as intercessors, see Cairns, 106; Balentine (1984) 161–173, who argues that the prophets were not intercessors, apart from Moses, Samuel and Jeremiah. Olson (1994) 57–58, understands Moses' role as a vicarious one.

273 Compare Braulik (1986) 80. He does not match vv26b, 29 which form a "rhetorical envelope" for the prayer. See Christensen (1991) 191; Weinfeld (1991) 417; Greenberg (1977–78) 31. Boorer, 288, argues that vv26, 29 have different functions. The motif of impotency is absent in Exodus but derives from the spies incident in Numbers 14. See Greenberg (1977–78) 33; Boorer, 366. Compare Peckham's analysis, (1975) 42; and Boorer's structure, 283. Skweres, 155–170, argues that 9:28 deliberately changes Numbers 14:16, substituting דִּבֶּר for נִשְׁבַּע. This was to dissociate 9:28 from the patriarchal promise because the context is of a promise to Israel, not the patriarchs.

274 Craigie (1976) 197; Minette de Tillesse, 60; Driver, 116. Both verses also mention in similar terms Yahweh's גָּדְלְךָ and יָדְךָ הַחֲזָקָה, another link between chapters 8–10 and 1–3.

David. More specificially, and in common with Genesis 15:2, 8, "they concern respectively Abraham's descendants and the fate of the people".[275] This address shows that Moses' intercession concerns the faithfulness of Yahweh to his promises even when they are under threat. Indeed Moses here brings Yahweh's attention to his own character and faithfulness.[276] Also, as mentioned, vv26b, 29 have common vocabulary and content regarding inheritance and redemption, forming an inclusio for the prayer, setting it into a context of grace.[277]

One of the striking things about this prayer is that there is no repentance, forgiveness or pledge to act better in the future.[278] Israel's sin is starkly mentioned in v27b, described as stubbornness, wickedness and sin, referring back to vv6–7.[279] Yahweh is asked simply to overlook this, a striking divergence from Exodus 32, where no mention of Israel's sin is recorded.[280] Unlike Exodus 32:11–13 and Numbers 14:13–19, which are like standard lament prayers, Deuteronomy is a pure intercession.[281] This lack of repentance and forgiveness in Deuteronomy is a recognition that Yahweh's standards are too high.

> (T)he Deuteronomist excludes references to forgiveness because it is his view that Israel is doomed from the start.... It is not forgiveness which dominates, but Yahweh's faithfulness.[282]

Millar may be reading too much into this, for although Israel is not explicitly forgiven, the fact that this prayer is answered is an implicit acknowledgement of forgiveness.

The key is the grounds of forgiveness. Yahweh does not forgive because of any merit in or repentance or pledge by Israel. Indeed v27b is a clear statement of Israel's inherent sinfulness. This is not covered over by Moses.[283] Unlike Exodus 34:6–7, the grounds of forgiveness are not primarily Yahweh's compassion. Instead, Deuteronomy highlights

---

275 Hagelia, 30.

276 Cairns, 106.

277 Braulik (1986) 81. On פָּדָה in Deuteronomy, see Kalland, 82; Weinfeld (1972) 326; (1991) 417. The verb also occurs in 7:8; 13:6; 15:15; 21:8; 24:18.

278 Millar, 238, 244, suggests this is consistent with the rest of Deuteronomy where forgiveness is suppressed. However there is no forgiveness mentioned in Exodus 32:9–14. Compare Exodus 32:32. So von Rad (1966e) 78. Also Balentine (1985) 69–70; Greenberg (1977–78) 32. See Davis, 75. On retribution and forgiveness in Exodus 32–34, see Boorer, 259–261.

279 Peckham (1975) 44.

280 Greenberg (1977–78) 31–32. However the mention of sin in v27b is hardly a statement of confession, as he claims. See Peckham (1975) 44.

281 Braulik (1986) 80–81; Greenberg (1977–78) 25.

282 Millar, 238.

283 Miller (1994) 270.

Yahweh's faithfulness to the patriarchal promises as the grounds of forgiveness.

> The appeal to the divine memory is an appeal to the faithfulness of God who keeps promises. The prayer assumes, therefore, that the faithfulness of God is a more controlling dimension of the divine character than the wrath or even the justice of God.[284]

This faithfulness of Yahweh is explicitly linked to the patriarchal promises in v27.[285] At the heart of this prayer is the simple request: זְכֹר לַעֲבָדֶיךָ לְאַבְרָהָם לְיִצְחָק וּלְיַעֲקֹב. This statement has occasioned some debate. Though the promises to the patriarchs are not explicitly mentioned,[286] they seem to be implied. The expression, זָכַר plus לְ, can mean "to think in favour of someone".[287] Yet it is unlikely that this verse is an appeal to the merit of the patriarchs.[288] Despite the fact that the patriarchs are uniquely here called servants and not fathers,[289] every time Abraham, Isaac and Jacob are mentioned by name in Deuteronomy, the context is of the promises to them, and especially the land. This reference is grounded on 9:5 where another explicit mention of patriarchal promise is made.[290] The theology of 9:1–6 demonstrated that Israel is no different from other nations

---

284 Miller (1994) 93–94. Also D. Schneider, 116; Rennes, 215. See Van Seters (1994) 351.

285 Greenberg (1977–78) 31, regards this as the central passage of the prayer, though see our comments on structure above. Compare Van Seters (1972b) 452–453; (1994) 309, who regards the reference to the patriarchs here as "intrusive" by comparison with Exodus 32:11ff. Of the seven explicit references to the patriarchs in Deuteronomy, which Braulik says are all strategic, this is the central one. Van Seters notes that this is the only explicit reference to the patriarchs which is not an appositional phrase. See Braulik (1991a) 47.

286 Braulik (1986) 81, thinks this is striking. Compare Exodus 32:13. See Moberly (1983) 50. On appeal to patriarchs in other prayers, see Minette de Tillesse, 83; Plöger, 77.

287 Weinfeld (1991) 403, 415. Greenberg (1977–78) 26, notes that the prepositional object with לְ is usually a person, not a thing. Other examples include Psalms 25:7; 132:1; 136:23; Jeremiah 2:2; 2 Chronicles 6:42.

288 Brichto (1983) 9, that "ancestral merit is now invoked on behalf of the generation which has again demonstrated its unworthiness". Greenberg (1977–78) 26–27, suggests that the sense can be "reward someone for their good deed", as in Psalm 132:1. He suggests, 28–29, that 9:27 is "a plea to ignore the wickedness of the children out of consideration for their meritorious fathers". Contrast Rose (1994) 512.

289 Braulik (1986) 81, suggests that "servants" is a dignified title denoting true followers. Greenberg (1977–78) 27, suggests that the loyalty of the patriarchs is "hinted at obliquely by the epithet 'Your servants'". Brueggemann (1961) 229, notes that only Moses (3:24) and the patriarchs (here) are called servants in Deuteronomy.

290 Seitz, 54.

with respect to righteousness. This is borne out in this intercession in that Moses makes no comment about Israel's inherent merit. As in 9:5, the patriarchal promise is decisive. Further, given the statement by Yahweh in v14 to make of Moses a great nation, which runs in the face of the promise of nationhood to Abraham, it suggests that v27a is referring to Yahweh's promises, not Abraham's merit.[291] More conclusive for this reading of v27 is the parallel in Exodus 32:13. There the patriarchs are also called servants and quite probably Deuteronomy takes its vocabulary from there. Indeed Boorer argues that v27a is a "blind motif", presupposing knowledge of Exodus 32:13.[292] That verse goes on to appeal explicitly to the promise to Abraham of nationhood. The oath to the patriarchs as the ground of pleading,

> is elsewhere employed only for and by sinners, who have no merit of their own and so must fall back on God's promise for support.[293]

We conclude then that Deuteronomy 9:27a is conscious of Exodus 32–34 and its abbreviated reference to the patriarchs is filled out by Exodus 32:13. The grounds of the intercession are the promises to the patriarchs, not their merit.[294]

That the prayer revolves around covenantal promises is also illustrated by the importance placed on personal pronouns in the prayer. These take as their starting point Yahweh's statement to Moses in 9:12, to go down the mountain כִּי שִׁחֵת עַמְּךָ אֲשֶׁר הוֹצֵאתָ מִמִּצְרָיִם.[295] The issue is whose people they are. Yahweh disavows ownership of them in vv12–13, as in Exodus 32:7, 9, making Moses responsible for the people. Moses takes issue with this and in his intercession and states they are Yahweh's people and Yahweh must take responsibility for them. So in v26 Moses repeats the verb שחת (piel in v12; hiphil in v26, also in 10:10), says to Yahweh that the people are עַמְּךָ (the exact reverse of v12), even calling them נַחֲלָתְךָ, and attributes the redemption from Egypt to Yahweh and not himself (פָּדִיתָ בְּגָדְלֶךָ, אֲשֶׁר־הוֹצֵאתָ). The servants Abraham, Isaac and Jacob in v27 are עֲבָדֶיךָ. In v28, Moses identifies himself with the people, again a refutation of Yahweh's disowning of them in v12.[296] Then v29 underlines the point again: עַמְּךָ, נַחֲלָתֶךָ, אֲשֶׁר הוֹצֵאתָ בְּכֹחֲךָ, בִּזְרֹעֲךָ הַנְּטוּיָה.[297]

The threat that the nations will consider that Yahweh hates Israel is an ironic allusion to 1:27 where the people express this very same thought in

291 Compare Olson (1994) 97.

292 Boorer, 305. Compare Weinfeld (1991) 415; Van Seters (1994) 309, who also lists appeals to God to remember the patriarchs in the Holiness Code.

293 Greenberg (1977–78) 27. An example is Leviticus 26:45.

294 Compare Boorer, 316.

295 Ridderbos, 137; Kalland, 82; Maxwell, 166.

296 Braulik (1986) 81.

297 Balentine (1993) 138–139; Greenberg (1977–78) 31.

the midst of the spies' report and subsequent rebellion of the people.[298] This allusion to the spies incident makes it even clearer how motivated by grace Yahweh is. For the people have already expressed the very lie which the nations may be expected to utter. There are no grounds at all in Israel's character, behaviour or past history which merit the favourable answer of Moses' prayer. Any answer will be pure grace.

The report of Moses' intercession is necessary within the narrative of the golden calf. It would have been insufficient to have only v18 as the reference to Moses' praying, for without vv26–29, the future for Israel would be inexplicable and Yahweh's justice would be challenged.[299] 9:26–29 shows why Yahweh acts as he does. It is the content of Moses' prayer, not the fact that Moses prayed, which is important.[300] That the prayer was answered validates its content. The bottom line is that because Yahweh has made promises to the patriarchs, Israel will survive this failure of the golden calf.

### *The Answer to the Prayer (10:1–11)*

No immediate answer to the prayer is explicitly recorded, in striking contrast to Exodus 32:14, 33; Numbers 14:20. Nor is the answer confined to 10:10–11.[301] It is demonstrated by the narrative which follows, a technique not unknown elsewhere in the Old Testament.[302]

10:1–5

Christensen argues that the seven occurrences of "tablets" occur chiastically as follows:[303]

---

298 Mayes (1979) 203. The reputation of Yahweh among the nations is often regarded as an exilic concern. So Balentine (1993) 132, 138; (1985) 68; Buis and Leclerq, 91. This motif also occurs in Joshua 7:9 and, as mentioned above, in Numbers 14:13–19. See Miller (1994) 121, 272. On both 1:27 and 9:28 as statements of the *vox populi*, see Crenshaw (1971) 32. Also compare 4:5–8; 29:25–28. See Alexander (1995) 183.

299 Contra von Rad (1966e) 79, who suggests 10:1ff may have originally followed 9:18.

300 Compare Driver, 116; Olson (1994) 57–58; Balentine (1993) 138; von Rad (1966e) 28, "Moses' struggle with God is at the centre of events". Driver, 124, emphasises the earnestness of Moses' prayer. Compare J.G. Janzen (1987a) 294; Brueggemann (1961) 226.

301 Von Rad (1966e) 77; Burden, 122. Rose (1994) 512, notes the prayer's answer is mentioned in v19.

302 Miller (1994) 139. See Exodus 17:4–7; Judges 15:18–19; 16:28–30; 2 Samuel 7:18–29; 17:14; 1 Kings 18:36–38; Nehemiah 4:6–22; Jonah 1:14–15.

303 Christensen (1991) 195. This grouping of seven is overlooked by Braulik (1991a).

| | | |
|---|---|---|
| A | 1 | “two stone tablets like the first ones” |
| B | 2 | “I will write on the tablets the words” |
| C | 2 | “on the first tablets which you broke” |
| D | 3 | “two stone tablets like the first ones” |
| C' | 4 | “on the tablets as at the first writing” |
| B' | 4 | “He wrote…the ten words” |
| A' | 5 | “I put the tablets into the ark I had made” |

Yet לוּחַ occurs twice in v3 and only once in v4. Christensen’s analysis here is misleading. The seven occurrences do not form a chiasm. Rather they balance the sevenfold occurrence of the same word in 9:9, 9, 10, 11, 11, 15, 17. This correspondence shows that the crisis of chapter 9 is now resolved by the events of 10:1–5.

The instructions to prepare two more stone tablets at the beginning of the chapter indicate that the prayer is answered.[304] The chapter begins בָּעֵת הַהִוא, linking the actions of 10:1–5 with Moses’ intercession, showing they are an answer to it. As before, this expression indicates a context of grace.[305] The people are completely restored to relationship with Yahweh without any conditions or qualifications. The renewal of the covenant is solely due to divine grace.[306]

Further, 10:1–5 stresses that the new tablets are to be identical to the original stone tablets. Thus, most notably, 10:4 repeats much of 9:10: הַדְּבָרִים אֲשֶׁר דִּבֶּר יְהוָה אֲלֵיכֶם/עִמָּכֶם בָּהָר מִתּוֹךְ הָאֵשׁ בְּיוֹם הַקָּהָל.[307] In addition the words and the second tablets are to be “like the first ones” (v1), “that were on the first tablets” (v2), “like the first tablets” (v3), “what he had written before” (v4). Thus it is the same covenant which is to be reinstituted.[308] These verses have as their parallel Exodus 34:1–4.[309] However, unlike that parallel, the ark is prominent here.[310] In Deuteronomy,

---

304 Christensen (1991) 196; Merrill, 198. Compare de Regt (1988) 59.

305 Brueggemann (1961) 248, “That day of intercession is an event in the history of the graciousness of Yahweh toward Israel”.

306 Kline (1963) 75; Driver, 117; Christensen (1991) 196.

307 Skweres, 28–29.

308 Blair (1964) 45; Peckham (1975) 49–51; Thompson, 144; Merrill, 198; Weinfeld (1991) 418. Mayes (1979) 204, argues that Deuteronomy is insisting that the laws of the renewed covenant were not those of Exodus 34 but of Exodus 20. Also Cairns, 108; Boorer, 319.

309 See Weinfeld (1991) 417–418, for details. Moberly (1983) 104, notes that the explicit identification of the words on the second tablets being the Ten Commandments occurs in Exodus only in 34:28 (compare 10:4), not in 34:1–4. Compare Van Seters (1994) 330.

310 In Exodus the ark is not constructed until Exodus 37. On “dischronologized narrative” in Deuteronomy, see Kalland, 84; Merrill, 199; Driver, 117; Weinfeld (1991) 417.

the ark is merely the depository of the tablets and its prominence here may suggest the preservation, security or permanence of this renewed covenant.[311]

10:6–7

10:6–7 is often regarded as a priestly parenthesis, resuming the travel narrative of chapters 1–3.[312] Yet its function here is to show the answer to Moses' prayer for Aaron referred to in 9:20. Though Aaron later died, that was not until the fortieth year of the wilderness. Significantly the priesthood was conferred on him after the golden calf incident. Thus the mention of Aaron here is another statement of grace.[313] Furthermore, after his death the priesthood continued. Eleazar, his son, is mentioned to show that the Aaronic priesthood continued, in addition to the restoration of the covenant demonstrated in 10:1–5.[314] The mention of travel in these verses also suggests a future for the people and, hence, answered prayer.[315] This is, therefore, the second section demonstrating answered prayer.[316]

10:8–9

Scholars disagree about whether these two verses carry on from 10:1–5 or whether they are part of the so-called parenthesis with 10:6–7.[317] In part this depends on what one understands to be the referent of "at that time". Probably it refers to v5, not vv6–7, as the Levites were selected long before Aaron's death. In this case, vv8–9 continues on from vv1–5. Thus vv8–9 have the function of showing the preservation of the covenant for future generations. This reflects Yahweh's commitment to an ongoing relationship with Israel, focused in the Levites whose נַחֲלָה is the LORD, repeating the noun from 9:26, 29.[318] Again we find divine grace at work.

---

311 Maxwell, 168; Peckham (1975) 48–49; D. Schneider, 120. Also Weinfeld (1972) 208. See Buis and Leclerq, 91.

312 See Driver, 119; Thompson, 145; Ridderbos, 138; Craigie (1976) 200; Kalland, 85; Christensen (1991) 196. Compare Weinfeld (1991) 419. Phillips (1973) 74; Driver, 119; Ridderbos, 139; König, 110. Compare 10:6–7 with Numbers 33.

313 Keil and Delitzsch, 340–342.

314 Thompson, 145. Compare Peckham (1975) 51.

315 Cairns, 108, suggests 10:6–7 balance 9:22–24. The places in 10:6–7 are not associated with death and apostasy, indicating that grace has prevailed. Braulik (1986) 83, suggests Moserah and Jotbathah recall 8:5, 7.

316 Craigie (1976) 200; Christensen (1991) 197; Cairns, 109.

317 As parenthesis, Seitz, 57. As resumption of vv1–5, see Merrill, 200; Driver, 121; Braulik (1986) 83; Ridderbos, 139; von Rad (1966e) 79; Watts (1970) 230; Keil and Delitzsch, 342; Steuernagel, 35.

318 Peckham (1975) 54.

10:10–11

Finally 10:10–11 makes it explicit that Moses' intercession is answered.[319] The covenant is renewed solely because of Yahweh's grace and faithfulness to his promises, as urged by Moses' prayer. The vocabulary repeated from 9:18, 25 about "forty days and forty nights" and "destroy" makes explicit what has thus far been implicit.[320] The detail about being on the mountain makes a similar point to 10:1–5, namely that the renewal of the covenant is identical in every way with the original (compare 9:9).[321]

As in 2:2, the resolution of the problem of Israel's sin is indicated by a command to continue the journey (10:11). This resumes 1:7–8, showing a return to the original situation, indicating that there remains a future for Israel. This instruction is the climax to the whole account of the golden calf.[322] Boorer suggests that where 10:10 resolves the golden calf episode, 10:11, by reference to the land, shows an explicit resolution of the spies incident, mentioned in 9:23–24 and, thus, all the problems of the past from Israel's sin are now resolved.[323]

The reinstatement of the covenant is now almost complete. The command to go shows that the promises to the patriarchs will be fulfilled despite the people's sin.[324] The section, indeed the whole golden calf incident, ends with another explicit mention of the patriarchal promises, showing yet again the motivation of Yahweh and reminding the hearers-readers why the prayer was effective. Future hope is grounded in the patriarchal promises.

## Deuteronomy 10:12–22

What remains to complete this episode is the renewed call to covenant fidelity. This occurs in 10:12–22. However the bleak diagnosis of Israel's condition in 9:1–7 still stands. Nothing has altered their stiff-neckedness. That is made clear in 10:16, a verse which hints at the ultimate solution to the problem of Israel's faithlessness. We turn therefore to a consideration of 10:12–22, again commenting on its structure in order to gain insight into its theology.

---

319 Craigie (1976) 201; Christensen (1991) 200.

320 Though 10:10 could follow 9:26–29, as Mayes (1979) 207, suggests, 10:1–9 does not make 10:10–11 redundant. If anything 10:1–9 contributes to seeing 10:10–11 as a climax for this whole narrative. Compare Driver, 124; von Rad (1966e) 80. In contrast, Bertholet, 34, suggests 10:10–11 refers back to 9:14.

321 Cairns, 110. Boorer, 285, 290, regards 10:10 as a reversal and summary of 9:9–29, especially alluding to 9:9, 19 and 25. Compare Rennes, 60.

322 Buis and Leclerq, 91; McConville and Millar, 67; Peckham (1975) 56–57; Dillmann, 283; Braulik (1986) 83; Rose (1994) 515.

323 Boorer, 295–296.

324 Ridderbos, 140; Craigie (1976) 203; Clifford, 64.

*Structure*

This section is framed with commands to fear and serve Yahweh (יָרֵא, עָבַד, vv12, 20) in the context of other basic covenantal requirements (vv12–13, 20).[325] Verses 21–22 concern the greatness of Yahweh, repeating words from earlier, "fathers", "great", "awesome". Thus vv20–22 appear to round off and envelope the section.[326]

Lohfink suggests that throughout 10:12–11:32, there is an alternation of six commands and six *Begründungen.*[327] Confining ourselves to 10:12–22, there are commands in vv12–13, 16, 19a, 20 and their *Begründungen* in vv14–15 (הֵן), 17–18, 19b, 21–22 (כִּי). However, the *Begründung* of vv14–15 does not belong to the first command. The emphatic הֵן suggests a break with the preceding vv12–13.[328] Rather vv14–15 belong to v16, where the command to circumcise is a perfect construction dependent on הֵן in v14.[329] The content of these verses also bears out this relationship. The election of the patriarchs in v15 fits well with the metaphor of circumcision in v16. Another link is established by לֵבָב. In v15, Yahweh's heart is set on the patriarchs and in v16, Israel's heart is to be circumcised.[330] We conclude that vv14–15 belong not to vv12–13, but to the central command, v16. This command is then further grounded by vv17–18. We have already noted that the command of v20 repeats part of the first (fear, serve) and the *Begründung* of vv21–22 picks up vocabulary from the others. Lohfink himself dismisses v19 as not fitting the pattern of the series.[331] If we follow that, the central command is v16, the command to circumcise the heart. Given the reference to heart in v12, v16 is the key to the fulfilment of the others. This, then, supports a concentric structure for vv12–22 as follows:[332]

---

325 On the verbs עבד and שמר together as Eden and sanctuary language, see Wenham (1986) 21; Alexander (1995) 21. They occur here in 10:12, 13.

326 Christensen (1991) 205, suggests an ABBA structure: A - vv12–13; B - vv14–16; B' - vv17–19; A' - vv20–22. However this ignores the command in 10:16 and does not explain the function of vv14–15, 17–19. On critical approaches to 10:12–22, see Mayes (1979) 207–208.

327 Lohfink (1963a) 220; Jacobs, 254; Braulik (1986) 84. McCarthy (1981) 165; Lohfink (1965) 37–38, suggest that the *Begründungen* form a temporal series beginning with the patriarchs (10:14–15) and leading to the land (11:10–12). Jacobs, 267, modifies this slightly by suggesting each command is followed by a cosmological reason and then a historical reason, though he also acknowledges that the pattern is not consistent.

328 Muraoka, 137–140; Weinfeld (1991) 436.

329 König, 111.

330 Braulik (1986) 85.

331 Lohfink (1963a) 223. He suggests v19 is dependent on v18 and may be a Levitical gloss.

332 Similarly Rennes, 62.

| | | |
|---|---|---|
| A | 12–13 | Basic command |
| B | 14–15 | Introductory reason for v16 |
| C | 16 | Command: circumcise the heart |
| B' | 17–19 | Supplementary reason for v16 |
| A' | 20–22 | Summary basic command and reason |

## *Theology*

The commands of 10:12–22 cancel out the golden calf incident and its effects.[333] Indeed 10:12–22 is a reinstatement of the Shema, if not also 5:29–6:17.[334] The repeat of these basic covenant stipulations is further evidence of a full renewal of the covenant after Israel's sin. This section begins וְעַתָּה, which signifies the transition from narrative to parenesis, history to application.[335] There is an abrupt return to the present.

> The adverb indicates a radical break between what precedes and what follows. There is no grammatical continuity between the two parts.[336]

The string of imperatives in vv12–13 represents the basic stipulation of the covenant in typical ANE treaty language.[337] The commands are all typical of Deuteronomy and the five interrelated verbs establish the basic themes of 10:12–11:32. Central is the command to love.[338] The right response, as seen before, is to stem from the heart, combining attitude and action.[339] Given the description of Israel's heart in the preceding two chapters, we cannot agree that 10:12–13 is "a practical possibility".[340] Rather, the

---

333 Braulik (1986) 84.

334 See Lohfink (1963a) 227–230, on the references to chapters 5 and 6. He notes that the same order of the five verbs in 10:12–13 occurs in 5:29–6:17. Also D. Schneider, 119; Keil and Delitzsch, 343.

335 Niccacci, 101, notes that this expression only occurs in speech and introduces "the result arising or the conclusion to be drawn concerning the present action from an event or topic dealt with beforehand. Also Brongers, 289–299; Blenkinsopp (1968) 109; L'Hour, 21; Rose (1994) 342.

336 Brueggemann (1961) 182. He also suggests, 183, that the וְעַתָּה gives urgency to what follows. See also 4:1; 5:25; 26:10; 31:19. Similarly von Rad (1966e) 83; Weinfeld (1972) 175; (1991) 435, 453–454; Thompson, 147. The same expression occurs in 10:22, providing a frame for this section. See Christensen (1991) 205. Jacobs, 252; Brongers, 289–299, suggest that וְעַתָּה ends a section rather than begins one. In addition to וְעַתָּה, יִשְׂרָאֵל indicates a clear structural break.

337 Baltzer, 37–38; Weinfeld (1972) 66; Kalland, 87; Craigie (1976) 204.

338 Rose (1994) 342. Christensen (1991) 206, argues this on the grounds of prosodic analysis. Contrast Merrill, 202.

339 See Weinfeld (1972) 332–334, 337, for other occurrences of love in Deuteronomy. On love in 10:12–11:32, see Craigie (1976) 204; Watts (1970) 231; Merrill, 201; Ridderbos, 141. See more fully the next chapter.

340 Cairns, 110.

> demand for fear, love, and reverence towards the Lord, is no doubt very hard for the natural man to fulfil, and all the harder the deeper it goes into the heart.[341]

These chapters have similarities with the covenant treaty structure. In particular, 9:7–10:11 is like the historical prologue to a covenant treaty where 10:12ff is the subsequent call to obey. Yet this prologue is full of failure. Though it is possible for a treaty prologue to include a case history of failure, and there are instances of vassal rebellion in the Hittite treaties, nonetheless it remains striking.[342]

> (T)he particular historical narrative in 9:9–10:11, as a story of covenant breaking, is not precisely the type of account one would expect as a historical prologue preceding the commandments.[343]

There has been no indication at all that Israel will be willing or able to keep the covenant. Its sin has been stated bluntly. It is portrayed as deep-seated. Its future beyond the golden calf apostasy is entirely dependent on Yahweh's grace. All this combines to create a pessimistic outlook for the future.

This is important for how we read the Moab covenant. Moab is a renewal of Horeb, not just because of a new situation, generation, or leader, but because of past failure. Deuteronomy itself is in effect a statement of the renewed covenant presupposing, indeed occasioned by, the sin and failure of Israel. It is not a neutral reactualisation of the covenant for each succeeding generation.[344] Every indication points to the fact that current Israel is unchanged. Its disposition is still an inclination towards failure. Horeb and Moab have "a shared pessimism about the ability of God's people to obey the commandments and laws of Horeb".[345] This pessimism is picked up in the central command to circumcise the heart. In chapter 8, the problem of the heart was linked to the command to keep the commandments in 8:1, 2, 6, 11. That same command occurs again in 10:13. The heart remains unchanged and the lessons of the wilderness have not been learnt.

The command to circumcise the heart (v16) is set in a context of grace and faithfulness to the patriarchal promise (vv15, 22) and the reference to circumcision itself conjures allusions to the Abrahamic covenant in Genesis

---

341 Keil and Delitzsch, 343.

342 Weinfeld (1972) 66, 70; Roberge, 109–110, 184. Weinfeld (1991) 407; Driver, 112; von Rad (1966e) 77, 83; Craigie (1976) 194; Jacobs, 259; McCarthy (1981) 165–167; McConville and Millar, 67; Ranck, 90, note this section has the same form-critical characteristics as 1–3, unlike 6–8. On a contrast between ANE literature and Genesis 1–11 which highlights human sinfulness, see Wenham (1990) 321–324.

343 Mayes (1979) 208. Also Lohfink (1963a) 224, 229; Mayes (1981b) 39. Jacobs, 259; Buis and Leclerq, 93, doubt that וְעַתָּה can refer to the preceding section. Minette de Tillesse, 37, argues that 10:12 refers back to 8:1–9:7a.

344 Compare Ranck, 217.

345 Olson (1994) 151.

17.[346] Verse 15 in particular is "a breathtaking sequence of elective terms" which stresses divine and sovereign grace.[347] That this grace is extended to the current generation is also made clear: וַיִּבְחַר בְּזַרְעָם אַחֲרֵיהֶם בָּכֶם. The current generation is being put in the place of the patriarchs. The command in v16 now follows almost naturally. "The metaphor of circumcision in this context seems to be prompted by the reference to the patriarchs in v. 15".[348]

The metaphor is explained by the second half of v16: וְעָרְפְּכֶם לֹא תַקְשׁוּ עוֹד. The allusion to 9:6, 13, 27 is unmistakable. What is clear is that the answer to the intercession and renewal of the covenant does not guarantee prevention of a repetition of sin. The generally adopted meaning of a circumcised heart is a heart which is submissive, responsive to God and humble.[349] The ideas of pride and humility are also important. An uncircumcised heart leads to pride (8:17–18) but a circumcised heart will recognise its inability and trust the all-powerful (10:14) Yahweh. Thus a circumcised heart will rely on grace and not itself. This central command recognises that "a true response to God is an affair of the heart" and, therefore, that Israel's problem is not an easy one to solve.[350] The centrality of this command within the section also makes it clear that "(w)ithout circumcision of heart, true fear of God and true love of God are both impossible".[351]

Deuteronomy 10 concludes with another statement of grace again focused on the fulfilment of patriarchal promise. Israel has become as numerous as the stars in the sky (v22). The promises to Abraham in Genesis 15:5–6 have been directly fulfilled. God is utterly faithful.[352]

---

346 Peckham (1983) 235; Brown, 139; Braulik (1986) 85.

347 Merrill, 203. On a comparison with 7:6–8, see Lohfink (1963a) 226. On the terms, see also Driver, 125; Weinfeld (1972) 327, 328. On the theme of election and grace in Deuteronomy, see Martin-Achard (1960) 334–336. Römer, 201, argues, following Rendtorff, that the election motif in Deuteronomy (namely 4:37–39; 7:6–11; 10:14–15) is generally regarded as very late. Also Seebass (1977b) 84. In comparison, Shafer, 25–28, following at different points Cross and Lohfink, argues that the election motif in Deuteronomy 10:15 is early.

348 Craigie (1976) 205. On the metaphor of circumcision elsewhere, see Driver, 125; Dillmann, 284; Exodus 6:12, 30; Jeremiah 4:4; 6:10; 9:25; Leviticus 26:41; Ezekiel 44:7, 9.

349 Merrill, 203; Thompson, 149; Kalland, 86; Maxwell, 172; Cunliffe-Jones, 77; Cairns, 111; Blair (1964) 45. It is more than dedication and cleansing. So von Rad (1966e) 84; Watts (1970) 233; Miller (1990) 125. Compare Ridderbos, 141; Cairns, 111. On circumcision in ANE, see Westermann (1985) 265.

350 McConville (1993b) 155.

351 Keil and Delitzsch, 344. See further the discussion of 30:6 below, pp163ff.

352 Craigie (1976) 207. Also Kline (1963) 77; Ridderbos, 143; Merrill, 205; Weinfeld (1991) 441; Braulik (1986) 86; Keil and Delitzsch, 345; Rose (1994) 347. Compare 1:10.

These verses raise the question of whether Israel is able but unwilling to keep the covenant requirements or, rather, both unable and unwilling to do so. At this point in Deuteronomy we must probably remain undecided. In itself, the notion of circumcision does not make an answer clear. That Israel is commanded to change may however suggest ability but an unwillingness hitherto. Indeed, the strength of the general rhetoric for obedience throughout Deuteronomy may also suggest that Israel is capable but unwilling. Yet the persistent deep-seatedness of its rebellion causes one to wonder if it is not something more than just unwillingness. The consistent grounds of hope in Deuteronomy have been Yahweh's grace and faithfulness to the patriarchal promises. This strong emphasis, and the contrast between Israel's faithlessness and Yahweh's faithfulness, suggests that Israel cannot rely on itself and its ability. Ultimately it has to rely on Yahweh. The context of grace in 10:12–22, in which the command to circumcise the heart is set, points away from Israel's ability to Yahweh. This question about Israel's ability/inability is one of the intriguing issues of the book. It reflects the tension between Yahweh's grace and human responsibility, between Yahweh's faithfulness and Israel's faithlessness. It is not until 30:6 that we will find its resolution.

## Conclusion

The restoration of the covenant is now complete. Israel's faithlessness is resolved purely by Yahweh's grace and faithfulness to the patriarchal promises. There is no optimism based on Israel's ability; all rests on Yahweh's grace. There is no suggestion that Israel has changed. Indeed 10:16 shows it has not. It remains a stiff-necked people. It is expected to fail. Yet Yahweh restores the covenant with it as an act of unconditional grace. He is keeping his promises and Israel's faithlessness will not annul them. His commands to Israel again serve to bring about the fulfilment of these promises. Law and grace are compatible. There is theological integrity in 8:1–10:22, as there was in chapters 1–3. Pessimism and optimism, faithlessness and faithfulness are not contradictory.

## CHAPTER 3

# Faithless Israel, Faithful Yahweh in Deuteronomy 29–30

The final, and most significant, section of this study concerns Deuteronomy 29–30. Unlike our previous two sections which recount past failures of Israel, this section anticipates future failure, described in 29:15–27. Chapter 30 deals with the resolution of that failure, grounded again in the grace and faithfulness of Yahweh. These chapters are the clearest expression of our thesis. Chapter 30 especially explores the relationship between Israel's faithlessness and Yahweh's faithfulness and shows that ultimately the resolution of the tension between the two is the circumcision of the heart by Yahweh. This chapter is the climax to the preaching of the book. Most of the main threads come together in this chapter as Israel is exhorted to choose life (30:19). Not only is Deuteronomy 30 significant for our thesis, it is also crucial for the book as whole.

The rationale for moving from Deuteronomy 10 to 29 is our concern with Israel's failure. The bulk of the intervening material is the lawcode. Though a discussion of how to read the law lies beyond the scope of this study, it is apparent that the overall negative assessment of Israel from the opening chapter of the book suggests that the reader-hearer should not expect Israel to keep the covenant requirements. The two accounts of Israel's failure, the spies and golden calf incidents, are failures with regard to land and law respectively. Especially the golden calf incident, therefore, raises serious doubts about Israel's ability and willingness to keep the law. The lawcode itself allows for failure, indeed in many cases it could be regarded as regulating failure, for example, case law on idolatry (chapter 13), murder (chapter 19) and sexual sin (chapter 22).[1] The law then starts from where people are as sinners.

> Since the framework to Deuteronomy's laws so forcefully portrays Israel's sinfulness, it is not strange that the laws themselves presuppose

1 McConville and Millar, 129. Deuteronomy 15:1–11 is another example of the tension between the ideal and the real with its comments about the presence of poverty, suggesting Israel's inability to keep this law. See Goldingay (1987) 156; Hals, 7.

> acts and events which are less than ideal. The common casuistic form of the laws (e.g., 13:1–2, 6–7, 12–13) assumes that Israel will sin; the laws' concern is with how that sin is to be dealt with, so as to eliminate the evil from Israel, deter others, and open oneself to Yahweh's mercy and blessing rather than his wrath.[2]

In other words, the law does not envisage that the Israelite will always love the LORD with all his heart or his neighbour as himself.

Chapters 27 and 28 suggest that curse and blessing are alternatives, a view which is changed in 29 and 30 where the inevitability of curse is clear. Nonetheless, the predominance of curses over blessings, and the setting up of the tablets and altar on Mount Ebal, the mountain of curse in 27:1–8, suggest that even in chapters 27 and 28, Israel is expected to fail.[3]

## Introduction to 28:69–30:20

Thus we turn to chapters 29 and 30. After a brief survey of approaches to these chapters we shall consider their theology section by section.

### *Survey of Approaches*

Few scholars argue for the unity of these chapters. 30:1–10 is sometimes regarded as the rightful continuation of chapter 28, not chapter 29. This is in part on the grounds of common singular address and vocabulary. Chapter 29 would then be a later plural insertion.[4] More often, 30:1–10, with its hope of return, is regarded as a later insertion between 29:1–20 and 30:11–20.[5] Disjunctions are identified between 29:20 and 21 and 30:10 and 11.[6] In the former, there is a move from a discussion of an individual to the nation as a whole. 30:11–14 is regarded as the strongest statement of Israel's ability to keep the law, possibly the oldest material in these chapters,[7] and thus as having a different perspective to 30:1–10. Knapp, for example, argues that 29:1–14, 15–27 and 30:1–10 are from three separate authors corresponding to the authors of 4:1–4, 9–14 and 4:15–16a, 19–28 and 4:29–

---

2 Goldingay (1987) 155. See generally, 153–166. Also Daube (1959). Compare Gowan, 123–124, who argues that the law in Deuteronomy presupposes wholeness and seeks to preserve the status quo.

3 On the theological significance of 27:1–8, see Ridderbos, 248–249.

4 Nicholson (1967) 35. Likewise Rofé (1985a) 311–312, who also notes that, apart from 30:7, there is virtually no link between chapters 29 and 30. Similarly Mitchell, 106–107. Contrast Steuernagel, 108; Knapp, 154; Nielsen, 270. See also Bee, 14.

5 Begg (1980a) 50, calls this the "literary-critical consensus". Similarly Lenchak, 36; Wolff (1961) 181. 29:21–27 is also commonly regarded as late. So Lenchak, 36. Compare the division into layers by Preuß (1982) 157–162.

6 Driver, lxxiii; Lenchak, 36.

7 Buis and Leclerq, 16; Driver, lxxv; G.E. Wright, 317–318.

35.[8] All these approaches are in large part attempts to resolve the tension between the pessimism of chapter 29 and the optimism of chapter 30. They seek to resolve diachronically this tension by the hypothesis of redactional layers.[9]

Typically these chapters are regarded as late, whether exilic or post-exilic, and understood as reflections upon and explanations of the exile.[10] One of the consequences of this is that it deprives these chapters of their essential future perspective. They are not a reflection on past failure but an expectation of future failure.

Some attempts at finding unity in chapters 29 and 30 have been made. In some respects, these chapters reflect the covenant treaty structure.[11] However this does not explain every part of the chapters. Nor are there covenant stipulations in these chapters.[12] Further, Deuteronomy 29 and 30 are primarily a discourse which uses "elements of covenant thought, language, and structure to encourage repentance".[13] So the "elements of the treaty which do appear here are not really formal parts of a treaty document".[14] Alternatively, a covenant cultic background is suggested as a unifying background for these chapters.[15] The liturgical nature of the

---

8 Knapp, 128–163. Begg (1980a) 49, notes that where chapters 29 and 30 change from singular to plural, the same change is found in 4:29. This coincides with a change from announcements of exile to a statement of restoration. Maybe the *Numeruswechsel* occurs to sharpen the distinction between the two, rather than being an indication of dual authorship. See Braulik (1978) regarding the unity of chapter 4.

9 See further Lenchak, 78–82, for a survey of approaches to these chapters.

10 For example, Mayes (1979) 359; Preuß (1982) 157–162.

11 Baltzer, 34–36. He maintains that 29:17b–20, 29:21–30:10 are later expansions. Similarly Rofé (1985a) 310–320.

12 Lenchak, 34–35; Mayes (1979) 358–359. Compare Wenham (1970) 175–178, who argues that chapters 29–30 are the recapitulation section of the covenant structure and conclude Deuteronomy. This recapitulation is unique to the Old Testament. It is found also in Exodus 23:23–33; Joshua 23 and 1 Samuel 12:20–25, and in Deuteronomy extends to 31:6. Also D.W. Baker (1989) 11, 14. Compare Rofé (1985a) 310–320, who argues that the Moab covenant consists only of chapters 29 and 30 which themselves are not a fundamental unity.

13 McCarthy (1981) 199. Also Preuß (1982) 158; Lenchak, 34–35. Compare Mayes (1979) 358–359.

14 Lenchak, 35. Compare McCarthy (1981) 202, that the Deuteronomistic school "has adapted the outlines of the covenant form to a speech".

15 Lohfink (1962) 49. He in fact argues for a unity extending to the end of chapter 32, though he acknowledges that this is not an original unity and tensions are explained diachronically. See also Mayes (1979) 358–359, though he rejects the inclusion of chapters 31 and 32 with 29 and 30. Lenchak, 113–114, suggests that לִפְנֵי יְהוָה in 29:9, 14 is a technical term for worship. Robinson, 112–124, considers that

chapters is seen in the recitation of salvation history (29:1–7), solemn charges to accept and choose (29:8–14; 30:11–20) and warnings (29:15–18).[16] The frequency of הַיּוֹם, thirteen times in these two chapters, is also regarded as liturgical.[17] The weakness of this approach, as with the covenant treaty structure approach, is that it neither explains every part of these chapters nor their theological integrity.

A more promising approach is the rhetorical analysis of Lenchak. He argues that whether or not the chapters are a diachronic unity, they "can be viewed rhetorically as a single unified discourse".[18] Certainly chapters 29 and 30 are hortatory, urging and persuading Israel to choose a correct course of action. While a cultic origin for exhortation is possible, perhaps more likely is the view that this exhortation "could have been used in a covenant renewal festival, even if it is not a proper liturgical text as it stands".[19] Lenchak's synchronic study concentrates on argumentation and rhetorical function. However, its weakness is that it is not concerned to resolve tensions within the text theologically. Either Lenchak ignores tensions as being outside his concern or he attributes them to diachronic developments of the text.[20] More importantly, he presupposes a high view of Israel's ability to live and choose correctly. This positive regard for human ability misunderstands theologically the relationship between Israel and Yahweh and thus the grounds for hope in these chapters.

As in previous chapters, our concern is theological and our method synchronic. Thus we seek to explore whether the tension between Israel's faithlessness and Yahweh's faithfulness can be explained theologically. We shall argue, for example, that, in order to be understood properly, 30:11–14 must be read in the light of 30:1–10, something that is rarely done.

### *28:69: Superscript or Subscript?*

In order to understand more carefully what is happening in chapters 29 and 30, we need to briefly discuss the contentious verse, 28:69. This will help clarify the relationship between these chapters and the rest of Deuteronomy.

The majority view among scholars is that 28:69 is a superscript to what follows rather than a subscript or colophon to the blessings and curses of

---

Lohfink's methodology regarding a cultic covenant ceremony it is without external evidence and is purely hypothetical.

16 Lenchak, 33; Lohfink (1962) 43–44. See also von Rad (1966e) 179; Mayes (1979) 360; Preuß (1982) 158–159; G.E. Wright, 502. Westermann (1994) 61, regards 29:1–8 as stemming from oral tradition.

17 Lenchak, 114. See 29:3, 9, 11, 12, 14, 14, 17; 30:2, 8, 11, 16, 18, 19. See also Brueggemann (1961) 267–268.

18 Lenchak, 81.

19 Lenchak, 33.

20 Lenchak, 77–78.

chapter 28.[21] The previous chapters make no mention of covenant renewal in Moab which is now announced in 28:69.[22] This verse is paralleled by 4:44–5:1 which is also a heading introducing, some would say, the Horeb covenant which runs to 28:68.[23] There are in fact four headings in Deuteronomy, 1:1; 4:44; 28:69 and 33:1, which, apart from 28:69, are clearly superscripts.[24] The key word בְּרִית ties 28:69 to 29:1–24 where the word occurs a total of seven times.[25]

A minority of scholars maintain that 28:69 is a subscript.[26] Van Rooy argues that דִּבְרֵי הַבְּרִית, which occurs in 28:69, always refers to covenant stipulations or curses. These, while presupposed in chapters 29 and 30, are not spelled out there. Thus 28:69 cannot be a superscript.[27] However there are only ten references to this expression and they are not all conclusive.[28]

---

21 So König, 195; Steuernagel, 105; Bertholet, 88–89; Rennes, 136; von Rad (1966e) 178; Mayes (1979) 360; Kline (1963) 129; McCarthy (1981) 199; McEvenue (1990) 132, 186; Nicholson (1967) 35; Braulik (1992) 210 (though Braulik suggests that in the earlier history of Deuteronomy, 28:69 may have been a subscript to the Horeb covenant before the Moab covenant was included in the book); Ridderbos, 263; Lenchak, 171–173. So too RSV, NIV, AV. See also Preuß (1982) 157–158; Seitz, 25; and Song, 188, for a list of other scholars. Thompson, 278, is undecided.

22 Ridderbos, 263. Lohfink (1992a) 49, says that before 28:69, בְּרִית refers either to the Decalogue, its first commandment or the patriarchal covenant but never Moab.

23 Rofé (1985a) 310–311. Also Bertholet, 88–89. Against the similarity of the headings, see Song, 189. Rofé also notes that the Sam Pent reads the verse as a heading. See also Lohfink (1962) 32–56; Cholewinski, 96–97; Olson (1994) 129.

24 Lohfink (1992a) 42. He, 42–45, accuses van Rooy of ignoring the internal structure of Deuteronomy. See Robinson, 112–113, for the importance of the superscriptions for Lohfink's analysis.

25 Lohfink (1962) 36. Also Seitz, 25; Mayes (1979) 360. Lenchak, 174, suggests that 28:69 forms an inclusio with 29:8. Lohfink (1992a) 50, follows Braulik's observation that there is a sevenfold occurrence of בְּרִית here, namely 28:69 (twice); 29:8, 11, 13, 20, 24. The central one is 29:11, a verse which has other vocabulary common to 28:69. Braulik (1991a) 46, notes that there are 21 occurrences of בְּרִית in Deuteronomy.

26 See Seitz, 25; Song, 188; Lenchak, 172. Others who regard 28:69 as a subscript include Driver, 319; Buis and Leclerq, 181; Mitchell, 105; Craigie (1976) 353; Brown, 267; Merrill, 373; Kutsch, 138–141; Nielsen, 256. Kutsch, 140–141, calls it a "vorwärtsverweisende Abschlußformel". Mayes (1981b) 44; Song, 190, both cite this quotation.

27 Van Rooy (1988a) 215–222. Also Kutsch, 138–141; Song, 190. Compare Mayes (1979) 359. Lohfink regards chapters 29 and 30 as part of a covenant renewal ceremony. This, says van Rooy, is never the referent of דִּבְרֵי הַבְּרִית. Van Rooy argues that 28:69 ties back to 1:1–5 and is thus a colophon for Deuteronomy 1–28. Also Bartholomew, 210.

28 Lohfink (1992a) 41, 46–48. He accuses van Rooy of inconsistency arguing that on van Rooy's own criteria, Deuteronomy 1–4, 27–28 cannot be part of the referent of 28:69. Lohfink in fact acknowledges that his earlier article on chapters 29–32

Also 28:69 could be regarded as forming an inclusio with 1:1, thus acting as a subscript.[29] Though there is no doubt about the closeness of 28:69 and 1:1; 4:44, it is much harder to determine function. Finally, the absence of stipulations in chapters 29 and 30 is not decisive as the referent of דִּבְרֵי הַבְּרִית can also be a ceremony.[30]

All things considered, the weight of evidence favours the traditional view that 28:69 introduces chapters 29 and 30. However, that there is debate indicates that the division between chapters 28 and 29 is not as great as some would make out. The importance of this discussion is its contribution to understanding the relationship between Horeb and Moab and, hence, what chapters 29 and 30 are about, in particular, their expectation of Israel's future.

### *Horeb and Moab*

We consider now the relationship between the Horeb and Moab covenants. The key question is whether Moab is to be understood as a supplement to or a replacement for Horeb.[31]

The relationship between the two covenants is most commonly understood to be that Moab renews, explains or confirms Horeb. It is a reapplication of Horeb to the current generation at a strategic point in history. Moses is about to die. The people are about to enter the land.[32] Such an understanding fundamentally identifies the two covenants. We accept this. This is indicated also by the absence of stipulations despite the basic covenant structure of Deuteronomy 29 and 30.[33] These chapters are

---

presupposed the superscript character of 28:69, rather than specifically arguing for it.

29 Lundbom (1975) 16, 141. He also argues that 4:44 forms an inclusio with 1:1 and that inclusios are common in Deuteronomy as rhetorical devices. See Lundbom (1976) 293–295; Seitz, 30.

30 Lohfink (1992a) 48–49. His argument is weakened by only considering דָּבָר and not דִּבְרֵי הַבְּרִית. Yet the fact that the stipulations are clearly presupposed in chapters 29 and 30 should allow the possibility that these chapters are in mind in 28:69. Also Lenchak, 172–173.

31 Preuß (1982) 158, "Soll die Moabberith außerdem dtr Ergänzung oder gar dtr Ersatz für die durch Israels Ungehorsam gebrochene Sinaiberith sein?" Seitz, 91, suggests that the redactor of the superscripts 1:1; 4:44; 28:69; 33:1 consciously attempted to contrast Horeb and Moab.

32 So Luther, 14; Munchenberg, 199, that Moab repeats Horeb; Craigie (1976) 353, that Moab renews Horeb; Cunliffe-Jones, 160, that Moab explains Horeb; Clifford, 154, and Ridderbos, 263, that Moab confirms Horeb; G.E. Wright, 502, that Moab supplements Horeb, renewing and extending it; Song, 191–193, that Moab renews Horeb and depends on it for its authority, hence the identity between them. Similarly Buis and Leclerq, 13.

33 Miller (1990) 210.

dependent on the earlier stipulations in Deuteronomy and presuppose them. There is no suggestion that Horeb is superseded or annulled. The obligations of Moab are largely the same. Indeed Deuteronomy as a whole is about this Moab renewal or ratification of the Horeb covenant. Further, the parallels between chapters 4 and 29–30 demonstrate the parallel relationship between Horeb and Moab. The same stipulations apply to both. Whereas in 4:9–14 Israel stands before Yahweh at Horeb, in 29:9–14 Israel stands before Yahweh at Moab. Both integrate history and law.[34] The absence of any mention of the Moab covenant elsewhere in the Old Testament is striking.[35] If Moab were a replacement for Horeb, then possibly we would expect more attention to Moab elsewhere. Since it is a renewal or supplement to Horeb, which remains the basis of the covenant, we need not be so surprised.

Against such identification stand Braulik and Cholewinski. Braulik argues that Horeb concerns only the Decalogue and that Moab expands this to include all the stipulations in Deuteronomy 5–26. This is on the basis of the occurrences of בְּרִית in the book.[36] Further, הַחֻקִּים וְהַמִּשְׁפָּטִים in Deuteronomy refers to the whole of the Mosaic preaching, uniting the Decalogue, laws and preaching under a single term. This is the Moab covenant expansion.[37] Cholewinski argues that Moab replaces Horeb. This is largely on the strength of מִלְּבַד in 28:69 which he says distinguishes Moab from Horeb.[38] Yet, to put this in perspective, this is the only place in the Old Testament where the two are distinguished.[39] It is not at all clear that the force of מִלְּבַד supports the argument that Moab replaces Horeb. Most commonly, מִלְּבַד has the sense of "in addition to" rather than "in place of".[40] So מִלְּבַד does not represent substantial grounds for arguing that Moab replaces, rather than supplements, Horeb. Like Braulik, Cholewinski also argues that Horeb comprised only the Decalogue, which Moab extended to include all the stipulations of Deuteronomy 5–26. Further, the impending death of Moses would require a new covenant according to the

---

34 Knapp, 130, 160. Also Nielsen, 264, on 29:1, 9–14 paralleling 5:1–5.

35 Preuß (1982) 158.

36 Braulik (1970) 43–45. Moab includes the notion of oath of obligation to that covenant. The occurrences of בְּרִית which refer to this notion are 28:69a; 29:8, 11, 13, 20. He includes 28:69b and 29:24 in the list of references to Horeb. It is unlikely that within the one verse, 28:69, בְּרִית could refer to two different covenants without some other explicit indication. Kutsch, 136–138, sees the same distinction in 28:69. Lenchak, 167, suggests that 28:69 creates a dissociation between the two covenants.

37 Braulik (1970) 61–62.

38 Cholewinski, 96. Also Phillips (1973) 199; Swanepoel, 380.

39 Preuß (1982) 158; Phillips (1973) 193.

40 Of 33 occurrences, the only time where the sense of "in place of" is possible is Daniel 11:4. Refer Even-Shoshan, 150.

ANE treaty patterns.[41] However it would be just as likely that a new covenant would be made after the death of the leader not before.[42] He argues that Deuteronomy is a positive response to the shattered Horeb covenant in the time of the exile. The Moab covenant provides hope beyond Horeb, giving it a dimension absent in the Horeb covenant.[43] This is also the position of Olson who states that the addition of Moab to Horeb means that "Deuteronomy in the end holds together law and human responsibility with promise and divine mercy".[44] However this fails to note, as we shall argue, that the hope expressed in these chapters is grounded not in a new covenant, but in the faithfulness of Yahweh to his promises made to Abraham. These promises also undergird Horeb, as we saw in Deuteronomy 1–3 and 8–10. So Moab is not postulating anything new at this point. Furthermore, the promise of the circumcision of the heart, the key to the hope expressed in these chapters, is a future event beyond the Moab covenant ceremony and after a period of blessing followed by further rebellion and curses. In the end, Cholewinski virtually identifies the Moab covenant with the new covenant anticipated by Jeremiah and Ezekiel.[45] Thus he asserts that Moab is clearly better than Horeb and is described in 4:8 as being the best in the world.[46] Similarly, Olson says, "Yahweh will create obedience through Moab (30:6) which humans could not achieve under Horeb".[47] Yet, as we shall see, that is not the case. The promise of 30:6 lies beyond Moab.

In further support of the identification of Moab and Horeb, and thus against the view that Moab is better than Horeb, is the observation that Deuteronomy 4 consciously fuses together the two covenants. So the mention of הַחֻקִּים וְהַמִּשְׁפָּטִים in 4:1 is ambiguous, referring, in part,

---

41 Cholewinski, 100–102.

42 Whilst ancient treaties dealt with issues of dynastic succession, for example the Esarhaddon treaty was most concerned that Ashurbanipal succeed Esarhaddon, covenant renewal occurred on the accession of the new sovereign. See Wenham (1970) 138–139. On the succession of Ashurbanipal in the Esarhaddon treaties, see Frankena, 128, 143–144.

43 Cholewinski, 102–106; Swanepoel, 380–381.

44 Olson (1994) 3, and 176, "The Moab covenant does not negate but decenters the Horeb covenant with an emphasis on the judging and saving action of God in the face of the failure and limitation of human obedience". He suggests, 155, that the focus shifts from human striving (Horeb) to divine action (Moab), and, 127, that the command has become a promise.

45 Similarly Lohfink (1962) 49, on the grounds that 29:9–14 is performative speech.

46 Cholewinski, 106–108. One of his points is that Moab is better in that it presupposes and copes with human sinfulness (31:16–21, 29). However, Horeb was not annulled by Israel's sin, as the reinstatement of the demands of Horeb in 10:12–22 showed. See further our discussion on Abraham and Sinai below, pp173ff.

47 Olson (1994) 176. He regards Horeb as law and Moab as promise.

vaguely to all of chapters 5–26 but also concretely to the revelation at Horeb in chapter 5.[48] In 4:5, the reference is more clearly to Moab. In 4:14, Moab is grounded in Horeb. Thus there is a deliberate identification of the events at Horeb with the preaching at Moab. The generations of each are also conflated.[49] So Deuteronomy wants to show that there is absolute continuity between the revelations. Moab is the new Horeb.[50] The two covenants are consistently fused together. The preaching of Deuteronomy is inseparable from the revelation at Horeb.

This is also seen in the rhetoric of הַיּוֹם, an important feature of chapter 29. The "you" who stood at Horeb are in effect the "you" who stand at Moab.[51] This is especially seen in the parallel between 5:3, "not with our fathers that the LORD made this covenant, but with us", and 29:13–14, "I am making this covenant, with its oath, not only with you...but also with those who are not here today".[52] Such a link indicates further support for our contention that the covenant at Moab, described in chapter 29, is much the same as the Horeb covenant. The fusion of covenants is accompanied by the conflation of generations.[53] This generational conflation is particularly prominent in chapter 29, as illustrated by the high frequency of הַיּוֹם, occurring in vv9, 11, 12, 14 (twice).[54] This emphasises the contemporaneity of the event. "Past events are actualised in the present to take later readers of the book back to the border and include them in the address".[55] The repeated "today" revitalises the covenant relationship through the renewal

48 McConville and Millar, 38–39.

49 McConville and Millar, 44, 46, 53–60. Commenting on 5:3, Millar, 58, says "the correspondence between Horeb and Moab is made totally explicit – the current generation is not to think of the covenant at Horeb as a mere memory, but as *a memory which is actualized in the present at Moab.*"

50 McConville and Millar, 49. Compare Weinfeld (1985) 76–78.

51 McConville and Millar, 42–43. Knapp, 142, suggests 29:1 indicates that the exodus generation is still alive.

52 For example, Miller (1990) 210; Cairns, 256; Craigie (1976) 257; Braulik (1992) 213; McConville and Millar, 53; Knapp, 145. Compare Lenchak, 104. On הַיּוֹם in Deuteronomy, see DeVries (1975a) 164–186. He, 178, argues that the function of הַיּוֹם in these verses is "to aim the parenesis at the late generation experiencing the covenant confrontation anew in liturgical celebration". It is usually understood that 29:13–14 refers to future generations rather than those absent for other reasons or at home. See Lenchak, 103–104; Knapp, 145; Nielsen, 266. Rofé (1985a) 312, considers v14 to refer to "members of the community who, for some reason, did not participate in the ceremony". Kearney, 6; Welch, 164, state that those absent were in exile.

53 Deurloo, 44–45; Braulik (1992) 214; McConville and Millar, 49; DeVries (1975a) 262.

54 Lenchak, 177.

55 Miller (1990) 209–210. This is also the effect of including future generations in v14.

of the old covenant, rather than in the sense of making a new covenant.[56] There is probably a sense of urgency suggested,[57] especially leading up to the climactic plea to choose life in 30:19.

Another argument in favour of identifying Moab and Horeb is that of Stek. He suggests that ANE covenants were made when

> circumstances *occasioned doubts* concerning desired or promised courses of action. The specific purpose of 'covenants' was to add a guarantee of fulfillment to commitments made.[58]

This certainly applies to Israel at Moab. Questioning why the Sinai covenant takes the form of "an oath-bound commitment on the part of the vassal people", he answers, "Because history had shown the unreliability of this people". Thus, "Covenant as an instrument of kingdom administration ministered to human weakness".[59] If Stek's suggestions are valid, then this reinforces our argument about the nature of the Moab covenant. It is fundamentally a confirmation of the Horeb covenant for a new, and fearful, generation. It is also addressed to an unreliable and fallible people. The expectations of this covenant remain that Israel will fail. The new generation is no better than the old. The same theological framework applies for Moab as for Horeb, namely the inevitability of Israel's sin but Yahweh's faithfulness to the Abrahamic promises as the sole grounds of hope.

In the light of these arguments, we assert that the Moab covenant is not fundamentally different in character from the Horeb covenant. Rather than annulling and replacing Horeb, it serves to confirm it, showing that Horeb applies not just to the previous generation which experienced the theophany at Horeb, but to this next generation as well.[60] Indeed the obligations of Moab could even be regarded as more demanding than those of Horeb, whether Horeb is the Decalogue alone or whether, as we prefer, Horeb is more than this. Yet "it is still the same people who must try to obey". So, "why should the outcome be any different?"[61]

56 Craigie (1976) 357.

57 Maxwell, 311.

58 Stek, 25. He argues that this principle applies to all the biblical covenants.

59 Stek, 33.

60 Millar is inconsistent at this point. He argues, 248, that Moab has replaced Horeb but, 118, disagrees with Preuß who speaks of Moab 'replacing' Horeb.

61 Millar, 249–250.

## Deuteronomy 29:1–8

The first section we shall consider is 29:1–8.[62] In particular, v3 is a crucial verse both for this study and Deuteronomy 29–30 as it is a statement of Israel's inability to keep the covenant. It establishes "the exigence of the rhetorical situation". All communication arises from an exigence. That of Deuteronomy 29–30 is the lack of proper insight and understanding.[63] Thus arises the serious danger of apostasy with resulting threat of punishment.[64] In our consideration of these chapters, we are concerned to see how this lack will be met. The first issue to consider is whether this is a statement which still applies at the time of address at Moab. The structure of 29:1–8 helps to clarify this.

### *Structure*

Begg suggests that vv1–3 show that the events of the exodus were insufficient for Israel to gain a sure understanding or recognition of God, as v3 admits. So the wilderness experiences, referred to in vv4, 5a,

> were designed as a supplementary measure to ensure Israel's coming to that perception of Yahweh as her God which the events of the Exodus had not of themselves been sufficient to effect.[65]

This explains, he says, the strange combination of bread, wine and strong drink. Bread leads to satisfaction which dulls the dependence on God (as in 8:3) and wine and strong drink also dull the senses and obscure proper recognition of God. The deprivation of these items in the wilderness was thus to ensure the right acknowledgement of God.[66] Thus it seems that in Begg's understanding, v3 represents the end of the first stage of prehistory rather than a statement of the current situation at the point of address of chapters 29 and 30.

There are a number of arguments against this. Firstly, Childs argues that the "signs and wonders" formula in Deuteronomy is used in a broad sense, that is, its referent is not only the plagues and the exodus but the whole event from Egypt to Moab.[67] If he is right, and his argument is substantial,

---

62 Lohfink (1962) 37, argues that 29:8 belongs with vv1–7. Lenchak, 161–162, 174, suggests that 29:1b forms an inclusio with 29:8. He notes that the threefold אַתֶּם delineates the beginning of sections in 29:1b, 9, 15. Also Knapp, 144, 147.

63 Lenchak, 112.

64 Kearney, 1–8, argues that Deuteronomy 29 suggests that "infidelity is dangerously close" because it is full of allusions to the Gibeonites and to the sin of Achan. Though his conclusion fits our thesis, his evidence is speculative. See also Mayes (1985) 324–325.

65 Begg (1980b) 273.

66 Begg, 273–274.

67 Childs (1967) 30–39.

this suggests that vv1–2 do not strictly refer to the pre-wilderness period. Therefore v3, "up to this day" would clearly mean the day at Moab, not pre-wilderness, and hence is a statement of the current situation.

Secondly, there are some important structural parallels between vv1–3 and vv4–6a. Both sections begin with a statement of place (Egypt, wilderness); both end with a statement referring to the present (עַד הַיּוֹם הַזֶּה; אֶל־הַמָּקוֹם הַזֶּה);[68] both change from singular to plural and back to singular; both conclude with a theological interpretation. Time (v3) and space (v6a) are the particular axes of this history.[69] This parallel of vv1–3 and vv4–6a suggests not so much a two-stage development, as Begg indicates, but rather a twofold parallel statement of the lack of proper acknowledgement and recognition of Yahweh. This view is strengthened by consideration of the expression עַד הַיּוֹם הַזֶּה (v3).

Quite commonly in Deuteronomy הַיּוֹם is used adverbially meaning "today". A number of times this is strengthened by the addition of הַזֶּה.[70] The reference is always to the present day. This is a significant feature of Deuteronomy, contributing to the book's existential and urgent style.[71] The particular phrase, עַד הַיּוֹם הַזֶּה, occurs six times in Deuteronomy.[72] Each time there is no suggestion that the situation pertaining "up to this day" is either about to change or is in the process of already changing. In 2:22, the descendants of Esau have lived in their place "up to this day" and still do so.[73] The same may be said about Bashan being called Havvoth Jair (3:14), the work of the Levites (10:8), the lasting destruction of the LORD against the Egyptians (11:4) and the knowledge of Moses' grave site (34:6). The sense of each of these is clearly that the situation so described as "up to this day" still applies. This is also the obvious way to read 29:3. Like the exodus, the wilderness has failed to bring Israel to a right knowledge, recognition and acknowledgement of Yahweh. Thus 29:3 stands as a statement of the current state of affairs and, contra Begg, not as a statement

68 A weakness of this parallel is that syntactically, אֶל־הַמָּקוֹם הַזֶּה belongs with v6b and not vv4–5.

69 Lohfink (1962) 37–38. Lenchak, 174, regards 29:1b–3, 4–5, 6–8 as three parallel sections describing three events in three different places each leading to a reflection, though he, 184, notes that vv6b–8 break the parallel pattern. Yahweh is no longer the actor; Israel is. Also Braulik (1992) 212; Mayes (1979) 361; Lohfink (1963a) 127–128.

70 DeVries (1975a) 165, counts 59 occurrences of היום used adverbially with or without הַזֶּה in Deuteronomy, excluding set expressions such as עַד הַיּוֹם הַזֶּה. McConville and Millar, 43, list 62 references.

71 Von Rad (1966a) 28–29.

72 Even-Shoshan, 453, lists 2:22; 3:14; 10:8; 11:4; 29:3; 34:6.

73 That they still do so is part of the purpose of the verse.

pertaining to Israel's pre-wilderness condition before being changed by that wilderness experience.[74]

That this is the right way of understanding 29:3 is also supported by noting that 29:4–5 recalls 8:2–5 in referring to the wilderness and, importantly, the purpose of the wilderness experience as a time of testing and discipline that Israel would יָדַעְתָּ עִם־לְבָבֶךָ.[75] Both 8:5 and 29:3 have יָדַע with לֵב/לֵבָב, both significant words in the respective pericopes, 8:2–5 and 29:3–5. There is other significant vocabulary which occurs in both pericopes. This includes the hiphil of הָלַךְ (8:2; 29:4, only elsewhere in 8:15; 28:36), אַרְבָּעִים שָׁנָה (8:2, 4; 29:5, only elsewhere in 2:7), בַּמִּדְבָּר in 8:2; 29:4 (nine times elsewhere), and לֶחֶם in 8:3; 29:5 (six times elsewhere). The similarity between שִׂמְלָתְךָ לֹא בָלְתָה מֵעָלֶיךָ in 8:4 and לֹא־בָלוּ שַׂלְמֹתֵיכֶם מֵעֲלֵיכֶם in 29:4 should also be noted.[76] Despite the fact that one is singular and the other plural and that different words for mantle are used, the verb בָּלָה is used only in these two verses in Deuteronomy. Further, each of these clauses leads into a related clause about feet. In 8:4, the feet did not swell. In 29:4, the sandals did not wear out on the feet. The general ideas are identical.[77] We conclude that 8:2–5 and 29:4–5 reflect the same understanding about the wilderness experience and its purpose.

The reason for drawing this parallel here is that there is no suggestion in chapter 8 that Israel had learned and changed as a result of the wilderness period. This reinforces what has been said above in response to Begg. Thus 29:3 reflects the current state of affairs.

### *Responsibility for Knowledge*

As it stands, v3 attributes no blame to Israel. It is simply said that right knowledge, sight and hearing are a gift from God.[78] This is an acknowledgement that unless God acts, Israel is unable to respond to God properly. By itself, the verse could suggest that Israel's lack of right

---

74 Cairns, 255, raises the possibility of understanding עַד הַיּוֹם הַזֶּה as "*from* 'this day'. Similarly von Rad (1966e) 179, suggests that only now is Israel beginning to understand. Amsler, 21, suggests that 29:3 is fulfilled by the Deuteronomic preaching.

75 For example, Mitchell, 106; von Rad (1966e) 179; Miller (1990) 204; Mayes (1979) 361; Steuernagel, 105; Preuß (1982) 160; Burden, 124–125; Lenchak, 115; Kearney, 6. Lohfink and Braulik, privately, have suggested that it is significant that in 29:1–8 the wilderness reference does not mention Israel's sin. This need not suggest a different redaction, as they imply. Rather, presupposing chapters 1, 8 and 9, the rhetoric of chapter 29 builds towards its positive climax in 30:15–20. On יָדַע plus כִּי elsewhere in the Old Testament, see Hagelia, 111.

76 Lenchak, 115.

77 Weinfeld (1991) 390, following Blau, 98–99.

78 Compare Isaiah 19:14; 29:9–10. Blenkinsopp (1968) 119.

knowledge is due solely to Yahweh who has not given Israel the gift.[79] However, a consideration of the wider context of thought in Deuteronomy, shows that Israel is ascribed blame for the failure to know God properly. Two lines of argument are relevant here.

Firstly, the parallel structure of vv1–3 and vv4–6a noted above links vv3 and 5b: לְמַעַן תֵּדְעוּ כִּי אֲנִי יְהוָה אֱלֹהֵיכֶם. Thus v5b shows what knowledge is intended by v3. The verb יָדַע does not have an object in 29:3; we understand it by the parallel with 29:5b.[80] Indeed, v5b draws attention to itself by the change to first person and rare use of אֲנִי.[81] The purpose of the wilderness experience was the right knowledge of Yahweh by Israel. 29:5b attributes responsibility to Israel for gaining this knowledge so its lack is its own fault. Various reasons for Israel's failure to achieve this end have been offered including Israel's disobedience and hardness of heart,[82] its ingratitude,[83] and that true understanding only comes with "the perspective of time".[84]

The second line of argument which shows that some blame must be attributed to Israel derives from the tension between 29:1–2 and 3. This tension turns on עֵינַיִם and רָאָה. Verses 1–2 stress three times what Israel has seen: אַתֶּם רְאִיתֶם (v1, an emphatic expression[85]), לְעֵינֵיכֶם (v1) and רָאוּ עֵינֶיךָ (v2).[86] However v3, "in an almost contradictory fashion", says that Israel does not have "eyes to see". "The tension between the verses is obvious."[87] This tension makes sense only if the meaning of "eyes to see" in v3 is different from the preceding.[88] Clearly something other than physical sight is meant in v3, despite the fact that physical sight is

---

79 Kline (1963) 130; Miller (1990) 206.

80 This is rare in Deuteronomy. Compare 31:13.

81 Driver, 321; Mayes (1979) 361. This occurs only in 12:30 and chapter 32. Lenchak notes, 11, 106, 139, 183, that the first person and the unusual אֲנִי draw attention to Yahweh's statement and intertwine the roles of Moses and Yahweh. Compare Polzin (1980) 55, 57. Von Rad (1966e) 22, suggests the change to Yahweh speaking is inadvertent. Kearney, 2, suggests it is a deliberate allusion to 8:3. Similarly Rennes, 136.

82 Thompson, 279. Similarly Driver, 321; Kline (1963) 130. Payne, 159, suggests that Israel's blame lay with the fact that it took pride in the achievements of the exodus.

83 König, 195, suggests that Yahweh's withholding the gift is an act of punishment to Israel.

84 Craigie (1976) 356. See also Merrill, 376.

85 König, 195.

86 Lenchak, 133.

87 Miller (1990) 204.

88 Lenchak, 158.

important in Deuteronomy. Thus v3 is referring to a "proper understanding of what has been witnessed".[89]

In v3, eyes is part of the triplet, לֵבָב/לֵב, עֵינַיִם, אָזְנַיִם which occurs elsewhere in the Old Testament only four times, in Isaiah 6:10; Jeremiah 5:21 and Ezekiel 40:4; 44:5.[90] Though the triplet is unique in Deuteronomy, the individual components are not rare. We shall now discuss each of these components in order to understand better their significance in 29:3.

### *A Heart to Know*

The first component of the triplet in 29:3 we discuss is the heart to know. The words יָדַע and לֵבָב are collocated six times: 4:39; 8:2, 5; 13:4; 18:21 and 29:3. In 4:39, the object of יָדַע is

כִּי יְהוָה הוּא הָאֱלֹהִים בַּשָּׁמַיִם מִמַּעַל וְעַל־הָאָרֶץ מִתָּחַת אֵין עוֹד.

This compares with 29:5b, כִּי אֲנִי יְהוָה אֱלֹהֵיכֶם, and thus indirectly with 29:3. However, the actual expression in 4:39 is וְיָדַעְתָּ הַיּוֹם וַהֲשֵׁבֹתָ אֶל־לְבָבֶךָ. Thus יָדַע is distanced from לֵבָב by the hiphil of the verb שׁוּב. So even though the object of knowledge in 4:39 reflects that of 29:5b, and hence 29:3, it is not an exact parallel. In 18:21, the relationship between יָדַע and לֵבָב is also indirect, לֵבָב relating directly to the verb אָמַר. In 8:2 and 13:4, the subject of יָדַע is Yahweh, not Israel. Finally, in 8:5, Israel is commanded וְיָדַעְתָּ עִם־לְבָבֶךָ and the object of this knowledge is the fatherly discipline of Yahweh. Even though לֵבָב is not the subject of the verb (Israel is) and by the preposition, עִם, לֵבָב is only indirectly related to יָדַע, and the object of the knowledge is not the same as in 29:5b, 8:5 is the closest we come to the sense of 29:3, לֵב לָדַעַת.[91]

The examples where יָדַע occurs without לֵבָב, with a sense of deep knowledge, have been surveyed in the previous chapter when discussing 8:2–6. These are 4:9, 35, which also combines יָדַע and רָאָה; 7:9; 8:3; 9:3, 6; 11:2 (twice), again in association with the verb רָאָה. What these verses reflect is a concern within Deuteronomy for knowledge being a right recognition or acknowledgement of Yahweh behind the events experienced or seen. This sense of יָדַע is what 29:3 is about: "il s'agit de savoir et de comprendre la pleine signification des actions de Yahweh dans l'histoire

---

89 Lenchak, 158. Also Driver, 321, "Israel's possession of the organ of physical sight (v2) suggests the thought of its deficiency in the faculty of spritual insight."

90 Watson, 405. Thompson, 279, also lists Jeremiah 1:17–19 and Ezekiel 3:4–11 as comparable passages. Lenchak, 136, 216; Kearney, 1, considers the threefold statement to be emphatic, an example of *copia*.

91 On the two pericopes, 8:2–6 and 29:1–5, see above. Mayes (1979) 362, says that in thought, יָדַע in 29:3 is closest to 8:3 and also 9:24 in a technical sense of "legally recognize, acknowledge". Also Dhorme, 506. König, 196, says that 29:5a is an illustration of 8:3. Also Bertholet, 89.

d'Israël".[92] 29:3 suggests therefore that despite Israel knowing, in the sense of experiencing, various events, it does not have the deep and proper recognition of Yahweh.

A further consideration concerns the statements in Deuteronomy about other gods or nations "אֲשֶׁר לֹא־יְדַעְתֶּם". This expression, or similar, occurs in 11:28; 13:3, 7, 14; 28:64; 29:25 and 32:17 in reference to other gods and in 28:33, 36 to other nations. The subject, the current generation of Israelites, can be singular or plural and, in three cases, also includes the fathers or past generation(s).[93] By contrast with other gods, this expression implies that Israel, in some sense, knows or has known Yahweh. Yet 29:3, by parallel with 29:5b, admits that Israel is yet to know that Yahweh is the LORD its God. This suggests that the two levels of sense for יָדַע occur here. Israel has known Yahweh in the sense of having experienced his acts of redemption and discipline in the desert and receiving his commandments. Yet Israel does not know Yahweh in the sense of a proper recognition of him as God.

Another possibility is that יָדַע has a technical sense for legal recognition of treaty obligations and relationships.[94] This could be either the suzerain knowing the vassal or vice versa. In the former category, Huffmon cites Deuteronomy 9:24 where, he argues, מִיּוֹם דַּעְתּוֹ אֶתְכֶם refers to when Israel entered into covenant at Horeb. However, in 9:7 the rebellion of Israel is traced back beyond Horeb to the exodus, and secondly, the reading דַּעְתּוֹ (rather than דַּעְתִּי) follows the Samaritan Pentateuch reading.[95]

If a technical treaty sense of a vassal knowing a suzerain is understood, we face the same dilemma as above. Does Israel know Yahweh? Huffmon argues that the technical treaty sense of יָדַע has to do with the recognition of Yahweh as the sole legitimate God.[96] This would fit the deeper sense of יָדַע mentioned above. If this is the case, it raises the possibility that the covenant renewal at Moab, which 29:1–8 is heralding, could be the time when Israel is given a heart to know Yahweh.[97] This would mean that the situation pertaining עַד הַיּוֹם הַזֶּה in 29:3 would be about to change. However, if the covenant at Moab does include a God-given heart to know,

92 Rennes, 136.

93 See Giles, 155–169. Clifford, 156, argues that the sense of "know" in these expressions is "confess".

94 Huffmon, 31–37; McCarthy (1981) 168, 186. For further Ugarit and Mari texts, see Huffmon and Parker, 36–38.

95 Huffmon, 35. The LXX reflects the Sam. Pent. reading. Weinfeld (1991) 403; Mayes (1979) 202, likewise argue that the MT reading is preferable. The first person reading makes Moses the subject. Huffmon also suggests 34:10 fits this category.

96 Huffmon, 35–36.

97 This would support the arguments of Miller (1990) 206; Lohfink (1963a) 128.

then the Moab covenant is significantly different from that of Horeb. We have argued above that Moab is identified with Horeb.

### *Eyes to See*

The second element of the triplet in 29:3 we discuss is eyes to see. There is considerable emphasis in Deuteronomy on eyewitness. Restricting ourselves to occasions where the object of this witness is the action of God, we firstly find a number of references to "before your eyes" (לְ + עֵינַיִם + pronominal suffix). These include Yahweh fighting in Egypt (1:30), all the things Yahweh did in Egypt (4:34), miraculous signs and wonders in Egypt (6:22), the breaking of the tablets (by Moses) at Horeb (9:17), and all that Yahweh did to Pharaoh (29:1). Each time the emphasis is on Israel being an eyewitness to the event. Secondly we find a number of references where עֵינַיִם (+ suffix) is the subject of רָאָה with some action of God as the object. Under this heading are 4:3, the things Yahweh did at Baal Peor;[98] 4:9, where the object is אֶת־הַדְּבָרִים; 7:19, the trials, signs and wonders with which Yahweh effected the exodus; 10:21, great and awesome wonders; 11:7, אֶת כָּל־מַעֲשֵׂה יְהוָה הַגָּדֹל; and 29:2, trials, signs and wonders. This expression is a rhetorical technique, characteristic in Deuteronomy, to put emphasis on Israel being an eyewitness to the great actions of Yahweh, even though it is the next generation which is ostensibly being addressed.[99]

However eyewitnessing is not the end but a means to an end. Firstly, the imperative רְאֵה is significant.[100] This imperative, always in the singular, has the force of an interjection, and often introduces a declaration of a gift or an appointment.[101] What is important in our context however is that each time (excluding 3:27 and 32:49 which are commands to Moses and not Israel), the purpose of "seeing" is some action of faith. So in 1:8, 21, Israel is to enter and take possession of the land. Both 2:24, 31 lead into commands to conquer Sihon. In 4:5, "seeing" leads to obedience. Similarly, in 11:26, what is to be seen are the blessing and the curse set before Israel.

---

98 Literally, עֵינֵיכֶם הָרֹאוֹת, "your eyes are those that see/saw" (Weinfeld (191) 195.) *GKC* §116q notes that 4:3 refers to the past.

99 Weinfeld (1972) 173, that the purpose of the "deuteronomic orator" is "to implant in his listeners the feeling that they themselves have experienced the awe-inspiring events of the Exodus; and he repeats these phrases again and again as if to hypnotize his audience."

100 Christensen (1991) 12, notes that the second person masculine singular imperative occurs six times in the so-called outer frame (1:8, 21; 2:24, 31; 3:27; 32:49) and three times in the so-called inner frame (4:5; 11:26; 30:15).

101 Weinfeld (1991) 134. The singular in 1:8 contrasts with the other imperatives in the verse which are plural, hence Weinfeld's view that this is an interjection. This also applies to 1:21; 2:24, 31; 4:5; 11:26 and 30:15. (Weinfeld, 451.) The LXX and Samaritan Pentateuch alter 1:8 to the plural.

The purpose is again obedience (11:32). 30:15 is similar to 11:26 where Israel is to see life and death and, in consequence, to obey. Thus what we have here is a suggestion of deeper sight, not purely at the physical, eyewitness level but a sight which leads to a right response of faith and obedience to Yahweh.[102] Regarding chapters 29 and 30, the imperative רְאֵה in 30:15 announces the climax of this speech and thus ties in with 29:1–3. It is the only imperative form in these chapters. The element of choice is signalled in the contrast between 29:1–3 and 29:16. Israel has seen Yahweh's actions and also the detestable images and idols. The choice comes to a head with the command of 30:15.[103] The same point is made without the imperative. What Israel has seen at Baal Peor should lead to obedience (4:2–5). Seeing Yahweh's great acts should lead to a lack of fear (7:19) and stimulate worship and fear of Yahweh (10:21). The emphatic "your own eyes saw" all these things (11:7) should lead to obedience (11:8).

Secondly, that sight should lead to a proper response to Yahweh is reflected in 4:34–36. In v34 the acts of God in Egypt לְעֵינֶיךָ are recalled.[104] In v35 the hophal of רָאָה with a purpose clause (infinitive construct of יָדַע + לְ) occurs showing that "seeing" is a means to an end, namely the deep knowledge discussed above. Then in v36 the hiphil of רָאָה contributes to the argument of 4:32–40, showing the purpose of Yahweh to be that Israel should acknowledge and recognise him alone as God in obedience and faith (vv39, 40).

A second hiphil of רָאָה in 5:21–26, again with Yahweh as subject, has as its goal the proper recognition of Yahweh in obedience and faith. In v21, the אֶת־כְּבֹדוֹ וְאֶת־גָּדְלוֹ which Yahweh הֶרְאָנוּ leads to a right, if temporary, response as demonstrated by Yahweh's words of approval in v26.

A third hiphil of רָאָה with Yahweh as subject occurs in 1:33.[105] We discussed this passage in chapter 1, noting that despite "seeing", Israel failed to believe (v32). In v30 the expression לְעֵינֵיכֶם refers to Yahweh fighting for Israel in Egypt. In v31, רָאִיתָ refers to the providence of God in the desert. Then in v33 the hiphil refers to the way Israel should go in the wilderness. Thus in these few verses, Israel's status as eyewitness of the acts of God is highlighted, strengthening the contrast with its unbelief in

---

102 Dhorme, 506.

103 Lenchak, 140–141, 158. He also suggests that the perfect forms in 29:8 (twice) and 30:19 function as imperatives. The imperative in 30:15 also functions like an interjection. Also see 203, 219.

104 Weinfeld (1991) 198, notes that the singular suffix here is inconsistent with the rest of the verse which is plural. This emphasises the idea of eyewitness.

105 The three other hiphils of רָאָה all have Moses as the object. These are 3:27; 34:1, 4. (Lisowsky, 1298.) The context in each is that Yahweh allowed Moses to see the land but not to enter it.

v32 and heightening the implication of its reprehensibility. Seeing is not believing; something more is needed.[106]

Throughout Deuteronomy we have an account of the failure of the eyewitness, for which 1:30–33 is the paradigm. The eyes of sight failed to become the eyes of faith, though the commands of the book show that this is Israel's responsibility.

### *Heart and Eyes*

Before we turn to the third part of the triplet of v3, we look further at the heart and eyes by noting verses where they occur together. These are 4:9; 11:18; 15:9; 28:65, 67.[107] So 4:9:

פֶּן־תִּשְׁכַּח אֶת־הַדְּבָרִים אֲשֶׁר־רָאוּ עֵינֶיךָ וּפֶן־יָסוּרוּ מִלְּבָבְךָ.

The parallelism between these two ideas suggests that what is seen is applied to the heart and that, in fact, Israel has done this correctly. The warning is that Israel must remain with these things permanently on its heart. It seems that Israel is, in fact, able to respond properly to Yahweh, if only fleetingly. In contrast, the "heart to know" and "eyes to see" of 29:3 points to a permanent and stable state and not one which fluctuates between faith and unbelief, obedience and disobedience.

In 11:18 the command שַׂמְתֶּם אֶת־דְּבָרַי אֵלֶּה עַל־לְבַבְכֶם is paralleled by הָיוּ לְטוֹטָפֹת בֵּין עֵינֵיכֶם. Whilst there is debate about whether the frontlet between the eyes is to be understood literally or metaphorically,[108] the idea of permanence and immovability is suggestive.[109] So Driver comments that the words are to be "as it were, imprinted there".[110] Thus we have the same idea as in 4:9. What is required is a permanent and fixed state of faith and obedience. Even though Israel may be able to respond sporadically to Yahweh aright, a permanent right response is beyond Israel without Yahweh's intervention. In 11:18, the eyes (and hands) are means of helping (*Hilfsmittel*) the heart to keep the word. Their importance lies in their ability to seduce man. Commonly in the wisdom literature, the eyes play a negative role.[111] Where heart and eyes occur together, they represent the close relationship between the inner process and the activity of man as a whole, whether positive or negative.[112]

---

106 Miller (1990) 205, "The issue is whether the eyes that see will become eyes of faith that *trust* this God." 16:19 suggests that bribes blind the eyes. Perhaps more generally human sinfulness is what prevents seeing becoming believing.

107 We shall deal with 28:65, 67 below, p130.

108 See below on 30:11–14.

109 The LXX translates טוֹטָפֹת by ἀσάλευτον, "immovable", reflecting the metaphorical interpretation. Weinfeld (1991) 335.

110 Driver, 92. He links this expression with the new covenant of Jeremiah 31:33.

111 Ogushi, 43. See Proverbs 6:17; 10:10; 21:4; 27:20; 30:17; Ecclesiaistes 2:10.

112 Ogushi, 44.

In 15:9, the heart and the eye are paralleled in the expressions דָבָר עִם־לְבָבְךָ בְלִיַּעַל and רָעָה עֵינְךָ בְּאָחִיךָ הָאֶבְיוֹן. By and large the word pairs are synonymous rather than antithetical, as is the case here.[113] Whilst this verse is not directly relevant to 29:3, it does reflect the fact that the word pair heart-eye is not unknown, and that the synonymity found in 29:3 is also found in 15:9.

In summary, the collocation of heart and eyes supports our case that 29:3 is concerned with proper and permanent response to Yahweh.

### *Ears to Hear*

The third element of the triplet in 29:3 is ears to hear. Unlike heart and eye, ear seldom occurs in Deuteronomy. Disregarding 15:17, which deals with pushing an awl through the ear of a slave, there are five occurrences of אֹזֶן apart from 29:3. Each is prefixed with a preposition, either לְ (31:11) or בְּ (5:1; 31:28, 30; 32:44) and translated "in (your) hearing".[114] Apart from 29:3, the only occurrence of אֹזֶן with שָׁמַע is 5:1. Only in 29:3 do אֹזֶן and לֵבָב coincide. Therefore the inclusion of אֹזֶן in 29:3 is somewhat striking. The addition of this third term perhaps lends emphasis to the importance of this verse and the seriousness of what it is saying.[115]

The verb שָׁמַע is very much more important in Deuteronomy than אֹזֶן.[116] Though its occurrences are spread throughout the book, the verb is especially prominent in chapters 4, 5, 28 and 30.[117] As alluded to in the previous chapter, it is important to note the frequent use of שָׁמַע plus בְּ, usually prefixed to קוֹל. Typically the קוֹל is that of Yahweh.[118] Possibly this expression derives from diplomatic letters and treaties of the ANE and expresses religious loyalty.[119] Regardless of its origin, by the expression שָׁמַע plus בְּקוֹל "die Beobachtung der Grundforderung des Yahwedienstes gemeint ist".[120] Thus the preposition בְּ gives שָׁמַע the deeper nuance of

---

113 Watson, 408.

114 In 5:1, the suffix is second person; 31:11 and 31:28 are third person; 31:30 and 32:44 are construct. All refer to Israel.

115 Lenchak, 216.

116 The verb appears in qal 85 times, in niphal once and hiphil four times. (Lisowsky, 1465ff.) Schult, 975, describes its frequency in Deuteronomy as "überproportional" and that it is "ein Schlüsselwort der dtn.-dtr. Schule".

117 Respectively 10, 9, 8 and 7 times.

118 The expression, "to listen to Yahweh's voice" occurs eighteen times in Deuteronomy: fourteen times in the singular: 4:30; 13:19; 15:5; 26:17; 27:10; 28:1, 2, 15, 45, 62; 30:2, 8, 10, 20; three times in plural: 8:20; 9:23; 13:5; once in first person: 26:14. See Begg (1980a) 41. The exceptions are 1:45; 21:20.

119 Weinfeld (1972) 83–84. The expression is not particular to Deuteronomy. Weinfeld notes that it occurs in JE; Bright (1951) 15–35, in Jeremiah.

120 Braulik (1978) 124.

obedience and heeding.[121] Where קוֹל is a direct object of שָׁמַע, it conveys only the idea of physical hearing. In particular, hearing Yahweh's voice at Horeb from the fire is common.[122] This parallels occasions where the direct object is קוֹל דְּבָרִים (or similar). In such cases, שָׁמַע again carries only the sense of hearing, rather than a fuller response of heeding or obeying.[123]

Another variation is שָׁמַע with an indirect object qualified by the preposition אֶל.[124] As with בְּ, the preposition אֶל gives to שָׁמַע the fuller sense of heeding and obeying. So, commonly, the indirect objects refer to commandments or words: הַחֻקִּים (4:1), הַמִּשְׁפָּטִים (4:1), מִצְוֹת (11:13, 27, 28; 28:13)[125], דְּבָרִים (13:4; 18:19). In each case, the context makes it clear that שָׁמַע has a full sense of obeying and heeding, rather than just listening. The same can be said for the other four occurrences of שָׁמַע plus אֶל. Here the indirect objects are not words or commands but persons. These are Moses (3:26; 10:10),[126] the priest (17:12) and Balaam (23:6). Again in each case, the context shows a fuller sense of heeding, obeying or responding.

Apart from the clear cases of שָׁמַע plus בְּ or אֶל, there are some occurrences of שָׁמַע where it is argued that the sense of the verb could be obey rather than merely hear. Weinfeld argues this to be the case in 5:1, שְׁמַע יִשְׂרָאֵל אֶת־הַחֻקִּים וְאֶת־הַמִּשְׁפָּטִים, and also in 4:1; 6:3; 9:1; 20:3 and 27:9. His argument derives from the "prevalent" use in wisdom literature of שָׁמַע in the sense of obey. He regards these verses as pedagogical expressions

---

121 This is also the sense in 1:45 and 21:20 where the noun in construct with קוֹל is not Yahweh. Schult, 977, makes only a little distinction between שָׁמַע with the direct object קוֹל and שָׁמַע with בְּקוֹל. The former is translated as "etwas/jemanden hören" and the latter as "auf etwas/jemanden hören". Earlier, on 976, he said, "daher ist שָׁמַע auch nur in Ausnahmefällen nicht mit »hören« übersetzbar". He goes on to say, 981, that within the relationship between Yahweh and Israel, the sense could be translated by "gehorchen, gehorsam sein". This comes out of the particular Deuteronomic and Deuteronomistic usage of the verb in connection with the commands and covenant of Yahweh. Compare KB, 991, where שָׁמַע with בְּ is listed under "listen to", "attend to", "readily hear", and שָׁמַע with בְּקוֹל is listed under "listen to" and "yield to, obey".

122 For example, 5:20, 21, 22, 23.

123 See for example 5:24, 25. In 5:25, the people's response to hearing the words is to say: שָׁמַעְנוּ וְעָשִׂינוּ. The addition of עָשָׂה to שָׁמַע suggests that שָׁמַע conveys a weaker sense here of hearing rather than the fuller sense of heeding and obeying, ideas taken up by עָשָׂה. This contrast in senses for שָׁמַע also occurs in chapter 4, where see vv6, 10, 12, 33 and 36. In these verses שָׁמַע has the sense of "von etwas hören", unlike 4:30 which carries the fuller sense. Braulik (1978) 125.

124 This occurs in 3:26; 4:1; 10:10; 11:13, 27, 28; 13:4; 17:12; 18:19; 23:6; 28:13.

125 Weinfeld (1972) 337, notes this group as characteristic Deuteronomic phraseology and translates שָׁמַע as "keep".

126 In both cases, the NIV translates the verb and indirect object as "listen(ed) to me". The context of each shows that the sense is not listening or hearing but rather heeding or, even, obeying.

reminiscent of the instruction by the wise man to his pupil.[127] His argument is not entirely convincing, failing as it does to note the syntactic significance of the preposition אֶל.[128] As well, the context in each case does not require the fuller sense of שָׁמַע. In 6:3, שָׁמַע is supplemented by וְשָׁמַרְתָּ לַעֲשׂוֹת. It seems more natural to understand שָׁמַע here in the weaker sense of hear or listen, for the sense of obey is carried by the following verbs. Likewise in 9:1; 20:3 and 27:9, it is more natural to read the sense of hear or listen rather than obey.[129] Also, in 4:1, the word order is significantly different from the other verses in Weinfeld's list. In 4:1 we have יִשְׂרָאֵל שְׁמַע and not vice versa. This order links the verb directly with the preposition and object and, as argued above, the presence of אֶל conveys the stronger sense of obey. In the other verses, apart from 5:1, שְׁמַע precedes Israel and does not have an object. Thus, Weinfeld has read in too much to the meaning of שָׁמַע in these verses, apart from 4:1. He has failed to note the syntactic significance of אֶל and the word order in 4:1. Moreover the context suggests the weaker sense of hear in the other verses.[130] Nonetheless, the weaker sense of hear is not unimportant. For example, the occurrence of שָׁמַע in 1:43 is part of the summary accusation against Israel concerning its lack of hearing which resulted in its rebellion.[131]

In 4:36, the hiphil of רָאָה and שָׁמַע occur. Extreme importance is placed on both seeing and hearing in chapter 4 in connection with Horeb. Of 68 occurrences of all forms of רָאָה, nine occur in chapter 4. For שָׁמַע it is ten of ninety. Whilst part of the focus of the chapter is that Israel did not see Yahweh or any form, with the resulting prohibition against the making of images and idols, v36 brings together the ideas that Horeb was both a visible and an audible event. Possibly the close connection of the two in chapter 4 leads to their association in 29:3 despite 29:1, 2 mentioning only seeing.[132]

---

127 Weinfeld (1972) 305. Compare, 176, where he argues that "Hear, O Israel" is a standard rhetorical term giving Deuteronomy the style of didactic speech.

128 Unlike all the other verses in his list, 4:1 has שָׁמַע plus אֶל. Weinfeld makes no comment on this difference.

129 For example, after 9:1, there is a narrative of what will happen when Israel crosses the Jordan. Thus it is more natural to read שָׁמַע in 9:1 as listen or hear. J.G. Janzen (1987b) 262, makes no comment on prepositional connotations. See also Sauer, 706.

130 This may imply a difference from the use of the verb in Wisdom literature, rather than a derivation from it.

131 On the priority of hearing over seeing in Deuteronomy, see our comments in the previous chapter.

132 Weinfeld (1991) 211–212, makes the interesting observation that 4:33 speaks of hearing the voice of Yahweh yet living, in contrast to Genesis 16:13; Exodus 33:20; etc, which speak of seeing Yahweh and living. Clearly the change in Deuteronomy would be to support the prohibition on images and idols though Weinfeld (1991)

Finally we consider occurrences of שָׁמַע with לֵבָב. Besides 29:3, there are six: 11:13; 13:4; 20:3; 29:18; 30:2, 10. In 11:13, שָׁמֹעַ תִּשְׁמְעוּ אֶל־מִצְוֹתַי is explained by the clause

לְאַהֲבָה אֶת־יְהוָה אֱלֹהֵיכֶם וּלְעָבְדוֹ בְּכָל־לְבַבְכֶם.

Thus the fuller sense of שָׁמַע parallels the use of לֵבָב which also reflects the full and proper response of Israel to Yahweh. Again in 13:4, the fuller sense of שָׁמַע, here שָׁמַע plus אֶל, is linked with אֹהֲבִים...בְּכָל־לְבַבְכֶם. In 20:3 a possibly weaker sense of שָׁמַע nevertheless leads to the prohibition אַל־יֵרַךְ לְבַבְכֶם. A negative connection exists in 29:18 where we read

וְהָיָה בְּשָׁמְעוֹ אֶת־דִּבְרֵי הָאָלָה הַזֹּאת וְהִתְבָּרֵךְ בִּלְבָבוֹ.

Then in 30:2 the closest connection exists:

וְשָׁמַעְתָּ בְקֹלוֹ כְּכֹל אֲשֶׁר־אָנֹכִי מְצַוְּךָ הַיּוֹם אַתָּה וּבָנֶיךָ בְּכָל־לְבָבְךָ.

Thus the fuller sense of שָׁמַע is firmly linked to the full response of the heart. A less direct link exists in 30:10.[133]

*Conclusion*

As we have indicated, 29:3 draws together many important motifs of Deuteronomy concerning Israel's response to Yahweh. Its tripartite statement is thus an entirely appropriate summary of Yahweh's demands in Deuteronomy. Indeed the verse is only fully understood in the light of the rest of the book. In drawing these threads together, v3 highlights Israel's failure to meet Yahweh's demands. Despite Israel experiencing, seeing and hearing the acts and commands of God, it has failed to apply this properly and to take the extra step of acknowledgement, faith and obedience. Though there are rare hints that at times Israel did, albeit fleetingly, respond properly, nonetheless Israel has "up to this day" failed to exercise the proper response to Yahweh.

Yet, without denying human responsibility, 29:3 has a glimmer of hope, for it attributes to Yahweh the possibility of giving what is lacking.[134] This possibility of hope is also suggested by noting that 29:3 picks up many important words from chapter 28, hinting at a possible reversal of the curses. Thus we find in chapter 28 the following: לֵב/לֵבָב (four times), יָדַע (three), שָׁמַע (eight), רָאָה (five), עַיִן (seven), נָתַן (seventeen).[135] Though not all are directly relevant to 29:3, their frequency suggests a possible

---

204, is wrong in saying "according to Deuteronomy there was nothing to see". See 4:3, 9, 35, 36.

133 Compare Weinfeld (1972) 245–246, on לֵב שָׁמַע in 1 Kings 3:9.

134 Miller (1990) 208, speaks of the juxtaposition of human act commanded and divine act promised.

135 Though these are common words, they are quite frequent in chapter 28: לֵב/לֵבָב (2nd most frequent chapter); יָדַע (6th); שָׁמַע (3rd); רָאָה (4th); עַיִן (1st); נָתַן (1st).

*Leitwortsystem* may be at work.[136] With regard to blessings, in 28:1–14, we note the requirement to שָׁמַע as a prerequisite for blessing, with בְּקוֹל in 28:2, 15, and in an emphatic sense with finite and infinite forms together in 28:1. The curses, on the other hand, will follow Israel not obeying (שָׁמַע plus בְּקוֹל in vv45, 62). The curses the Israelites will see (רָאָה and עַיִן) will wear out their eyes and drive them mad (vv32, 34). These curses will involve confusion of לֵבָב (v28) and are in part caused by a bad heart (v47).

The verb נָתַן is particularly prominent in chapter 28. Usually its subject is Yahweh.[137] Yahweh gives various things with regard to blessings, (vv7, 8, 11, 12, 13) and with regard to curses (vv24, 25, 31, 32 [assuming that Yahweh is the subject of the passive participles], 48, 52, 53). Finally, and most importantly, in v65, Yahweh will give Israel לֵב רַגָּז וְכִלְיוֹן עֵינַיִם וְדַאֲבוֹן נָפֶשׁ. Here we have two of the three anthropological terms from 29:3 and, as in that verse, as objects of נָתַן.[138] The same word pair, heart and eyes, occurs in v67 in the expression

מִפַּחַד לְבָבְךָ אֲשֶׁר תִּפְחָד וּמִמַּרְאֵה עֵינֶיךָ אֲשֶׁר תִּרְאֶה.

This repeated word pair comes in the culmination of the curses of the chapter. One effect of this repeated word pair is to highlight 29:3 as a contrast to the curses threatened in chapter 28.

Though 29:3 is not itself a promise that Yahweh will give the right heart and eyes, chapters 29 and 30 lead in effect to such a promise in 30:6. Quite possibly the intended effect of 29:3, following on from 28:65, 67, is to create a sense of longing or desire for this gift of Yahweh. The heart and eyes of 29:3 thus give a positive alternative to the suffering heart and eyes under the curses of the previous chapter. The addition of וְאָזְנַיִם לִשְׁמֹעַ may then be intended to give a sense of assurance or certainty for, in chapter 28, blessings and curses depend on whether Israel שָׁמַע or not. So 29:3 implies or suggests the possibility of blessings.

This is also borne out by noting that 29:8 is the conclusion to the section. It is a call to obedience, using two perfect verbs, שָׁמַר and עָשָׂה, imperatively.[139] The right heart, eyes and ears will result in obedience. This verse is also important within the strategy of chapters 29 and 30 for the verb עָשָׂה not only occurs twice here but also in 29:28; 30:8, 12, 13, 14.[140] This vocabulary link indicates that the lack expressed in 29:3, affecting Israel's fulfilment of the law, is resolved in 30:6, as 30:8, 12, 13, 14 will show.[141]

---

136 It is perhaps significant that the less common word לֵב is used in 28:65 as well as 29:3. See Braulik (1978) 99.

137 The exceptions are 28:1, 55, 67 (twice in the idiom מִי־יִתֵּן).

138 Watson, 404–405, notes 28:65 and 29:3 (though by error he has 28:25) as the only triple sets involving heart and eyes in the Old Testament.

139 Lenchak, 141, 161–162.

140 Lenchak, 195.

141 Lenchak, 203–204.

We have argued that in 29:3 the deeper sense of each of the verbs is intended. In the case of the heart knowing, this is clearest from the parallel in 29:5b. For the eyes seeing, this is clearest from the tension between what is seen in vv1, 2 with inability to see in v3. For the ears hearing, this is implied from being in parallel with the heart and eyes in 29:3. As well, for each of the three, there are ample examples within Deuteronomy to show that though Israel has experienced, seen and heard, each was insufficient in that it should have led to a full and permanent sense of acknowledging, believing and obeying. So the eyes to see are eyes of faith. The ears to hear are ears of obedience. The heart to know perhaps encompasses both.[142]

## Deuteronomy 29:9–28

We turn to a consideration of the theology of the rest of the chapter, focusing our attention on issues relating to Israel's faithlessness and Yahweh's grace. The first section we consider is 29:9–14.

### *29:9–14*

This paragraph is centred on "*die Bundesformel*" in v12, the centre of a chiasm whose outer part is לִפְנֵי יְהוָה in vv9, 14, plus אֱלֹהֵי with different pronominal suffixes.[143] The other element comprises בְּרִית, אָלָה and כֹּרֵת in vv11, 13. A fourth element could be the list of participants in vv9, 10 which is balanced by the reference to future generations in v14.[144] The centrality of the covenant formula to this section, and the chapter, underlines the importance of the patriarchal promise for its theology. The patriarchs are frequently mentioned in Deuteronomy in the context of land but in the context of בְּרִית, they are mentioned only in 4:31; 7:12; 8:18 and here.[145] Though chapter 29 is largely pessimistic, its grounds of hope lie in Yahweh's promises and faithfulness to them.[146] This is what we have found elsewhere in Deuteronomy. Moab is not a new covenant but is grounded in

---

142 Miller (1990) 205. The three things denote acknowledgement, faith and obedience. Driver, 321, "*the eyes* and *the ears* are named as figures for the capacity of moral and spiritual perception (Isa 6:10; 32:3)."

143 Lohfink (1962) 39. Also Braulik (1992) 213; Lenchak, 175. On this twin-element covenant formula and its derivation, see Skweres, 129–137, 178–180. Compare Genesis 17:7; 19:21; Exodus 19:5f. Also Kutsch, 147–148. Nielsen, 266, suggests v11 refers to Genesis 15:7ff.

144 Mayes (1979) 362; Lenchak, 186.

145 Driver, 323; Kutsch, 106–107. Compare 4:37 and 7:8.

146 Böhmer, 95.

the patriarchal covenant.[147] Rather than being the actual "central act of covenant ratification", this paragraph describes the purpose of the Moab covenant renewal as the establishment of covenant relations with this generation in fulfilment of the patriarchal promises.[148]

The formality of this section, signifying its importance, is illustrated by נִצָּבִים in v9, a formal term, perhaps suggesting a parade.[149] הַיּוֹם is especially frequent here, occurring five times in six verses. The effect of this, as noted above, is to contemporise Horeb, identify Moab with it and conflate the generations in a rhetorical and urgent parenesis.

The unusual expression וּבְאָלָתוֹ, which stands in parallel with בִּבְרִית in v11, requires comment. Often these two words are translated as a hendiadys, "sworn covenant".[150] The two words, אָלָה and בְּרִית, are semantically close.[151] אָלָה can be translated as either oath or, as in v20, curse. Possibly "a self-cursing formula to guard against disobedience" lies behind this.[152] Its use here is probably suggested by the content of chapter 28. It may then be another hint at an expectation of failure for Israel.[153] The addition of the word for oath here expresses the threats against possible disloyalty in the sharpest way.[154] The expression "sworn covenant" occurs three times in Deuteronomy 29 but not at all in chapters 1–28, suggesting that it is shorthand for the covenant of chapters 1–26 and for the curses of chapter 28.[155] The relationship between covenant and oath has been much discussed, but it seems that an essential characteristic of a covenant is that it was established through an oath.[156] The hendiadys here adds an extra

---

147 Cairns, 258, suggests the unity of the patriarchs and Horeb is rare in Deuteronomy. Compare McConville and Millar, 79, "The covenant at Moab is also presented as a fulfilment of the promise to Abram in Genesis 15."

148 Kline (1963) 130. Compare Lohfink (1962) 38, that this "ist ein fast juristisch gemeinter, präzis formulierter Text, eine Art Protokoll". He, 49, and Braulik (1992) 212, argue that this is performative speech. So von Rad (1966e) 179–180. Kalland, 183, notes that הָקִים "is used in Deuteronomy to describe establishing, confirming, or performing something actively and effectively". He cites 8:18; 9:5; 22:4; 25:7. Of 29:12 he says, "it speaks of an effective confirmation or establishment of the covenant".

149 Craigie (1976) 356. Also Driver, 322; Thompson, 281; Cairns, 257.

150 For example, Mayes (1979) 363; Cairns, 256; Weinfeld (1972) 62–63; Merrill, 379; Brichto (1963) 24–25. Scharbert, 264; Braulik (1970) 44.

151 Naylor, 380–395. Also Hugenberger, 202–203.

152 Mayes (1979) 363. Knapp, 133, 145, suggests that the different sense of אָלָה in v20 shows a different author to vv11, 13.

153 Thompson, 281.

154 König, 196. Braulik (1992) 213, suggests that the oath/curse links the destiny of the transgressor with that of the divided animals in covenant making ceremonies.

155 Cairns, 258.

156 Hugenberger, 202–204. On allusions to Genesis 15, see Hagelia, 152–158, 163–164.

dimension of solemnity or seriousness about the infringement of covenant stipulations.

The relevance of this is as follows. Moab is described in ways which show that it is fundamentally identical to Horeb and, furthermore, is closely linked to the patriarchal covenant. Israel is being urged to pledge itself to this covenant which has been expounded throughout Deuteronomy. However, as 29:3 stated, up to this day Yahweh has withheld the means for Israel to be able to make a proper and lasting response. Now, however, Yahweh is about to act, for it is Yahweh, not Israel, who כֹּרֵת this sworn covenant. In this entire paragraph, the only thing which Israel is doing is standing (נִצָּבִים, v9; עֹמֵד, v14) before Yahweh. All other verbs either have Yahweh as the subject or represent part of the purpose and intention of the ceremony. The onus in this paragraph remains clearly on Yahweh.[157]

Verse 12 spells out the purpose (לְמַעַן) of this action of Yahweh. This is stated as the two sides of the covenant relationship, firstly, הָקִים־אֹתְךָ הַיּוֹם לוֹ לְעָם and, secondly, וְהוּא יִהְיֶה־לְּךָ לֵאלֹהִים.[158] This stated purpose relates to that of v5b which, we have argued, expresses the substance of v3. The fulfilment of the promise of covenant relationship, to "this day" unrealised, ultimately depends on the action of Yahweh.[159] Though Israel does stand and "pass over"[160] into this covenant, the bottom line is that Yahweh's action is decisive.

This covenant renewal does not rectify Israel's lack in 29:3. The covenant relationship of these verses is an external affair. Israel's lack expressed in 29:3, despite the covenant relationship, is as yet unmet. The rest of the chapter shows this. In conclusion, the new generation is being invited to enter into a relationship with Yahweh grounded not on its own merit but on the patriarchal promises.

### *29:15–20*

We continue our discussion of the theology of chapter 29 by looking at the next paragraph, 29:15–20. The rhetorical style of this paragraph is markedly

---

157 Yahweh occurs 38 times in 49 verses in chapers 29–30. Lenchak, 127.

158 The hiphil of קוּם speaks of ratifying an already existing covenant. This supports the contention that Moab and Horeb are complementary. Compare Genesis 6:18; 9:9, 11; 17:19, 21; Exodus 6:4; Deuteronomy 8:18 and 9:5. Merrill, 379–380; Dumbrell (1984) 25–26; Rose (1994) 552.

159 That action is circumcision which, in Genesis 17, is the sign of the covenant established with Abram earlier. See Rose (1994) 346.

160 עָבַר plus בְּ, in the context of the covenant, is unique here in the Old Testament. See Driver, 323; Mayes (1979) 363. Kline (1963) 130, suggests Genesis 15:17 as a parallel though the verb has בֵּין not בְּ. Also Steuernagel, 106.

different from the preceding.[161] Structurally, the paragraph could be viewed as a microcosm of the covenant formula, namely prehistory (v15), basic demand (v17) and the threat of curse (vv18–20).[162] The basic demand is the prohibition against serving other gods. No further stipulations are detailed.[163] Yet even this basic demand is alluded to rather than commanded.[164]

This paragraph repeats some of the vocabulary of 29:3. The emphatic[165] אַתֶּם יְדַעְתֶּם in v15 refers to the past in Egypt and the journey to the plains of Moab, corresponding to 29:1–8. יָדַע in v15, which in some sense parallels the use of רָאָה in v1, carries the weaker sense of experience. שָׁמַע occurs in v18 with the sense of "hear" rather than "obey" for the hearing of the oath is associated with downright disobedience. This hypothetical person has obviously not been given "ears to hear". לֵב/לֵבָב occurs three times in vv17–18.[166] This emphasis is to move the hearer-reader from external participation in the covenant ceremony in vv9–14 to an internal participation of the heart in the covenant of Yahweh.[167] This again reflects the concerns of 29:3.

There is a development of ideas associated with the heart of the hypothetical person in vv17, 18. Firstly the heart פֹּנֶה הַיּוֹם מֵעִם יְהוָה אֱלֹהֵינוּ. That a heart can turn away from Yahweh suggests that it was directed towards Yahweh in the first place. Possibly this reflects the external nature of the covenant relationship being established in vv9–14.[168] Israel, at times, did respond properly to Yahweh. However this was only temporary or fleeting. On its own Israel, or an individual Israelite, had limited capacity to respond properly to Yahweh. The capacity depends on Yahweh giving "a heart to know". This hypothetical person may indeed come from a position of a right relationship with Yahweh but he has not been given "a heart to know". Hence his response will only be temporary and he is vulnerable to his heart turning away.

The second stage is indicated by הִתְבָּרֵךְ (v18) which describes the heart,

---

161 Lohfink (1962) 39, calls this a splendid specimen of rhetoric. Similarly Braulik (1992) 214; Preuß (1982) 160.

162 Lohfink (1962) 39; von Rad (1966e) 180; Thompson, 282.

163 Miller (1990) 210. Braulik (1992) 214, says this demand for exclusive worship of Yahweh is the kernel of both Horeb and Moab.

164 Mayes (1979) 364, "This is the only allusion in this chapter to a specific demand, that of the sole worship of Yahweh; yet it is an allusion to a demand rather than a demand itself. The latter is presupposed as already given and accepted."

165 Driver, 323.

166 Braulik (1992) 214; Lohfink (1962) 39.

167 Braulik (1992) 214. Also Cairns, 259; Lohfink (1962) 39.

168 The same expression occurs in 30:17 on which see p205 below.

das sich in einem Gegensegen (wie in einem Gegenzauber) absichernde Herz (so ist das Hitpael von *brk* vielleicht zu verstehen).[169]

This then leads to the third stage in v18 where the person says כִּי בִּשְׁרִרוּת לִבִּי אֵלֵךְ (v18). This is "das sich verstockende Herz".[170] שְׁרִירוּת, or other forms derived from שָׁרַר, with לֵבָב/לֵב occur "always in the bad sense of stubborn or persistent evil resistance to the Lord".[171] Occurrences in Jeremiah indicate that שָׁרַר involves abandoning Torah, abandoning Yahweh, not listening to and despising Yahweh's word. Each is an unacceptable assertion of autonomy and independence.[172] So the expression, שְׁרִירוּת לֵב, denotes "obstinate thought or reflection". The sense of the verse is that the person will keep his evil thoughts to himself and, since no-one will know, he will remain unpunished.[173]

The succession of these three ideas suggests that sin strengthens its grip and places the person in a position of entrenched opposition to Yahweh. Sin is like a contagious infection, a common portrayal in the Old Testament.[174] Its power and purpose are seen in the way that the "*result* of the idolator's action is represented, ironically, as being his *design*" (לְמַעַן).[175] This highlights guilt.[176] The punishment in this case will come from Yahweh himself (v19). In chapter 13, the people are the agents of punishment because the person there sins publicly. Here, however, the person's thoughts are kept to himself. Hence Yahweh himself executes punishment.[177]

The power of sin is perhaps reflected in the use of רָבַץ in v19. The sense of the verb is to stretch out or lie down, often with the idea of rest, being settled or lying in wait. There are just two occasions where the subject of this verb is abstract, here and Genesis 4.[178] In Genesis 4:7, in Yahweh's warning to Cain, its subject is, probably, sin.[179] In 29:19 it is הָאָלָה. In

---

169 Lohfink (1962) 39. Also Driver, 325; Maxwell, 314. Compare 8:17. Brueggemann (1985) 21, 29.

170 Lohfink (1962) 39. Brueggemann (1985) 20, suggests that שָׁרַר parallels (rather than develops) the hithpael "bless himself".

171 Kalland, 184. Also Driver, 325; Cunliffe-Jones, 162; Lenchak, 127–128. The combination occurs in Jeremiah (eight times) and Psalms (once).

172 Brueggemann (1985) 19–20.

173 Weinfeld (1972) 105–106. Similarly Kopf, 283.

174 Koch, 57–87, especially 68. He argues that sin has built-in consequences for disaster (Sin-Disaster-Construct).

175 Driver, 325. Also Ridderbos, 267; Cunliffe-Jones, 162.

176 Bertholet, 90.

177 Weinfeld (1972) 105–107.

178 See BDB, 918. The verb occurs 30 times in the Old Testament. Typically its subject is animate.

179 The problem is the lack of gender agreement between the masculine participle and feminine noun. Wenham (1987) 94, notes that grammatically the two should agree.

Genesis 4, the context is the power and mastery of sin which is personified as a force. It "is waiting like a hungry lion ready to leap" and "is an aggressive force ready to ambush Cain".[180] Possibly רֹבֵץ here in Deuteronomy is an oblique allusion to that passage or at least to the power of sin which takes hold of and masters people.[181] If so, Cain may be regarded as a model of Israel's sin.[182]

The power and force of sin is also highlighted by the analogy of the root.[183] Verse 17 is divided into two parallel parts, each beginning with פֶּן־יֵשׁ בָּכֶם.[184] The hypothetical person, clan or tribe is thus depicted as a root producing poison.[185] The individual has the potential to be the source of destruction for others.[186] This is because sin is powerful and Israel is vulnerable to it and its control.[187] The metaphor "indicates the permeation of evil throughout Israel because of the action of an individual, family or tribe".[188]

The seriousness of the threat posed by the sinful individual is seen in the expression סְפוֹת הָרָוָה אֶת־הַצְּמֵאָה. There are three main possibilities for understanding this expression.[189] Firstly, and most commonly, the two opposites are understood as a merismus indicating that nothing will escape disaster.[190] However, this would be harsh judgment on the innocent which

---

V.P. Hamilton, 225–227, who finds support from *GKC*, §122r, says, "nouns which are feminine morphologically are sometimes treated as masculine". Compare Speiser, 32–33.

180 Brueggemann (1982a) 57.

181 Driver, 326, suggests the metaphor is forced and considers the alternative reading of דָּבֵק (𝔊) to be correct. This is unnecessary. König, 197, says this expression personifies the curse. Also Lenchak, 165.

182 Van der Toorn, 53, links the idea of personification in both places.

183 Ginsberg, 74–75; Craigie (1976) 358, suggest that שֹׁרֶשׁ could be translated as "stock" rather than "root". See Koch, 69–74. Lenchak, 144, suggests that the rhetoric here conveys disdain, contempt and even horror at the sinner. Nielsen, 266, suggests the root implies hidden growth.

184 Lohfink (1962) 39.

185 Kalland, 182; Ridderbos, 266; Craigie (1976) 358; Lenchak, 214. Compare Hebrews 12:15. Thompson, 282, agrees that the root is the person. He identifies the plant with idolatry. Merrill, 382, identifies the root with idolatry and the poison with the golden calf. Miller (1990) 210, identifies the root with "an act of stubborn disobedience" rather than the person. Similarly Driver, 324. Cairns suggests that as a root is hidden, this suggests the notion of secret sin here.

186 Compare 19:10; 21:1. Ridderbos, 266.

187 Israel's capability of sin does not imply freedom not to sin, as Lenchak, 240, suggests.

188 Craigie (1976) 358.

189 Cairns, 259. On the difficulty of this expression, see Rennes, 138.

190 Payne, 161; König, 197; Craigie (1976) 359; Driver, 325; Blair (1964) 74; Merrill, 382; Honeyman, 15; Lenchak, 149–151; Rose (1994) 553.

would contradict v20. Secondly, it could mean the person's evil will cancel out his good, so the reference is to the totality of the sinner's life.[191] The third possibility is that the evil person is speaking the words and that they express his expectation that his deeds will be undetected or covered by the righteousness of the people.[192] None of these fully fits the argument of the paragraph. It seems wisest to understand this expression in the light of the poison-bearing root in v17. The root, which is the offender, if left undetected or unpunished, will infect the rest of the community with the poison of sin. Thus all would be drawn into sin and, therefore, all would face the disaster of v18.[193] The punishment will then justly be against all sinners. This metaphor highlights the vulnerability of Israel to sin. To blot out a name from under heaven (v19) is very serious and is the punishment usually reserved for Israel's enemies.[194] The loaded language portrays the sinner in a damning light, a device intended to dissuade the audience from such a course.[195]

In conclusion, despite entering into this covenant, Israel is vulnerable to sin. The heart, eyes and ears which would ensure a permanent and proper response to Yahweh are not yet given. Though Israel on its own is capable of temporary or fleeting faithful obedience, the power and strength of sin makes it always vulnerable to turning away.

### *29:21–27*

This section shifts the focus from the individual to the nation. Yahweh's anger, which was a feature of Deuteronomy 1–3, 8–10, and the land are highlighted here.[196] The style shifts from contingency to prediction.[197] In

---

191 Mayes (1979) 365, argues that the watered or moist is "the man's life in covenant with Yahweh…while the 'dry' or 'thirsty' is his life away from Yahweh". Similarly Munchenberg, 202–203. This seems to be an artificial division, one never conceived in Deuteronomy.

192 Rofé (1985a) 313, suggests that "the sated, irrigated land will feed the thirsty, dry-land". Similarly Nielsen, 266.

193 Dillmann, 381. Compare Cairns, 259, "No sin is purely private: it inevitably involves the community".

194 So 7:24; 25:19. See Kalland, 184; Driver, 323; Cairns, 259. Payne, 161, comments that idolatry makes a person, in effect, a foreigner.

195 Lenchak, 164, 190–191. The sinner is portrayed as an anti-model, one not to follow. Kearney, 8, suggests that the model is Achan, seeing allusions to Joshua 7. Also Mayes (1985) 324–325.

196 Lenchak, 143, 176, 195. On Yahweh's anger in Deuteronomy, see our comment on 3:26 in chapter 1. Words from the root קצף, occur in Deuteronomy only in 1:34; 9:7–22; 29:27, linking the three sections of our discussion together. Other words for anger occur elsewhere.

chapter 28 the blessings, as an alternative to the curses, are listed first. In 29:26–27, and 30:1–10, the curses precede the blessings, not as an alternative but as an historical succession.[198] The abruptness of these shifts need not suggest a discontinuity between vv20, 21.[199] Disaster coming on all the land has been hinted at in v18. This would be the result if the sin of the hypothetical individual was left undetected or untreated. Sin would spread to others, like the poison from the root spreading. Frequently in the Old Testament, individual and collective responsibility are intertwined.[200] So here, the responsibility of an individual is part and parcel of that of the nation. The abruptness seems to emphasise the potency of sin. "(T)he Writer evidently contemplates the case of the 'poison' of v17 (18) having completed, only too thoroughly, its baneful effects."[201]

This is also reflected in the mention of Sodom and Gomorrah in v22, alluding to Genesis 19:24–29. There, as here, punishment involves fire, salt and sulphur.[202] An emphasis of the Sodom and Gomorrah account in Genesis is Abraham's pleading with God not to destroy Sodom and Gomorrah if there were even a few righteous people left there. Its destruction showed this not to be the case. The suggestion then, in Deuteronomy, is that the poison of sin would spread to all people. This is a severe warning about the power of sin. That v22 sharply interrupts vv21, 23 also draws attention to the seriousness of the devastation.[203]

It is common to read these verses as exilic and retrospective. However a final form reading requires us to read them as a future prediction. Consistent with what we have seen throughout this chapter, Israel is expected to sin and, therefore, the curses of the covenant will surely come.

---

197 Driver, 326, "the dreaded contingency is now pictured as a certainty"; Kalland, 184; Braulik (1992) 215; von Rad (1966e) 180; Thompson, 283.

198 Braulik (1992) 215; Lohfink (1962) 41. Cholewinski, 107, regards the succession of curse and blessing as a feature of Moab and not Horeb.

199 So Ridderbos, 267. Compare Rofé (1985a) 313–315; Driver, 326.

200 Joyce, 82–83.

201 Driver, 326. Likewise Payne, 161. Lenchak, 192, suggests that the rhetorical effect of the abrupt change from individual to nation is to draw the audience into an acceptance of the cause-effect sin-punishment relationship which applies to the nation and not just the individual.

202 See Weinfeld (1972) 110–111, 122. Also Cairns, 261; Driver, 327; Mayes (1979) 366.

203 Craigie (1976) 359, "The terseness of v. 22 is an effective rhetorical device to accentuate the horror of the devastated land."

### *29:28*

Verse 28 is rather enigmatic. Typically the "secret things" is understood to be referring to the unknown future.[204] Other explanations include "the hidden causes which motivate God to discipline His people",[205] and a wisdom maxim about the limits of human wisdom.[206] Less convincing is Rofé's suggestion that the "secret things" are hidden sins of the individual, referring back to vv19–20. That they concern God means that "the Lord will single out the sinner and punish him". In contrast, overt acts are the responsibility of the community to deal with.[207] Also unconvincing is Weinfeld's suggestion that the verse is about the two copies of the covenant and that the secret "thing" is God's copy and the revealed one is Israel's.[208]

Commonly this verse has been considered in some isolation.[209] This has no doubt contributed to the difficulty in understanding it. It is helpful to see this verse in relationship to 30:11–14. Access to the law or word is for the purpose of obedience (v14). 29:28 contains the same idea and purpose.[210] Though 30:11–14 is much more detailed than 29:28 and there is no significant overlap in vocabulary,[211] it seems reasonable to suppose that 29:28 is preparation for 30:11–14 and is therefore best interpreted by it.[212] The argument that these two sections relate to each other, and thus form a

---

204 Driver, 328; Bertholet, 90; Cunliffe-Jones, 164; Payne, 162; G.A. Smith, 326; Craigie (1976) 360–361; Mayes (1979) 368; Lenchak, 152. Rennes, 140–142, suggests that the present and the future are both in mind and that this verse is similar to what the New Testament calls "mystery".

205 Maxwell, 315.

206 Von Rad (1966e) 180; McCarthy (1981) 201; Cairns, 262, who calls it "timeless wisdom"; Mayes (1979) 368. See the survey in Lenchak, 152.

207 Rofé (1985a) 313. He argues this was the standard ancient Jewish understanding and accuses Dillmann of leading "astray three following generations of critics". Rofé's understanding falls on two grounds. God ultimately deals with all sin. His interpretation depends on omitting vv21–27.

208 Weinfeld (1972) 63–64. This interpretation requires the reading of the singulars הַנִּסְתֶּרֶת and הַנִּגְלֵת in place of the plurals. There are no grounds for this. As Mayes (1979) 368, points out, this would identify the secret with the revealed. The point of the verse is that the two are different. Labuschagne (1985) 123, suggests that the secret things have to do with Deuteronomy's complex numerical system.

209 Compare Lohfink (1962) 41; G.A. Smith, 326; Cairns, 262; Clifford, 153; Kearney, 7. Levenson (1975) 208, calls this verse "a pious gloss". McCarthy (1981) 201, says this verse is "a gloss, a meditation in the Wisdom style on the mystery of God's way with man, and not part of the over-all structure".

210 Steuernagel, 108. Also Kalland, 185.

211 Compare דָּבָר, on which see p183 below on 30:11–14. Further, 29:28 is first person plural; 30:11–14 is second person singular throughout.

212 So Mayes (1979) 367; Miller (1990) 212; Cairns, 262; Braulik (1992) 216; Ridderbos, 268; G.E. Wright, 507; Merrill, 385; Rennes, 140; Nielsen, 270. Hals, 9, suggests both 29:28 and 30:11–14 raise potential excuses for not obeying.

frame for 30:1–10, is strengthened by the observation below that 30:1–10 is constructed palistrophically. So v28 is saying that revelation has been given for the purpose of obedience. The "revealed things" is perhaps therefore a reference to Deuteronomy itself, law, parenesis and history which all serve to exhort obedience. The secret things remain undefined. Whatever they are, they are not necessary for man to know. God has revealed all that is needed for obedience. 30:11–14 makes this same point.

This verse functions as a transition between the generally negative chapter 29 and the more optimistic chapter 30.[213] There is vocabulary common to this verse and 28:69; 29:8 (דִּבְרֵי הַבְּרִית), 29:20; 30:10 (תּוֹרָה), 29:18; 30:1 (דִּבְרֵי) which indicates the pivotal role of 29:28 in these chapters. In particular, עָשָׂה links back to 29:8 and forward to 30:8, 12, 13, 14.[214] Thus 29:28 hints at the solution to the problem of 29:3 which prevents Israel fulfilling its obedience (עָשָׂה) as expressed in 29:8. That solution will be spelled out in 30:1–10.[215]

### *Conclusion*

The renewal of covenant relations with the current generation in 29:9–14 is an act of Yahweh's grace. He is the one who initiates covenant renewal in order to fulfil the patriarchal promises. This covenant renewal does not in itself resolve the problem of 29:3. That is clear from what follows in 29:15–28 where Israel's vulnerability and inevitable fall into sin is depicted. Sin is portrayed as powerful and contagious. Israel's vulnerability is attributed to the absence of, in effect, "a heart to know, eyes to see and ears to hear". The individual who falls into sin is repesentative of the people as a whole. The metaphor of the poisonous root demonstrates this. The reference to Sodom and Gomorrah makes the seriousness of this clear. 29:9–28 is largely pessimistic. Israel's faithlessness is suggested by the inevitability of the curses. The final verse of the chapter is a transition to the next chapter where the resolution to this inevitable failure is described. We turn now to a discussion of 30:1–10.

## Deuteronomy 30:1–10

This section is of the utmost significance for this study. Chapter 29 has established that Israel lacks a "heart to know". Therefore it will inevitably fall into sin and incur the wrath of Yahweh. In contrast, 30:1–10 raises the

---

213 Lenchak, 153, 174.

214 Lenchak, 195.

215 29:28 is not itself the answer to 29:3, as Kearney, 7, argues. It is not a statement that Israel has already overcome its lack of understanding, rather that it will depend on a revelation from God.

possibility of a resolution to this future failure, grounding hope in Yahweh's grace and faithfulness to the patriarchal promises. Yahweh will provide a "heart to know" by circumcising Israel's heart (30:6). Our concern is to show theologically how the faithfulness of Yahweh relates to the faithlessness of Israel.

### *Structure*

Our concern to understand the theology of 30:1–10 is aided by observing its structure. This section is certainly highly structured. Vanoni argues for a fivefold concentric structure as follows:[216]

| | | |
|---|---|---|
| A | 1–2 | Protasis |
| B | 3–5 | Apodosis |
| C | 6–8 | Centre |
| B' | 9 | Apodosis |
| A' | 10 | Protasis |

The framing sub-sections, AA', have you (= Israel) as their subject, apart from the relative clause in v1c. In contrast, BB' have only Yahweh as the subject, apart from Israel being the subject of יָרַשׁ in v5b. The middle sub-section moves from having Yahweh as the subject in vv6, 7 to Israel as the subject in v8, introduced by an emphatic וְאַתָּה in v8a.[217]

In deriving this structure, Vanoni first considers the syntax of this section. He argues that the occurrences of third person singular pronominal suffixes show strong connections between clauses. Thus, for example, there are strong links within v2 because קֹלוֹ in v2b refers back to Yahweh in v2a. Likewise Yahweh is explicitly the subject of שׁוּב in v3a and is also the unnamed subject of the verbs in vv3b, 3c, 3d, thus providing a strong syntactic link between all parts of v3. Similarly, he also finds strong links between vv4b, 4c, 5a to 5d, 8b and 8c, 9b and 9c. None of these links goes beyond the sub-sections noted above. Vanoni also considers the natural links of dependent clauses (vv1a and 1b, 4a and 4b), the strong links provided by demonstrative elements, for example the repeated occurrence of מִשָּׁם in vv4b, 4c which ties all of v4 together, and the taking up of the same word but with a changed function in consecutive clauses, for example, הַדְּבָרִים, which changes from subject to object in vv1b, 1c. Weaker links between clauses are provided by ו-consecutives with the same subjects of the verbs.[218]

---

216 Vanoni, 76. Also Mayes (1979) 367; Braulik (1991a) 38–39; (1989) 331.

217 Vanoni, 76, 79.

218 Vanoni, 73–74.

Strong indications of disjunction are subject changes between clauses. These occur between vv1c and 2a, 2b and 3a, 3d and 4a, 4a and 4b, 5b and 5c, 5c and 5d, 7 and 8a, 8c and 9a, 9c and 10a.[219] A weaker indication of disjunction is where a subject is expressed nominally rather than assumed in the verb. Taking all these syntactic observations into consideration, Vanoni evaluates the strength of connection between consecutive clauses in the section. He concludes that the clearest breaks occur at the end of vv2, 3, 7, 8, 9, with a weaker break at the end of v4.[220] He also considers the clauses in 30:1–10, noting that the subject change in v3a signals the change from protasis, introduced by כִּי in v1b, to apodosis. Vanoni also notes the use of כִּי in v9b introducing a *Begründungssatz* for v9a. He suggests that the continued use of כִּי in vv10a, b could provide further grounds for v9a.[221] These suggestions of breaks do not exactly correlate to the structure given above. The analysis of the syntax is only a first step.

Vanoni then considers vocabulary distribution, his most decisive criterion for determining the structure of 30:1–10.[222] The verb שׁוּב is crucial. It occurs seven times in either qal or hiphil. With Israel as subject, it occurs in vv1c, 2a, 8a, 10b, that is, only in ACA'. With Yahweh as subject, it occurs in vv3a, 3c, 9b, that is, only in BB'.[223] Other keywords show a similar distribution. Only in BB' occur references to the fathers. The keyword לֵבָב occurs six times (vv1c, 2b, 6 (three times), 10b), only in ACA'. נֶפֶשׁ similarly occurs only in ACA'. The demonstrative pronouns אֵלֶּה (vv1b, 7) and זֶה (v10a) occur only in ACA'.

The same situation occurs with words concerning law and obedience. שָׁמַע plus בְּקֹל occurs only in ACA'.[224] The combination אֲשֶׁר אָנֹכִי מְצַוְּךָ הַיּוֹם occurs only in AC.[225] This expression however is tied to another expression for law, namely, מִצְוֹתָיו וְחֻקֹּתָיו (v10a), which repeats מִצְוֹתָיו from v8c where it is the antecedent of the אֲשֶׁר mentioned above.[226] Thus again we find an ACA' pattern. Thus all expressions and words for law, *Promulgationssätze*, and verbs for *Gesetzesbeobachtung* occur only in ACA'.[227] We can be even more precise in noting that in C, all these legal

---

219 Vanoni, 74.

220 See his summary table, 74.

221 Vanoni, 75.

222 Vanoni, 75–76.

223 Braulik (1992) 219.

224 Vanoni, 81, notes all other words for *Gestezesbeobachtung* occur in sub-sections ACA', namely, עָשִׂיתָ in v8c and לִשְׁמֹר in v10a.

225 There are three *Promulgationssätze* in 30:1–10, the other in v1b (A) with נָתַן.

226 Vanoni, 80, discusses the selection of words for law used in 30:1–10 and their occurrence in chapters 4–28.

227 Vanoni, 80–81.

terms occur only in v8.[228]

Vanoni also considers verbs about blessing (*Verben im Segenshinweis*).[229] In this category he lists, from 30:1–10, יָרַשׁ, בּוֹא, רָבָה and יִיטַב. The occurrences of these verbs are limited to BB'. He also notes חַיֶּיךָ (v6) which, though a nominal variant of חָיָה, a verb in this blessing category, occurs in C and not BB'.[230] Sub-section C, as we have noted, effects a transition between Yahweh as subject and Israel as subject. This noun occurs in the part of C where, like BB', Yahweh is the subject.

The biggest question about Vanoni's structure is where B ends. Given that Yahweh is predominantly the subject of all of vv3–7, it could be argued that B should include vv6, 7 and that v8 alone should be C. After all, we have noted that much of the vocabulary common to Vanoni's ACA' occurs only in v8 of C. Also his C includes a significant change from Yahweh to Israel as the subject. His syntactical analysis argued for a clear break after v7 but not after v5. So, possibly, all of vv3–7 could be regarded as Yahweh's response to Israel's action in vv1, 2. The effect of this would be to understand the circumcision of the heart as one of a number of blessings given to Israel by Yahweh as a result of Israel's turning and obedience.[231] This is how Lohfink outlined the structure of 30:1–10.[232] Appealing though this structure may be, Vanoni has rightly seen that the subtlety of this passage is reflected in his structure.

---

228 These categories are not unrelated. Given that the law and observation of it applies to Israel, and not Yahweh, then we would expect mention of it to occur in passages where Israel is the subject. On identical ideas in the centre and extremes of a chiasm, see Lund, 41. He noted that in a chiasm of seven elements, the odd and even may carry distinctive elements. Though we have just five elements here, the same principle mostly applies.

229 The term is from Lohfink (1963a) 81–85.

230 More commonly the verb occurs, for example, 4:1; 5:30; 8:1; 16:20; 30:19. See Driver, 330. Compare 30:16.

231 So Schenker, 100–103; Lenchak, 198. Contrast Köckert, 517.

232 Lohfink (1962) 41. His structure is as follows:

| | | | |
|---|---|---|---|
| A | 1f | Premise | The people return and hear Yahweh's voice |
| B | 3–6 | Apodosis | Yahweh's turning; the fathers |
| C | 7 | further apodosis | |
| D | 8 | Premise | The centre; keywords as in A |
| C' | 9a | Apodosis | |
| B' | 9b | further apodosis | Keywords as in B |
| A' | 10 | Premise | Keywords as in A, D |

This structure fails to see the tension in this passage between conditional and unconditional statements. Compare Robinson, 119–121, who questions Lohfink's methodology here, and offers his own suggestion regarding the structure of 30:1–10. Lenchak, 75, argues that linguistic patterns are more significant in Hebrew rhetoric than in Western rhetoric.

Interestingly Vanoni does not make a detailed case for all of vv6–8 being the central part and he fails to comment on the links between AA' being concentrated in v8. However the key to this structure is the occurrences of לֵבָב in v6 of C. The word also occurs in AA'. The same applies to חַיִּים in v6, mentioned above. This points to the fact that v6, and not v8, is the centre of vv1–10. Within v6 the subject changes from Yahweh to Israel. לֵבָב ties the two subjects together, uniting the action of Yahweh with the action of Israel throughout all of vv1–10.[233]

Vanoni's arguments for this five-part structure to 30:1–10 are persuasive. The consistency of the distribution of vocabulary between the sub-sections is clear. The significant changes in subject between Yahweh and Israel are crucial, not only for determining this structure but also the theological relationships of the sub-sections. The changes between protasis and apodosis fit well Vanoni's structure.[234] The details of the structure as outlined will help determine the theological thought of this section. In particular, his inclusion of v6 in the central section, vv6–8, indicates the priority of Yahweh's action on Israel's heart to enable Israel's right response. We now consider in more detail various indications in 30:1–10 of the priority of Yahweh's grace over Israel's response.

### *The Priority of Yahweh*

Typically, interpretations of 30:1–10 suggest that the initiative for a restored relationship with Yahweh must come from Israel. That is, if Israel of its own volition repents, then Yahweh will respond.[235] This reflects an optimistic expectation about Israel's ability to restore the covenant bond. 30:1–10 is thus sometimes seen to be different from statements in, say, Jeremiah 31 and Ezekiel 36 where the initiative lies clearly with Yahweh. So, for example, Meyers says:

> One biblical tradition (Deut 30:1–10) regarded the people's repentance in the exile as the basis for reestablishing a proper relationship with Yahweh. Another view (Ezek 36:24–31) leaves all initiative to Yahweh, who brings the people back to himself and to the land through his own divine actions and spiritual cleansing. In the latter view, God's actions will cause the people to repent of their evil ways and so return to Yahweh.[236]

We recognize that the majority view in Old Testament scholarship, and not least in modern Jewish scholarship, is that ancient Israel was able to keep the Old Testament law. Such an optimistic view of ancient Israel fits with

---

233 See further our discussion below, pp163ff.

234 Compare Lenchak, 196–197, 215, who suggests 30:1–3 is chiastic.

235 Levenson (1975) 208; Payne, 164–165; Craigie (1976) 363; Driver, 328; van Rooy (1988b) 875–876, 881; Polzin (1980) 70.

236 Meyers, 99.

the view of Levenson, Polzin and others, just outlined, that attributes to ancient Israel the initiative and ability of its own volition to repent and turn to Yahweh. However we are arguing that this is not the correct way to read Deuteronomy in general or 30:1–10 in particular. The prevailing view of Israel's ability to keep the law is most clearly challenged by 29:3, 17–27 already discussed, and 31:16–29, beyond the scope of this book, among other passages in Deuteronomy. Therefore we are arguing that the best sense is made of 30:1–10 when it is understood consistent with the expectation of Israel's future failure expressed in the book. Indeed we shall argue that the text itself, as well as its structure, demand that it be read in such a way. Thus it is our contention that 30:1–10 does not reflect an optimistic view of Israel's ability and that the maintenance, or restoration, of the covenant bond depends ultimately on Yahweh and not Israel's ability.

### שׁוּב

The priority of Yahweh's action is indicated by the occurrences of the verb שׁוּב in 30:1–10. This is clearly the most important verb in the section, occurring seven times in vv1c, 2a, 3a, 3c, 8a, 9b, 10b.[237] Holladay classifies every occurrence of שׁוּב in the Old Testament by meaning. He places the hiphil in v1c with preposition אֶל and object לֵבָב into a category with the meaning "bring back (to one's heart that)" or "recall". There are just seven instances of this sense of שׁוּב in the Old Testament.[238]

The focus of Holladay's study is the occurrence of שׁוּב in a context of covenantal relationship. This occurs in vv2a, 10b, where the occurrences of שׁוּב are two of 62 identified by Holladay with the meaning of "return" or "repent".[239] Many of these are followed by the prepositional phrase "to God". In v2a the preposition is עַד; in v10b it is אֶל. He makes no semantic distinction between the different prepositions.[240]

---

237 Compare Mayes, 368, who counts six occurrences and omits v1c. The verb occurs 35 times in Deuteronomy, 21 qal, 14 hiphil. Therefore 20% of its occurrences occur in these ten verses. Braulik (1982) 155, notes that the frequency of שׁוּב in this section exceeds any other place in the Old Testament. See Rofé (1985a) 311. This is another of Braulik's groupings of seven, (1991a) 38–39. "Yahweh" occurs fourteen times in these ten verses, significant in the light of the fact that it is absent in 30:11–14 and occurs just four times in 30:15–20. See Lenchak, 199.

238 Holladay (1958) 101. Also 4:39. Some instances have עַל.

239 Also 4:30. Holladay (1958) 147, concludes that the technical sense of "repent" for שׁוּב does not occur before Jeremiah where the covenantal usage of שׁוּב is a marked feature. However the sense of "return (to God)" which occurs in vv2a, 10b occurs as early as the eighth century prophets.

240 Holladay (1958) 78–79. Wolff (1982) 97; Vanoni, 83, note that שׁוּב with עַד occurs in DtrH only here and 4:30.

In vv8a, 9b, שׁוּב occurs with what Holladay suggests is the sense of "again", repeating an action. He acknowledges that in some instances such as vv8a, 9b, there is doubt that this sense is the right one.[241] Though Holladay identifies four different syntactical structures in this category, none of these exactly fits these two verses.[242]

We consider v8a first. Given the importance of the verb in 30:1–10 and the clear sense of "repent, return to God" in vv2a, 10b, the context of v8a suggests that a sense of repent or return is also present there. In vv2, 8, 10, שׁוּב occurs in collocation with שָׁמַע בְּקֹל. In vv2, 10, שׁוּב has a prepositional phrase "to God". This is absent in v8. However the repeated association with שָׁמַע בְּקֹל suggests that the same notion is present. That is, Israel will return and obey, implying that it will return "to God", as in vv2, 10.[243] A further argument in favour of understanding v8a in this way is that it is not clear that Israel has substantially obeyed Yahweh in the past. If the sense of שׁוּב in v8a is that Israel "will again obey the LORD",[244] one wonders what past obedience is in mind. Though at times Israel temporarily or fleetingly did obey Yahweh, the general impression we get from Deuteronomy is that its history was one of disobedience. Thus we conclude, against Holladay, that in v8a the sense of שׁוּב is, as in vv2, 10, repent or return to God.

The notion of return is less apparent in v9b. Here Yahweh will "again delight" in Israel. Though the occurrence of שׁוּב here deliberately links Yahweh's action to Israel's, there is a sense in which Yahweh has never turned away from Israel. What Yahweh does is not turn to Israel but turn Israel's fortunes around. So the idea of repetition fits much better here than that of turning. The verb שׂוּשׂ, to delight, occurs in Deuteronomy only here and 28:63, where the reference is to a past delight by Yahweh in Israel which will be ended by the curses. Now, in v9b, subsequent to the curses, Yahweh will again delight in Israel. The association with שׂוּשׂ in 28:63 makes it clear that the notion of repetition is intended in v9b rather than the notion of return.[245]

The remaining two occurrences are in v3. The second of these could have the sense of "again",[246] though Holladay lists it under a category of special meanings, linked to the sense of again, but with the meaning of "reversal", that is, reversing the direction of the accompanying verb. In this case the accompanying verb is a hiphil of פּוּץ in v3d. Certainly the sense of

241 Holladay (1958) 66–70. Also Rofé (1985a) 311.

242 Holladay (1958) 67.

243 Compare BDB, 997, "come back and do so and so".

244 For example, NIV; Mayes (1979) 368.

245 So Driver, 330; Mayes (1979) 368.

246 The syntax fits exactly one of Holladay's categories, namely, שׁוּב followed by וְ plus the same form of another verb, in this case קִבֵּץ. Both verbs are third person masculine singular perfects.

"again" would be strange as one wonders when Yahweh has in the past gathered Israel from the nations where it had been scattered.[247] Holladay argues that the force of שׁוּב is to demonstrate that קָבַץ (hiphil) in v3c reverses the action of פּוּץ.[248] Though it is debatable that שׁוּב is necessary to make this reversal clear,[249] it does appear likely that שׁוּב is used, as in v9b, to tie Yahweh's actions to Israel's in the preceding verse but without necessarily intending to connote an actual return of Yahweh. In v2a, Israel turns to Yahweh. In v3c, Yahweh's actions are linked to Israel's, through the repetition of שׁוּב, but not meaning an identical action.

The final occurrence is in v3a in the expression וְשָׁב יְהוָה אֱלֹהֶיךָ אֶת־שְׁבוּתְךָ. The major difficulty with this expression is the derivation of the noun שְׁבוּת which could derive from either שׁוּב or שָׁבָה, "to take captive". Thus the expression could mean either "bring about the restoration of" or "return the captivity of".[250] Holladay notes that contextually, in most places, either translation is feasible, as here. Following Dietrich, Holladay argues that שְׁבוּת derives from שׁוּב, the expression meaning "render a restoration". Because of the focus on restoration from exile, as well as possible manuscript confusion, the noun שְׁבוּת was confused with שְׁבִית which derives from שָׁבָה. The application to the exile is late. Certainly we agree that both possibilities fit the context and that the evidence seems inconclusive. However, given the importance of שׁוּב in 30:1–10, and the relative paucity of words obviously derived from שָׁבָה in Deuteronomy,[251] we incline towards the meaning "bring about the restoration of" or "restore the fortunes of".[252] As with the occurrence of שׁוּב in v3b, so here its occurrence is to tie in with those of vv1c, 2a.

We have discussed the meaning of each occurrence of שׁוּב in 30:1–10. However, in order to understand the use of שׁוּב in these verses, we need to consider its subject. Our aim is to appreciate the relationship between those occurrences with Israel as subject and those with Yahweh as subject.

---

247 Craigie (1976) 363–364, suggests the first gathering is from Egypt. This does not fit with the notion of scattering among a number of nations. Compare NIV, "gather you again"; Mayes (1979) 368.

248 Holladay (1958) 68–69.

249 There are many co-occurrences of פּוּץ and קָבַץ in Isaiah, Jeremiah and Ezekiel, without שׁוּב, where the two verbs are antonyms. In some of these verses, Jeremiah 23:3; Nehemiah 1:9 and Zephaniah 3:20, שׁוּב occurs but clearly meaning return or bring back. It thus has some synonymity with קָבַץ.

250 Holladay (1958) 110–112.

251 Lisowsky, 1395–1398, lists שָׁבִיתָ (21:10), שְׁבִי (21:10, 13; 28:41) and שִׁבְיָה (21:11; 32:42).

252 Compare McConville (1992) 75. Driver, 329, argues that regardless of its derivation, the expression refers to "a decisive *turn*, or change, in a people's fortune." Also Mayes (1979) 369.

In vv1c, 2a, in a protasis, Israel is the subject. In the apodosis (vv3a, c), it is Yahweh. The use of שׁוב with both serves to link Yahweh's action to Israel's "turning". A similar relationship exists between v10b, a protasis, with Israel as subject, and v9b, the apodosis with Yahweh as subject. The most significant occurrence is v8a, in the central section, an unconditional statement with Israel as subject. The verb שׁוב is therefore used, with various nuances, to tie together this section and, in particular, the action of Yahweh with the action of Israel. The task in this paper is to determine the precise connection between Yahweh's action and Israel's turning. Whatever that precise relationship happens to be, that Israel and Yahweh are each the subject of the verb shows that both human responsibility and divine action fit together. It is not a case of either/or.[253]

The conditional statements of Israel's return in vv1, 2, 10 must be considered in the light of the unconditional statement in v8. Verse 8 indicates that "the return is plainly part of the promise. The presupposition in 4:30f. as in 30:2f. is Yahweh's watchful compassion".[254] Similarly, "daß die volle Umkehr Israels erst nach YHWHs Zuwendung möglich ist".[255] Wolff suggests that the conditional nature of vv1, 2 is because of the imminence of Yahweh's compassion breaking through. The fundamental character of the call to return is promise or kerygma.[256] Sklba makes much the same point, namely,

> conversion is in fact promised as a gracious gift of Yahweh, both the spiritual reality of the renewed relationship and the geographical transposition back to the land of promise.[257]

We shall explore further below the nature of the condition when we discuss the sense of כִּי. We shall later also discuss how to read the conditional statements of vv1, 2, 10 in the light of the promise in v8. At this point we are raising the issue created by the tension between conditional and unconditional statements regarding Israel's return. We shall argue below that the resolution lies in v6.

The priority of Yahweh's action is also supported by the stress in vv3, 4 on Yahweh gathering (קָבַץ) Israel. It is not that Israel has to return all the

---

253 Joyce, 33–77, discusses the same issue in Ezekiel. He argues, 50–51, that an emphasis on human responsibility implies the possibility of repentance and that Ezekiel is attempting to move the people to admit their responsibility. Thus the call to repent both underlines Israel's responsibility, 60, and offers just a hint of hope, 70.

254 Wolff (1982) 98. Wolff only considers the occurrences of שׁוב with Israel as the subject. Olson (1994) 36, "This new hopeful finding and returning to God is not grounded in the people's character and activity but in the character and activity of God".

255 Vanoni, 90. He also notes רִחֲמֶךָ in v3b.

256 Wolff's thesis is that "return" is the kerygma of DtrH. Compare Diepold, 147–150.

257 Sklba, 72.

way to Yahweh or the land. Rather Yahweh goes to gather his people and bring (בּוֹא hiphil, v5) them back to the land. Indeed Yahweh's action is highlighted by the reference to the extent to which he will go: מִכָּל־הָעַמִּים (v3) and אִם־יִהְיֶה נִדַּחֲךָ בִּקְצֵה הַשָּׁמָיִם (v4) with the repeated מִשָּׁם.[258] Physically then, Israel's return is dependent on the initiative of Yahweh.

> Wo der Terminus שׁוּב in 4,30 und 30,1–10 die Bekehrung Israels bezeichnet, ist sie eine Frucht göttlicher Begnadigung vor allem Gesetzesgehorsam.[259]

Human responsibility and co-operation on the part of Israel are not abrogated by the priority on Yahweh here, for Israel's return is largely synonymous with its hearing Yahweh's voice. The two expressions stand in parallel in v2 and, in reverse order, in v10, with the prepositional phrase בְּכָל־לְבָבְךָ וּבְכָל־נַפְשֶׁךָ interchanged. The two expressions are also paralleled in v8, though without any prepositional qualifying phrase. This linking of the two verbs and the interchangeability of the prepositional phrase suggests closeness of meaning. To return to Yahweh is, in effect, to obey his voice.[260] Repentance necessitates obedience. Both remain Israel's responsibility.[261] It is important here to distinguish between grounds and responsibility. The grounds of this return lie with Yahweh, not Israel. In this passage this is expressed primarily in Yahweh circumcising the heart. That is the grounds which makes possible Israel's response. Yet it is Israel's responsibility to co-operate for this return to be effective.[262] Thus there is a sense in which return and restoration do depend on Israel's repentance and obedience though the ultimate grounds lie with Yahweh and his grace. There is a fine balance between these two which underlies much of this section.[263] The dilemma between human responsibility and divine grace may be put thus:

---

258 Braulik (1982) 157; Vanoni, 75. Kalland, 187, says that the particle אִם "is often used to make a very strong assertion."

259 Braulik (1989) 321.

260 Schenker, 98, "Umkehren heißt für *Israel*, sich der Tora des Sinai zu beugen (*V, 2, 8*: umkehren und auf JHWHs Stimme hören stehen *parallel*)". Also Wolff (1982) 98, "In Deuteronomy 4:30 and 30:2, 8, 10 'turning back' and 'listening to the voice of Yahweh' have become an indissoluble combination"; Braulik (1982) 152–153.

261 Compare Braulik (1989) 325–327, who argues that where Israel is in exile, the commandments do not apply. Hence the turning of Israel cannot be grounded in its obedience. He suggests that this is an initial exilic point of view which was slack in respect to the law. Another redactor, DtrN, corrects this exilic slackness. This Nomistic redactor acknowledges the inability of Israel to keep the law without Yahweh preceding and accompanying it.

262 Compare Schenker, 98–99, for whom the initiative and grounds lie with Israel.

263 Goldingay (1987) 145, advocates that Deuteronomy is ambivalent about whether the relationship between Yahweh and Israel is ultimately dependent on Yahweh or on Israel's repentance and obedience. He suggests that this tension is found within

how may a new act of redemption, conceived as an answer to the people's earlier persistent inability to maintain covenant faithfulness, both overcome the problem thus posed by the failure of the human will and preserve the reality of human responsibility?[264]

To summarise thus far, שׁוּב is the only significant word, apart from Yahweh, which occurs in each of the five sections of 30:1–10. In the central section, vv6–8, שׁוּב occurs in an unconditional statement which, we will argue below, is part of a promise of Yahweh. What this hints at is that the priority, even initiative, for return is the action of Yahweh and not Israel.

### וְהָיָה כִי־יָבֹאוּ עָלֶיךָ כָּל־הַדְּבָרִים הָאֵלֶּה

Another indication of the priority of Yahweh is found in v1a. At first sight, Israel's return to Yahweh in vv1, 2 appears to be the condition for Yahweh's return to Israel. This is suggested by the syntax of vv1, 2 as protasis. However Israel is not the subject of the first verb in the protasis in v1a. It is the object. The subject is כָּל־הַדְּבָרִים הָאֵלֶּה הַבְּרָכָה וְהַקְּלָלָה. This refers back at least to 28:1–68.[265] Thus the prompt for Israel's return is Yahweh's words which come upon Israel. "Genaugenommen geben »diese Worte«...den Anstoß zur Reflexion." Braulik goes on to say, that this "Öffnung für Gott, ist vermittelt durch Gottes Wort, das den Glauben erst ermöglicht."[266] This is much the same as in the closely related passage, 4:29–31, where Yahweh's compassion is the presupposition for his action.[267] So it fair to say for both passages:

> Nicht Israel wird Jahwe finden, sondern Jahwes Worte werden Israel finden. Israel muß nicht umkehren, damit Jahwe sich ihm wieder zuwen-

---

30:1–10 and that "one should not try to resolve" it. The relationship between Yahweh and Israel begins with Yahweh's initiative, needs Israel's response but that response is inspired by Yahweh and yet remains Israel's own response. The two poles of Yahweh's initiative and Israel's response will come into focus in varying degrees at different places.

264 McConville (1993a) 175. The question applies equally as well here as to Jeremiah 30–33.

265 Driver, 328; Wolff (1982) 94; Skweres, 70. Compare Blank, 79, who sees a reference between 30:1 and 29:26. See Braulik (1989) 331.

266 Braulik (1982) 156. He qualifies his remarks by saying of Israel, "Der von Gott Getrennte kann sich zwar für den Empfang der Bekehrungsgnade disponieren – konkret: das von Jahwe abgefallene Israel kann sich auf die von Gott bewirkte Bekehrung vorbereiten". Similarly Merrill, 387. Whilst Schenker, 100, acknowledges that Israel's return will be "unter dem Eindruck der eingetroffenen Flüche", he fails to observe that the initiative for this lies with Yahweh. See Braulik's response to Schenker, (1982) 156.

267 So 4:30: מְצָאוּךָ כֹּל הַדְּבָרִים הָאֵלֶּה. Like 30:1–2, 4:29–31 also mentions בְּכָל־לְבָבְךָ וּבְכָל־נַפְשֶׁךָ (v29), שַׁבְתָּ עַד־יְהוָה אֱלֹהֶיךָ וְשָׁמַעְתָּ בְּקֹלוֹ (v30) and רַחוּם (v31). See Braulik (1982) 154–155.

det, sondern wenn Jahwes Worte Israel finden, dann wird Israel die Gnade der Umkehr gewährt werden.[268]

Thus the final grounds of Israel's return belong to Yahweh, rather than Israel's own ability.

The character and function of כָּל־הַדְּבָרִים הָאֵלֶּה need clarifying. These words may refer to the law and urge obedience to it.[269] However in their function as prompting Israel to return to Yahweh, they are disciplinary, bringing Israel back to Yahweh. In this they act as "das »Evangelium« für ein schuldig gewordenes Volk".[270] The words, then, are not fundamentally a demand for obedience to the law. כָּל־הַדְּבָרִים הָאֵלֶּה prompt repentance and are Yahweh's means of effecting a reconciled relationship with his people. In a sense they are a call to rely on Yahweh's enabling grace. They are an invitation to and promise of conversion.[271] "In this passage, the gospel of God's pursuing, redemptive, empowering love is eloquently set forth."[272]

Ultimately Israel's return to Yahweh depends on Yahweh. The close connection between שׁוּב with Yahweh as its subject and שׁוּב with Israel as its subject is not a simple conditional relationship. The priority of Yahweh's action is reflected in the movement of his words to come over Israel, prompting and inviting repentance and obedience. Israel's return is a response to Yahweh's word and not a free act of its own independent volition. Thus the immediate context of vv1, 2 makes it clear that a purely conditional reading of v2 is inappropriate.

29:28

The wider context also makes such a reading inappropriate. This wider context is supplied by the connection between 29:28 and 30:1. We noted above the tendency to see 29:28 in isolation. We also noted the approaches which link 29:28 with 30:11–14 as a frame for 30:1–10. Now we note the link between 29:28 and 30:1 provided by the common word דְּבָרִים.[273] In 29:28, דְּבָרִים is in construct with הַתּוֹרָה. Though not the case in 30:1, we

268 Lohfink (1965) 113.

269 Schenker, 96–97.

270 Braulik (1982) 155. Braulik (1984) 11, objects to Schenker's view, saying it implies "Israel can once again shift itself, by means of conversion, into the proper relationship with God, thereby justifying itself." On the use of perhaps anachronistic theological language, see Braulik (1989) 332–333.

271 Braulik (1982) 153, understands שׁוּב in 4:30 and 30:1–10 in its religious sense, meaning conversion. Also Christensen (1991) 95. This argument ties in with our interpretation of 30:15–20 below.

272 Blair (1964) 74.

273 Vanoni, 70, notes this common word as "bewußt anknüpfend". He also notes other common vocabulary between 29:21–28 and 30:1–10. Wolff (1982) 100, comments that 29:28 functions to introduce 30:1–10.

note the common purpose between 29:28 and 30:1–10 and the repetition of תּוֹרָה in 30:10.[274] In 29:28, the revealed things are for doing the words of the law. The same verb, עָשָׂה, occurs in 30:8. So, 29:28 leads into 30:1–14, and indeed connects it with 29:21–27.[275]

We have already seen that the purpose of כָּל־הַדְּבָרִים הָאֵלֶּה in 30:1 is disciplinary, to lead to obedience. The revealed things are דִּבְרֵי הַתּוֹרָה הַזֹּאת which comprise the curse and the blessing. The purpose of תּוֹרָה is obedience but, as we have argued above, here this has a grace or gospel sense rather than a legalistic sense. "This revealed word now contains the summons to return".[276] The theological significance of seeing the connection between 29:28 and 30:1 is the emphasis given in 29:28 to revelation. The initiative clearly comes from Yahweh. He has revealed or given all that is needed for obedience. The נִגְלֹת underline the fact that Israel's return is not entirely its own effort or volition but is prompted and initiated by Yahweh.

## THE SEQUENCE OF CURSE–BLESSING

The wider context of curse and blessing also indicates that a purely conditional reading of v2 is inappropriate since it shows an expectation that Israel is unable to keep the covenant. In 11:26–32 and 28:1–69, the curses and blessings are held out as "alternative possibilities dependent on disobedience or obedience".[277] However in chapters 29 and 30, these conditional curses and blessings have become "future facts".[278] The significance of this shift is that Deuteronomy

> takes for granted that the people will indeed fail to be the true people of the covenant and that this will result in the full force of the curses of ch. 28 falling on them.[279]

The blessing is now not an alternative but a period in Israel's history successive to the inevitable curse.[280] Blessing will only arise out of, and after, the curses. This sequential outlook has a prophetic, rather than hortatory, style, deriving from Moses' experiences of the past and his notion of the potential future.[281]

---

274 Vanoni, 70, notes that 29:28 connects the expressions הַכְּתוּבָה בַּסֵּפֶר הַזֶּה in 29:26 with הַכְּתוּבָה בְּסֵפֶר הַתּוֹרָה הַזֶּה in 30:10 since 30:10 extends the notion of 29:26 by including the notion of תּוֹרָה from 29:28. See also Köckert, 497.

275 Lohfink (1962) 41; Wolff (1982) 100.

276 Wolff (1982) 100.

277 Mayes (1979) 368.

278 McCarthy (1981) 201, also notes parallels in Assyrian texts. See Driver, 326; Braulik (1992) 215; von Rad (1966e) 180; Thompson, 283; Schenker, 98.

279 McConville (1993b) 135.

280 Mayes (1979) 368.

281 Craigie (1976) 364. See also von Rad (1966e) 183; Blair (1964) 74; Kalland, 187. Jacobs, 109, notes that there remains a persuasiveness about 30:1–10 as a call to

That curse is now regarded as inevitable is not surprising. The bulk of chapter 28 is curse, possibly suggesting that Israel will in fact fail.[282] Indeed the syntax of 28:45–48 suggests not just a conditional possibility but "a declared state of fact that will happen in the narrated future".[283] Further, the placing of the plastered stones with the law on them on Mount Ebal, the mount of curse, indicates that Israel will inevitably fail for the law exposes Israel's sin and brings it under a curse.[284] Thus the inevitability of curse is not incompatible with chapters 27 and 28.

The above needs to be qualified with the observation that the perspective of 30:1–10 is of a sequence of blessing-curse-blessing. 30:1 notes that both blessing and curse will come upon Israel, in that order, before the final blessing of restoration.[285] This, perhaps, is an acknowledgement that Israel may initially but temporarily obey Yahweh but the lasting, deep obedience discussed above, is absent.[286] Curses will inevitably follow. The muted optimism for some qualified obedience is overshadowed by the pessimism expecting the curses.

As the change from condition to certainty underscores Israel's inevitable failure, so too the sequence of curse-blessing underscores the certainty of Yahweh's grace. As the curse is now shown to be inevitable, so too is the blessing which is a deliberate reversal of the curses in chapter 28.[287] The curse is inevitable because of Israel's inability; the blessing because of Yahweh's promise.

---

repent. Certainly 30:1–10 is not a detached statement of the future. It impinges on the present, as with any prophetic statement.

282 Goldingay (1987) 155. However the preponderance of curse to blessing is common to many ANE treaties, though McCarthy (1981) 173, notes this is not the case with Hittite treaties. See Noth (1966) 122–126; Olson (1994) 119–120.

283 Olson (1994) 122–123; McCarthy (1981) 178. McEvenue (1990) 144, argues that the syntax changes from conditional to certain at v47.

284 Olson (1994) 117; Ridderbos, 249.

285 This point is not commonly observed, though see Driver, 329; Jacobs, 98.

286 McConville (1993b) 136, suggests that this sequence of blessing-curse sheds light on David and Solomon whose reigns were characterised by such a sequence.

287 Cairns, 263, notes the curses of chapter 28 reverse the blessings of the same chapter. Thus "the blessings of 30:3–5 in their turn constitute a reversal of those reversals". See Buis and Leclerq, 185, for details of links between 30:1–10 and chapter 28. Similarly Wolff (1982) 94–95; Vanoni, 82–90; Craigie (1976) 363; Skweres, 70–71; Driver, 330; Jacobs, 98, 106–107. Vanoni and Wolff (1982) 94–95, argue for a closer relationship between 30:1–10 and 28:45–69 which they regard as the later section of chapter 28. Rofé (1985a) 311–312; Mayes (1979) 369; McCarthy (1981) 137, note that 30:1–10 also reverses the curses of 29:20–27.

### כִּי

We have argued that the conditional statements in vv1, 2 should not be read as pure conditions. We turn now to consider the precise nature of the conditional statements in 30:1–10. The particle כִּי occurs in vv1a, 10a, 10b.[288] In each case it is better to understand כִּי temporally rather than conditionally. Usually commentators translate the particle in v1a temporally ("when")[289] but those in v10 conditionally ("if").[290] It is better to be consistent and translate all three as temporal.

It is frequently difficult to decide between the two senses for a particular כִּי clause.[291] In part, any decision will be subjective.

> The border line between conditional and temporal is, however, extremely vague – particularly in cases referring to the future.... A temporal interpretation and the rendering 'when' would seem appropriate, when our understanding of the context suggests a higher probability that the contents of the כי clause will actually occur.[292]

Verse 1a has a high degree of probability about it. The curses, as shown above, will now definitely come upon Israel. They are no longer just a possibility. The sequence blessing-curse-blessing has made this clear. Further, v1a begins וְהָיָה כִּי, a combination found in 6:10; 11:29; 15:16; 26:1 and 31:21, all temporal statements.[293] All but one of these speaks of an obviously certain event. 6:10; 11:29 and 26:1 refer to the entry into the land in definite terms; 31:21 refers to coming disasters. The context of 15:16

---

288 כִּי with causal function in v9b does not concern us here.

289 So Craigie (1976) 361; Ridderbos, 271; Driver, 328 (though he concedes some doubt); von Rad (1966e) 182; Merrill, 386.

290 So Craigie (1976) 362; Ridderbos, 271; von Rad (1966e) 182; Merrill, 386. Driver, 330; Miller (1990) 213, both translate v10 temporally.

291 Joüon (1991) 621; Waltke and O'Connor, 637; Schoors, 269. Compare Braulik (1992) 216, "Die Wenn-Formulierungen (die für verschiedene, aber ebenso schillernde hebräische Wörter stehen) können nicht eindeutig auf konditionalen oder temporalen Sinn festgelegt werden (einmal legt sich sogar konzessiver Sinn nahe). Die sprachliche Schwebelage scheint beabsichtigt zu sein."

292 Aejmelaeus, 197. The context of these comments is כִּי clauses which precede their main clauses (196). Similarly Schoors, 269.

293 See Lambdin, 123. Aejmelaeus, 198, comments that וְהָיָה כִּי is the general rule in narration in the Pentateuch and could be conditional or temporal. Schoors, 268–269, lists 6:10 and 31:21 as temporal but notes that generally the construction could be either temporal or conditional. Diepold, 92–93, argues that for a majority of cases, כִּי in the context of land is temporal but that, given the assumed reality of Israel already in the land, the sense becomes conditional.

suggests this clause could be either conditional or temporal.[294] The context and syntax of 30:1a both suggest a definite future event.[295]

In verse 10, the repeated כִּי governs שָׁמַע בְּקֹל and שׁוּב. Both these verbs were also governed by כִּי in vv1–2. Given the concentric structure of vv1–10, which associates v10 with vv1–2, where the temporal sense is clear, it thus makes more sense to understand the two parts in like manner, that is temporally. The context of vv1–2 thus determines the sense of v10. Apart from וְהָיָה כִּי, elsewhere in Deuteronomy there are clear examples of temporal כִּי: 4:25; 7:1; 12:20, 29; 17:14; 18:9; 19:1; 20:1, 10, 19; 21:10; 26:12; 31:20; 32:36.[296] Many of these refer to events such as land possession and war. So כִּי need not be purely conditional.[297] Joüon, in fact, seems to indicate that כִּי is more often than not temporal, rather than conditional.[298] We conclude that the syntax of 30:10 could just as easily fit a real conditional sense as a temporal sense, but that the context of v10, in its relationship to vv1–2, demands a temporal and not conditional sense.[299]

A different possibility is that each כִּי in v10 introduces a further *Begründungssatz* in support of v9a. The parallels between vv9b, 10b also suggest this.[300] We have already noted that כִּי in v9b is causal. Aejmelaeus argues that the position of the כִּי clause in relation to the main clause is an important factor for distinguishing function.[301] כִּי clauses following the main clause, as in vv9–10, are predominantly causal rather than circum-

---

294 Schoors, 270–271, lists this verse as conditional.

295 Merrill, 387, on 30:1, says, "The grammatical pattern suggests a lack of any true conditionality here" and "the conditional clauses of vv. 1–6 require a nuance not of contingency but of time".

296 כִּי occurs 275 times in Deuteronomy. The majority of these, over 150, introduce a motivation or are translated as "for", "because" or "since"; 33 introduce nominal clauses; over 50 are in casuistic laws, translated usually "if" though "when" is often a possibility here. כִּי occurs in combination with other particles about a dozen times. This leaves 28 times where כִּי could be translated "when". See Aejmelaeus, 207; Lohfink (1963a) 114.

297 Compare Merrill, 389, who states, without explanation, that syntactically, the dependent clause in v10 "is highly conditional". He refers to Williams, 86, and Craigie (1976) 364, though Craigie does not argue for the verse being "highly conditional". See further Williams, 72, §446; Lambdin, 277; compare Waltke and O'Connor, 638.

298 Joüon (1991) 627.

299 On the significance of a preceding וְהָיָה or וַיְהִי, see Williams, 72; Joüon (1991) 627. Contrast BDB, 473; Waltke and O'Connor, 643. Joüon (1991) 627, suggests that in Late Biblical Hebrew, the introductory וְהָיָה or וַיְהִי is frequently omitted.

300 Vanoni, 75. He suggests that כִּי יָשׁוּב יְהוָה in v9b parallels כִּי תָשׁוּב אֶל־יְהוָה in v10b.

301 Aejmelaeus, 196.

stantial.[302] Having said that, Aejmelaeus then goes on to say that the exception to this rule is Deuteronomy.

> Otherwise, it is only in Deuteronomy that כי is found introducing a condition after the main clause, and these are always to be found in the same type of context, Israel's obedience as a condition for promises concerning the future.[303]

Her argument fails to consider that the order of clauses in vv9, 10 may be to balance chiastically vv1–3. Less weight should therefore be given to the order of main and subordinate clauses. All things considered, we consider that the links between vv1, 2 and 10 render a temporal reading most appropriate. This is also appropriate in light of our discussion below about the centrality of the circumcision of the heart by Yahweh which enables Israel's return and obedience. Therefore, unlike most scholars, we prefer to read v10 as "when Israel..." rather than "if Israel...". We also note there is no formal distinction in Hebrew between temporal and causal clauses. The certainty of Israel's return means that v10b could also carry a sense of causality. This is similar to Braulik who argues that כִּי in vv10, 11 should be translated by "denn", rather than "wenn". He regards all the clauses as parallel *Begründungssätze*.[304]

The effect of this reading is that the so-called conditional nature of vv1, 2, 10 is best understood temporally and causally. Future hope is definite in 30:1–10, resting as it ultimately does on Yahweh and not Israel. Verses 1, 2, 10 do not detract from that confidence.

### בּוֹא

One further indication of the priority of Yahweh's grace in 30:1–10 is the occurrence of בּוֹא in v5a. Here, בּוֹא occurs as a hiphil with Yahweh as its subject and אֶל־הָאָרֶץ as its prepositional object. Every other occurrence of this combination in Deuteronomy is either in a conditional clause, expressing obligation through an imperative, or in a negative clause.[305] Here, however, it occurs in an independent clause. This is unique in the book, even though בּוֹא is such a common word.[306] 30:1–10 uses common Deuteronomic language but in a markedly different way. The avoidance of

302 Aejmelaeus, 199. The term "causal" is used broadly to cover nuances such as cause, reason, motivation and explanation. See Claassen, 29–46.

303 Aejmelaeus, 207–208. She includes 30:10 as an example. See also Lambdin, 276–279; Waltke and O'Connor, 636–638.

304 Braulik (1992) 216–217.

305 Vanoni, 90–91. Occurring in כִּי clauses: 6:10; 7:1; 8:7; 11:29. He does not list 31:20, 23. The negative clauses are 9:28; 31:21. Other hiphils of בּוֹא with Yahweh as the subject in the general context of giving the land are 4:38; 6:23; 9:4; 26:9. On the avoidance of imperatives in 30:1–10, see Braulik (1989) 331.

306 Also noted by Köckert, 517; Braulik (1982) 157. בּוֹא occurs 83 times in qal and 22 in hiphil. Lisowsky, 181–202.

בּוֹא in qal with Israel as the subject, and the lack of condition attached to its use in v5a, highlights the nature of the land as a gift and that a successful return is the work of Yahweh, not Israel.[307] Even without the different syntax of v5a, occurrences in Deuteronomy of בּוֹא in the hiphil with Yahweh as subject already stress the "theme of Yahweh's agency in Israel's progress".[308] So, "Dabei betont בּוֹא Hif. den reinen Geschenkcharakter der Landgabe".[309] We conclude that the use of בּוֹא in the hiphil with Yahweh as subject in v5a adds weight to the thesis of Israel's clear dependence on Yahweh for its return and restoration.

## *The Heart*

Having argued for the priority of Yahweh's action in restoring Israel, we turn now to the issue of how Yahweh deals with Israel's faithlessness. We noted above in our discussion about the structure of 30:1–10 that לֵבָב is the decisive word for determining that vv6–8 comprise the central section and not just v8. לֵבָב is what unites the action of Yahweh with the action of Israel throughout all of vv1–10. The resolution to the tension between Israel's faithlessness and Yahweh's faithfulness is found here.

Apart from שׁוּב, לֵבָב is the other key word in 30:1–10, occurring six times, in vv1c, 2b, 6 (three times), 10b. In vv2b, 6b, 10b, it occurs in the expression בְּכָל־לְבָבְךָ וּבְכָל־נַפְשֶׁךָ.[310] The three occurrences outside v6 all occur in AA' in the protases of conditional sentences. This word is so crucial, we will firstly discuss its importance in Deuteronomy generally, before looking at its occurrences in vv1, 2, 10 and, finally, in v6.

### לֵבָב IN DEUTERONOMY

Deuteronomy is an appeal to the heart, from which both sin and obedience derive.[311] Important though the preaching of the law and the demands for obedience are, the goal of Deuteronomy is the transfer of that law into the heart.[312] In Deuteronomy, לֵבָב occurs "in almost every case in contexts which the writer evidently intended to be emphatic".[313] Certainly לֵבָב is a

---

307 Vanoni, 91.

308 McConville (1984) 33–34. This is also the case with the occurrences of בּוֹא in qal with Israel as subject, especially in collocation with יָרַשׁ, a verb which occurs in v5. Occurrences of בּוֹא in qal with Israel as subject are often coupled with יָרַשׁ especially in chapters 1–11.

309 Köckert, 517.

310 Also 4:29; 6:5; 10:12; 26:16 (singular); 11:13; 13:4 (plural).

311 Von Rad (1962a) 225, "It is in the heart and the understanding that Israel's belonging to Jahweh comes about." Also Eichrodt (1967) 149; McConville (1993b) 155. See the note on לֵבָב and לֵב in the previous chapter.

312 Stek, 37.

313 Toombs, 401.

most important word in the theology of Deuteronomy and the most important in Hebrew anthropology.[314] It has a variety of senses. The word can refer to the physical organ. Metaphorically it can refer to the emotions. More common than either of these is its reference to the rational faculties.[315] Especially in Deuteronomy, the heart is the locus of moral response.[316]

On a number of occasions, לֵבָב is the subject of verbs which express, either positively or negatively, relationship to Yahweh. So, for example, the heart is the subject of יָרֵא and שָׁמַר in 5:26 where Yahweh expresses his desire that Israel's heart would constantly be right.[317] There are warnings against Israel's heart becoming proud (רוּם, 8:14) and deceptive (פָּתָה, 11:16), both of which result in disobedience and lack of faith.[318] In 15:7–10, לֵבָב occurs three times, once as the subject of רָעַע, in a context which makes plain that the right response to Yahweh is not a superficial obedience but an obedience which derives from the heart. In 17:17, the king's לֵבָב is the subject of סוּר in the context of turning from Yahweh. A similar sense is behind 29:17 and 30:17 where לֵבָב is the subject of פָּנָה with all Israel in mind. In 29:17 the object is מֵעִם Yahweh. No object is specified in 30:17.[319] לֵבָב is also the subject of רָכַךְ (20:3, 8). In all these cases, the action of the heart represents a response to Yahweh.

The heart is also the object of various verbs in Deuteronomy. These include מָסַס (1:28), the effect of which is to bring disobedience and lack of trust (1:29–32), as also in 20:8; אָמַץ (piel, 2:30; 15:7), where the result in each case is opposition to God; and נָתַן (28:65; 29:3) with Yahweh as the subject.

לֵבָב is also an indirect object. With בְּ it is the object of אָמַר (7:17; 8:17; 9:4; 18:21). In the first two of these Israel is permitted to say something in its heart but a warning follows about remembering and not forgetting Yahweh. In 9:4 there is a prohibition against self-righteousness being said in the heart. In 18:21 a question is allowed to be said in the heart. Of these four occurrences, the first three are concerned with an appropriate response to Yahweh. We have noted above the hithpael of בָּרַךְ plus בְּ in connection with Israel's sin (29:18). With בְּכֹל, לֵבָב is the object of אָהַב (6:5; 13:4; 30:6); דָּרַשׁ (4:29); עָבַד (10:12; 11:13); עָשָׂה (26:16); שָׁמַע (30:2); and שׁוּב (30:10). These are all key verbs in Deuteronomy, specifying the most important terms of response to Yahweh. With all of these verbs, the

314 Wolff (1974a) 40. Also Dhorme, 489–508.

315 BDB, 523–525; Dhorme, 502–507; Joyce, 108.

316 Joyce, 120.

317 5:26 suggests that Israel will not always have such a heart.

318 On the idiom in 11:16, see Driver, 131; Weinfeld (1991) 447; Craigie (1976) 210.

319 סוּר and פָּנָה are important verbs in Deuteronomy occurring 15 and 16 times respectively. Also in 4:9, לֵבָב is the indirect object of סוּר (with מִן).

repeated expression, בְּכׇל־לְבָבְךָ וּבְכׇל־נַפְשְׁךָ, underlines the importance of the heart in responding to Yahweh. Deuteronomy emphasises that the heart is the seat of Israel's response to Yahweh, whether that response is correct or not.

Deuteronomy mentions a number of influencing factors on the heart. For good, these include the things Israel has seen (4:9), the commandments (6:6), the experience of the wilderness (8:5), circumcision (10:16; 30:6), "these words" (11:18; 32:46), care (15:9), reading the law (17:19–20), decrees and laws (26:16), the words of blessing and curse (30:1), the word (30:14). In a number of these, teaching is a significant influence (4:9; 6:6; 11:18–9; 32:46). Also Yahweh acts on the heart (29:3; 30:6). For evil, they include the words of others which cause fear (1:28), forgetfulness (8:14), lack of care (11:16), a king's many wives (17:17), the faint-heartedness of others (20:8), the lure of idols (29:17, 18; 30:17), as well as the action of Yahweh in judgment (2:30; 28:28, 65).

The condition of the heart, therefore, is the determinative factor for Israel's response to Yahweh. This is perhaps best expressed in 8:2, where the purpose of the wilderness experience was that Yahweh might לְנַסֹּתְךָ לָדַעַת אֶת־אֲשֶׁר בִּלְבָבְךָ, that is, הֲתִשְׁמֹר מִצְוֺתוֹ אִם־לֹא.[320] The heart is that which reveals the basic condition of the person, indeed the nation. Thus far we have found Israel to be lacking a right heart. Now, at the climax of the book, Yahweh addresses the problem.

### לֵבָב IN 30:1, 2, 10

We turn now to the occurrences of לֵבָב in 30:1–10. Before looking at those in v6, we consider those in vv1, 2, 10. In v1c, לֵבָב occurs in the expression וַהֲשֵׁבֹתָ אֶל־לְבָבֶךָ meaning "bring back (to one's heart that)" or "recall". In v2, לֵבָב occurs in the phrase, בְּכׇל־לְבָבְךָ וּבְכׇל־נַפְשֶׁךָ qualifying שָׁמַעְתָּ בְקֹלוֹ. The repetition of לֵבָב in vv1, 2 underlines the link between כׇּל־הַדְּבָרִים הָאֵלֶּה and Israel's obedience. Israel's obedience with all its heart (v2) derives from Yahweh's words being taken to heart (v1).[321] Thus there is a two-way movement. Yahweh's words penetrate into Israel's heart; out of Israel's heart will come obedience. In v10b, the same phrase, בְּכׇל־לְבָבְךָ וּבְכׇל־נַפְשֶׁךָ occurs, this time qualifying שׁוּב. We have already noted above the interchangeability of שׁוּב and שָׁמַע בְּקוֹל. In v10 the order of the two verbs is reversed from v2. The same two verbs occur in v8 where they are the result of the circumcision of the heart in v6. This interchangeability suggests that as with שָׁמַע בְּקוֹל, so also שׁוּב is effected by Yahweh's words penetrating Israel's heart. This confirms our argument above about

---

320 See also 13:4.

321 The importance of Yahweh's words is also suggested by the relative clause in v2: כְּכֹל אֲשֶׁר־אָנֹכִי מְצַוְּךָ הַיּוֹם. Also Lohfink (1962) 41, "Das Volk kehrt um und hört auf Jahwes Stimme entsprechend dem Gebot Moses".

the priority of Yahweh. Both Israel's obedience and its return must stem from the heart.

Thus we suggest again that 30:1, 2, 10 rests ultimately on Yahweh's words and not on Israel's ability and volition. As mentioned above, these are not simple conditional statements: If Israel...then Yahweh. The occurrences of לֵבָב in v6 show more clearly how Yahweh's words penetrate the heart to effect return and obedience.

### לְאַהֲבָה בְּכָל־לְבָבְךָ

The third of the three occurrences of לֵבָב in v6 is, like vv2, 10, in the prepositional phrase בְּכָל־לְבָבְךָ וּבְכָל־נַפְשְׁךָ. As in those verses, the sense of לֵבָב is clearly that of the seat of moral response. On this occasion, the verb it qualifies is אָהַב, as in 6:5 and 13:4. It is commonly recognised that Deuteronomy has a stock of key verbs to denote the basic response of Israel to Yahweh. These include יָרֵא, אָהַב, דָּבַק, עָבַד, עָשָׂה, שָׁמַר and שָׁמַע. There is obviously some synonymity and overlapping senses with these verbs in Deuteronomy.[322] Often they seem interchangeable. The various, and different, lists of some of these verbs in Deuteronomy is probably a rhetorical device so that the use of one or more of the words is intended to imply all the others as a "total package" denoting Israel's comprehensive response to Yahweh.

Perhaps אָהַב is the most important of all these verbs. It is the only one qualified by this prepositional phrase three times. It is the most recurrent demand in Deuteronomy, both to God and others,[323] yet outside Deuteronomy, the injunction to love God is rare.[324] It is the verb highlighted in 6:4, 5, the Shema, which is so important as the centrepiece of Deuteronomy's concern.[325] Probably significantly, it is the central term in the important summary in 10:12, 13.[326] It occurs three times in chapter 30, which is the rhetorical climax of the book. It is a verb which is used with Yahweh as subject and Israel as object as well as vice versa,[327] showing that Israel's response to Yahweh is a response in kind.[328] Yahweh's love for

---

322 Compare Lohfink (1982b) 49; Lyonnet, 93, "expressions practiquement équivalentes".

323 Myers, 29, notes, "The term 'love' occurs more frequently in Deuteronomy than in any other book of the Old Testament". Also Toombs, 402; Rennes, 247.

324 Willoughby, 80, suggests thirteen passages; Bamberger, 53, lists eleven.

325 Köckert, 502–503; Zobel, 52–54. Merrill, 389, argues that 30:6 refers back to the Shema.

326 See p103 above on 10:12–13.

327 With Yahweh as subject and Israel as object: 4:37; 7:8, 13; 10:15; 23:6; with Israel as subject and Yahweh as object: 6:5; 10:12; 11:1, 13, 22; 13:4; 19:9; 30:6, 16, 20. Lisowsky, 28–30. Compare שָׁמַר, Lohfink (1963a) 170.

328 McBride(1973) 299. Similarly Lohfink (1982b) 51; Wiéner, 40; Rennes, 197; Toombs, 402. Compare L'Hour, 38–40, 43–45. Zobel, 76; Amsler, 16–17, make the

Israel is tied to his election of Israel through the covenant. Israel's response of love is also covenantal. For Israel to love Yahweh is to accept his covenantal love.[329]

Love is commonly understood as the supreme ethic, "the fundamental motive of human action".[330] Alternatively there are those for whom love is understood purely as an emotion, "an inner response of affection and gladness".[331] The problem with this is that love, unlike a pure emotion, is commanded. Thus it is better to understand the character of love in Deuteronomy as "love which is seen in reverential fear, in loyalty and in obedience",[332] denoting both attitude as well as action. This demand to love is a covenant term denoting the obligation on a vassal to show steadfastness to his suzerain.[333] So love is

> the zealous allegiance to Yahweh's exclusive, divine kingship which underlies the manifold decrees, statutes and ordinances of the Deuteronomic torah.[334]

Thus it is the verb which best of all sums up the demands made on Israel in Deuteronomy.[335] As such it makes clear that Israel's response to Yahweh

---

observation that love for God is never motivated in Deuteronomy with mention of the love of God.

329 Merrill, 75–76. On the contrast with love in Hosea, see Andersen and Freedman, 576. Moran (1963b) 78–81, notes that love in Deuteronomy does not occur within the context of the Father–Son relationship nor in the context of a marriage relationship between Yahweh and his people. Compare McCarthy (1965) 144–147, that "the picture of the father–son relationship as applied to Yahweh and Israel corresponds to the Deuteronomic definition of covenant love". Similarly McKay, 433. See further Zobel, 51–87; McCurley, 299; Wiéner, 39–40; Schmid, 8; Rennes, 195.

330 Driver, 91. Similarly Nicholson (1967) 46; Clements (1968) 82.

331 Cunliffe-Jones, 60. Similarly von Rad (1966e) 63; Eichrodt (1961) 91. Thomas, 57–64, suggests that the root of the verb originally meant something to do with breathing and emotions.

332 McCarthy (1965) 145; Moran (1963b), 78; McCurley, 299. McKay (1972) 426–435, quite simply equates love with obedience. Zobel, 61–64, says the relationship between love and obedience is made explicit in 11:13, 22; 19:9; 30:16, and is implied by the context in 6:5; 30:6 (through 30:8). Love is also the motive for obedience. Obedience concretises love. Also C.J. Wright (1990) 20–21. Wiéner, 43, considers that the fact that love is commanded in Deuteronomy shows that it is unnatural for the hearers-readers of the book.

333 McCarthy (1981) 160–161. McKay, 433, argues that Deuteronomy is not only dependent on covenant terminology but also on wisdom ideas which have given a "new twist to the verb אָהַב". Also Malfroy, 49–65. McCarthy (1981) 161, acknowledges that wisdom influence does not preclude treaty influence. See Lohfink (1963b) 417. Compare Brekelmans (1978).

334 McBride (1973) 300–301. Zobel, 54, 75, argues that exclusivity of relationship is a key to the notion of love for Yahweh. Similarly, Kooy, 111; L'Hour, 38–40.

can never be an external affair only. Rather it is to be a total commitment, an affair from the heart, an idea which is further enforced by the prepositional phrase in 30:6.[336] It is an impossible ideal.[337] Furthermore, the reciprocity of love between Yahweh and Israel, sums up the theological relationship between the two and highlights that the priority of action lies with Yahweh, not Israel.[338]

Each time in Deuteronomy when Israel is the subject and Yahweh the object of אָהַב, the verb is either expressed as a commandment (6:5; 11:1), or an infinitive construct, לְאַהֲבָה, dependent on a verb of command (10:12; 11:13, 22; 19:9; 30:16, 20) or a participle with similar effect (13:4).[339] The one exception to this is 30:6b. Here the infinitive construct appears with a consecutive function.[340] Now for the first time in the book, love is no longer a command but a statement. Israel's capability to love is grounded in and enabled by Yahweh's action in v6a.[341]

This is extremely important for understanding this section. Not only is Israel's ability to love Yahweh in v6b dependent on Yahweh's action in v6a, but so too is its return and obedience. The concentric structure of vv1–10 focuses on the central sub-section, vv6–8. Thus vv1, 2, 10 ultimately rely on vv6–8.[342] Ridderbos has misunderstood the place of the circumcision of the heart in this passage. Failing to see this structure, and therefore v6 as the kernel of vv1–10, he understands Israel's conversion in v2 as preceding the circumcision of the heart in v6. Thus circumcision, in his opinion, is about "a continuing renewal" and not "the once-for-all renewal". This is in contrast to 29:3. Though Ridderbos's distinctions are not entirely clear, he has failed to appreciate the relationship between the

335 Moran (1963b) 78; Willoughby, 81. Compare Jones, 281–285, for whom "service" is the key summary word to denote Israel's response to Yahweh. See further Bamberger, 39–53, on fear and love. On the notion in ANE covenant parallels and elsewhere in the OT, see Moran (1963b) 84–85.

336 Kooy, 113–114; Wiéner, 42.

337 Merrill, 389.

338 Köckert, 503, "Damit wird das Verhältnis Gott/Volk als allein in Jahwes Liebe gegründete".

339 Vanoni, 93. In 30:20 the infinitive construct with לְ has a gerundive or modal or epexegetical function, explaining the nature of choosing life yet ultimately dependent on the command בָּחַר in in the previous verse. See Soisalon-Soininen, 87–88; Joüon (1991) §124o. Köckert, 503, also includes 5:10 and 7:9 in the list of participial occurrences.

340 Vanoni, 93; Baltzer, 36. Compare Zobel, 51.

341 Vanoni, 93, "Erst aufgrund der Tat YHWHs in 6A ist Israel überhaupt fähig, ihn zu lieben *bkl lbb= wbkl npš=* (6B)". Also Wiéner, 45–46.

342 Contra Okeke, 155, for example, who says that "the point to note is that Yahweh's action was very much dependent on Israel's returning (v. 2).... So ultimately the situation depended on human initiative."

circumcision of the heart and conversion.[343] The interplay between Israel's action of repentance and Yahweh's circumcision of the heart is that "repentance in itself will not be sufficient to insure future loyalty and obedience to God".[344]

In summary, 30:6 shows that Israel's ability to love Yahweh depends upon Yahweh's action on Israel's heart in v6a. Indeed we have argued that all the covenant requirements demanded in Deuteronomy are summed up by the word "love". Thus the fulfilment of all of these depends on the circumcision of the heart. From this action derives the ability for Israel to repent or return as well as to obey. We need now to consider what is meant by the metaphor of circumcision of the heart.

### CIRCUMCISION OF THE HEART

We focus now on the act of circumcision itself.[345] The statement in v6a, וּמָל יְהוָה אֱלֹהֶיךָ אֶת־לְבָבְךָ וְאֶת־לְבַב זַרְעֶךָ, is unconditional. It is in effect a statement of future fact or promise. This is significantly different from the only other occurrence of this idea in Deuteronomy (10:16) where Israel is the subject of the verb expressed as a command. The meaning of this metaphorical expression is suggested by 10:16b: וְעָרְפְּכֶם לֹא תַקְשׁוּ עוֹד. Here the stiffening of the neck refers back to 9:6, 13 where Israel is described as having been stiff-necked constantly from the time of leaving Egypt.[346] This stiff-neckedness is, in the context of chapter 9, associated with rebellion and disobedience provoking Yahweh to anger. Stiff-neckedness is a state of hardness against God. To be uncircumcised is therefore to be in opposition to God.[347] This, then, is a statement of both Israel's past and present condition, for there is no indication at all that Israel has changed. This is also reflected in the threat of future rebellion in 29:17–18, where the heart is determinative in causing the disobedience and apostasy predicted there. Thus if Israel is to change, the root of the problem, and not the external symptoms, must be addressed. Thus the heart is the organ to be changed.[348]

To change the condition of stiff-neckedness and rebellion, Israel must circumcise its heart (10:16). This is to remove the state of hardness and

343 Ridderbos, 270. See pp175ff below on the permanence of circumcision.

344 G.E. Wright, 508.

345 See our discussion on 10:16 for further details about circumcision.

346 In 9:6, 13 and 31:27, the adjective קָשֶׁה is collocated with עֹרֶף. In 10:16 the hiphil of קָשָׁה occurs with עֹרֶף. These are the only occurrences of עֹרֶף in Deuteronomy. קָשָׁה occurs in qal in 1:17 and 15:18; and in hiphil in 2:30, with Yahweh as subject and Sihon's spirit as object.

347 Compare Weinfeld (1991) 438, who implies that lack of circumcision denotes a neutral or insensitive position. Compare Christensen (1991) 206.

348 See Le Déaut, 179–183.

rebellion against God.[349] It is to make the heart responsive to God, with a renewed capacity to obey and love, rather than remaining hard.[350] The term means "to strip from the heart...the overlay of flesh that makes it dull and irresponsive". Its effect is to break the chain of inevitability of Israel falling again and again into sin and rebellion.[351]

In 30:6, the reference to the circumcision of the heart is significantly transformed from 10:16. Rather than Israel being the subject, Yahweh is. Rather than a demand, it is an unconditional statement or promise.[352] The implication of 30:6 is that Yahweh will now do what Israel is incapable of doing in its own strength or ability. Or, better, Yahweh will act on Israel's heart to enable it to do what it is otherwise unable to do, namely that which is required to keep the covenant. Israel's stubbornness and stiff-neckedness stem from the heart. To change the heart is too big a task, an impossible task, for Israel alone, for its sin is rooted there. Only Yahweh can change the heart. The circumcision of the heart by Yahweh in 30:6 is therefore the resolution to the problem of Israel's inability and infidelity to the covenant.[353]

However, if the expectation is that Israel is unable to circumcise its heart as 10:16 demanded, then we must ask why it is commanded to do so in the first place. A diachronic solution is that an expectation of inability (such as 30:1–10) is exilic, and thus later than 10:16 which is more optimistic in its outlook.[354] So, for example,

> certain passages suggest a rewriting from the exilic perspective, stressing the inevitability of sin and perhaps also of destruction.[355]

Such a solution fails to address the tension adequately.[356] It almost denies it. Our concern is to understand theologically the subtleties and significance of

---

349 Le Déaut, 182–203, gives examples in versions, targums, Qumran and early Greek translations which simply translate circumcision by 'remove hardness' or similar.

350 See Joyce, 111, on the "new heart" in Ezekiel 11:19–20; 36:26–27.

351 Clifford, 157. Also Wiéner, 45.

352 Weinfeld (1976) 35, says "There is apparently no significant difference between God's circumcising the heart of Israel and Israel's circumcising their own heart". He gives no reasons for this statement. Compare Joyce, who addresses the parallel issue in Ezekiel, with the demand to get a new heart in chapter 18 and the promise of a new heart from Yahweh in chapter 36. These are what Joyce, 125, calls the "twin poles" of Ezekiel.

353 Freedman, 431. Similarly McConville (1993b) 137; (1993a) 82. He calls it, (1993a) 95, the "theology of illogical grace".

354 This is the standard critical position regarding 30:1–10 as we mentioned in the introduction to this chapter.

355 Levenson (1975) 212. He includes 29:21–30:20 in this. It is not clear that 30:1–10 must be late given Hittite parallels and also parallels in the eighth-century prophets. See Wenham (1970) 190, on the Hittite treaties of Boghasköi; and Wenham (1970) 209; Clements (1965) 106–107; Ackroyd, 71, on the eighth-century prophets.

these tensions throughout the whole book regarded as a synchronic unity. The demand of 10:16 directs Israel to its fundamental need for a changed heart, something it cannot of itself rectify. Thus the demand exposes need and directs attention ultimately to Yahweh who now promises to meet that need by circumcising the heart himself. The circumcision of the heart is thus an act of grace. Especially in the light of the demand of 10:16, it is clear that Yahweh does what Israel of itself cannot do. The contrast between command and promise is in effect the same contrast between Israel's faithlessness and Yahweh's faithfulness. 30:6 shows that Yahweh's grace resolves the problem of Israel's faithlessness.[357]

We are now in a position to draw together the threads of our argument concerning the central section of 30:1–10, namely vv6–8. In our acceptance of Vanoni's analysis of the structure of 30:1–10, we noted that the middle sub-section C (vv6–8) bore most similarity with AA' (vv1–2, 10). It is more precise, however, to note that the links between C and AA' are mostly limited in C to v8. The chief exception to this is לֵבָב which occurs in AA' but in C occurs in v6.[358] In AA', Israel is the subject of action related to its heart. This is also the case for the third occurrence of לֵבָב in v6. However in the first two occurrences in v6, Yahweh is the subject of action related to Israel's heart. We noted above that BB' (vv3–5, 9) had Yahweh as their subject; AA' had Israel. Sub-section C changes from Yahweh to Israel within v6.[359] That which links the actions of Yahweh and Israel in this section is the circumcision of Israel's heart. Thus it is this action by Yahweh on Israel's heart which ties this entire section together. It is the kernel of the whole section. "Im literarischen und theologischen Zentrum... stehen die Herzensbeschneidung und die Gottesliebe".[360]

The importance of the circumcision of the heart is also reflected in the relationship between C and BB'. In particular, חַיִּים in v6c is the only "*Segenshinweis*" not to occur in BB'.[361] In BB', hints of blessing are construed as conditional on Israel's return and obedience. Now they are

356 For a comment on this approach with regard to Judges and 1 Samuel, see McConville (1993b) 105, 115–116 respectively.

357 See below, pp175ff, on the relationship between grace and law.

358 Vanoni, 76. The same also applies to נֶפֶשׁ.

359 Verse 7 reverts to Yahweh as the subject and v8 returns to Israel. It is the change within v6 which concerns us here.

360 Braulik (1992) 217. He argues this applies also for vv1–14, on which see p186 below.

361 This is the only time לְמַעַן חַיֶּיךָ occurs in Deuteronomy. Jacobs, 103, takes it to be the equivalent of "that you may live", לְמַעַן תִּחְיוּ.

shown to be dependent on the grace of Yahweh's action on the heart which enables the love resulting in the blessing of life.[362]

Life is a significant theme in Deuteronomy. Just as "love" sums up the demands of Deuteronomy, so "life" sums up its blessings. The noun occurs twelve times, five of which are in this chapter; the verb occurs eighteen times, twice in this chapter.[363] Life can be considered a result of and motivation for obedience (4:1; 5:30; 6:24; 8:1; 16:20; 30:16, 19). Life can also be considered as given by God. So Israel finds that it can hear God's voice and yet live (4:33; 5:21, 23). Yahweh's word gives life (8:3; 32:47). Yahweh himself brings to life (32:39). Yahweh offers life as an option (30:15, 19). Finally Yahweh himself is Israel's life (30:20). Life is tied to the land in Deuteronomy and that association is not lost in 30:1–10.[364] The wilderness experience was intended to show Israel the true nature and source of life (8:1–3). As 29:1–8 indicated, Israel failed to appreciate that. The emphasis on life in chapter 30 resolves that ignorance. From the circumcision of the heart will flow an understanding of life and its source and the enablement to choose it and experience it. It is a gift of grace which is received through the proper response of Israel, namely, love (30:6).[365] Summing up the blessings of Deuteronomy, life is the goal of the restoration promised in 30:1–10.[366] Verse 6 therefore shows that not only does the fulfilment of the demands of Deuteronomy on Israel, summed up in the word "love", flow from the circumcision of the heart (as argued above), but so too do the blessings of restoration, summed up in the word "life".[367]

Verses 7, 8 describe further consequences of the circumcision of the heart in v6a.[368] As Yahweh's circumcision of Israel's heart enables Israel to love and, hence, to have life (v6), so will it lead to Yahweh placing the curses on Israel's enemies. Furthermore, Israel's ability to return and obey is expressed in v8 as a further consequence enabled by the circumcision of the heart in v6. Thus, "the circumcision of the heart through God precedes

---

362 Jacobs, 103, notes that despite the "natural" relationship between love and life in 30:6, that is a relationship simply formed by action and result, "(e)ven here Yahweh's grace is made to stand out".

363 The noun occurs in 4:9; 6:2; 16:3; 17:19; 28:66 (twice); 30:6, 15, 19 (twice), 20; 32:47. The verb occurs in qal in 4:1, 33, 42; 5:21, 23, 30; 8:1, 3 (twice); 16:20; 19:4, 5; 30:16, 19; 33:6; in piel in 6:24; 20:16 and 32:39. Compare Jacobs, 12–14.

364 Jacobs, 7, 108. See further on 30:15–20 below, pp206ff.

365 Jacobs, 105.

366 Vanoni, 78.

367 Vanoni, 93–94.

368 As are vv9, 10. See Le Déaut, 181–182.

the conversion of Israel".[369] It also precedes Israel's ability to obey and heed Yahweh's voice. So the circumcision of the heart

> eine radikale innere Erneuerung bewirken und damit die Voraussetzung für Israels »Liebe« und seinen vollen Gehorsam schaffen.[370]

Thus blessings are no longer conditional but certain, as we have seen. Again we note that Yahweh's creating the possibility does not abrogate Israel's responsibility to effect the actuality.[371] Yet without Yahweh's grace, Israel is unable to make actual the repentance and restoration required.

In effect we have found that Yahweh's "turning" has preceded Israel's turning and not the other way round. We saw in our discussion above of שׁוב that when Yahweh was the subject, the sense of turning was not necessarily foremost in mind. The word functioned rather as a literary feature to tie Yahweh's action to Israel's. Israel does not need to wait for Yahweh to turn. He has never turned away.

30:6 AND 29:3

This act of Yahweh is seen as the fulfilment of Israel's lack expressed in 29:3. As discussed above, Israel was dependent on Yahweh for a right heart, eyes and ears all of which he had yet to give. This verse expressed the exigence which 30:6 now meets. About 30:6, Buis and Leclerq note, "L'idée...rejoint l'affirmation de 29,3 sur la nécessité de la grâce".[372] So the "heart to know" is the circumcised heart.[373] The association of 30:6 with 29:3 reinforces what we found in 29:1–8 that "up to this day" (29:3) suggests that no change has yet occurred. This also reinforces our contention that the change will not come in the cultic act of the Moab covenant renewal itself.[374] The anticipation of right heart, eyes and ears lies further in the future, beyond the curses.[375]

The right heart, eyes and ears are not three independent organs, for the circumcised heart will enable right hearing, שָׁמַעְתָּ בְּקֹלוֹ (30:8), remembering that this verse is a statement and not a condition or command. Thus the

---

369 Braulik (1984) 14. Similarly Thompson, 285. Contrast Vanoni, 94, "Voraussetzung der Beschneidung/Entschleierung des Herzens ist die Umkehr des Menschen zu YHWH/zum Herrn".

370 Braulik (1992) 218.

371 Miller (1990) 208.

372 Buis and Leclerq, 187. Also Rose (1994) 551.

373 Driver, 330, says that to circumcise the heart is to "remove its dulness of spiritual perception", thus fulfilling the lack expressed in 29:3. Also Miller (1990) 206–208.

374 Compare Miller (1990) 206, "Only now in this (cultic) act does the Lord give the grace truly to see, to hear, and to comprehend and acknowledge". Also Lohfink (1963a) 128.

375 Schmid, 9–15, argues that Israel's future is understood existentially and qualitatively rather than temporally. See Zimmerli's critique, (1971) 75–78.

right heart yields the right ears. This connection is also suggested by the notion of stiff-neckedness. In 10:16, the circumcision of the heart counters stiff-neckedness. We noted above that being stiff-necked denotes rebellion against Yahweh. There are parallelisms in Jeremiah, Zechariah and Nehemiah which show that not to bend the neck is a parallel to not inclining the ear to hear the words or voice of Yahweh.[376] Though this parallel of stiff-neckedness and not inclining the ear to hear is based outside Deuteronomy, it applies readily here as well. The two notions of stiff-neckedness and inclining the ear are both linked to the circumcision of the heart, the former in 10:16 and the latter in 30:6–8. Further, in 9:23, part of the summary indictment against Israel is its not hearing Yahweh's voice. This summary links back to 9:6–7, the opening summary where stiff-neckedness is mentioned, and these two summaries bracket the narrative of the golden calf episode. The circumcision of the heart enables the inclination of the ear to hear by preventing stiff-neckedness. Thus both the heart and ears, which are not yet given in 29:3, are given in Yahweh's circumcision of the heart in 30:6.

We saw above that Israel did occasionally, though fleetingly, respond properly to Yahweh.[377] What it lacked was the ability permanently to trust and obey. The issue of permanence is touched on in 30:6. Firstly the metaphor of circumcision suggests a once only act. It is not an ongoing act, nor one needing repetition. Circumcision is permanent. Secondly the reference to the succeeding generations also having their hearts circumcised highlights the notion of permanence. Thus circumcision will not be an act for one generation only but an on-going and permanent state for Israel.

> Die Herzensbeschneidung aber wird im übrigen nicht nur einmalig als eine Zuwendung Jahwes der Exilsgeneration zugesagt, sondern auch den jeweiligen künftigen Geschlechtern zugesichert.[378]

In summary, the circumcision of the heart deals with the central lack expressed in 29:3, that is of an enduring and consistent right response to Yahweh on the part of Israel.

### *The Patriarchal Promises*

We have seen that the act of circumcision of the heart meets the need expressed in 29:3 and resolves the problem of Israel's faithlessness. We have seen that this represents the priority of grace. However our investigation is not yet complete. In both Deuteronomy 1–3 and 8–10, the

---

376 Couroyer (1981) 216–225. He argues that the origin of the expression does not lie with yoked animals or stubborn mules. Rather this expression only applies to humans in the Old Testament. Also Weinfeld (1991) 407.

377 For example 5:26. Driver, 330, associates this verse with the effects of 30:6.

378 Braulik (1982) 158. Also (1984) 14; (1989) 332.

problem of Israel's faithlessness was resolved on the grounds of the patriarchal promises. This is the case here also. Though there are many references and allusions to the patriarchal promises in 30:1–10, surprisingly this is not always noted. For example, Braulik asserts that in 30:1–10, "not even the covenant with the fathers is mentioned as the reason for the grace granted to Israel".[379] We turn now to these allusions and references.

The first allusion to the patriarchal promises is that of circumcision itself. Circumcision derives from the injunction to Abraham in Genesis 17:9–12 to circumcise every male. This was to be a sign of the covenant which God had just repeated to Abram at the beginning of the same chapter.[380] Deuteronomy has appropriated this physical sign and applied it metaphorically to Israel's heart, recognising that the covenant relationship depends on the internal state of Israel's heart and not mere external obedience. "What had been externally symbolized in circumcision…would be spiritually actualized by the power of God."[381] So the circumcised heart belongs to a person standing under the Abrahamic covenant.[382] This also fits with the covenantal context which we noted at the beginning of chapter 29.

This notion of circumcision is linked to Abraham in yet more specific ways. As we saw in 10:16, the injunction to circumcise the heart immediately follows a reference to Yahweh's love and election of the forefathers and a reference to the forefathers' זֶרַע. This is an allusion to Abraham.[383] The inclusion in 30:6 of the phrase וְאֶת־לְבַב זַרְעֶךָ, speaks of future descendants in an analogous way to which 10:15 speaks of Abraham's descendants, thus recalling deliberately the Abrahamic covenant.[384]

---

379 Braulik (1994e) 111; (1989) 331. Van Seters (1994) 468, states that the patriarchal promise as a basis for hope occurs for the first time in Second Isaiah.

380 Kline (1968) 39–49, argues that circumcision was a covenant-ratifying oath-sign which symbolised on the one hand the curse of being cut off from among his people (Genesis 17:14), and on the other hand a pledge of consecration. Also Hugenberger, 214–215. Le Déaut, 179, argues that 'covenant' and 'circumcision' are so intimately related that 'covenant' is often interpreted by the word 'circumcision'.

381 Kline (1963) 132. Similarly Christensen (1991) 206.

382 Kline (1968) 47–48. Le Déaut, 183, "la circoncision signifiait l'incorporation dans l'alliance, la consécration et l'appartenance à Yhwh"

383 Weinfeld (1976) 34. Though Abraham is not explicitly mentioned in 10:15, he is in 1:8 and 34:4, both times in collocation with זֶרַע. Thus the mention of the fathers in general and also זֶרַע in 10:15 ties the circumcision of the heart to a covenantal context with Abraham.

384 On the importance of זֶרַע in Genesis, see Alexander (1993) 254–270. He notes, 266, that the fulfilment of the Abrahamic promises is associated with the 'seed' of Abraham. Deuteronomy picks up on this.

אֲבֹתֶיךָ in vv5 (twice), 9 also call to mind the Abrahamic covenant.[385] These references occur in BB' in the context of Yahweh's restoration of Israel. They deal with land, prosperity and progeny, each of which suggests that the restoration of Israel will be based on the promises to the fathers and thus a renewal of the Abrahamic covenant.[386]

The notion of land in Deuteronomy is clearly a reference to the Abrahamic promises. One of its most common qualifications in Deuteronomy is that which associates it either with the fathers generally or with Abraham, Isaac and Jacob specifically, through Yahweh's gift or oath.[387] It is important, then, to see that future hope and restoration are clearly tied to a return to this land. The promise of land to Abraham still stands.[388] It is noteworthy that the hope of 1 Kings 8:46–53 and the new covenant in Jeremiah 31:31–34, both of which are often compared to Deuteronomy 30:1–10, omit any mention of a return to the land.[389]

The notion of prosperity is not obviously Abrahamic. However recent discussion has shown that טוֹב is a word taken from the ancient treaty language, often to denote good relations and friendship between two parties.[390] So טוֹב

> expresses fidelity to the formal treaty (covenant) relationships on the part of Yahweh and of Israel. The term 'good' is used in the oldest traditions of Deuteronomy to describe the covenant when both parties were faithful.[391]

טוֹב and related words occur 32 times in Deuteronomy, most commonly as an adjective qualifying אֶרֶץ.[392] In 30:1–10, the hiphil of יָטַב (v5) and טוֹב

385 Braulik (1982) 157; (1989) 331; Watts (1970) 280; Polzin (1980) 70–71, argue that the mention of the fathers in 30:5 is not a reference to the patriarchs but to the pre-exilic ancestors of the exiles. On this issue, see our discussion in chapter 1.

386 Munchenberg, 207–208.

387 See the discussion in chapter 1 on patriarchal oath and land.

388 Craigie (1976) 364. Seebass (1977a) 220–223, argues that one Deuteronomic feature of the land promise is that it emphasises election certainty and the ongoing validity of the Abrahamic promises of Genesis 15, despite current loss of land. This emphasis is not contradicted by a stress on acquiring the land through obedience for obedience is a confession of trust.

389 McConville (1992) 67–79, argues that 1 Kings 8:46–53, taking up the Deuteronomy 30 passage, deliberately holds back from expressing a hope in the return to the land. Buis, 3, misses this point. Contrast Weinfeld (1991) 217–221, 223–224.

390 Moran (1963c) 173–176; Hillers, 46–47; Fox, 41–42; Millard, 115–117; Brueggemann (1968) 389. Hillers argues that Deuteronomy 23:7 fits this notion of "amity established by treaty".

391 Brueggemann (1968) 389.

392 There is sometimes difficulty deciding whether the word is an adjective, noun or verb. Even-Shoshan, 411–414, lists 30:9b as an adjective. BDB, 373, 375, lists 30:9a under טוֹבָה (n.f. welfare).

(v9, twice) occur.[393] In 30:5, יָטַב expresses a gift of Yahweh.[394] In v9b לְטוֹב occurs.[395] Here, again, the good is promised through Yahweh's action and is not conditional on obedience. In v9a, לְטוֹבָה follows from הוֹתִירְךָ at the beginning of the verse. What was conditional in 28:11, to which this verse refers, is now promised through Yahweh's action in 30:9.[396] The covenant treaty background of טוֹב suggests that v9 is an expression of the continuation of the covenant.[397] At one level, Israel is commanded to "do good". This "good" is all-inclusive. It involves land, prosperity, goods and life itself.[398] However at another level, the "good" stresses the grace of Yahweh, especially because this future blessing is greater than past blessings.[399] Yahweh's "good" is grace, covenant grace. This idea is another reference back to 9:6 where the land is described as a good gift in association with Israel's unrighteousness.[400] Thus, although we do not find an explicit Abrahamic connection with the notion of prosperity, nonetheless covenant relations are in mind. The point to make here is that the sense of טוֹב is broad, relational, covenantal and concerns both grace and the outcome of obedience.[401]

The notion of progeny also alludes to the Abrahamic promises. We have noted the reference to seed in 30:6 which refers back to Abraham. In v5, Yahweh will make Israel more numerous (רָבָה hiphil) than its fathers.[402] The hiphil of רָבָה also occurs with Yahweh as the subject and Israel the

---

393 יָטַב occurs in the hiphil with Yahweh as subject and Israel as object elsewhere in Deuteronomy only in 8:16 and 28:63.

394 Vanoni, 85; Jacobs, 100–101. In contrast, the qal of יָטַב with Israel as the object is always conditional dependent on Israel's obedience. In אֲשֶׁר clauses: 4:40; 6:3; in לְמַעַן clauses: 5:16, 26; 6:18; 12:25, 28; 22:7.

395 Compare 6:24; 10:13. Vanoni, 87; BDB, 375. Compare Even-Shoshan. Jacobs, 247, takes 6:24 and 10:13 to be infinitive constructs and, 101–102, 30:9b as nominal.

396 Vanoni, 86–87; Jacobs, 101. Vanoni also refers to 7:13; 28:4, 18 where this three-fold blessing is mentioned.

397 Jacobs, 127, says that the return to the land "promises the 'good' known formerly by the patriarchs" and "the covenant remains as the life-giving relationship even for these ('future') exiled Israelites".

398 Brueggemann (1968) 387–392; Jacobs, 5–6.

399 Braulik (1982) 159; (1989) 332, states that v9 in fact expands on v5 which already had promised greater blessings than the past. Lenchak, 159, suggests vv5, 9 make different comparisons with the past.

400 Brueggemann (1968) 392–395. Similarly Rose (1994) 556.

401 See McConville (1984) 14–15, for a discussion on טוֹב and צְדָקָה as near synonyms. Brueggemann, (1968) 388, 401–402, argues that טוֹב balances שׁוּב as twin kerygmata of DtrH. Compare Wolff (1982) 83–100.

402 Buis, 6–7, suggests that Jeremiah envisages a return to life as it was pre-exile whereas Ezekiel anticipates a future which is better and more prosperous. Deuteronomy would, in that case, align itself to Ezekiel.

object in 1:10; 7:13; 13:18 and 28:63.[403] The first three of these are explicitly connected to the promise to the fathers; the last is linked to the same promise through 28:62 which, like 1:10, refers to Genesis 15:5. רָבָה in the hiphil occurs a number of times elsewhere in the Pentateuch in the context of patriarchal promise: Genesis 17:2, 20; 22:17; 26:4, 24; 28:3; 48:4; Exodus 32:13; Leviticus 26:9.[404] A similar case can be made for the occurrences of the qal of רָבָה with Israel as a subject.[405] In Deuteronomy, apart from 30:5, all of these occurrences, when anticipating the future, are conditional on Israel's obedience.

Another connection with Abraham is Yahweh's compassion (רִחֲמֶךָ, v3) on which the hope of restoration is grounded. Words from the רחם root occur just four times in Deuteronomy. In 4:31 the adjective רַחוּם describes Yahweh. This is the grounds for Israel's return mentioned in the previous verse. Verse 31 goes on to link Yahweh's compassion with his covenant sworn to the fathers. Thus Yahweh's compassion derives from his faithfulness to the Abrahamic covenant.[406] In 13:18 we read that Yahweh נָתַן־לְךָ רַחֲמִים וְרִחַמְךָ. The context here is of destroying all who seek to lead others to apostasy. However Yahweh will be compassionate if Israel is obedient. His compassion is linked to increasing Israel's numbers. Both are then tied to כַּאֲשֶׁר נִשְׁבַּע לַאֲבֹתֶיךָ. So again we find Yahweh's compassion derives from his faithfulness to the Abrahamic covenant. In 30:3 however there is no direct association between Yahweh's compassion and the Abrahamic covenant. Nonetheless, given the association in 4:31, especially since the context of 4:29–31 is so similar to that of 30:1–10, and 13:18, it seems likely that the Abrahamic covenant lies behind the reference to compassion in 30:3.

The verb אָהַב in v6 also alludes to the Abrahamic covenant. We have noted above that Yahweh loves Israel and Israel is to love Yahweh. On five occasions Yahweh is the subject and Israel the object of love. In four of these the context is the Abrahamic covenant. These are 4:37; 10:15, where the object is the fathers; 7:8, 13, where the object is the current generation. This love in 7:8 derives from Yahweh's faithfulness to his oath to the fathers and, in 7:13 will be a demonstration of his faithfulness to his covenant of love he swore to the fathers (v12). The exception is 23:6. Since

---

403 Vanoni, 85.

404 Compare Driver, 16; Mayes (1979) 121, who link this promise only to JE in Genesis 22:17; 26:4; Exodus 32:13.

405 Namely 6:3; 8:1; also 30:16. רָבָה in qal in the context of patriarchal promise occurs also in Genesis 35:11; 47:27; Exodus 1:7, 10, 12, 20. Compare with the creation and post-flood occurrences of רָבָה in qal in Genesis 1:22, 28; 8:17; 9:1, 7. Lohfink (1963a) 84, notes the association of רָבָה in Deuteronomy 8:1 with both Genesis 1 and the patriarchal promises.

406 On the connection between God as merciful and his faithfulness to the covenant sworn to the ancestors, see J.G. Janzen (1987a) 292.

Israel's love is to be a response to Yahweh's, which in turn usually is tied to the promises to the fathers, we would suggest that the statement in v6 that Israel will love Yahweh alludes again to the Abrahamic covenant.[407]

All these allusions and references suggest that the grounds for future hope and restoration expressed in 30:1–10 lie not just with Yahweh's grace in general, but specifically with Yahweh's faithfulness to the Abrahamic covenant.[408] This should not be surprising given that the whole book is riddled with references to Abrahamic promises.

> The covenant with the patriarchs may provide for (the Deuteronomist), as for the Holiness Code (Lev 26:42), a divine commitment which even covenant violations cannot cancel, in other words, an ancestral covenant other than the royal grant to David. It is interesting to note that even Dtn conceives of the promise to the patriarchs as a pool of grace which prevented the destruction of the generation of the rebellions in the wilderness (Deut 9:4–5).[409]

The point to note here is that hope and restoration beyond covenant breach depend on Yahweh's faithfulness to the Abrahamic promises. This is consistent with what we have found in Deuteronomy 1–3 and 8–10.

These appeals to the Abrahamic covenant raise the issue of its relationship to the Sinai covenant. This is not a simple matter and we will make only cursory comments here.[410] The Abrahamic covenant is usually regarded as a one-sided, unconditional covenant.[411] It stands regardless of Israel's faithlessness "and therefore could be invoked even in the time of sin".[412] Yet the Abrahamic covenant embraces the Sinai covenant which relates to the patriarchs in a positive and integrated way. Sinai and Abraham are not opposed to each other. It is too simplistic to see in Abraham and Sinai the opposition of grace and law. Likewise it is too simplistic to argue that Yahweh's anger and jealousy derive from the Sinai covenant and his mercy and compassion from the Abrahamic.[413] Rather, the Sinai covenant functions as a confirmation of the Abrahamic covenant and

---

407 Schmid, 7–9, "So ist das menschliche Verhalten in die Erfüllung der Verheißung inkorporiert". He refers to 6:3.

408 Jacobs, 108. Hagelia, 125, suggests another allusion in that the possibility of subjugation in 30:1 alludes to Genesis 15:14.

409 Levenson (1975) 232. Also J.G. Janzen (1987a) 293.

410 A related issue is the relationship of the Exodus-Conquest tradition with the Sinai-Law tradition, famously separated by von Rad (1966a). For a critique, see C.J. Wright (1990) 5–9, 13–15, 24–43.

411 Contrast Kline (1968) 39–49, that the Abrahamic covenant was conditional. Similarly Wenham (1978) 4.

412 Weinfeld (1991) 210. Similarly Schenker, 96, "Der Väterbund ist das Bleibende und die Bürgschaft JHWHs, daß die Geschichte Israels von ihm her nie aufhören wird."

413 Lohfink (1965) 113–114.

is the means through which its promises are fulfilled and protected.[414] As we saw in Deuteronomy 1–3, law and promise serve the same end.[415] "At Sinai a new instrument for administering (the existing relationship between Yahweh and Israel) was put in place. That is all."[416] Thus there is fundamental continuity and agreement between the two covenants.[417]

At one level, Israel's faithlessness results in a break in the Sinai covenant.[418] However, we have also found that Sinai itself still stands beyond Israel's faithlessness. So in Deuteronomy 8–10, the resolution of failure at the golden calf incident results in the continuation of the Sinai covenant, as the renewed call to obey in 10:12–22 showed. The covenant renewal at Moab is also a ratification of Sinai. Sinai is therefore a permanent offer, not destroyed by Israel's faithlessness, but resting on the permanence of the patriarchal covenant.[419] Having said this, the importance of the Abrahamic covenant in Deuteronomy is often overlooked, not only in 30:1–10.[420] The hope of Deuteronomy rests without apology on the Abrahamic promises.

We recognise that the tension between the two covenants is usually resolved diachronically. A typical view would be that

> the Deuteronomists repudiated any attempt to set the patriarchal covenant in the forefront of Israel's existence, and very forcibly stressed its subordination to that of Horeb.[421]

However, as with P, in exilic times the Abrahamic covenant came to assume "a radical new importance" for Israel and its hope, though unlike JE and P, Deuteronomy makes no mention of the eternal or everlasting nature of the patriarchal promises.[422] Thus in "the later introductory section of Deuteronomy", "the permanent validity of the patriarchal promise is

---

414 Fensham (1967) 311; McComiskey, 165; Clements (1967) 68. Also Cazelles (1977) 79.

415 Compare Clements (1967) 68.

416 Stek, 33.

417 Stek, 33; McComiskey, 165. See also Roberge, 115, who notes that Hittite treaties often appeal to previous generations in a similar way to which Sinai appeals to Abraham.

418 Fensham (1967) 310; Freedman, 429.

419 Schenker, 96. Compare Freedman, 429, who suggests that the Abrahamic covenant "was discharged when its terms were fulfilled in the conquest and settlement in the land" and that thereafter "the fate of Israel was contingent upon its obedience to the terms of the Covenant made at Mount Sinai". See also Clements (1968) 40. However there is no suggestion in Deuteronomy that the Abrahamic promises have been discharged. Nor is there a suggestion that on fulfilment of these promises the Abrahamic covenant would become void.

420 McComiskey, 173; Martens (1981) 240–242.

421 Clements (1967) 66.

422 Weinfeld (1993) 249, 258. He suggests this is significant, yet fails to say why. See Hugenberger, 194, for a list of the occurrences of "an everlasting covenant". See Tsevat, 71–82, on the limits of meaning of עוֹלָם in covenantal contexts and its relationship to conditionality.

affirmatively declared".[423] In place of such an approach, we have sought to relate Abraham and Sinai theologically and, in Deuteronomy, synchronically. In our opinion, Deuteronomy integrates Abraham and Sinai. The latter rests on, and derives from, the former.

### *Grace and Law*

This understanding of Deuteronomy 30:1–10 and the Abrahamic and Sinai covenants raises the issue of the nature of and relationship between law and grace in Deuteronomy. All too commonly, law and grace are seen as opposites, the Old Testament being characterised by the former, the New Testament by the latter. This is an unfortunate distinction.[424] At one level we could say that in Deuteronomy there is a priority of grace over law for it is Yahweh's actions on which Israel ultimately depends rather than its own obedience and effort. Law and obedience could then be regarded as the response to grace.[425]

This relationship between Yahweh's activity and Israel's activity is illustrated by the nature of the promised land in Deuteronomy. There are two strands of thought in Deuteronomy which stand in some tension together. The first is the indicative, that the land is a free gift of divine grace. The second is the imperative, that Israel must take possession of the land. The latter relates the land to Israel as conditional on its obedience. These two strands are related by a covenant theology which shows that the imperative is a requirement of the grace of Yahweh.[426]

> Die Realität des Bundes ermöglicht es, Indikativ und Imperativ nach beiden Seiten hin voll zu entfalten, so daß der Indikativ nicht zur billigen Gnade wird, aber auch so, daß der Imperativ nicht zur Werkgerechtigkeit entartet.[427]

---

423 Clements (1967) 68–69. Also Lohfink (1991b) 21, 32. Also Zimmerli (1960) 277–279, regarding P.

424 Braulik (1982) 127–128, discusses this in reference to Aquinas and Luther. Luther's distinction was that law was essentially self-redemption and gospel was redemption by God. Eichrodt (1966) 302–321, argues, 310, that the notions of commandment and covenant "belong essentially together" and that it is apparently "no contradiction that a communal relationship with mutual rights and duties can be seen at the same time as a gracious benefaction of the superior party". He continues, 313, 315, to argue that the notion of commandment should not be allowed to degenerate into a nomistic legalism but rather properly regarded as a gift of prevenient grace. On the other hand, law and grace are not totally conjunctive, as Werblowsky, 156–163, seems to think. There remains some disjunction between the two, as Perlitt (1990a) 37, notes.

425 Plöger, 83; Diepold, 96–102; L'Hour, 112–116.

426 Diepold, 76–102.

427 Diepold, 100. Similarly L'Hour, 102–106.

In addition, we maintain that this applies throughout Deuteronomy. That is, the imperative and the indicative must be seen in this mutual relationship where the priority lies with Yahweh's grace, even if in individual verses the future, or land, seems only conditional on obedience.[428] So in Deuteronomy 30, the priority lies with Yahweh's grace; Israel's obedience is, at first, a response to that.[429]

However, the priority of grace is deeper than this. Israel's obedience to the law depends on Yahweh's grace and is not merely a response to it. Yahweh's grace, as we have seen throughout 30:1–10, enables obedience to the law.[430]

We can take yet a step further. We noted that כָּל־הַדְּבָרִים הָאֵלֶּה in 30:1 refers at least back to the curses and blessings of chapter 28. The related reference in 4:30 is about "the covenant's central commandment pertaining to Israel's relationship with God".[431] That is, that "all these words" is, or at least includes, law. Since these words which come upon Israel will lead to repentance, these words constitute gospel or grace. The point is that law and grace are not in any way opposed. It is not merely that law is a response to grace. Nor is it even that law depends on grace. Rather, the character of law is itself grace or gospel.[432]

> Das wahrhaft geinnerte deuteronomische Gesetz ist »Wort des Glaubens« (Romans 10:8), also »Evangelium« (Romans 10:16).[433]

This is also clear in the regiving of the law to a failed people. Whether this is to the exiles or to those about to enter the land under Joshua, this proclamation of the law is an act of grace, a declaration of renewed relationship with Yahweh.[434]

As we have suggested above, law exposes Israel's inability. The requirements in Deuteronomy, stemming from the heart, are absolute in their demands. The very impossibility of keeping them exposes Israel's inherent sinfulness. This renders it unable to meet the covenant demands on its own. The character of Deuteronomic law, therefore, presupposes the sinfulness of Israel. Yet Deuteronomy does not leave that exposed need

---

428 Regarding land, for example, see 6:18; 8:1; 11:8, 13, 22. Diepold, 185, goes on to say, "Gegenüber dem Dt bedeutet das *Deuteronomistische Geschichtswerk* theologisch eine Reduktion der dt Bundestheologie auf die Kategorie des Gesetzes". With respect to Deuteronomy 1–3, we argued in chapter 1 this is not the case.

429 On the ethic of response (*Antwort*), see L'Hour, 32–48.

430 Braulik (1989) 332; Christensen (1991) 95.

431 Braulik (1984) 12. Christensen (1991) 95, fully accepts Braulik's thesis repeating much of his argument in almost the same words. Braulik (1982) 156; (1989) 331, notes that the referent in 30:1 is more precisely the curses and blessings rather than the whole covenant.

432 Compare 4:5–8.

433 Braulik (1982) 160.

434 Braulik (1994a) 24–25.

unmet. It addresses it above all in 30:1–10. Israel's inability is met by a gracious creation of possibility. But this creation of possibility, through the circumcision of the heart, only makes sense in the context of the exposed need throughout the rest of the book. The law exposes need, because Israel has a basic incapacity to fulfil the demands of the law, and thus functions as gospel to a guilty people by pointing to Yahweh to resolve the dilemma.[435]

Certainly Israel's responsibility to respond with obedient faith is not abolished or usurped by Yahweh's action on its heart.[436] So promise does not annul law but "law and promise co-operate unto the salvation of God's people".[437] Israel's response of repentance and obedience is its own work, a work of co-operative response. This is perhaps illustrated by the emphatic וְאַתָּה at the beginning of v8. The contrast which וְאַתָּה stresses is not between the enemies in v7 and Israel but between Yahweh's action in v6 and Israel's response in v8.[438] So וְאַתָּה stresses the "gegenseitige Abhängigkeit" between Yahweh's action and Israel's response.[439] Certainly there is a double focus on Israel's restoration. Firstly, there is Yahweh's action, which creates the possibility. Secondly, in response to and enabled by the first, there is Israel's repentance and obedience, which creates the actuality.[440] Brueggemann writes,

> The problem of kerygma in this tradition is the balance between the *graciousness* of the 'good' motif and the demand of the 'repent' motif.[441]

---

435 Braulik (1984) 12. Compare Galatians 3:19–25.

436 Braulik (1982) 158; (1989) 332; Miller (1990) 213. Contrast Schenker, 101, who writes, "Beschneidet JHWH die Herzen der kommenden israelitischen Generationen, so festigt er sie in der Unterwerfung unter die Tora und macht eine neue dunkle Zwischenzeit des Abfalls unmöglich." On the priority of divine grace but the obligation of human responsibility in the Old Testament in general, see Schmidt (1989) 11–28.

437 Kline (1968) 30–31, and "in the very process of securing for his chosen the covenant's blessing of life, God honors his original covenant of law in its abiding demand for obedience as the condition of life and with its curse of death for the covenant breakers."

438 Mayes (1979) 369; Vanoni, 75. On contrast with the enemies of v7, see Driver, 330. Vanoni, 72, notes that if v7 is omitted, as Dillmann suggested, then the emphatic וְאַתָּה becomes meaningless since Israel is the subject of v6b. Verse 6 itself juxtaposes Yahweh and Israel as subjects. The likelihood is that the emphasis in v8a is a contrast with v7. Yet this need not be with the enemies but with Yahweh who is the subject of v7.

439 Vanoni, 75. Also, 76, "Die Verteilung der handelnden Subjekte auf die Abschnitte mag wieder die gegenseitige Abhängigkeit und Verflochtenheit der Umkehr Gottes und der Menschen betonen." Also L'Hour, 112–116, 119–121.

440 Miller (1990) 208. Similarly Watts (1970) 281, says of 30:6, that "the Lord promises to give the people the possibility for faith. He will prepare their hearts to believe and remove the barriers to full commitment and faith."

441 Brueggemann (1968) 389. Also Jacobs, 104–105.

This action by Yahweh on Israel's heart and the obedience which flows from that correspond to what the New Testament calls justification and sanctification.[442] Whilst it is true to an extent to say that hope depends on Israel's response, ultimately the grounds of hope derive from Yahweh's grace.[443]

Thus far we have spoken of the circumcision of the heart in terms of enabling Israel to repent, love and obey. We must ask whether the circumcision of the heart does more than this, that is whether it also guarantees obedience. As we have argued, this primary act of God's grace does not do away with the responsibility of Israel to respond properly to Yahweh. This is demonstrated in the change of subjects within v6. Yahweh circumcises; Israel loves. It remains Israel's responsibility to love.[444] Yet the certainty of the statements about Israel's love and obedience in vv6b, 8 suggests a sense of guarantee as well.[445] Verses 6–8 function almost as a promise that Israel *will* love and obey, not just that they *can*. How is this guarantee to be understood? Perhaps an eschatological perspective is helpful here.[446] The New Testament makes it clear that the circumcision of the heart is associated with identification in Christ's death and the giving of the Spirit.[447] Yet it is also clear that Christians do not yet perfectly love and obey. Perfection belongs to the eschaton. However with the giving of the Holy Spirit after Pentecost, the eschaton has broken into the current age. The changing of the heart by Jesus' death and the giving of the Spirit is a guarantee of perfect obedience in the end. This is the end of a process called sanctification, rather than the immediate result of a single action. This perspective of a gradual process is not apparent in Deuteronomy 30. It anticipates the one future event, guaranteeing perfect obedience.

### *The Frame of the Law*

Before concluding this section, we turn our attention to some of the implications of the theology of 30:1–10 for the rest of the book. In

---

442 Miller (1990) 213. Compare, 208, "Circumcision of the heart is a way of speaking about conversion and transformation." Kline (1963) 133, speaks of the "spiritual gifts of regeneration, conversion and sanctification".

443 Braulik (1992) 217. Vanoni, 78–79, stresses mutuality but fails to give priority to the action of Yahweh.

444 Köckert, 517, "Die Tat Jahwes macht Israel allererst fähig, Jahwe zu lieben". Compare Joyce, 127–128, on Ezekiel, who says that in the end, human responsibility is subsumed in the divine initiative of Yahweh. The tension between the two defies rational resolution.

445 Joyce, 127; Steuernagel, 109, "sodass erneuter Abfall unmöglich ist".

446 On Israel's unchanged nature contributing to reading Deuteronomy eschatologically, see MacKenzie, 301.

447 See Romans 2:25–29; Colossians 2:11–14. Also Merrill, 388.

particular we are interested in the implications for reading the law in Deuteronomy. Our comments are based on the frame for the law created by 30:1–10 and the closely related passage 4:29–31.

Without doubt, the section of Deuteronomy most like 30:1–10 is 4:29–31.[448] It is possibly significant that these two places, most clearly dealing with Yahweh's grace and Israel's return or conversion, provide a frame for the entire Deuteronomic legal corpus.[449] The key issue is the function of this frame for the book as a whole. Diachronic methods tend to attribute these sections to an exilic redactor but generally fail to discuss the impact of this layer on how to read other layers or strata in the book. Our synchronic and theological concerns mean we seek to relate this frame to the law which it surrounds. These passages deliberately frame the bulk of Deuteronomy, providing a filter for understanding the whole book.

One diachronic critic who does make an attempt to relate theologically this frame with the law is Levenson. He argues that the theological position of the exilic frame regards the law

> not as the program gloriously realized by royal fiat, but as a bill of indictment against a sinning nation prosecuted by a God who calls on heaven and earth to witness against them (Deut 4:25ff. , 30:19ff. , 31:28ff. ). In its present position, Dtn is a cause not for self-congratulation, but for self-reproach.[450]

Certainly the law does expose sin. The question is how to interpret this. The weakness of this diachronic approach is that it reads Deuteronomy as an interpretation of the past only. Thus law exposes past sin as an explanation of failure and a bill of indictment. We have argued that Deuteronomy 29 and 30 should be read as oriented to the future. They are a statement of Yahweh's perfect standards which a faithless people will be unable to meet in their own strength. This frame then, in our view, suggests that the commandments are to be understood in terms of Israel's current and future inability to keep them. The law is given, and the exhortations are made, knowing that failure will be the response. The law then functions to drive the people to trust in Yahweh and not themselves. It points to righteousness from Yahweh rather than from oneself. The law, which is from God, is

---

448 Von Rad (1966e) 183; Driver, lxxvi, 328; Weinfeld (1991) 207, 209; Craigie (1976) 363; Ridderbos, 268; Kalland, 188; Wolff (1982) 96; Schenker, 94–95; Cross, 287; Begg (1980a) 49–50. Van Rooy (1988b) 876, argues 30:1–10 takes 4:29–31 further.

449 Braulik (1984) 11; (1989) 330–331; (1992) 217; Weinfeld (1991) 216–217; Lenchak, 35; Cross, 278; Cairns, 256; von Rad (1966e) 183. Christensen (1993) 9, illustrates this through the concentric structure of the whole book. Levenson (1975) 212–217, notes many strong lexical links between the two sides of the frame. On the unity of chapter 4, see Braulik (1978). Contrast Begg (1980a) 10–55; Mayes (1981b).

450 Levenson (1975) 232.

therefore righteous; the people are not.[451] In sending Israel to trust in Yahweh and not itself, the law cannot be divorced from the gospel, for it is a demonstration of the need for grace and, in Deuteronomy, to be understood in association with a promise of grace. The Deuteronomic law, then, cannot be understood in simple terms of retribution of curse and blessing.

In contrast, Levenson's diachronic approach fails to see the depth of Yahweh's grace. For him, the message of the exilic redactor is that Israel "can yet return to God through observance of the commandments they have thus far spurned".[452] This view grounds hope in Israel's moral freedom.[453] Israel is fundamentally able to keep the law. Even though Levenson is concerned to emphasise grace in 30:1–10, his failure to appreciate the inherent faithlessness of Israel weakens his understanding of grace.[454] We would maintain that a correct view of Israel's inability to keep the law heightens grace further. As acknowledged above, Levenson is far from alone in advocating the ability of Israel to keep the law. However, in order to accommodate such a view, he has to read 30:1–10 as exilic and looking to the past rather than, as the text functions, future in outlook. In effect, his diachronic approach undercuts the thrust of the passage and weakens the force of Yahweh's grace in 30:1–10.

The framing of the law with the "life" motif contributes to this fuller appreciation of grace. The vocabulary associated with "life" is most frequent in "programmatically significant" chapters including 4 and 30. This "stylistically determined motif" with "a determinable intention in view" is employed

> in a deliberate attempt to enclose the Deuteronomic law with the promise and assurance of 'life' and to demonstrate the relationship between the two.[455]

In effect, then, this framing of the law with the "life" motif sets the law into a context of grace, acknowledging that the source of life is ultimately Yahweh and that life is not the straightforward result or outcome of obedience. In summary, we argue that a synchronic approach stands a better chance of integrating theologically the threads of Deuteronomy. In particular, the implication of our thesis about the relationship between Yahweh's faithfulness and Israel's faithlessness is that the law must be read

---

451 See 4:8; 9:6.

452 Levenson (1975) 221. Weinfeld (1991) 215–221, argues that the theology of repentance in chapters 4 and 30 "is anchored in liturgy and prayer as practiced in times of national disaster, beginning with the fall of Samaria in the eighth century". See Mayes (1981b) 45–46; Begg (1980a) 49–50.

453 Levenson (1975) 232.

454 Levenson (1975) 233, "To the man who discovers he has sinned, the grace of God is his sole hope, a hope which requires that he reembrace the norm he has spurned."

455 Jacobs, 14. Also Lenchak, 35–36. On the life motif, see below, pp206ff.

in the light of an expectation of failure. Its function is therefore to expose sin and, in so doing, to drive Israel to Yahweh, the source of life.[456]

## *Conclusion*

Deuteronomy 30:1–10 is the strongest and clearest statement of hope in the book. This hope is precisely defined. It lies only beyond the judgment of curse and exile. Israel will fail, through its own inability, to keep the covenant and procure its blessings. However grace will abound. Yahweh will act, faithful to his promises to Abraham. These promises are not annulled by Israel's disobedience. They remain always valid. They are the enduring basis of hope.

One of the implications of this analysis is that Deuteronomy 30 shares much the same theological position as the promise of the new covenant in Jeremiah 31.[457] Though the terminology is different, there is theological harmony between the two passages.[458] The same Mosaic law is in view and both passages address its internalisation in the hearts of God's people.[459] Both passages acknowledge the inability of Israel. The major difference is that Deuteronomy rests on the Abrahamic covenant while Jeremiah postulates a new covenant.[460]

There is optimism throughout Deuteronomy about the future, but always in creative tension with an underlying pessimism about Israel's capacity to obey faithfully. This tension is ultimately resolved in 30:1–10 in the promise of the circumcision of the heart. 30:1–10 "picks up the essential attitude of the entire book".[461] It draws together all the major ideas and motifs of Deuteronomy. These include land, entry, possession, obedience, love, life, prosperity, blessing and curse, heart, soul, offspring and the Abrahamic promises. These major Deuteronomic themes are combined in a final statement of hope which resolves the book's tensions. The gracious promise of the circumcision of the heart resolves the dilemma caused by Israel's inability both to obey and repent, and yet preserves the reality of human responsibility.

---

456 We shall comment further on the source of life below, pp206ff.

457 Contra Schenker, 101–104; Vanoni, 86–90; Coppens, 21. See also Böhmer, 76–77. On Jeremiah as Deuteronomistic, see Cholewinski, 109–111; Lyonnet, 92–94; Nicholson (1970) 82–84; Hoppe (1985) 109. Compare von Rad (1962a) 229–231; Okeke, 237; Potter, 350–355; Rowley, 200–208; Cazelles (1951–52) 5–36. See also Lohfink (1991b) 49; Braulik (1994a) 213.

458 McConville (1993a) 19–20, 82–83, 91, 97; Le Déaut, 181; Kline (1968) 75.

459 Swetnam (1974) 111–115; Buis, 5; Martin-Achard (1962) 90–91; (1974) 156.

460 See Köckert, 518; Buis, 12. Weinfeld (1976) 34–35, suggests Deuteronomy 30:6 hints at a new covenant without using that expression.

461 Watts (1970) 280.

## Deuteronomy 30:11–14

### *The Relationship of 30:11–14 to 30:1–10*

If 30:1–10 is the clearest statement of Israel's inability to keep the covenant, 30:11–14 is "the most explicit statement in the whole book of *their ability* to obey his commands".[462] In a highly rhetorical way, these four verses appear to stress the ease by which Israel should be able to keep the covenant commandments. The stress on this ease has led to the assertion that vv11–14 affirm the opposite of vv1–10.[463]

A difficulty in relating this section to the preceding has to do with the time scale involved. 30:1–10 has a future perspective. In vv11–14, it is claimed, "(t)he emphasis returns once again to the present, the renewal ceremony being enacted on the plains of Moab."[464] This is especially through the occurrence of "the typical urgent 'today'" in v11.[465] Such an understanding of these two paragraphs, seeing contrast and uneasy juxtaposition, raises questions such as, How does this apparent present ability relate to the expected future inability? And conversely, "How does a vision of a still future empowering of Israel by God affect the present generation…?"[466] Schneider comments,

> Die Schwierigkeit für eine einfühlsame Erklärung dieses Abschnittes besteht darin, daß man sich erstaunt fragt: Wie kann eben erst davon geredet worden sein, daß der Gehorsam eine Frucht der endzeitlichen Umkehr Israels ist, und dann im nächsten Augenblick davon, daß dieses »Wort« so nahe beim jetzigen im Land Moab befindlichen Israel ist, daß sein Nichtbefolgen außerhalb des Denkmöglichen ist?[467]

The juxtaposition of these two sections has led some scholars to suggest different dates and origins for each as though the two are mutually incompatible. So Driver suggests that vv11–14 are only "loosely connected with v.1–10".[468] Some suggest that passages which reflect an optimism about Israel's ability are very early. Pessimistic passages would then be later, reflecting the failure of Israel's history.[469] Others suggest that

---

462 McConville (1993b) 137.

463 Schenker, 99.

464 Craigie (1976) 364. Also Merrill, 390.

465 McConville (1993b) 137. Also Schenker, 99; von Rad (1962a) 231.

466 McConville (1993b) 137. Similarly D. Schneider, 269.

467 D. Schneider, 271–272.

468 Driver, 330. Also Vanoni, 71; Köckert, 499–500; Cunliffe-Jones, 166. Lohfink (1962) 42–44, notes the striking preaching character of these verses in distinction from 30:1–10. Friedman, 183, argues that 30:11–14 belongs with 29:28 and derives from a separate layer to 30:1–10, 15–20. Rofé (1985a) 318, notes that 30:11–14 is "extraneous to its present context" on the grounds of diction and content.

469 So Köckert, 499–504, though see 516 where he seems to suggest the possibility of 30:11–14 being much later. Lohfink (1962) 44, suggests a cultic background for

optimistic passages such as vv11–14 are even later again, possibly reflecting the hopes of the exilic or post-exilic age.[470]

Our concern is to deal theologically with the final form of the text and thus to understand vv11–14 in its relation to vv1–10. We will argue that these two paragraphs are not contradictory. It is our contention that both structurally and theologically, vv11–14 are dependent on, and must be read in the light of, vv1–10. We shall argue for this on a number of grounds.

The first argument is the relationship between 30:11–14 and 29:28. We commented above that 29:28 bears some similarity to 30:11–14.[471] This is mainly thematic rather than verbal. However דָּבָר occurs in both 29:28 and 30:14. Though plural construct in 29:28 and singular in 30:14, nevertheless the same idea is in mind.[472] This is further suggested by the fact that both 29:28 and 30:14 conclude with a purpose clause with לַעֲשׂוֹת.[473] Both verses are, in general terms, about the revelation of the law and its purpose, namely obedience. We argued above for a concentric structure for 30:1–10. Following on from this, 29:28 and 30:11–14 can be regarded as the outer layer or frame for 30:1–10.

A further argument concerns vocabulary links between 30:1–10 and 11–14. The idea of God's revealed words leading to obedience also occurs in 30:1–10. There the revealed words (הַדְּבָרִים) of blessing and curse come upon Israel (v1) with the goal of Israel's return and ultimate obedience (v2). We saw earlier that this theme, and the repetition of דָּבָר, links 29:28 to 30:1–10. Now we see it also links vv11–14 and vv1–10.

Vanoni has described the common vocabulary between vv1–10 and vv11–14 as accidental.[474] We cannot entirely agree with this. The words in common, which he identifies, are as follows: לָקַח (vv4, 12, 13), עָשָׂה (vv8, 12, 13, 14), שָׁמַיִם (vv4, 12 (twice)), מִצְוָה (vv8, 10, 11) and לֵבָב (vv1, 2, 6

---

29:1–20; 30:11–20 but understands 29:21–30:10 as a later Deuteronomistic insertion. McCarthy (1981) 15, 229, argues that 30:11–14 belongs to UrDt, affirming that total obedience is possible. In contrast, 30:1–10 is late. Compare Sklba, 72.

470 For example, Cunliffe-Jones, 166. Payne, 166, argues that this section is an optimistic challenge to counter the pessimism of the exile.

471 For example, Braulik (1992) 219; Kline (1963) 134; Blair (1964) 75; Ridderbos, 271; Craigie (1976) 365; Thompson, 286; Miller (1990) 212; Mayes (1979) 370; Brown, 281; Friedman, 183.

472 Braulik (1970) 45–49, analyses the use of this word in Deuteronomy. In 30:14, דָּבָר stands in parallel to מִצְוָה in v11. Both refer to the whole legal corpus, including parenesis. This is the same as for דְּבָרִים in 1:18; 6:6 and 11:18. He does not consider 29:28. There is no semantic distinction between plural and singular uses. As we will note below, pp189ff, 6:6 is an important parallel to 30:14.

473 Braulik (1970) 59, "Alle Ausdrücke für 'Gesetz' aber, mit denen עָשָׂה als einziges Verb der Gesetzesbeobachtung im Dtn verbunden wird (1:18; 26:16; 29:28; 30:8, 14), bezeichnen das ganze 'Gesetz'."

474 Vanoni, 71.

(three times), 10, 14). The relative clause, אֲשֶׁר־אָנֹכִי מְצַוְּךָ הַיּוֹם, occurs in vv2, 8 and 11.[475] In addition to Vanoni, we note that שָׁמַע occurs in vv2, 8, 10, 12 and 13.[476] There may well be no significance in the occurrences of לָקַח and שָׁמַיִם here. Yet, even though the other words are quite common in Deuteronomy, they are nonetheless important. Admittedly in vv12, 13, שָׁמַע occurs in hiphil and without the preposition בְּ. However in each of vv8, 12 and 13, the verbs עָשָׂה and שָׁמַע occur in collocation. This seems unlikely to be coincidental. Obedience is obviously a central issue to both sections. Verses 11–14 extrapolate on vv1–10 showing how the obedience expected in v8 may happen.[477] The hiphils of שָׁמַע reflect this. We are told that Israel will hear (שָׁמַע qal, vv2, 8 and 10). This is now shown to be because Yahweh will make Israel hear (שָׁמַע hiphil, vv12, 13). This is not by a messenger going and getting the commandment and making Israel hear. That is denied by vv12, 13. Rather, Yahweh himself makes Israel hear by putting the word in its heart and mouth (v14). The repeated verb עָשָׂה in vv12, 13, 14 shows that the putting of the word in the mouth and in the heart has the same effect as causing Israel to hear.[478]

The object of obedience in both sections is the commandment. Nor is this coincidental. Chapter 30 is bringing to a head the issue of response to all of the commandment contained throughout Deuteronomy. The singular מִצְוָה implies the "whole revelation in Deuteronomy of the divine will".[479] All but two of the fourteen occurrences of the singular מִצְוָה in Deuteronomy refer to the whole of the law, including the parenesis. 30:11 is not one of these exceptions.[480] Frequently in Deuteronomy, the singular מִצְוָה is qualified by כֹּל, stressing this completeness.[481] Even though the noun occurs in the plural in vv8, 10, there is no significant semantic distinction between the plurals there and the singular in v11. All three refer to the whole law.[482]

475 Weinfeld (1972) 356, lists 31 occurrences of this clause, or variants, in Deuteronomy.

476 Compare Braulik (1992) 218.

477 Braulik (1992) 218.

478 Craigie (1976) 362, translates v12, "It is not in the heavens, so that it might be said: Who will ascend to the heavens for us and bring it to us? – then he will make us listen to it and we will do it!" Similarly Mayes (1979) 370. NIV translates the verb as "proclaim", though BDB, 1034, prefers "cause to hear".

479 Von Rad (1966e) 184; (1962a) 231; Thompson, 286; Kalland, 189. Compare Watts (1970) 281, who regards the singular as an indication that only the command for exclusive worship is intended. Mayes (1979) 174, suggests that the singular means the whole law only in later parts of Deuteronomy.

480 Braulik (1970) 53–56.

481 Thus 5:28; 6:25; 8:1; 11:8, 22; 15:5; 19:9; 26:13; 27:1; 31:5. With זאת: 6:1, 25; 11:22; 15:5; 19:9 and 30:11.

482 Braulik (1970) 56–60. There are six exceptions to thirty occurrences of the plural noun which refer only to the Decalogue.

This is reinforced by the repeated relative clause, אֲשֶׁר־אָנֹכִי מְצַוְּךָ הַיּוֹם, in vv2, 8 and 11. Thus the verbs עָשָׂה and שָׁמַע, the occurrence of מִצְוָה in vv11–14 and the repeated relative clause show that this section continues on from and is to be read in the light of vv1–10.[483]

This discussion helps us to appreciate the apparent shift in time perspective from future to present. The impact of this shift is weaker than often thought, for the "today" of v11 belongs to the same "*Promulgationssatz*" clause which occurs in both vv2, 8. The function of the clause, including הַיּוֹם, is "to provide an identifying characterization of the general parenetical situation".[484] Thus הַיּוֹם in v11 has the function of identifying the commandment under discussion and does not have the function of stressing the present tense any more than הַיּוֹם in vv2, 8.[485] Rather than creating a tension with the preceding, the "today" of v11, and the relative clause in which it occurs, are links of similarity between the paragraphs rather than marks of contrast. We thus question whether there is a present tense urgency here in contrast to vv1–10. The heightened rhetoric of vv11–14[486] may in fact function to emphasise in a dramatic way the striking results of the circumcision of the heart in v6. In other words, vv11–14 may be understood proleptically as being addressed to those who have experienced the circumcision of the heart by Yahweh.

The close relationship between the two paragraphs is further indicated by the use of כִּי in vv10, 11. Those wishing to contrast vv11–14 and vv1–10 have understood the particle כִּי in v11 in an emphatic or asseverative way.[487] Such a translation tends to highlight the present sense of vv11–14, strengthening any contrast with the preceding paragraph.

> V.11–14 ('For'…) clearly states the reason for a *present* duty; in view of the contents of the four verses, it is exceedingly unnatural to suppose that they explain why Israel should find it easy to return to Jehovah in the future contingency contemplated in v.10. It is next to impossible, therefore, that v.11–20 can have been originally the sequel of v.1–10.[488]

This is unconvincing. As we have already seen, the present sense in vv11–14 is not as pronounced as often thought and the connections in vocabulary and contents suggest a stronger link between the two sections than usually supposed. This statement also fails to see that the כִּי of v11 is part of a sequence of כִּי clauses in vv9–11.[489] In light of the other arguments for the

---

483 For a list of repeated vocabulary in chapters 29 and 30, see Lenchak, 132.

484 DeVries (1975a) 186. On the *Promulgationssatz*, see Lohfink (1963a) 59–63; DeVries (1974) 301–316.

485 Compare McConville (1993b) 137; Schenker, 99.

486 Braulik (1992) 219.

487 For example, NIV: "Now…". Similarly Köckert, 499. See further Claassen, 29–46, on the use of כִּי in Biblical Hebrew.

488 Driver, 330–331.

489 Also overlooked by Lenchak, 134. Compare Steuernagel, 109.

association of vv11–14 with the preceding, it seems fair to treat the particle as causal or evidential, that is, giving further reason for the expected blessing and restoration expressed in v9a.[490]

> Das dreifache satzeinleitende כִּי in 30:10f, das die EÜ (Einheitsübersetzung) zweimal mit »wenn« übersetzt (10), einmal nicht weiter berücksichtigt (11), wird wohl besser mit »denn« wiedergegeben. Dann stehen am Ende mehrere parallele Begründungssätze, die immer wieder das gleiche Urdatum von verscheidenen Seiten her ins Auge fassen, aber keine Bedingungen.[491]

This further supports our argument about the sense of certainty in v10. Yahweh will make Israel prosperous (v9a) for (כִּי evidential, v9b) he will restore Israel's fortunes when (כִּי temporal, v10a) Israel obeys and when (כִּי temporal, v10b) Israel returns for (כִּי evidential, causal, v11) the word is in Israel's heart.[492] Thus vv11–14 are further evidence that Israel will surely return and obey Yahweh.

We argued above that the certainty of future hope rests on Yahweh's promise to circumcise the heart. Hence v8 expressed Israel's return and obedience as certain future events. Now vv11–14 elaborate on the nature of that circumcision, giving a more detailed reason and explication for such confident expectation. These verses explain what the circumcision of the heart does and why it enables obedience. So vv11–14 deal with the same issue as vv6–8 but in different terms and they "greifen dann nochmals weiter zurück und führen aus, wie es denn möglich ist, daß man »hören« und »tun« kann".[493] Thus the כִּי of v11 refers back to the preceding section and binds the two sections together.[494] Verses 11–14 complement vv1–10.

The final connection in vocabulary between 30:1–10 and 11–14 is לֵבָב. This is the most important vocabulary connection. A pattern exists in its occurrences in vv1–14 as follows:[495]

A take the word to heart (1)
  B return and obey with all your heart (2)
    C heart circumcision and subsequent love (6)
  B' return with all your heart (10)
A' the word is in your heart (14)

---

490 On distinguishing between causal and evidential senses of כִּי, see Claassen, 29–46; Joüon (1991) §170d; BDB, 473–474, 3c.

491 Braulik (1992) 216–217.

492 Alternatively, v10, "for Israel will obey and will return" conveys even more strongly the sense of certainty. On כִּי clauses in Deuteronomy 1–30 as predominantly causal, see de Regt (1988) 115. The כִּי clause in 30:14a, he says, is adversative.

493 Braulik (1992) 218.

494 Ridderbos, 271.

495 Braulik (1992) 217–218.

This structure suggests not only that vv11–14 belong with vv1–10, but also how they are to be understood in relation to that section. The optimistic expectation that Israel is able to obey, reflected in vv11–14, thus derives from the circumcision of the heart in v6. So the word is placed in the heart by the circumcision of the heart. As with vv1–10, vv11–14 are also concerned with a change of heart (*Herzensverwandlung*).[496] As the action on Israel's heart in v6 enables obedience, so v14 expresses the same idea. The near word is a result of the circumcision of the heart and not a cause for it.

So, on grounds of theme, vocabulary, time perspective, syntax, and theology, vv11–14 may be understood as dependent on vv1–10 and an elaboration of its key idea. The two paragraphs are complementary not contradictory.

### *The Grounds for Israel's Capacity to Obey*

There is general agreement that vv11–14 deal with Israel's capacity to obey the covenant commands of Yahweh. However the grounds of that capacity need clarification. One view is that Israel's capacity to obey derives from its having received, learnt, and understood the torah which has been given to it. That is, the grounds are external to Israel, and involve both the easiness of the torah and its revelation. The second view is that Israel's capacity to obey rests on a change of heart which enables obedience. In this case, the grounds are internal to Israel. Given our argument above that vv1–10 and vv11–14 are complementary, we argue for the latter of these two views.

#### NEARNESS

The usual interpretation of the near word in v14 is that nearness is a result of revelation by agents of God. So the word has been brought near "by prophets and other teachers, and especially in the discourses of Dt.".[497] Alternatively, the nearness of the word is due to its being written.[498] Similarly, the nearness of the word lies in the lucidity and intelligibility of the faith expounded through clear Deuteronomic preaching.[499] However the nearness is not a reflection of its being written but rather that it is in the

---

496 Braulik (1992) 218. Also Miller (1990) 213.

497 Driver, 331. Similarly Lenchak, 200; Blair (1964) 75. On a link between 30:14 and 4:7, see Cairns, 265; Schenker, 99; Thompson, 286; Buis and Leclerq, 187; Mayes (1979) 370. Compare Friedman, 183.

498 Cairns, 265; Lenchak, 241. Compare Moore, 83, who argues that nearness "seems to depend upon the immediacy of Moses' role of *speaking 'to you this day'* (v.11)".

499 Amsler, 21.

mouth and heart.[500] Indeed v14 does away with the need for a messenger or agent of revelation by positing an alternative to the agent of vv12, 13.

Up to this point in Israel's history, namely the covenant in the Plains of Moab, the word of the law has been revealed, delivered and is about to be written. Yet 29:3 and 30:1–10 have shown that more is required for Israel to obey. The revelation which they have received through Moses is insufficient for obedience, as the golden calf incident demonstrated. The circumcision of the heart is what is required. This act of Yahweh still lies in the future. We have seen above that the references to heart in 30:1–14 link together and focus on the centre point, v6. So the nearness of the word is a consequence of the circumcision of the heart and not the result of reading, writing or reciting the law. As we have noted above, vv11–14 elaborate on the nature of this heart circumcision. In different words they explain what a circumcised heart means and why it enables obedience. To circumcise the heart is in effect the same as placing the word on the heart.[501] Perhaps it is helpful to see vv6, 14 as complementary. In v6 the heart is dealt with to make it receptive. In v14, what that heart is actually receptive to is addressed. The heart and the word go together. So the placing of the word on the heart in v14 cannot therefore be equated with the revelation of the law through Moses, prophets, teachers or in writing. An inner possession of divine revelation is the issue.[502]

### MOUTH AND HEART

This point also influences our understanding of what it means for the word to be in the mouth and in the heart. One possibility is that mouth and heart comprise a merismus, that mouth and heart are antithetical, mouth referring to the external and heart to the internal.[503] However the majority of commentators, understanding nearness as a result of revelation through teachers and prophets, take the reference to the mouth to mean that the word is recited or repeated. So, "La Loi pourra être dans la bouche de tous par la répétition méditative".[504]

The reference to the word being "in the heart" is understood in a variety of ways. If the heart is understood primarily as the seat of understanding, then the word being in the heart is understood as follows:

---

500 Ridderbos, 271.

501 Compare Jeremiah 31:31–33. So König, 201; von Rad (1966e) 184; Nielsen, 272. Compare Schenker, 99; Couroyer (1983) 424.

502 König, 201. Köckert, 501–502, suggests the idea is similar to 8:3 where life stems from the word from God's mouth.

503 BDB, 523, "*the inner man* in contrast with the outer".

504 Buis and Leclerq, 187. Similarly Kalland, 189; Schenker, 99; D. Schneider, 272. Cairns, 265, suggests it refers to cultic recital and domestic catechism.

> Jahweh wants obedience admittedly; but he also wants men who understand his commandments and ordinances, that is, men who assent inwardly as well.[505]

The more common interpretation of "in the heart" is that this refers to the word being memorised, understanding the heart as the seat of memory.[506] Couroyer distinguishes between "in" and "on" the heart. When something is "in the heart", as here, memory is intended. By contrast, "on the heart" denotes an aid to memory, probably a pendant hanging on the chest. In such cases, "heart" is not the internal organ but the external chest.[507]

To support the contention that v14 refers to repetition and memorisation, many appeal to 6:5–9.[508] The heart is mentioned in both passages and though the mouth is not mentioned in 6:5–9, functions of speaking and reciting do occur.[509] Couroyer states that 6:5 refers to memory, understanding "heart" in its proper, that is, internal, sense. In contrast he argues that heart in 6:6 is used in its improper sense, that is, referring to the chest, paralleling the external aids in 6:7–9.[510] If his distinction is valid, then 6:6 is not a parallel to 30:14 as 6:6 refers to the commandments being עַל־לְבָבֶךָ and 30:14 speaks of the word בִּלְבָבְךָ. Indeed there would be a significant progression from the former to the latter. The word would be merely external in 6:6, an aid to memory as perhaps illustrated in 6:7–9, but fully internal in 30:14.

However there are important connections between the two passages. 6:6 is a command to Israel, following the command "to love with all your heart" in 6:5. Thus there is a relationship between הַדְּבָרִים הָאֵלֶּה אֲשֶׁר אָנֹכִי מְצַוְּךָ הַיּוֹם (compare 30:11) being on the heart and loving Yahweh with all the heart. The same connection exists in 30:1–14. We have seen that the placing of the word in the heart (30:14) is the same thing as circumcising the heart (30:6) which enables the love of Yahweh with all the heart. So Braulik says, "Dabei ist 30:11–14 in ähnlicher Weise auf das Liebesgebot in 30:6 bezogen, wie 6:6f an das Liebensgebot in 6:5 anschließt".[511] The significant development from chapter 6 to 30:11–14 is that whereas in the earlier chapter the people are commanded to put the commandments on their heart, in chapter 30, Yahweh does it for them. This is the same change

505 Von Rad (1962a) 198. Also Kalland, 189.

506 Ridderbos, 271; Cairns, 264, "dynamic remembering"; Buis and Leclerq, 187; Payne, 166. Schenker, 99, combines understanding with memory.

507 Couroyer (1983) 416–434.

508 Schenker, 99; König, 201; Mayes (1979) 370; Driver, 331. Couroyer (1983) 420–421, among others, also discusses 11:18–20.

509 Mayes (1979) 370; Driver, 331.

510 Couroyer (1983) 420–421.

511 Braulik (1992) 220. He, 219, argues that in 6:6 the law is to be learnt only outwardly (in contrast to 30:14) and permanently recited. These two functions parallel the heart and mouth reference in 30:14.

we saw from 10:16 to 30:6 regarding the circumcision of the heart. What was commanded of the people is now promised by Yahweh.[512] If there is any semantic distinction as Couroyer advocates, then one could argue that Israel is commanded to do a lesser thing, namely an external act, which is surpassed by what Yahweh does for them, namely an internal change. In either case, there is no need to conclude from the links with 6:5–9 that mouth and heart in 30:14 must be understood as recitation and memory.

In our opinion, the teaching, talking, tying and writing of the commandments in 6:7–9 are a means to an end and not the end in itself. The end is expressed in v6. This is the right internal state of the heart.[513] So vv7–9 are not a parallel to v6. This is suggested by the fact that the external acts of vv7–9 are excessively demanding.[514] Such an extreme demand suggests a rhetorical purpose, almost indeed to point to the impossibility of fulfilling the command of 6:6. Scholars dispute whether these acts were intended to be taken literally or figuratively.[515] It seems more appropriate to understand them figuratively. Throughout, Deuteronomy is concerned for an inner disposition of the heart and soul towards Yahweh. This is to be expressed in external action, but that is not in itself a sufficient response. The acts of recital and memorisation in 6:7–9 are indications of how the heart may be influenced and, further, how important is a right inner disposition, though they are no guarantee of such a disposition. The *aides mémoire* are necessitated by the inherent weakness of Israel.[516] They are an acknowledgement of Israel's proclivity to sin and forgetfulness. Thus that disposition can only be brought about through Yahweh's action on the human heart. That is what 30:11–14 expresses.

Therefore 30:11–14, like 30:1–10, reflects the point of view that Israel's capacity to obey is dependent on a change of heart effected by Yahweh.

---

512 Augustine: "*du quod iubes, et iube quod vis*".

513 Miller (1990) 104, says, "Verses 8 and 9 may be easily understood as indications of an external appropriation, but the symbolic acts referred to there are only in the context of an internal appropriation that makes this instruction second nature".

514 Compare von Rad (1966e) 64.

515 Couroyer (1983) 420–421, takes them literally. The LXX translates frontlets in v8 figuratively. See Weinfeld (1991) 341–343, for a discussion on this issue. He notes that Rashbam understood v8 figuratively but Weinfeld agrees with Ibn Ezra that v8 is literal. On the possibility of understanding the head and arm phylacteries as apotropaic, see Miller (1970) 129–130. The Samaritans understood v8 figuratively but v9 literally. Among modern commentators, Driver, 93, understands vv8–9 literally. Also Mayes (1979) 177–8; Payne, 47. Craigie (1976) 170–171, is undecided. Miller (1990) 104–105, says it makes little difference. Also Christensen (1991) 144–145. Von Rad (1966e) 64; Cairns, 85, take these verses figuratively. Also Thompson, 123, "What was given originally as a metaphor became for later Jews a literal injunction."

516 Millar, 240.

The revelation of the torah, through Moses, or other agents, whether orally or in writing, does not sufficiently enable obedience. Thus we reject the view that

> the covenant people *have* the capacity to achieve what is required of them, for they possess a completely sufficient map for the way, namely, the God-given torah,[517]

and that obedience is "possible because the people know the commandments".[518] These statements have misunderstood the thrust and significance of this section. Yahweh's revelation of the torah is one thing but it is insufficient for obedience. What is needed is the torah on the human heart.[519]

"NOT TOO DIFFICULT"

Verse 11 says the torah is "not too difficult", לֹא־נִפְלֵאת. Most frequently this is taken to mean that the law is able to be understood and is "nothing abstruse or incomprehensible, like the complicated structure of the human frame (Ps 139:6)".[520] Weinfeld suggests a sapiential background to the expression. He translates נִפְלֵאת as "wondrous", meaning beyond comprehension. The writer of Deuteronomy is emphasising that "the wisdom embodied in his teaching may be easily understood by all".[521] Whether or not the background is sapiential, these explanations wrongly place the emphasis on the ability of man to understand.

The niphal of פָּלָא occurs thirteen times in the Old Testament and נִפְלָאוֹת 44 times.[522] Predominantly these occurrences refer to God's astonishing acts, whether creation, the miracles of the exodus or his wonders generally. Almost invariably Yahweh is the subject or cause of these acts.[523] These wonderful things belong to the realm of Yahweh rather than man. They are impossible for man but not for God who is often praised for them.[524] Yet often there is expression of amazement, astonishment or incomprehension at them. So, for example, in Genesis 18:14, in the context of the announcement that Sarah will bear a child, God says, "Is anything

---

517 Cairns, 264.

518 Ridderbos, 271. Also Kline (1963) 133.

519 Luther, 277–278; Aho, 48.

520 Driver, 331. *GKC*, §133c, notes נִפְלָא מִן־ also occurs in Genesis 18:14; Deuteronomy 17:8; Jeremiah 32:17 and Proverbs 30:18. Compare Psalm 139:6. Also Kalland, 190. Von Rad (1966e) 184, says that the law "is something that is evident; it can be comprehended and talked about"; see also his (1962a) 228. Compare BDB, 810.

521 Weinfeld (1972) 258–260. The writer of Deuteronomy is contrasting the law with wisdom, Weinfeld says. Also Thompson, 286; Ridderbos, 271.

522 Lisowsky, 1154, 942–943.

523 Though see Deuteronomy 17:8; 2 Samuel 1:26; 13:2; Daniel 8:24; 11:36.

524 For example, Psalms 9:2; 26:7; 40:6; etc.

too hard (הֲיִפָּלֵא) for the LORD?" The implied answer is "No". What God is able to do is astonishing, so surprising that Sarah laughs. She thinks the suggestion impossible. But with God, it is not. Zechariah 8:6 also draws a clear distinction between what is marvellous to the people and yet not so astonishing for God. The נִפְלָאוֹת are the things God does which man can neither do nor comprehend. They are things which, in a sense, belong to God. With man they are impossible; with God, they are possible.[525]

This discussion sheds some light on Deuteronomy 30:11. To say that what is being commanded is לֹא־נִפְלֵאת is to say that it does not require a miracle to do it. Ridderbos suggests that v12 explains the first negative of v11. So the law is not "too wonderful to be grasped or understood and it is thus not part of the secret things" because it has been revealed.[526] Though this places the emphasis on Yahweh's revealing, rather than Israel's ability, Yahweh's making possible is deeper than simply revealing the law. The torah is not difficult, not because of something inherent in the torah itself, nor only because of its being revealed, but because of Israel having its heart circumcised. So vv11–14, acknowledging

> that the 'nearness' of the commandment was attributable to the gift of God,...affirms Israel's capacity to respond adequately to God's command, because it knows that in the end God will 'circumcise [their] hearts' (30:6).[527]

What is impossible for man, נִפְלָאוֹת in fact, God makes לֹא־נִפְלֵאת by both revelation and the circumcision of the heart. Indeed the notion is almost paradoxical: Yahweh performs the miracle so that Israel does not have to. The view that the law itself is easy, mentioned above, denies the need for the grace of God which enables love of the law.[528]

It is important to remind ourselves again that the expression of ability in 30:11–14 is due to the circumcision of the heart in 30:6. Though McConville recognises this in part, he states that "Deuteronomy 30:11–14 state a truth in principle, but one that is negated in history by the character

---

525 See also, for example, Jeremiah 32:17, 27. Compare Deuteronomy 29:28.

526 Ridderbos, 271. He takes v13 as a parallel to the second negative of v11. He translates נִפְלֵאת as "wonderful", rather than "difficult". Similarly Mayes (1979) 370, says that נִפְלֵאת refers to things beyond human comprehension. This is overcome by revelation. Maybe another way of understanding these verses is to see both vv12, 13 explaining the second negative of v11. Possibly v14 elaborates on the first negative of v11. This would give an ABA' structure to vv11–14. It is more likely that v14 is a summary verse for the section as a whole. Similarly Lenchak, 179, suggests a simple chiasm ABB'A'.

527 McConville (1993b) 156.

528 Luther, 277–278. Compare Watts (1970) 281, "But it is not *hard* to keep if one loves it devotedly". Unlike Luther, Watts fails to identify from where the capacity to love comes. Compare Buis and Leclerq, 187; Diepold, 101.

of Israel".[529] The implication of this sentence however is that the grounds of Israel's capacity to obey rest in the revelation and easiness of the torah, that is, the external grounds, rather than in the change to Israel's heart. He has failed to see the proper relationship between these two paragraphs and hence is forced to try and reconcile what are seen to be tensions, if not contradictions, between the two. We would prefer to say that 30:11–14 states a truth *yet to be effected by Yahweh.* Perhaps McConville is suggesting this when he says,

> The exhortation remains absolute, though we know that it can only ever have validity in a new arrangement that lies beyond both sin and judgment.[530]

30:11–14 comes to reality only when Yahweh circumcises Israel's heart. The present tense of vv11–14 is not in contrast to vv1–10 but rather highlights rhetorically the certainty of this future event and its effects for obedience. Rather than saying that the character of Israel in history negates this truth, Israel's character in history demonstrates the need for this truth still to come into effect.

This emphasis on divine grace does not negate human responsibility here. 30:11–14 preserves the same balance between divine initiative and human responsibility which exists in vv1–10. So v14 shows that the purpose of the grace of God is that Israel will obey.[531]

> (S)uch obedience cannot come without God's gift of a heart to know and obey. But the responsibility so to act as God's people is no less incumbent upon each individual.[532]

Possibly the rhetorical questions of vv12, 13 are expressions of an evasion of human responsibility. That is, they could be read as excuses for not keeping the law.[533] If so, then their negation in vv12, 13 asserts human responsibility. There is no excuse for ignoring or not keeping the law.[534] Taken on their own, these verses may imply a theology of salvation by human effort and works. However we have argued that these verses must be read in the wider context of, and deriving from, 30:1–10. So human capacity depends on divine grace, namely Yahweh's circumcision of the heart.[535]

---

529 McConville (1993b) 138.

530 McConville (1993b) 138.

531 Craigie (1976) 365.

532 Miller (1990) 213.

533 Craigie (1976) 365; Cranfield, 525. Hals, 9, includes 29:28 with vv11–14 as excuses for dodging the choice. Lenchak, 220, argues that these questions expect a negative answer and rhetorically function to coerce the audience into agreeing with 30:14. He suggests that 30:11–14 is a refutation to some unspoken objection on the part of the audience.

534 On the ANE background, see Craigie (1976) 365; Thompson, 286; von Rad (1966e) 184; Cairns, 264; Kalland, 190; Weinfeld (1972) 259–260.

535 Toombs, 401. Similarly Sklba, 73; McConville (1993b) 138.

### *Deuteronomy 30:11–14 in Romans 10*

Further support for our understanding of Deuteronomy 30:11–14 is found in St Paul's interpretation of this passage. Paul understands 30:11–14 in much the same way as we have argued for above. We consider that finding support from St Paul is not invalid. From a Christian perspective, there is an authority in the New Testament and its understanding and use of the Old Testament which gives it a privileged position above other interpretations of the Old Testament. Thus we appeal to Romans 10 for support of our understanding of 30:11–14.[536] We shall not attempt an analysis of Paul's argument through Romans 10. Nor are we primarily concerned with Paul's use of 30:11–14. Rather, we shall confine ourselves to the issue of Paul's understanding of 30:11–14 and what light that sheds on our understanding of this passage.

Frequently it is asserted that Paul in Romans 10:5–7 is contrasting law/works and faith/grace by setting against each other Leviticus 18:5 and Deuteronomy 30:11–14.[537] This is usually maintained on the basis of the γὰρ...δὲ construction in 10:5, 6.[538] However this construction in Romans more often than not carries little or no adversative force and therefore 10:5, 6 should be read in parallel rather than in contrast.[539] This means that Paul has a view of law and faith which holds the two together harmoniously.[540] This is supported by reading τέλος as "goal" without a temporal sense.[541]

---

536 Sanday and Headlam, 286, 289, suggest Paul's language is not a quotation but an allusion or general reference to 30:11–14. Similarly Barrett, 198–199, that Paul exercises great rhetorical freedom. Also Cranfield, 523. See the discussion in Käsemann, 284; Badenas, 126. Compare Suggs, 300–302, that Paul undertakes a serious attempt to cite and exegete Deuteronomy 30. Also Seifrid, 25–27.

537 For example, Cunliffe-Jones, 166; Thompson, 287; Kalland, 190; Bruce, 201; Murray, 51; Morris, 382. Cranfield, 520. Compare McConville (1993b) 154, that Leviticus 18:5 is close to Deuteronomy 4:1; 6:24 in thought. Also B. Schneider, 163–207.

538 For example, Seifrid, 16–17.

539 G.N. Davies (1990) 190–191, 199. In any case, δέ when adversative in force is weak. Compare Dunn, 602. He notes, 612–613, that the absence of attribution of the second quotation in 10:6 to Moses intends to heighten the contrast. Compare Davies, 199–200, that the reference to Moses in 10:5 is a "double affirmation" covering 10:6 as well. Also Martin, 138–139. McComiskey, 121–128, argues that Paul has a bi-covenantal structure in mind and is contrasting the covenant of administration (Sinai) which operates by law and the covenant of promise (Abraham) which operates by faith.

540 Kline (1991) 433–456; Martens (1992) 21–22; Selman, 19.

541 W.S. Campbell, 77–78; Flückiger, 153–157. Also Badenas, 121–125; Barth, 245; Hays, 75–76.

In 10:6–8, Paul applies the nearness of the word to Christ, rather than to the torah.[542] At a basic level, some simply note that nearness is a result of Christ's incarnation and universal offer of salvation.[543] Yet Paul's understanding goes much further than this. The nearness of Christ is not simply a result of his incarnation. Calvin regards Romans 10:6–7, citing Deuteronomy 30:12–13, as a reference to Christ's death and resurrection rather than incarnation. So it is through his death and resurrection that Christ is near. Thus Calvin says, "The word of the law is never of itself in our heart...until it is ingrafted in us by the faith of the Gospel."[544] This idea is certainly consistent with the rest of Paul's argument in Romans. At the heart of Paul's gospel is not the incarnation but the crucifixion and resurrection. In Romans 2:25–29, Paul argues that true circumcision is circumcision of the heart. This is accomplished by the Spirit and not the written code. The giving of the Spirit is made possible only through the death and resurrection of Jesus.[545] These ideas support the view that the nearness spoken about both in Deuteronomy 30:11–14 and in Romans 10 is a result of God's work, by the Spirit, in the circumcision of the heart.[546] This is consistent with what we found above, that law and faith are held together by Paul. He understands that Deuteronomy 30:11–14 does the same.[547]

Paul discusses the Deuteronomy passage under the title of "the righteousness that is by faith" (10:6). Braulik sees in this that Paul has rightly understood 30:11–14 as a statement of justification by faith since he has read it in the light of 30:1–10.[548] Paul then understands 30:11–14 as grounding the capacity of Israel to obey the law in God's grace and not in its own ability. He understands the law, at least in Deuteronomy 30, not as mere legalism but in a broad way, as a word of gospel and faith. Yet it is

---

542 On the wisdom motifs which link Christ and torah, see Suggs, 304–311; Weinfeld (1972) 259–260. In response to Suggs, see Seifrid, 25–26.

543 So Payne, 167; Cunliffe-Jones, 166; Thompson, 287; Cranfield, 525; Murray, 53. Payne argues that Romans 10:5–13 reinforces the point of Deuteronomy 30:11–14 in arguing for the universal availability of the God's self-revelation. Similarly, Cairns 265. Barrett, 199, argues that the descent mentioned in Romans 10:6 is a reference to the incarnation. Against the notion of incarnation, see Dunn, 605, 615; Martin, 140.

544 Calvin, 224. Also, 225, "The benefit of Christ's death and resurrection is now communicated to us by the Gospel." Merrill, 391, speaks of both incarnation and resurrection.

545 Colossians 2:11–14 makes even clearer the link between circumcision of the heart and the death and resurrection of Jesus.

546 See Dunn, 614. On the law and the heart in Romans, see 2:15; 6:17.

547 McComiskey, 125.

548 Braulik (1992) 218–219. Likewise Calvin, 225.

commonly alleged that Paul's understanding of this passage is careless or inept, even "a drastic and unwarrantable allegorizing".[549]

Paul does exercise freedom of quotation, especially in 10:7. He also omits 30:11 and the end of v14, "so that you may obey it", in his reference.[550] It is suggested that this is a deliberate devaluation of the importance of keeping the commandments.[551] To some minds therefore, Paul has distorted the meaning of 30:11–14.[552] However, the way he introduces 10:6a by "Do not say in your heart" indicates he has correctly understood Deuteronomy 30:11–14 as not legalistic.[553] This expression "reproduces exactly the opening words of two verses of the LXX version of Deuteronomy (8:17 and 9:4)." Both these verses conform to a doctrine of justification by faith and refute the claims of Israel to self-righteousness.[554] Also the notion of the circumcision of the heart in Deuteronomy 30:6 is picked up by Paul in Romans 2:29, showing that Paul saw all of Deuteronomy 30 "as anticipatory of righteousness by faith". So in "a comprehensive and creative way, he is just developing a theme suggested by the text itself." Further, "(i)f the real will of God for his people was the way of faith..., applying this to Christ, Paul remained faithful to the Deuteronomy text".[555] In Paul's time, Deuteronomy 30 would have been understood as a promise of return from exile, which is shown to be fulfilled in Christ. Thus Paul understands Deuteronomy 30 correctly.[556]

---

549 Black, 9, quoting Kirk. See Suggs, 299.

550 For complete details, see Badenas, 125.

551 McConville (1993b) 154; Dunn, 613.

552 Bruce, 203–204, wrongly understands Deuteronomy 30:11–14 to be a statement of righteousness through the law, as is Leviticus 18:5. He suggests that Paul is misappropriating these verses. Similarly Calvin, 224; compare Sanday and Headlam, 289. See also Badenas, 126. Alternatively some scholars suggest that Paul is using a contemporary *pesher*-like interpretation to Deuteronomy 30:11–14. So Black, 8; Bruce, 204; Käsemann, 285. For a rejection of this, see Seifrid, 27–34. On other contemporary interpretation parallels, see Badenas, 126–128; Dunn, 604–605. See Seifrid, 23–25, for a rejection of the view that the Targums offer a parallel to Paul's method here.

553 Dunn, 614. McConville (1993b) 154, says, "Paul focuses on the terms 'word' and 'heart' in the Deuteronomy passage in order to pursue his main point that righteousness – a true relationship with God – comes not by the effort of keeping the Law, but by faith."

554 Cranfield, 523; Badenas, 129–130; McConville (1993b) 155; G.N. Davies (1990) 201. Likewise Hays, 78–79, "these words evoke an earlier word of God to Israel, in which the Lord God warns them against the presumption of their own righteousness and reminds these 'stiff-necked' people that the initiative in deliverance and covenant making is his, not theirs. The message is so apt for Paul's argument...". See Seifrid, 36; Käsemann, 288; Romans 10:3.

555 Badenas, 130. Similarly McConville (1993b) 155–156.

556 N.T. Wright, 245.

Though Paul has dropped the end of 30:14 from his quotation, the exhortation to respond remains, expressed in Romans 10:9, 10. So Paul is not down-playing the requirements demanded but transforms them into believing in Christ. Also the inclusion of the introductory phrase from Deuteronomy 9:4 "maintains the individualized hortatory tone present in Deut 30:11–14".[557] So Paul is faithful to Deuteronomy and its theology in a broad context.[558]

Thus we conclude that Paul in fact understands Deuteronomy 30:11–14 in the way we have argued above. He does not have to distort its meaning to bring it in line with his argument, even if he is selective in its citation.

> In writing the words which he here borrows from Deuteronomy Paul knows that they revolve around a thought which is completely in conformity with the doctrine of 'justification by faith', which consists essentially in not claiming before God a 'righteousness of one's own'.[559]

Righteousness is a gift from God. That, we have seen, is the hub of the argument of Deuteronomy 30. Deuteronomy 30 is not legalistic and Paul does not interpet it thus.[560]

> The appropriateness of Paul's use of the passage thus emerges the more strongly.... Moses knew that some new act of God was needed in order to achieve the goal; Paul knows that that act is the coming of the gospel of Christ.[561]

Since Paul understands Christ as the true substance of the law, the same divine grace lies behind the gift of the law and the incarnation. His interpretation of Deuteronomy 30:11–14 is justified.[562]

The relationship between law and faith therefore, often described as antithetical, is perhaps not so polarised. "The law is not nullified by faith but fulfilled by it."[563] We argued in a previous section that law in Deuteronomy 30 is also gospel to a guilty people. Law and faith are not mutually exclusive alternatives. The faith which both Deuteronomy and Romans desire is obedient faith which stems from a heart changed by God. So Deuteronomy 30:11–14 fits Paul's argument.[564] The antithesis is between self-righteousness and the righteousness which is a gift from God.

---

557 Seifrid, 22–23.

558 Seifrid, 36.

559 Leenhardt, 268–269. And, 270, "Paul has recognized the real bearing of the Deuteronomic text, whereas his modern detractors have failed to see it". Similarly Calvin, 225; Morris, 382–383.

560 Murray, 52.

561 McConville (1993b) 156.

562 Cranfield, 524–525.

563 McConville (1993b) 155. Also Dunn, 613.

564 Dunn, 615. Also G.N. Davies (1990) that the nature of faith in Romans is that of "the obedience of faith". Also Cunliffe-Jones, 166; Calvin, 224–225, "for the observance of the law springs from faith in Christ".

Both Deuteronomy and Romans are of a common mind on this. They reject the former and propound the latter.[565]

### *Conclusion*

In conclusion we find that Paul's understanding of Deuteronomy 30 is not contrived or misconstrued but rather he understands the passage properly. This supports our thesis that 30:11–14 is dependent on 30:1–10 and therefore grounds Israel's capacity to obey the law in the circumcision of the heart by Yahweh. We have rejected the view that 30:11–14 stands in temporal contrast to 30:1–10. Rather it describes the consequence of the circumcision of the heart. It therefore denies human capacity to fulfil the covenant demands. It is not a statement that the law is easy to fulfil. Nor is the law's accessibility due to revelation. Being in the mouth and heart is not a reference to memorisation or recital. Rather, v14 is a statement of the effect of the circumcision of the heart in v6. Ultimately, the fulfilment is the work of God, in Christ, as Paul argues in Romans 10:4. Thus the optimism of 30:11–14 derives from the hope of God's gracious, and future, work.

## Deuteronomy 30:15–20

We turn now to the final section of Deuteronomy 30. It is in this paragraph, 30:15–20, that the focus returns to the present, bringing the future possibilities, promises and warnings to bear on Israel's choice in the present.

### *Introduction*

This paragraph is the rhetorical climax of Deuteronomy.[566] It is the end of the third speech of Moses. The next chapter begins another speech which, along with all the remaining four chapters, focuses on issues of transition of leadership and the death of Moses.[567] Moses' exhorting Israel to obey the covenant demands comes to a climax in 30:15–20. Whether these verses

565 McConville (1993b) 155.

566 Miller (1990) 213; Selman, 15; McConville and Millar, 83, "the zenith of the exhortation of the book is reached here". For possible chiasm here, see Lenchak, 179. He also suggests, 177, that the blessings and curses of 30:19 form an inclusio with 30:1, also with the expression נָתַתִּי לְפָנֶיךָ.

567 In a sense, the final four chapters form an appendix. Wenham (1970) 213–216; Mayes (1979) 371; Rofé (1985a) 310–320; McConville and Millar, 83; Miller (1990) 213; Jacobs, 47. Compare Lohfink (1962) 32–56.

formed the original conclusion to Deuteronomy,[568] or whether it is Deuteronomistic in origin,[569]

> the verses do clearly function as a conclusion. They bring together the covenant themes of the whole book: commandments, blessing and curse, witnesses, and end with an appeal for obedience so that the ancient promises to the patriarchs might be fulfilled.[570]

The character of these verses is hortatory. Though this does not rule out a cultic background,[571] since preaching often occurs in a cultic context, it is the preaching character of these verses, rather than the liturgical, which is at the fore.[572] This is not a ceremony where the people respond with a formal pledge of commitment. Rather what we have here is a final and urgent appeal to a life of faithfulness.[573] First and foremost, it is a plea for decision. There "is no independent evidence that such a cultic ceremony ever actually took place".[574]

The occurrences of הַיּוֹם in vv15, 16, 18, 19 are significant.[575] הַיּוֹם occurred in 30:2, 8, 11 in the identical promulgation clause, אֲשֶׁר אָנֹכִי מְצַוְּךָ הַיּוֹם, which identified the commandment being given. This same relative clause occurs in v16, with the same function.[576] The repetition of the clause serves to tie together this paragraph with the preceding. The occurrences of הַיּוֹם in vv15, 18, 19 are of a different category. DeVries comments that these occur at points of special stress, though he does not elaborate on that claim.[577] He argues that the last two are time-identifiers, a late feature of Deuteronomy, which "compare the present day of parenetic appeal with either the past or the future".[578] Verse 18 is a solemn curse-formula, reminiscent of 4:26 and 8:19, though the governing verb in those two verses is הַעִידֹתִי, the same as in 30:19. Rhetorically, הַיּוֹם as a time-identifier

---

568 So Steuernagel, i–ii; Bertholet, 91; Preuß (1982) 161; von Rad (1966e) 184; Buis and Leclerq, 187; Zobel, 64.

569 So Preuß (1982) 161; Mayes (1979) 370.

570 Mayes (1979) 370. Similarly Cunliffe-Jones, 166.

571 On a liturgical background to these verses, see Lohfink (1962) 42. Similarly von Rad (1966e) 185; Clifford, 157; Blenkinsopp (1968) 119; Braulik (1992) 220; Brueggemann (1961) 276–278. See also our introduction to this chapter.

572 See Robinson, 116; Tiffany, 1–29.

573 Buis and Leclerq, 187; D. Schneider, 273; Miller (1990) 215.

574 Robinson, 123. Also Childs (1979) 219.

575 McConville and Millar, 43. Also von Rad (1966a) 26; Grassi, 24. On הַיּוֹם as liturgical, see Murphy, 28.

576 The text of v16 is disputed. See Mayes (1979) 370; Driver, 332; Kalland, 190; Buis and Leclerq, 186; BDB, 83–84; Jacobs, 58–60.

577 DeVries (1975a) 178.

578 DeVries (1975a) 261. Moses is depicted "standing in the present, solemnly warning his hearers of the consequences of a future apostasy that, from the writer's point of view, is certain to come because it has already come"(!).

heightens the urgency of the exhortation and is concerned to bring the current generation to accept the appeal.[579]

DeVries defines הַיּוֹם in v15 as having an epitomising function which acts "as the fulcrum either of the entire composition or of one of its important elemental units".[580] Here, v15 "epitomizes not only the present pericope but the entire Deuteronomic parenesis".[581] This is supported by the opening words of the verse, רְאֵה נָתַתִּי. 11:26, a parallel to this section, begins, רְאֵה אָנֹכִי נֹתֵן.[582] The perfect of נָתַן in 30:15 suggests that what was being given (participle) in 11:26 has now been given.[583] Thus 30:15 brings all the preceding law and commandment together, epitomised in this verse. As in 1:8; 4:5 and 11:26, רְאֵה in 30:15 occurs in a context urging a decision to go forward.[584] Each occurrence is strategic. רְאֵה here is the only pure imperative form in chapters 29 and 30, bringing the rhetoric to a climax. The verse draws attention to itself.[585] Thus vv15–20 are fundamentally hortatory. All that has gone before in Deuteronomy is brought into a dramatic climax.

We argued that 30:11–14 is a consequence of the action of Yahweh in 30:6. Though there was a present sense to 30:11–14, which we consider best understood proleptically, its basic orientation was to the future, dependent on 30:1–10. That cannot be said for 30:15–20. The rhetoric of an urgent choice "today" compels us to read this paragraph in the present sense.

### *Israel's Choice*

"Nowhere is the choice facing Israel so starkly presented".[586] In v15 the contrast is between חַיִּים and טוֹב on the one hand and מָוֶת and רַע on the

---

579 DeVries (1975a) 179, 261–262. He says, 165, "Inasmuch as it is the parenesis that aims to close this existential circle between the past and the present, it is quite naturally the parenesis that also makes the most frequent use of *hayyôm* and *hay-yôm hazzeh*, sometimes with emphasis, sometimes not." Also Polzin (1987) 92–94.

580 DeVries (1975a) 261.

581 DeVries (1975a) 179. This function occurs only in 11:26; 26:3, 17, 18; 27:9.

582 Driver, 331; Mayes (1979) 370. On this formulaic expression, see Braulik (1994a) 3, 200.

583 DeVries (1975a) 179. Braulik (1992) 220, suggests that the opening of v15 is performative speech. Compare Lohfink (1960) 34, "Perfekt der Koinzidenz".

584 McConville and Millar, 39. Miller (1990) 214, notes the parallel with 1:8 and comments that setting the land before Israel is the same as setting before it life. "That is the fundamental kerygma of Deuteronomy: the offer of life on the land that God gives."

585 Lenchak, 140–141, 203. He notes, 219, that the imperative itself is not part of the persuasion.

586 McConville and Millar, 81. Also Watts (1970) 282.

other. Here the two positives are put together and precede the two negatives. In v19 the choice is between חַיִּים and בְּרָכָה on the one hand and מָוֶת and קְלָלָה on the other. Here the grouping is in two pairs of contrasts with the positive preceding the negative each time.[587] It is clear that Israel does not face a free choice. It is to make the right decision and choose life.[588] The seriousness of this choice is suggested by the appeal to heavenly witnesses.[589] As is well known, ANE treaties acknowledged divine witnesses for their ratification. Since Israel's covenant was with God himself, heaven and earth are appealed to instead.[590]

Many commentators suggest that the language of choice is sapiential in background. Parallels are suggested in Proverbs in particular.[591] Yet it is also noted that in the Wisdom literature, the choice is an individual one; in Deuteronomy it is corporate and national.[592] בָּחַר is an important word in Deuteronomy. It occurs 31 times, more than in any other book in the Old Testament.[593] Twenty-nine times the subject is Yahweh.[594] Apart from 23:17, where a refugee slave is the subject, 30:19 is the only occurrence in Deuteronomy where Yahweh is not the subject.[595] It is therefore a striking verse. In 30:19, בָּחַר occurs in qal perfect. However the force is clearly imperative.[596] Perhaps the singularity of the vocabulary is to draw attention to the seriousness of the decision and that this is the climax of the book.[597] The solemnity of the first person singular also contributes to this.[598]

It is clear from the choice presented that blessings and curses, which were alternatives in chapter 28 and sequential in chapter 29 and the

---

587 Lenchak, 202, suggests that the pairing of antonyms in 30:19 forces the choice. See Lenchak, 211–213, on pairs in chapters 29 and 30.

588 Nielsen, 272. On this passage as the background to Mark 3:1–6, see Derrett, 174–178.

589 Blair (1964) 75; Clifford, 157; Craigie (1976) 366.

590 See Thompson, 287; Merrill, 393. Compare 4:26 and 32:1, Driver, 332; Mayes (1979) 370. Further, Braulik (1992) 220; Weinfeld (1972) 147.

591 For example, Weinfeld (1972) 308–311; Mayes (1979) 370. Craigie (1976) 366, notes ANE parallels in the Hymn to Aten and Gilgamesh. See also Thompson, 288; Buis and Leclerq, 187; Jacobs, 71–73, for prophetic parallels.

592 Weinfeld (1972) 308; Thompson, 288, though he notes that 30:15–20 is singular. Compare Buis and Leclerq, 187.

593 Lisowsky, 208–209. Compare Thompson, 288, who says the call to choose is common to both testaments.

594 With place: 12:5, 11, 14, 18, 21, 26; 14:23, 24, 25; 15:20; 16:2, 6, 7, 11, 15, 16; 17:8, 10; 18:6; 26:2; 31:11; with you: 7:6, 7; 10:15; 14:2; with priests: 18:5; 21:5; with descendants: 4:37; with king: 17:15.

595 Cairns, 266; Rennes, 197. Jacobs, 71, fails to note 23:17.

596 Jacobs, 75; Craigie (1976) 366; König, 201; Lenchak, 219.

597 Lenchak, 113. He also notes, 224, the odd word order in v19 of two direct objects followed by a verb followed by two more direct objects. Also de Regt (1991) 158.

598 Lenchak, 144.

beginning of chapter 30, have become alternatives again. The renewed possibility of rebellion, apostasy and wrong decisions suggests that this paragraph is addressing people who are yet to receive the circumcision of the heart.[599] This confirms what we noted above, that the time reference has changed from 30:1–14. Now the present is in focus rather than the future. What is the point of presenting such an alternative if the preceding paragraphs have spoken of the inevitability of the curses? Certainly the rhetoric of this paragraph makes it clear that Israel does have a real decision to make and a serious one at that. The future may be inevitable but human responsibility is never denied.[600]

A common way of understanding this chapter is to suggest that we have here an exilic choice in the light of past failure. So Jacobs concludes that the Deuteronomistic 30:15–20 states that life is still available, even after exile. Past judgment was deserved but it is past. There remains hope of future life.[601] Jacobs' solution, implying that hope lies in Israel's ability to choose correctly, fails to grasp that the grounds of hope lie with Yahweh's grace. Nor does he read this paragraph as consequential to 30:1–14. We want to take seriously the future perspective of 30:1–14 and not diminish it by simply subsuming the future into the past, even if there is reflection on the past involved.[602] As we have it, 30:15–20 urges a decision in the light of a predicted future failure. That is quite different from treating the failure as only a past event. The text as it stands places Israel's choice in a particular light. We must deal with that if we are to understand its theology properly.

### *Absence of Israel's Reponse*

Unlike similar passages elsewhere, the people's response to the demand to choose is not recorded. In Exodus 19:3–9, the people respond to Moses' appeal by affirming their intention to obey. In Exodus 24:3, 7, the people respond by affirming their resolve to do everything commanded of them. In Joshua 24:16–18 the people pledge their obedience to Yahweh. This is then reiterated in vv21, 24.[603] By contrast, no mention is made of the people responding in Deuteronomy 30. If this section were primarily a liturgical account, such a response would be anticipated. Its absence is further

599 Compare Millar, 253, who seems less convinced about the present time reference here.

600 Craigie (1976) 366; Cairns, 266; Jacobs, 70; McConville (1994) 227.

601 Jacobs, 83–85.

602 Compare von Rad (1962a) 231; Murphy, 29. Millar, 254, "The Israelites are confronted with a decision in the light not only of their failures in the past, but also the Deuteronomist's gloomy prognosis for the future".

603 Miller (1990) 215; Lenchak, 113. Wenham (1970) 211–212, notes Exodus 24 and Joshua 24. He suggests that the people's response in Deuteronomy would come at 31:1. Also Mayes (1979) 370.

evidence that we are dealing with parenesis. The passage leaves open the question about whether Israel will respond in obedience or not. We need therefore to consider what this silence may suggest.

One possibility is that the silence about Israel's response is intended to contemporise or existentialise the exhortation. The decision is for "today", for the current reader, in his or her own situation. Thus no response can be recorded, for the reader must decide.[604] This suggestion fits in well with the emphasis in vv15–20 on "today".[605] A simple narrative giving the required response would be less engaging or demanding of the reader.[606]

However chapters 29 and 30 are not entirely existential. The historical situation of Israel in the Plains of Moab remains important. At one level, the silence creates suspense. What will Israel decide? The unanswered question invites the reader to continue reading into Joshua, and beyond, to find out the answer. This is especially so if we regard Deuteronomy as the first instalment of DtrH extending to 2 Kings. Yet this also leads to ambiguity. On the one hand, Joshua portrays the fulfilment, by and large, of the Deuteronomic commands relating to the conquest of the land.[607] The impression is that Israel has answered correctly and chosen life, the incidents of Achan and the Gibeonites notwithstanding. However Israel's faithful obedience in Joshua is incomplete and temporary, creating a tension which diachronic approaches attribute to different editions. So there are two Deuteronomistic editions of Joshua, the first triumphal, the second restrained and conditional.[608] Unlike a diachronic approach which resolves the issue of tension by separate editions, Polzin finds that this tension between promise of land and its fulfilment is central to Joshua's ideology. He notes that as Israel was imperfectly obedient, so was the fulfilment of the promise imperfect. Thus the polarity between success and defeat, promise fulfilled and threatened, is integral to the book's own reflection.[609]

---

604 Miller (1990) 215.

605 DeVries (1975a) 178; McConville and Millar, 43; Millar, 253; von Rad (1962a) 231; McConville (1994) 227.

606 Olson (1985) 151, notes that Numbers also ends with an "unresolved character of the future of the new generation" which "invites every succeeding generation to identify itself as the new generation of God's people." However Deuteronomy's style makes this identification more compelling than the narrative style of Numbers which leaves the reader standing at a distance.

607 Wenham (1971) 140–148. Also Lohfink (1994b) 234–247; Noth (1981) 36–41, who described Joshua as a triumphalist ideology. Compare Lenchak, 242.

608 Mayes (1983) 40–57. McConville (1993b) 93, argues that Noth ignored passages such as 13:1ff.; 15:63; 16:10; 23:16; 24:19–20.

609 Polzin (1980) 80–86. He says, 80, "The fact that the book describes that fulfillment as considerably less than the promise outlined in chapter 1 is central to the ideological position of the Deuteronomist vis-a-vis the occupation of the land". See further McConville (1993b) 91–102.

So the two strands stem from the same Deuteronomic tradition and the editors of Joshua did not see such tension as a problem.[610] As in Deuteronomy,

> the tension between the ideal inheritance and the actual possession was used by the editor of the book of Joshua in a homiletical fashion to urge continuous obedience.[611]

Beyond Joshua the balance shifts. Israel fails more and more, though not totally. The same tension exists between obedience and disobedience, success and failure. By the end of DtrH, Israel is in exile. Pessimism has overtaken optimism.[612] Thus for Deuteronomy 30, there remains ambiguity. The silence of Israel's response, which directs the reader to keep reading, fails to provide a clear answer.

The silence is also ambiguous because within Deuteronomy itself there is uncertainty concerning what Israel's response will be. The optimism of Deuteronomy's rhetoric is tempered by this silence about Israel's response. Indeed this moderation is quite marked, especially after the highly positive and optimistic preceding paragraph. Having declared the possibility of obedience enabled by Yahweh's grace in 30:11–14, one might well expect an expression of willingness to obey. However the silence is deafening. Despite all the promises of grace, the exhortation, encouragement and persuasion, Israel fails to respond at the end of chapter 30. This silence can be read pessimistically.

> Since the appeals for Israel to respond are relatively infrequent, and the characterizations showing her responsible to respond are relatively frequent, one again receives the impression that the actuality of her affirmative response is highly questionable in the pareneticist's mind.[613]

Perhaps we can be more definite. At Sinai, Israel was all too willing to state its pledge of unconditional allegiance and obedience to Yahweh (Exodus 19:8; 24:3, 7). Yet this willingness was matched by its eagerness to act in disobedience, notably by building a golden calf. Deuteronomy has not been shy in reminding Israel of this event, and also its persistent stubbornness throughout the wilderness years. Verbal pledges of obedience, as recorded in Exodus 19, 24 and Joshua 24, no matter how enthusiastic, are meaningless if the practice does not follow suit. In the light of this background, the silence of response in Deuteronomy 30 may be intended to sound a note of pessimism.[614] At Sinai/Horeb Israel responded vociferously

---

610 Childs (1979) 249.

611 Childs (1979) 251. Also Gunn, 107–110; Curtis, 81–84.

612 Wolff (1961, 1982); Lohfink (1981); Brueggemann (1968).

613 DeVries (1975a) 263.

614 McCarthy (1981) 264–276, argues that Exodus 24:1–11 and 19:3b–8 are pre-Deuteronomistic. Also Childs (1974) 30–361, 499–502; Muilenburg (1959) 347–365. Compare Durham, 260, 340–342. Baltzer, 28–31, is cautious about the dating

to covenant demands, yet immediately failed. As we have seen, chapters 29 and 30 make it clear Israel has not changed. As Israel failed in the past, so will it in the future. It does not even verbally pledge to do otherwise. The prognosis, then, is not optimistic. Israel is expected to fail.

This expectation of failure is also suggested by noting that the threat of rebellion in vv17–18 links back to chapter 29.[615] We noted above that a pattern exists in the occurrences of לֵבָב in 30:1–14.[616] We now can add an outer layer to this. In 29:17, לֵבָב occurs with the verb פָּנָה. The same combination occurs in 30:17.[617] Thus there is a distinct progression in the way the heart is dealt with in these two chapters. So we can expand the structure as follows:

A heart turning away (29:17)
  B take the word to heart (30:1)
    C return and obey with all your heart (30:2)
      D heart circumcision leading to love (30:6)
    C' return with all your heart (30:10)
  B' the word is in your heart (30:14)
A' heart turning away (30:17)

The key to this structure remains 30:6. That verse determined how to read 30:11–14. The same can be said for 30:17. Without a circumcised heart, Israel has a heart which is vulnerable to turning away. Indeed, as the sequence in chapter 29 showed, Israel inevitably would turn away. Quite possibly the deliberate allusions back to 29:15–27 are intended to reflect the expectation that Israel will fail to choose correctly.[618] In 29:15–27, apostasy and curses were regarded as inevitable. Nothing has changed in the meantime to suggest otherwise. Though viewed as an alternative in 30:17–18, one can hardly help thinking Israel will fail and choose wrongly. Yet it will be without excuse.[619] It has been warned and exhorted. Though the promise of circumcision remains in the future, this does not abrogate Israel's responsibility in the present.

This reading also has implications for the existential reading of this paragraph. The lack of response does not just force the contemporary reader

---

of both 19:3–8 and 24:3–8. Levenson (1985) 25–26, disagrees with Perlitt that covenant theology arose only with Deuteronomy.

615 Compare Buis and Leclerq, 187, "Après une longue interruption, la prédication de 29, 1–20 trouve ici sa conclusion normale". We disagree that 30:1–14 is an interruption.

616 Braulik (1992) 217–218.

617 Driver, 332; Weinfeld (1972) 304.

618 For example, the combination הִשְׁתַּחֲוָה and עָבַד in 30:18 also occurs in 29:25. See Kalland, 190.

619 McConville (1994) 227.

to decide for himself. In the light of Israel's failure, and the suggestion that Israel's lack of response is itself an indication of pessimism, the existential reading is also pessimistic. The reader of any age is in the same situation as Israel at Moab. "This 'today' means both the time of Moses and that of Deuteronomy taken together".[620] Like Israel, the reader is also expected to fail.

The call to decision combined with the uncertainty of response creates tension in these verses. This same tension exists throughout chapters 29 and 30, indeed the whole book, and is resolved only in Yahweh's grace in circumcising the heart. For all its confident exhortation,

> it remains true that the whole of Deuteronomy is pervaded by the feeling of a great anxiety lest Israel might possibly throw this claim (to God's grace) to the winds and forfeit her salvation.[621]

Further tension is created by the change of time reference. 30:1–10 primarily refers to the future. 30:11–14 continues this future outlook but with bold statements in the present, referring proleptically to the future. The present sense is clearly more pronounced in 30:15–20. Thus this paragraph creates tension with the preceding, similar to the relationship between indicative and imperative found throughout the Bible.[622]

> If vv. 15–20 do refer to the present and vv. 11–14 primarily to the future, the subtle juxtaposition of the calls to obedience has the effect of preserving the Deuteronomic tension between the need for divine transformation in the future and powerful exhortation in the present.[623]

We have already seen a similar tension between the imperative in 10:16 for Israel to circumcise its heart and the promise in 30:6 that Yahweh would do it. In order to understand the nature of the exhortation, we must look at precisely what Israel is being exhorted to choose.

### *The Source of Life*

On the face of it, the call to Israel to choose suggests an optimism about its ability to do so. This would run counter to our thesis that the grounds of optimism lie with Yahweh and not Israel. However the call to choose in 30:15–20 does not in fact allow for optimism grounded in Israel. This is because Israel is called to choose Yahweh and his grace, thus implicitly acknowledging its own inability. We see this through the important motif of "life".

---

620 Von Rad (1962a) 231. Also Polzin (1987) 92–94.
621 Von Rad (1962a) 231.
622 Von Rad (1962a) 231. Compare Rennes, 238–239.
623 Millar, 253.

The motif of "life" is very important in Deuteronomy. It occurs at key places throughout the book.[624] At this point we are concerned with the חָיָה, חַי, and חַיִּים vocabulary.[625] These words occur 18 (15 qal; 3 piel), 8 and 12 times respectively in Deuteronomy.[626] In 30:15–20, the qal verb occurs in vv16, 19; and the noun in vv15, 19, 19, 20.[627]

At a first level, life is simply the *result* of obedience, that is the consequence of the verbs in v16. In this case to choose life is to choose to obey which then brings the consequence of life.[628] If this were the total situation, there would be a straightforward, retributional relationship between the two. Obedience leads to life.[629] This would ground optimism in Israel's ability.

However the relationship is more subtle than this. At the second level, the law is itself life.[630] This is most clearly expressed in 32:47 where "all the words of this law" are equated with "your life". Jacobs argues that this same idea pertains in 30:15, 16, reading the MT without the LXX addition and translating אֲשֶׁר as "for".[631] This does not deny the necessity of human response in order for "life" to exist. This is demonstrated in v16 on either reading. "But *what* was commanded was life and good".[632] There is thus a closer relationship between the law and life than one of simple cause and effect.[633] Though Jacobs tries to show that the simple cause-effect relation-

---

624 Jacobs, 339–345. Under this motif, Jacobs, 4–8, includes not just the vocabulary of חָיָה, חַי, and חַיִּים, but also טוֹב, בֵּרַךְ, יָטַב, רָבָה, אֹרֶךְ יָמִים, and שָׂכַל.

625 אֹרֶךְ יָמִים also occurs in 30:18, 20. See Jacobs, 166.

626 Lisowsky, 482–487.

627 Jacobs, 4–5, defines the motif by the criteria (i) life "as result or reward of specified courses of action" and (ii) "in relation to the law, the covenant, or a particular commandment".

628 Weinfeld (1972) 307. Also Driver, 331.

629 Jacobs, 61. Martens (1992) 9–10, dismisses the view that perfect obedience is the prerequisite to life. Rather he uses the terms "embracing the law" and "paying attention to the law" to denote what brings life.

630 Thompson, 288, "Life consists in loving God, obeying his voice, cleaving to him". Fretheim, 25, "an *intrinsic* relationship is perceived between obedience to the commandments and life". McComiskey, 152–153, says that life is granted through the covenant of promise and not through law. His separation of law and promise, obedience and faith, does not do justice to the positive connection of law and life in Deuteronomy. See Selman, 17.

631 Also Kalland, 190. Compare 11:26–27.

632 Jacobs, 61–62, 70.

633 Jacobs, 76. He, 64–65, argues that the standard relationship in Deuteronomy is a neutral one. "This is precisely what Klaus Koch has called the *Tat-Ergehen Zusammenhang*". See Koch, 57–87. The exception is when Yahweh is the subject of בֵּרַךְ which is stressed in 30:1–10, 16b.

ship is inadequate, he fails to appreciate fully the freedom and initiative of Yahweh in blessing.[634] This is best expressed in v20.

In v20 we read כִּי הוּא חַיֶּיךָ. There are two possibilities here for the antecedent of הוּא. One is the three infinitves לְאַהֲבָה, לִשְׁמֹעַ, and לְדָבְקָה.[635] Syntactically this is possible. In that case obedience is identified with life, agreeing with the second level we have observed above. The other possibility is that the antecedent is Yahweh.[636] Yahweh is mentioned in association with each of the three infinitives, firstly by name and then in pronominal suffixes. Jacobs rules out this second possibility in part on theological grounds.[637] However we have seen that the relationship between life and law/obedience is variously nuanced. This verse makes another contribution to that which in fact is not out of character for Deuteronomy. This is the third level of this relationship.

The idea that "Yahweh is your life", does occur in Deuteronomy. In 32:39, Yahweh says, אֲנִי אָמִית וַאֲחַיֶּה. Yahweh is the life-giver. The law is the means of life. Yahweh is its source. So life is identified not only with law but here with Yahweh himself.[638] At the culmination of this rhetorical section it should not surprise us that Moses directs attention to the ultimate source of life, Yahweh.[639] Israel is really being exhorted to choose Yahweh, for life comes from him.[640] The preceding verses show that to choose death is to choose other gods. Conversely, to choose life is to choose Yahweh, the antecedent of הוּא.[641]

The theological significance of this is important. By ultimately directing Israel's attention to Yahweh the life-giver rather than the law, Moses is in effect saying that Israel must depend on Yahweh and not on itself. Its life will come from him and not from its own work.[642] This does not deny the

---

634 Jacobs, 67–68, "Obedience is (only) the necessary presupposition to the blessing; Yahweh blesses, gives life (in his order)". Also 76. See L'Hour, 99–106, 112–116, 119–121.

635 So Driver, 332; Perlitt (1981) 423.

636 Jacobs, 75, rules this out syntactically but does not state why this is the case. Compare NIV; Lohfink (1962) 42; König, 201; McConville (1994) 227.

637 Jacobs, 75.

638 So Cairns, 266, "'Life' is virtually a title for Yahweh: to choose life is…to choose Yahweh…".

639 Compare 30:15, Yahweh is the source of life since it is given (נָתַתִּי) by him.

640 This idea is also found in 8:3 which we discussed in the previous chapter. See Köckert, 501–502; Craigie (1976) 185.

641 Jacobs, 73–74, "the verb בָּחַר may be used as the proper response to the covenant, a response seen as a choice for Yahweh". Also Jacobs, 336.

642 Compare Joshua 24, a parallel Jacobs notes. There Israel pledges its allegiance to Yahweh but is brought down to earth by Joshua's rebuke that it is unable to serve the LORD. That covenant renewal ceremony elaborates and makes explicit what is

need for human responsibility. Obedience is not ignored and Israel must make a real choice. Yet there is a subtle acknowledgement that obedience will fail to bring life because Israel lacks the power to obey. Yahweh is whence Israel's life will come. Related to this point is the appreciation that the real character of obedience is a confession of trust and faith in Yahweh.[643] Obedience does not seek to earn life in as much as it seeks to express reliance on Yahweh, the source of life. This then confirms what we have been arguing, that Israel's choice does not reflect a positive view of its ability but rather an acknowledgement of its weakness. All grounds for optimism about the future belong to Yahweh. Hence Israel is exhorted to choose Yahweh.

### *The Context of 30:15–20*

We have been arguing that Israel is exhorted to choose Yahweh who is the source of life. This argument is confirmed by looking at the wider context provided by 30:1–14. The vocabulary common with 30:1–14 establishes that the things Israel is to choose are things which 30:1–14 says Yahweh will himself provide and do. This context explains further that the choice to be made by Israel is a choice for Yahweh, for his grace and is thus an implicit acknowledgement of dependence on him.

The first key term is life itself. In v6, חַיִּים is promised as a result of Yahweh's grace in circumcising the heart. Though human responsibility is not denied in v6, the possibility of life depends ultimately on Yahweh's grace. The occurrence of חַיִּים in v6, which we noted above was striking, prepares the reader for the concentration of "life" vocabulary in vv15–20 and sets the exhortation of vv15–20 into context. Thus in v19, Israel is being asked to choose what Yahweh has already promised. It is not being asked to do something, or achieve something. Rather it is being asked to receive what Yahweh wants to give. Since life is a result of the circumcision of the heart, Israel is implicitly being asked to acknowledge its own weakness and rely on Yahweh's grace. There is no sense that Israel can in and of itself be faithful. Thus there is an implicit acknowledgement that there can be no bright future for Israel without Yahweh's grace and faithfulness.[644]

That vv15–20 are to be read in the light of v6 is also suggested by the repetition of זֶרַע in v19. With the sense of "descendants", the word occurs

---

here in Deuteronomy 30, namely that Israel, despite all the exhortation, is unable to serve the LORD. It requires Yahweh's grace.

643 Seebass (1977a) 222.

644 L'Hour, 120, "Der Beitrag Israels besteht darin, sich dem Handeln Jahwes immer mehr zu unterwerfen". He also, 32–33, states that Israel's first ethical act is to acknowledge its dependence on Yahweh's Lordship.

ten times in Deuteronomy, referring to the descendants of the patriarchs (1:8; 4:37; 10:15 and 11:9), of Israel (31:21), of Moses (34:4) and the current generation, which is included along with its descendants (28:46, 59; 30:6, 19). In both 30:6, 19, life is the context. This is further support for our contention that the context of vv15–20 is found in the early part of the same chapter. The perspective of future generations enjoying life is consistent in both parts.[645] So again, Israel's choice is in the context of Yahweh's promise and grace.

That vv15–20 are to be read in the context of vv1–10 is further seen in other common vocabulary. The content of the "life" motif is only minimally concerned with being alive (חָיָה, v16).[646] Life is national, rather than individual.[647] "Life" in vv15–20 consists of טוֹב (v15), doing the three verbs of v16 (loving, walking and keeping), increase (רָבָה, v16), blessing (בֵּרַךְ piel, v16 and בְּרָכָה, v19), doing the three verbs in v20 (loving, listening and cleaving), and longevity (אֹרֶךְ יָמֶיךָ לָשֶׁבֶת, v20).[648] Significantly, many of these terms have already arisen earlier in chapter 30.

The first is טוֹב which occurred twice in v9. Both times it referred to what Yahweh promises to give Israel as a result of him circumcising its heart and Israel's consequent obedience. We also saw in our discussion that טוֹב suggests both covenant faithfulness and grace.[649] Now in v15, Israel is exhorted to choose הַטּוֹב. Though paired with רַע, the sense is not moral.[650] It is to do with prosperity, hence *Heil und Unheil*.[651] In context, Israel is to choose what Yahweh promises to give in the future. So again, it is not so much to choose to do something as to choose to receive something.[652] As vv6–9 made clear, טוֹב is a gift from Yahweh. So the choice is for grace. The question is whether Israel will decide to accept Yahweh's grace or not.

The only other occurrence in Deuteronomy of טוֹב with רַע is in 1:39. In that verse, in contrast to the adults, the children are described as those אֲשֶׁר לֹא־יָדְעוּ הַיּוֹם טוֹב וָרָע. The expression, in apposition to בְּנֵיכֶם, is probably simply a way of defining children.[653] However that this particular expression is used,[654] as well as its context in chapter 1, sheds light on 30:15. The previous generation, knowing good and evil, failed to choose good. That is, they did not trust the promise of Yahweh to give them the land. In effect,

---

645 Driver, 332; Clifford, 157.

646 D. Schneider, 273.

647 Ridderbos, 272.

648 Jacobs, 57, 76–78.

649 Brueggemann (1968) 387–402; Braulik (1982) 159; McConville (1984) 14–15.

650 Thompson, 287; Mayes (1979) 370; Driver, 331; Bertholet, 92.

651 Bertholet, 92.

652 Compare Jacobs, 77, 278, who identifies הַטּוֹב with the Deuteronomic Code. Also L'Hour, 119–121.

653 Jacobs, 353–354. See our discussion in chapter 1.

654 It does not occur in Numbers 14:29–31.

this was their choice.[655] Forty years later, the generation which did not know good and evil at Kadesh is in the same situation in the plains of Moab. Now, however, they know good and evil, as the exhortation to choose between them implies. While this change could just suggest they are now adult, it seems that more is involved in the expression.[656] They know Yahweh's promise. The exhortation to choose good is fundamentally an exhortation to trust Yahweh's promise, and so to act on that trust. This the previous generation failed to do. Jacobs is too limited in his appreciation of this. He makes the connection between 30:15 and 1:39 but limits the content of "good and evil" to the law and commandments. For him, the key is obedience to the commandments.[657] Yet, as 1:32 makes clear, trusting the promise is basic. Disobedience is an expression of lack of trust. Of course it may be coincidental that these two verses alone in Deuteronomy have both words. Yet Jacobs argues that we must at least consider the possibility that 1:39 foreshadows 30:15.[658] Certainly he draws attention to a key point, though failing to give it the full weight. Both 1:36–39 and 30:15–20 are about the faithfulness of Yahweh to his word.[659] His promise still stands. That, we maintain, is what Israel is being urged to respond to above all.

The second important word is אָהַב. In each of vv6, 16, 20, we have לְאַהֲבָה אֶת־יְהוָה אֱלֹהֶיךָ. In v6, this was the result or even purpose of Yahweh circumcising Israel's heart. In v16, לְאַהֲבָה is dependent on צִוָּה and is part of Israel's choice. לְאַהֲבָה in v20 is dependent on בָּחַר in v19.[660] As with טוֹב, Israel is not so much deciding to do something as to receive something. The ability to love is a result of Yahweh's action. Israel is now being asked to choose to receive what Yahweh has earlier promised to do and give. Yahweh's love is tied to his election or choice of Israel. Indeed, love is virtually a synonym of election.[661] Now Israel is to choose and love Yahweh. That is, it is to accept the covenant relationship established by Yahweh.[662]

---

655 See 1:32 and the emphasis on promise of the "good" land in 1:34. Jacobs, 354.

656 Jacobs, 355, "it must be argued that the Deuteronomistic author wished to give it (the expression 'to know good and evil') a particular content other than its meaning 'of age'." He notes that the insertion of הַיּוֹם into the expression after the verb suggests Deuteronomy has its own conception of the clause. Also Clark, 267.

657 Jacobs, 356–359. So, 358, "From the immediate context of 1:19–46 it is possible only to see this much about רַע and טוֹב – that Yahweh's command is essential".

658 Jacobs, 360–364. He suggests, 361, "Dtr saw the event of this covenant ceremony as the event of the 'coming of age,' as it were, of this generation".

659 Jacobs, 361.

660 The infinitive construct plus לְ here has a gerundive or modal or epexegetical function, explaining the nature of choosing life, yet ultimately dependent on בָּחַר in v19. See Soisalon-Soininen, 87–88; Joüon (1991) §124o; Vanoni, 93.

661 Merrill, 202; Moran (1963b) 77–87. Also Zobel, 77; Rennes, 195.

662 See further, Merrill, 75–77; Selman, 16.

The next connection with vv1–14 is the infinitive construct of שָׁמַר which occurred in v10 with object
מִצְוֹתָיו וְחֻקֹּתָיו הַכְּתוּבָה בְּסֵפֶר הַתּוֹרָה הַזֶּה.
A similar object, מִצְוֹתָיו וְחֻקֹּתָיו וּמִשְׁפָּטָיו, occurs with the infinitive construct in v16. We have argued that v10 is best understood as a temporal clause. The actions expressed in it are consequent on the circumcision of the heart in v6. As with אָהַב, so with שָׁמַר, though the latter occurs only in v16 and not v20. In v16, Israel is being exhorted to do what vv1–10 have shown is to be the result of the circumcision of the heart.

The qal of רָבָה in v16 refers back to the hiphil of the same verb in v5. There Yahweh was the subject. The sentence was an unconditional promise to Israel of what Yahweh would do in the future. It is also an appeal to the Abrahamic promises.[663] It is this context which explains v16. The qal with Israel as subject reflects the means by which the increase will occur. As v5 showed, the ultimate cause of increase is Yahweh. Again Israel is being asked to accept what Yahweh promised in vv1–10.

The noun בְּרָכָה occurs in vv1, 19. In v1 it referred to blessing which preceded the curses which in turn preceded the circumcision of the heart and the restoration of Israel. Given the return in v19 to viewing blessing and curse as alternatives rather than sequentially, it is difficult to be certain what the precise notion behind blessing is. The blessing mentioned in v1 was temporary. However since that verse, all mention of related ideas and concepts seem permanent, depending as they do on Yahweh's grace. The context of vv15–20 suggests this is in mind here as well.

Finally שָׁמַע בְּקוֹל, which occurred in vv2, 8, 10, occurs again in v20. We argued above that the occurrences in vv2, 10 are structurally dependent on that of v8 which is a statement, not a condition, and is a result of the circumcision of the heart. Again, therefore, in vv19–20, Israel is being asked to choose what Yahweh himself has promised he will enable. It is not a simple choice to obey. Rather Israel is being asked to choose Yahweh and his grace which will enable obedience. Again, the choice to be made is an acknowledgement of Israel's faithlessness.

All these points of vocabulary suggest that the choice the Israelites are being asked to make is not fundamentally a pledge to obey and rely on their own effort but to entrust themselves to the grace and faithfulness of Yahweh who has promised that he will enable the obedience which Israel requires. So, "the possibility of life is entirely because of Yahweh's faithfulness alone in his word".[664] This highpoint of Deuteronomy's rhetoric, though positively urging Israel to choose, is an acknowledgement that there is no hope without Yahweh. The rhetoric of choice may look

---

663 It was noted above that רָבָה (qal) with Israel as subject is in the context of the Abrahamic promises. This is one of a number of allusions to these in this verse.

664 Jacobs, 338.

optimistic, suggesting that Israel can choose rightly. However the context established by 30:1–14 makes it clear that the choice is between Yahweh's grace and faithfulness on the one hand and Israel's faithlessness on the other. There is no possibility grounded in Israel's ability to be faithful. That is only a possibility enabled by the grace and faithfulness of Yahweh.

This point is further strengthened by the end of v20. The exhortation of vv15–20 ends with another reference to Yahweh's faithfulness to the patriarchal promises.[665] In this case the patriarchs are mentioned by name. Unusually in Deuteronomy, the patriarchs, rather than the current generation, are the recipients of the promised land.[666] In Deuteronomy there is no conception of life apart from the land.[667] Death is not necessarily destruction but life outside the land which is thus not real life.[668] The significance of finishing this sermon on this note is to underline the point yet again: all hope derives from Yahweh's faithfulness to his promises to Abraham. This faithfulness, which will ultimately lead to the circumcision of the heart, resolves the tension between hope and Israel's faithlessness.

30:1–10 established that Israel's future hope, the promise of restoration and the circumcision of the heart, all depend on the Abrahamic covenant and Yahweh's faithfulness to it. Israel is now being called to trust the promise. The importance of the theme of the faithfulness of Yahweh in Deuteronomy is not always given its full due. The tension we have described above between optimism and pessimism, causing uncertainty about the future, is really a tension between the faithfulness of Yahweh and the faithlessness of Israel. The resolution of the tension is a triumph of the faithfulness of Yahweh. To conclude the exhortation with this appeal to the

---

665 Kline (1963) 134, "Over and over again Moses traces the work of salvation which God was accomplishing through him to the covenant promises sworn unto Abraham." Also Braulik (1992) 220; Seebass (1977a) 222.

666 In 11:21 and 30:20, only, are the recipients of both the promise and the land identified as the patriarchs. Most commonly the Patriarchs are the recipients of the promise with the current generation the recipients of the land. See Brettler, XII–XVIII.

667 Compare Clifford, 157, who understands this whole section liturgically and hence that life in the liturgical sense is proximity to the Lord; death is to be absent from the Lord.

668 D. Schneider, 273, "Das Leben, das Israel angeboten wird, ist nicht bloßes Dasein, sondern Leben im gesegneten Land, und zwar in langer zeitlicher Dehnung. Tod und Unheil meinen hier: *nicht lange werden eure Tage währen in dem Land*, also nicht Auslöschung der Existenz, denn das Leben muß nun außerhalb der Grenzen Israels stattfinden." Jacobs, 68–69, considers the theme of land to be the fifth essential ingredient in the motif of "life" in Deuteronomy. His five points are (i) the covenant is conducive to life; (ii) the relationship between covenant and life is expressed in neutral terms, that is, Yahweh does not intervene to bring or promise life; (iii) human response is entailed; (iv) Israel as a nation is addressed; and (v) life is in the land.

patriarchal promises and Yahweh's faithfulness sets Israel's choice in the framework of grace again. Deuteronomy has made it clear that Yahweh can be trusted. The future is certain because of this. Israel is called to trust this and choose this.

This raises the question of what it means for uncircumcised Israel to choose. Schneider sees the command to choose in v19b as "die gradlinige Fortsetzung von V.14", meaning that the near word makes possible and effects the choice for God.[669] However we have argued that vv11–14 speak of the future whereas vv15–20 return to the present. We noted above that at times Israel did obey and have faith but that these times were fleeting and temporary. The promise of the circumcision of the heart addresses that and creates the possibility of permanent obedient faith. Israel is able to choose of its own accord. Yet its ability to obey permanently and love God is flawed. That is why the choice is to receive God's promise and grace rather than, primarily, a pledge to obey forever. The latter is impossible; the former is not. For, as v20 concludes, if Israel chooses Yahweh, he will give all he has promised.

We see then that the exhortation to Israel in Deuteronomy is not pointless. Though it is expected that Israel cannot perfectly obey, the exhortation to do so is in effect a plea to turn to Yahweh for help. This is exactly the case with Christian preaching. The preacher exhorts certain responses knowing full well that sinful Christians cannot meet God's requirements perfectly. Yet the exhortation has some effect in furthering obedient faith in the context of directing the listeners to trust God. For until the heart is perfect, the possibility of renewed rebellion, as in vv17–18, remains real. Thus the emphasis on exhortation in Deuteronomy does not presuppose an optimistic assessment of Israel's capability, as it has tended to be understood. Exhortation in fact presupposes Israel's inability to keep the covenant without Yahweh's grace.

### *Conclusion*

30:15–20 brings the exhortation of Deuteronomy to a climax. Though on the surface the urgent appeal to choose life looks optimistic, we have seen that underlying Israel's choice is an implicit acknowledgement of Israel's faithlessness and inability. It is asked to choose Yahweh and his grace, to choose what 30:1–14 has already said Yahweh promises to do and give. Israel is thus being asked to rely on Yahweh's grace and to receive what he

---

669 D. Schneider, 273. He sees v19b as "die innere Mitte dieses Abschnittes". Schneider does not recognise that for Israel the promise is yet to be fulfilled. Similarly McConville and Millar, 82, "Ultimately divine action is necessary for the consistent fulfilment of the spirit and letter of the law. In the immediate present Israel is equipped to 'choose to serve Yahweh'."

promises to give. The exhortation does not presuppose Israel's ability. The priority lies with divine grace, though human responsibility is not lost.[670] The possibility of a future for faithless Israel is due entirely to faithful Yahweh. So the faithlessness of Israel does not annul the faithfulness of Yahweh. "Will their lack of faith nullify God's faithfulness? Not at all!" (Romans 3:3–4).

---

670 Compare Joyce, 127, who argues that in Ezekiel, "the responsibility of Israel has been subsumed in the overriding initiative of Yahweh". Even if he is correct about Ezekiel, this is not the case with Deuteronomy. Human responsibility is preserved to the end.

# Conclusion

This study has investigated the portrayals of Israel and Yahweh in Deuteronomy. Approaching the book synchronically, we have attempted to relate the portrayals theologically. This study has limited itself to three passages in Deuteronomy which focus on an account of Israel's failure and the resolution of that failure.

In chapter 1 we discussed Deuteronomy 1–3. We argued that the concentric structure of Deuteronomy 1, based on the speeches, highlighted the perversity of Israel's refusal to enter the land after the report of the spies. Deuteronomy's unqualified spies' report, in contrast to Numbers, further cast Israel's refusal in a particularly damning light. Israel's failure was seen to be a failure of faith, portrayed in terms of Holy War and Exodus in reverse. Moses' own exclusion from the land is not attributed to his sin but "because of you", contributing to the portrayal of Israel's culpability. This failure was depicted paradigmatically, suggesting that Israel in the future would repeat its sin. The strategic placing of this account at the beginning of Deuteronomy also contributes to this sense. An important feature of Deuteronomy is its conflation of generations, identifying the current addressees in Moab with their parents who died in the wilderness. This feature, which Lohfink, Brueggemann and others consider cultic, functions rhetorically to suggest that this next generation is unchanged from its forebears. It too will fail.

Yahweh's response to this failure was anger and punishment, limited however to that one generation. The renewal of hope for the next generation was not due to Yahweh's character of mercy and compassion in general but was particularly grounded in his promises to Abraham. Thus we argued that these promises undergird his commands. Deuteronomy 1–3 is careful to highlight Yahweh's faithfulness. Thus his promise of a multitude of descendants for Abraham has been fulfilled, his faithful protection of Edom, Moab and Ammon is a model for how he will be faithful for Israel, and the defeat of Sihon and Og, whose land is ambiguously described in terms of the promised land, is another demonstration of his willingness and ability to keep his promise of land. Indeed these victories, and the archaeological notes in chapter 2, address Israel's fear of giants and fortifications expressed in 1:28. Important for this study was to show that the success of Israel in chapters 2 and 3 derived not from its obedience, but ultimately from Yahweh's promises. This was reflected in the schema of command and execution applying to each of the five encounters with the five nations. These parallel panels mirrored the movement of Israel under Yahweh's impulse. However, this priority on divine grace and initiative does not usurp human responsibility as the reports of Israel's victories over Sihon and Og showed.

In chapter 2 we discussed Deuteronomy 8–10. Though the focus of our concern was the golden calf episode and its resolution, chapter 8, in particular 8:1–5, also discusses the wilderness. The descriptions of the wilderness in these verses highlight Yahweh's gracious provision, a model for that promised in the land. This is also the focus of the important v3. This grace is despite Israel's disobedience in the wilderness, alluded to by mention of manna and water, and suggested by the ambivalence regarding the result of the wilderness test. Allusions to the spies incident also suggested Israel's expected failure. We outlined a number of attempts to elucidate the structure of this chapter, noting in particular the importance of v11 and the movement from positive to negative which indicates some pessimism about how Israel will act.

Deuteronomy 9 is the clearest statement in the book in support of our thesis that Israel is expected to fail. The golden calf incident is demonstrably not an isolated incident of failure but is prefaced and framed by statements of Israel's insistent stiff-neckedness. Both the consistency and seriousness of Israel's sin are addressed. The golden calf incident, like that of the spies, is regarded paradigmatically. The two represent sins in the context of land and law, two of Deuteronomy's major themes. The resolution of this account of failure is through Moses' intercession. The contents of this prayer are delayed, highlighting both Israel's sin and, then, the prayer itself. Central to the prayer is the appeal to the patriarchal promises. The vocabulary of the prayer draws on various sources, again suggesting its paradigmatic or universal importance. The answer to the prayer is indicated via the replaced tablets, the continuity of the Aaronic priesthood, the renewed commands to journey and the renewed exhortation to covenant obedience, showing a reinstatement of both the Decalogue and the Shema. We argued throughout this chapter that Yahweh's grace is fundamental for Israel's future, that the current generation is no different from its predecessor and that human responsibility is not abrogated by grace. Israel's sin does not annul the covenant relationship which is grounded in the Abrahamic promises. We also noted the importance of Israel's heart in Deuteronomy 8–10, noting the ambivalence of chapter 8 to it, the clearer suggestion of its corruption in chapter 9, made explicit in 10:16 which links the uncircumcised heart with being stiff-necked. We argued that the command to circumcise the heart in 10:16 was both central to 10:12–22 and was based on a fulfilment of the Abrahamic promises.

The most important part of this study is Deuteronomy 29–30 which chapter 3 addresses. We argued that Deuteronomy 29 demonstrated that the current generation of Israel was in the same state as its predecessor. This was indicated by both generational conflation and the identification of the Moab covenant with the Horeb covenant. The failure of the past generation in response to Horeb was symptomatic of what the future would hold for the next generation in response to Moab. In particular Israel stood in need of a changed or new heart (29:3). This verse expressed the key exigence of these chapters, and of the covenant renewal of Moab. The verse reflects an acknowledgement that a right heart can only come from Yahweh. We also argued that Deuteronomy's concern was for a permanent right response to Yahweh. Though Israel seemed capable of a temporary right response, Yahweh's prior action was needed for that to be permanent. The inevitability of Israel's sin was suggested by the change from blessing and curse as alternatives, as in chapter 28, to being sequential. The later half of Deuteronomy 29 portrays the power and contagion of sin.

Deuteronomy 30:1–10 is often misunderstood. Typically it is regarded as expressing a theology of repentance and restoration initiated by Israel itself. Often initial impressions are that Yahweh's response is conditional on Israel's repentance. We argued in detail that this is not so simple. The controlling verse is 30:6. This is argued on various grounds. Structurally, this is supported by Vanoni's concentric structure rather than Lohfink's. We noted that v6, and in particular לֵבָב, linked together Yahweh and Israel, and showed that the demands on Israel could only be met subsequent to Yahweh's action on Israel's heart. Syntactically, this is supported by noting that the rare unconditional statements of 30:6–8 result from the circumcision of the heart and thus provide the control for understanding the כִּי clauses in vv1, 9–10. Theologically, this is supported by noting that the impulse for Israel's return in v1 is Yahweh's words.

Braulik, among others, downplays the significance of the Abrahamic promises in 30:1–10. We argued that they are central. A number of allusions are made to them which demonstrate that Yahweh's actions are motivated by his faithfulness to his promises. Thus we found that the theological structure of 30:1–10 is much the same as for chapters 1–3, 8–10.

This raised questions about the relationship between grace and law, given that the promise of heart circumcision by Yahweh in 30:6 accomplishes what Israel was itself commanded in 10:16. We argued that law and exhortation do not presuppose ability to fulfil the commands. Rather the law exposes inability and pushes Israel to Yahweh for grace. We also discussed the implications of this for an integrated relationship of Sinai and Abrahamic covenants.

The circumcision of the heart is the theological resolution to the dilemma of a faithless people and a faithful God. The circumcision of the heart enables the fulfilment of the demands. Yahweh's grace both precedes Israel and enables Israel and ultimately ensures a faithful Israel and the absolute fulfilment of Yahweh's promises. Thus 30:6 is the key to the book of Deuteronomy. It is the verse which makes sense of the law and exhortation, both perfect in their demands, being addressed to a people who are far from perfect.

Our discussion of 30:11–14 we also consider significant. These verses are almost universally regarded as expressing Israel's inherent ability to keep the law. However we argued that this ease of keeping the law must be read in the light of the fulfilment of 30:6. We noted the extended palistrophe which tied 30:11–14 with 29:28, especially in its use of לֵבָב, as an outer frame for 30:1–10. The כִּי clause of v11 also links back to כִּי clauses in vv9–10. We also argued that the present sense of 30:11–14 is not as pronounced as often thought. We therefore argued that the grounds of obedience in 30:11–14 are not the revelation and ease of the torah itself but the circumcision of the heart. We supported our argument by discussing Paul's understanding of these verses as illustrated in Romans 10.

The final paragraph of chapter 30 brings to a climax the exhortation of the book. We argued that the vocabulary of these verses alludes back to 30:1–14 showing that Israel is being asked to choose what Yahweh has promised to give. Thus the command to choose is not asking Israel to rely on its ability to obey but in fact is demanding Israel to rely on Yahweh's grace which enables obedience. This paragraph thus sums up the exhortation of the book. It presupposes Israel's sinfulness and the priority of Yahweh's grace.

This study has been limited to three sections of Deuteronomy. The task still remains to investigate more thoroughly the rest of Deuteronomy to determine if the same theological relationship obtains, namely a presupposition of sinfulness, an optimism based on the patriarchal promises and Yahweh's faithfulness to them, and a call to reliance on his grace. In particular this will require an investigation of the law. This study has made only cursory comments about this.

The synchronic reading of Deuteronomy has challenged some of the premises of diachronic critical approaches. These usually presuppose univocal strands or redactions and regard pessimism and optimism as standing in tension and historically conditioned. We have suggested that the two are integrated harmoniously in Deuteronomy. We contend this need not indicate a combination of originally separate sources or circumstances. This also has implications for the reading of the Deuteronomistic History.

This study has touched on issues of covenant and the relationship between Horeb, Moab and Abraham in particular. It is beyond the scope of this study to interact with approaches to the origin and development of covenant theology and traditions in the Old Testament. However our thesis raises a possibility of a more integrated relationship than is often espoused.

Finally, the identification of 30:6 as the key to the dilemma of sinfulness and the promises of Yahweh raises eschatological questions about Deuteronomy. Not only does this suggest further consideration of the eschatology of other parts of the Old Testament. For the Christian intepreter of the Old Testament this also suggests a consideration of the consummation of this hope in the New Testament by Christ in whom "you were also circumcised" (Colossians 2:11).

# Bibliography

Aberbach, M. and Smolar, L.
1967 "Aaron, Jeroboam and Golden Calves", *JBL* 86:129–140

Achtemeier, E.
1987 "Plumbing the Riches: Deuteronomy for the Preacher", *Int* 41:269–281

Ackroyd, P.R.
1968 *Exile and Restoration: A Study of Hebrew Thought of the Sixth Century BC* (SCM Press)

Aejmelaeus, A.
1986 "Function and Interpretation of כִּי in Biblical Hebrew", *JBL* 105:193–209

Aho, G.
1983 "The Eighth Sunday after Pentecost: Deut 30:9–14", *CTQ* 47:48–49

Alexander, T.D.
1993 "Genealogies, Seed and the Compositional Unity of Genesis", *TynBull* 44:254–270
1994 "The Relationship between the Old and New Testament (sic) with Special Reference to the Abrahamic and Mosaic Covenants", Paper presented to the Tyndale Fellowship, July 1994
1995 *From Paradise to the Promised Land: An Introduction to the Main Themes of the Pentateuch* (Paternoster)

Amsler, S.
1977 "La motivation de l'éthique dans la parénèse du Deutéronome", *Beiträge zur alttestamentlichen Theologie: FS für W. Zimmerli zum 70. Geburtstag* (ed. H. Donner, R. Hanhart, R. Smend; Vandenhoeck & Ruprecht) 11–22

Anbar, M.
1982 "Genesis 15: A Conflation of Two Deuteronomic Narratives", *JBL* 101:39–55
1985 "The Story about the Building of an Altar on Mount Ebal: The History of its Composition and the Question of the Centralization of the Cult", *Das Deut* 304–309

Andersen, F.I.
1974 *The Sentence in Biblical Hebrew* (Moulton Publishers)

Andersen, F.I. and Freedman, D.N.
1980 *Hosea* (AB 24; Doubleday)

Anderson, B.W.
1963 "The New Covenant and the Old", *The Old Testament and the Christian Faith* (The Preacher's Library; ed. B.W. Anderson; SCM Press)

Aristotle
1926 *The "Art" of Rhetoric* (Loeb Classical Library; trans. J.H. Freese; Heinemann)

Ashley, T.R.
1993 *The Book of Numbers* (NICOT; Eerdmans)
Badenas, R.
1985 *Christ the End of the Law: Romans 10:4 in Pauline Perspective* (JSNTSup 10; JSOT Press)
Bailey, L.R.
1971 "The Golden Calf", *HUCA* 42:97–115
Baker, D.W.
1980 "Further Examples of the *Waw Explicativum*", *VT* 30:129–136
1989 "The Mosaic Covenant Against Its Environment", *ATJ* 20:9–18
Baker, J.A.
1984 "Deuteronomy and World Problems", *JSOT* 29:3–17
Balentine, S.E.
1984 "The Prophet as Intercessor: A Reassessment", *JBL* 103:161–173
1985 "Prayer in the Wilderness: In Pursuit of Divine Justice", *HAR* 9:53–74
1993 *Prayer in the Hebrew Bible: The Drama of Divine–Human Dialogue* (OBT; Fortress Press)
Baltzer, K.
1971 *The Covenant Formulary in Old Testament, Jewish and Early Christian Writings* (trans. D.E. Green; Blackwell)
Bamberger, B.J.
1929 "Fear and Love of God in the Old Testament", *HUCA* 6:39–53
Barr, J.
1974 "Etymology and the Old Testament", *Language and Meaning: Studies in Hebrew Language and Biblical Exegesis* (*OTS* 19; E.J. Brill) 1–28
Barrett, C.K.
1962 *The Epistle to the Romans* (BNTC; A&C Black [Rev Ed])
Barth, K.
1957 *Church Dogmatics, Vol 2: The Doctrine of God, Part 2* (ed. G.W. Bromiley, T.F. Torrance; T&T Clark)
Bartholomew, C.G.
1992 *The Composition of Deuteronomy: A Critical Analysis of the Approaches of E.W. Nicholson and A.D.H. Mayes* (Unpublished MA thesis; Potchefstroom University)
Bartlett, J.R.
1970 "Sihon and Og, Kings of the Amorites", *VT* 20:257–277
1989 *Edom and the Edomites* (JSOT/PEF Monograph Series 1; JSOTSup 77; JSOT Press)
Bee, R.E.
1979 "A Study of Deuteronomy Based on Statistical Properties of the Text", *VT* 29:1–22
Begg, C.T.
1979 "The Significance of *Numeruswechsel* in Deuteronomy and the 'Pre-History' of the Question", *EThL* 55:116–124
1980a "The Literary Criticism of Deut 4,1–40: Contributions to a Continuing Discussion", *EThL* 56:10–55
1980b "'Bread, Wine and Strong Drink' in Deut 29:5a", *BTFT* 41:266–275
1982 "The Reading *sbty(km)* in Deut 29:9 & 2 Sam 7:7", *EThL* 58:87–105
1983 "The Tables (Deut 10) & the Lawbook (Deut 31)", *VT* 33:96–97
1985 "The Destruction of the Calf (Exod 32,20/Deut 9,21)", *Das Deut* 208–251

Bellefontaine, E.

1975 "The Curses of Deuteronomy 27: Their Relationship to the Prohibitions", *No Famine in the Land: Studies in Honor of John L. McKenzie* (ed. J.W. Flanagan, A.W. Robinson; Scholars Press (for the Claremont Institute for Antiquity and Christianity) 49–62

Berg, W.

1988 "Israels Land, der Garten Gottes: Der Garten als Bild des Heiles im Alten Testament", *BZ* 32:35–51

Berlin, A.

1983 "Parallel Word Pairs: A Linguistic Explanation", *UF* 15:7–16

Bertholet, A.

1899 *Deuteronomium* (KHAT 5; J.C.B. Mohr [Paul Siebeck])

Birch, B.C.

1988 "Old Testament Narrative and Moral Address", *Canon, Theology and Old Testament Interpretation: Essays in Honor of Brevard S. Childs* (ed. G.M. Tucker, D.L. Petersen, R.R. Wilson; Fortress Press) 75–91

Black, M.

1971–72 "The Christological Use of the Old Testament in the New Testament", *NTS* 18:1–14

Blair, E.P.

1961 "An Appeal to Remembrance: The Memory Motif in Deuteronomy", *Int* 15:41–47

1964 *Deuteronomy, Joshua* (LBC 5; John Knox Press)

Blank, S.H.

1950–51 "The Curse, Blasphemy, the Spell and the Oath", *HUCA* 23:73–95

Blau, J.

1956 "Zum Hebräisch der Übersetzer des Alten Testaments", *VT* 6:97–99

Blenkinsopp, J.

1968 "Deuteronomy", *Jerome Biblical Commentary* (ed. R.E. Brown, J.A. Fitzmyer, R.E. Murphy; Prentice Ward) 101–122

1995 "Deuteronomy and the Politics of Post-Mortem Existence", *VT* 45:1–16

de Boer, P.A.H.

1982 "Some Observations on Deuteronomy vi 4 and 5", *Von Kanaan bis Kerala: FS für J.P.M. van der Ploeg* (AOAT 211; ed. W.C. Delsman, J.T. Nelis, J.R.T.M. Peters, W.H.P. Römer, A.S. van der Woude; Butzon & Bercker) 45–52

Böhmer, S.

1976 *Heimkehr und neuer Bund. Studien zu Jeremia 30–31* (GTA 5; Vandenhoeck & Ruprecht)

Boissonard, R. and Vouga, F.

1980 "Pour une éthique de la propriété: Essais sur le Deutéronome", *BCPE* 32:5–46

Boorer, S.

1992 *The Promise of the Land as Oath: A Key to the Formulation of the Pentateuch* (BZAW 205; W. de Gruyter)

Braulik, G.

1970 "Die Ausdrücke für 'Gesetz' im Buch Deuteronomium", *Biblica* 51:39–66

1978 *Die Mittel deuteronomischer Rhetorik* (AnBib 68; Biblical Institute Press)

1982 "Gesetz als Evangelium. Rechtfertigung und Begnadigung nach der deuteronomischen Tora", *ZTK* 79:127–160

1984 "Law as Gospel: Justification and Pardon According to the Deuteronomic Torah", *Int* 38:5–14

1985 "Zur deuteronomistischen Konzeption von Freiheit und Frieden", *IOSOT Congress Volume Salamanca 1983* (VTSup 36; ed. J.A. Emerton; E.J. Brill) 29–39

1986 *Deuteronomium I 1:1–16:17* (DNEB 15; Echter Verlag)

1989 "Die Entstehung der Rechtsfertigungslehre in den Bearbeitungsschichte des Buches Deuteronomium: Ein Beitrag zur Klärung der Voraussetzungen paulinischer Theologie", *ThPh* 64 (1989) 321–333

1991a "Die Funktion von Siebenergruppierungen im Endtext des Deuteronomiums", *Ein Gott, Eine Offenbarung: Beiträge zur biblischen Exegese, Theologie und Spiritualität: FS für N Füglister zum 60. Geburtstag* (ed. F.V. Reiterer; Echter Verlag) 37–50

1991b *Die deuteronomischen Gesetze und der Dekalog: Studien zum Aufbau von Deuteronomium 12–26* (SBS 145; Verlag Katholisches Bibelwerk)

1992 *Deuteronomium II 16,18–34,12* (DNEB 28; Echter Verlag)

1993 "The Sequence of the Laws in Deuteronomy 12–26 and in the Decalogue", *A Song of Power and the Power of Song: Essays on the Book of Deuteronomy* (SBTS 3; ed. D.L. Christensen; trans. L.M. Maloney; Eisenbrauns) 313–335

1994a "Wisdom, Divine Presence and Law", *Theology of Deuteronomy: Collected Essays of Georg Braulik* (BIBALCE 2; trans. U. Lindblad; BIBAL Press) 1–25

1994b "The Joy of the Feast", *Theology of Deuteronomy: Collected Essays of Georg Braulik* (BIBALCE 2; trans. U. Lindblad; BIBAL Press) 27–65

1994c "Commemoration of Passion and Feast of Joy", *Theology of Deuteronomy: Collected Essays of Georg Braulik* (BIBALCE 2; trans. U. Lindblad; BIBAL Press) 67–85

1994d "Some Remarks on the Deuteronomic Conception of Freedom and Peace", *Theology of Deuteronomy: Collected Essays of Georg Braulik* (BIBALCE 2; trans. U. Lindblad; BIBAL Press) 87–98

1994e "Deuteronomy and the Birth of Monotheism", *Theology of Deuteronomy: Collected Essays of Georg Braulik* (BIBALCE 2; trans. U. Lindblad; BIBAL Press) 99–130

1994f "Deuteronomy and Human Rights", *Theology of Deuteronomy: Collected Essays of Georg Braulik* (BIBALCE 2; trans. U. Lindblad; BIBAL Press) 131–150

Brekelmans, C.

1978 "Wisdom Influence in Deuteronomy", *La Sagesse de l'Ancien Testament* (BEThL 51; ed. M. Gilbert; Louvain University Press) 28–38

1985 "Deuteronomy 5: Its Place and Function", *Das Deut* 164–173

Brettler, M.Z.

1981–82 "The Promise of the Land of Israel to the Patriarchs in the Pentateuch", *Shnaton* 5–6: VII–XXIV

Brichto, H.C.

1963 *The Problem of 'Curse' in the Hebrew Bible* (JBLMS 13; Society for Biblical Literature and Exegesis)

1983 "The Worship of the Golden Calf: A Literary Analysis of a Fable on Idolatry", *HUCA* 54:1–44

Bright, J.

1951 "The Date of the Prose Sermons of Jeremiah", *JBL* 70:15–35

1966 "An Exercise in Hermeneutics: Jeremiah 31:31–34", *Int* 20:188–210

Brongers, H.A.

1965 "Bemerkungen zum Gebrauch des adverbialen וְעַתָּה im A.T.", *VT* 15:289–299

Brown, R.

1993 *The Message of Deuteronomy: Not By Bread Alone* (BST; IVP)

Brown, F., Driver, S.R. and Briggs, C.A.

1979 *The New Brown-Driver-Briggs-Gesenius Hebrew and English Lexicon* (Hendrickson)

Bruce, F.F.

1963 *Romans* (TNTC; Tyndale Press)

Brueggemann, W.

1961 *A Form-Critical Study of the Cultic Material in Deuteronomy: An Analysis of the Nature of Cultic Encounter in the Mosaic Tradition* (Unpublished ThD dissertation, Union Theological Seminary)

1968 "Kerygma of the Deuteronomistic Historian: Gospel for Exiles", *Int* 22:387–402

1974 "Israel's Sense of Place in Jeremiah", *Rhetorical Criticism: Essays in Honor of James Muilenburg* (PTMS 1; ed. J.J. Jackson, M. Kessler; Pickwick Press) 149–165

1977 *The Land: Place as Gift, Promise and Challenge in Biblical Faith* (OBT; Fortress Press)

1982a *Genesis* (Interpretation; John Knox Press)

1982b *The Creative Word: Canon as a Model for Biblical Education* (Fortress Press)

1985 "Imagination as a Mode of Fidelity", *Understanding the Word* (JSOTSup 37; ed. J. Butler, E. Conrad, B. Ollenberger; JSOT Press) 13–36

Brunner, H.

1958 "Was aus dem Munde Gottes geht", *VT* 8:428–429

Budd, P.J.

1973 "Priestly Instruction in Pre-Exilic Israel", *VT* 23:1–14

1984 *Numbers* (WBC 5; Word)

Buis, P.

1968 "La Nouvelle Alliance", *VT* 18:1–15

Buis, P. and Leclerq, J.

1963 *Le Deutéronome* (Sources Biblique; J. Gabalda)

Burden, T.L.

1994 *The Kerygma of the Wilderness Traditions in the Hebrew Bible* (AUS Series VII: Theology and Religion 163; Peter Lang)

Cairns, I.

1992 *Deuteronomy: Word and Presence* (ITC; Eerdmans/ Handsel)

Calvin, J.

1960 *The Epistles of Paul the Apostle to the Romans and to the Thessalonians* (trans. R. McKenzie; Oliver & Boyd)

Campbell, A.F.

1994 "Martin Noth and the Deuteronomistic History", *The History of Israel's Traditions: The Heritage of Martin Noth* (JSOTSup 182; ed. S.L. McKenzie, M.P. Graham: Sheffield Academic Press) 31–62

Campbell, W.S.

1979 "Christ the End of the Law: Romans 10:4", *Studia Biblica 1978 Vol III: Papers on Paul and Other New Testament Authors* (JSNTSup 3; ed. E.A. Livingstone; JSOT Press) 73–81

Carmichael, C.M.
1967 "Deuteronomic Laws, Wisdom, and Historical Traditions", *JSS* 12:198–206
1985 *Law and Narrative in the Bible* (Ithaca Press)
Carpenter, E.E.
1987 "Literary Structure and Unbelief: A Study of Deuteronomy 1:6–46", *AsTJ* 42:77–84
Carroll, R.P.
1977 "Rebellion and Dissent in Ancient Israelite Society", *ZAW* 89:176–204
Cazelles, H.
1951–52 "Jérémie et le Deutéronome", *RSR* 38:5–36
1958 *Le Deutéronome* (La Sainte Bible; Les Éditions du Cerf [2nd Ed, Rev])
1966 "Institutions et Terminologie en Deutéronome i 6–17", VTSup 15 (E.J. Brill) 97–112
1967 "Passages in the Singular within Discourse in the Plural of Deuteronomy 1–4", *CBQ* 29:207–219
1977 "Alliance du Sinai, Alliance de l'Horeb et Renouvellement de l'Alliance", *Beiträge zur alttestamentlichen Theologie: FS für W. Zimmerli zum 70. Geburtstag* (ed. H. Donner, R. Hanhart, R. Smend; Vandenhoeck & Ruprecht) 67–79
Childs, B.S.
1962 *Memory and Tradition in Israel* (Alec R. Allenson)
1967 "Deuteronomic Formulae of the Exodus Tradition", *Hebräische Wortforschung: FS für J. Baumgartner* (VTSup 16; E.J. Brill) 30–39
1974 *Exodus* (OTL; SCM Press)
1979 *Introduction to the Old Testament as Scripture* (SCM Press)
Chingota, F.L.
1991 *The Use of the Concept 'Fear' in Deuteronomy to denote the Relationship between God and Israel* (Unpublished PhD thesis; Aberdeen University)
Cholewinski, A.
1985 "Zur theologischen Deutung des Moabbundes", *Biblica* 66:96–111
Christensen, D.L.
1985a "Form and Structure in Deuteronomy 1–11", *Das Deut* 135–144
1985b "Prose and Poetry in the Bible: The Narrative Poetics of Deuteronomy 1,9–18", *ZAW* 97:179–189
1986 "The *Numeruswechsel* in Deuteronomy 12", *Proceedings of the Ninth World Congress of Jewish Studies. A. The Period of the Bible* (World Union of Jewish Studies) 61–68
1991 *Deuteronomy 1–11* (WBC 6A; Word)
1992 "New Evidence for the Priestly Redaction of Deuteronomy", *ZAW* 104:197–202
1993 "Deuteronomy in Modern Research: Approaches and Issues", *A Song of Power and the Power of Song: Essays on the Book of Deuteronomy* (SBTS 3; ed. D.L. Christensen; Eisenbrauns) 3–17
Claassen, W.T.
1983 "Speaker-Oriented Functions of כִּי in Biblical Hebrew", *JNSL* 11:29–46
Clark, W.M.
1969 "A Legal Background to the Yahwist's Use of 'Good and Evil' in Genesis 2–3", *JBL* 88:266–278
Clements, R.E.
1965 *Prophecy and Covenant* (SBT 43; SCM Press)

1967 *Abraham and David: Genesis XV and It Meaning for Israelite Tradition* (SBT [2nd Series] 5; SCM Press)
1968 *God's Chosen People: A Theological Interpretation of the Book of Deuteronomy* (RBC 182; SCM Press)
1989 *Deuteronomy* (OTG; JSOT Press)

Clifford, R.
1982 *Deueronomy, with an Excursus on Covenant and Law* (OTM 4; Michael Glazier)

Clines, D.J.A.
1978 *The Theme of the Pentateuch* (JSOTSup 10; JSOT Press)

Coats, G.W.
1976 "Conquest Traditions in the Wilderness Theme", *JBL* 95:177–190

Cody, A.
1964 "When is the Chosen People called a gôy?", *VT* 14:1–6

Cogswell, J.
1961 "Lest We Forget: A Sermon (Dt 8,11.14)", *Int* 15:32–40

Collier, G.D.
1983 "The Problem of Deuteronomy: In Search of Perspective", *RestQ* 26:215–233

Coppens, J.
1963 "La nouvelle alliance en Jér 31,31–34", *CBQ* 25:12–21

Couroyer, B.
1981 "'Avoir la nuque raide': Ne pas incliner l'oreille", *RB* 88:216–225
1983 "La tablette du coeur", *RB* 90:416–434

Craigie, P.C.
1969 "Yahweh is a Man of Wars", *SJT* 22:183–188
1976 *The Book of Deuteronomy* (NICOT; Eerdmans)

Cranfield, C.E.B.
1979 *The Epistle to the Romans* (ICC; T&T Clark; Vol II)

Crenshaw, J.L.
1969 "Method in Distinguishing Wisdom Influence Upon 'Historical' Literature", *JBL* 88:129–142
1970 "Popular Questioning of the Justice of God in Ancient Israel", *ZAW* 82:380–395
1971 *Prophetic Conflict: Its Effect Upon Israelite Religion* (BZAW 124; W. de Gruyter)
1981 "Wisdom and Authority: Sapiential Rhetoric and Its Warrants", *IOSOT Congress Volume: Vienna 1980* (VTSup 32; ed. J.A. Emerton; E.J. Brill) 10–29
1994 *Trembling at the Threshold of a Biblical Text* (Eerdmans)

Cross, F.M.
1973 *Canaanite Myth and Hebrew Epic: Essays in the History of the Religion of Israel* (HUP)

Cunliffe-Jones, H.
1951 *Deuteronomy* (TBC; SCM Press)

Curtis, A.H.W.
1994 *Joshua* (OTG: Sheffield Academic Press)

Daube, D.
1947 *Studies in Biblical Law* (CUP)
1959 "Concessions to Sinfulness in Jewish Law", *JJS* 10:1–13
1961 "Direct and Indirect Causation in Biblical Law", *VT* 11:246–269
1969a "*Repudium* in Deuteronomy", *Neotestamentica et Semitica: Studies in Honour of Matthew Black* (ed. E.E. Ellis, M. Wilcox; T&T Clark)

1969b "The Culture of Deuteronomy", *Orita* 3:27–52

Davies, G.I.

1974 "The Wilderness Itineraries: A Comparative Study", *TynBull* 25:46–81

1979 "The Significance of Deut 1:2 for the Location of Mount Horeb", *PEQ* 111:87–101

1990 "The Wilderness Itineraries and Recent Archaeological Research", *Studes in the Pentateuch* (VTSup 41; ed. J.A. Emerton; E.J. Brill) 163–175

Davies, G.N.

1990 *Faith and Obedience in Romans: A Study in Romans 1–4* (JSNTSup 39; JSOT Press)

Davies, W.D.

1974 *The Gospel & the Land: Early Christianity and Jewish Territorial Doctrine* (University of California Press)

Davis, D.R.

1982 "Rebellion, Presence and Covenant: A Study in Exodus 32–34", *WTJ* 44:71–87

Derrett, J.D.M.

1984 "Christ and the Power of Choice (Mark 3:1–6)", *Biblica* 65:168–188

Deurloo, K.A.

1994 "The One God and All Israel in its Generations", *Studies* 31–46

DeVries, S.J.

1974 "The Development of the Deuteronomic Promulgation Formula", *Biblica* 55: 301–316

1975a *Yesterday, Today and Tomorrow: Time and History in the Old Testament* (SPCK)

1975b "Deuteronomy: Exemplar of a Non-Sacerdotal Appropriation of Sacred History", *Grace Upon Grace: Essays in Honor of Lester J. Kuyper* (ed. J.I. Cook; Eerdmans) 95–105

Dhorme, P.

1922 "L'emploi metaphorique des noms de parties du corps en hébreu et en akkadien", *RB* 31:489–517

Diepold, P.

1972 *Israels Land* (BWANT (5th Series) 15; W. Kohlhammer)

Dillard, R. and Longman, T.

1994 *An Introduction to the Old Testament* (Zondervan)

Dillmann, A.

1886 *Die Bücher Numeri, Deuteronomium und Josua* (Verlag von S. Hirzel [2nd Ed])

Dion, P.E.

1970 "The 'Fear Not' Formula and Holy War, *CBQ* 32:565–570

Doron, P.

1978 "Motive Clauses in the Laws of Deuteronomy: Their Forms, Functions and Contents", *HAR* 2:61–77

Driver, S.R.

1902 *Deuteronomy* (ICC; T&T Clark [3rd Ed])

Dubarle, A.M.

1964 *The Biblical Doctrine of Original Sin* (trans. E.W. Stewart; Geoffrey Chapman)

Dumbrell, W.J.

1984 *Covenant and Creation: An Old Testament Covenantal Theology* (Lancer/Paternoster)

Dunn, J.D.G.

1988 *Romans 9–16* (WBC 38B; Word)

Durham, J.I.
1987 *Exodus* (WBC 3; Word)

Eichrodt, W.
1961 *Theology of the Old Testament* (trans. J.A. Baker; SCM Press; Vol 1)
1966 "Covenant and Law: Thoughts on Recent Discussion" (trans. L. Gaston), *Int* 20:302–321
1967 *Theology of the Old Testament* (trans. J.A. Baker; SCM Press; Vol 2)

Emerton, J.A.
1970 "A Consideration of Some Alleged Meanings of ידע in Hebrew", *JSS* 15:145–180

Eslinger, L.
1989 *Into the Hands of the Living God* (JSOTSup 84; Bible and Literature Series 24; Sheffield Academic Press)

Even-Shoshan, A.
1984 *A New Concordance of the Old Testament Using the Hebrew and Aramaic Text* (Baker [2nd Ed])

Eybers, I.H.
1970 "Some Examples of Hyperbole in Biblical Hebrew", *Semitics* 1:38–49

Fabry, H.-J.
1995 "לֵב, לֵבָב", *TDOT* (Vol 7) 399–437

Falk, Z.W.
1992 "Law and Ethics in the Hebrew Bible", *Justice and Righteousness: Biblical Themes and Their Influence* (JSOTSup 137; ed. H.G. Reventlow, Y. Hoffman; Sheffield Academic Press) 82–90

Fensham, F.C.
1962 "Malediction and Benediction in Ancient Near Eastern Vassal-Treaties and the Old Testament", *ZAW* 74:1–9
1963 Clauses of Protection in Hittite Vassal-Treaties and the Old Testament", *VT* 13:133–143
1966 "An Ancient Tradition of the Fertility of Palestine", *PEQ* 98:166–167
1967 "Covenant, Promise and Expectation in the Bible", *TZ* 23:305–322
1971 "Father and Son as Terminology for Treaty and Covenant", *Near Eastern Studies in Honor of William Foxwell Albright* (ed. H. Goedicke; John Hopkins Press) 121–135

Fletcher, V.E.
1971 "The Shape of Old Testament Ethics", *SJT* 24:47–73

Flückiger, F.
1955 "Christus, des Gesetzes τέλος", *TZ* 11:153–157

Forshey, H.O.
1973 *The Hebrew Root* NHL *and its Semitic Cognates* (Unpublished PhD dissertation; Harvard University)

Foster, R.
1987 *These are the Words… A Study in Deuteronomy* (College Communications)

Fox, M.V.
1973 "*Tôb* as a Covenant Terminology", *BASOR* 209:41–42

Frankena, R.
1965 "The Vassal Treaties of Esarhaddon and the Dating of Deuteronomy", *OTS* 14:123–154

Freedman, D.N.
1964 "Divine Commitment and Human Obligation: The Covenant Theme", *Int* 18:419–431
Fretheim, T.E.
1983 *Deuteronomistic History* (IBT; Abingdon Press)
Friedman, R.E.
1981 "From Egypt to Egypt: Dtr[1] and Dtr[2]", *Traditions in Transformations: Turning Points in Biblical faith: FS for F.M. Cross* (ed. B. Halpern, J.D. Levenson; Eisenbrauns) 167–192
Fymer-Kensky, T.
1983 "Pollution, Purification and Purgation in Biblical Israel", *The Word of the Lord Shall Go Forth: Essays in Honor of David N. Freedman in Celebration of His Sixtieth Birthday* (ASOR Special Volume Series 1; ed. C.L. Meyers, M. O'Connor; Eisenbrauns) 399–414
Fuhs, H.F.
1990 "יָרֵא", *TDOT* (Vol 6) 290–315
Gammie, J.G.
1972 "The Theology of Retribution in the Book of Deuteronomy", *CBQ* 32:1–12
1989 *Holiness in Israel* (OBT; Fortress Press)
García López, F.
1977 "Analyse littéraire de Deutéronome, V–XI", *RB* 84:481–522
1978 "Analyse littéraire de Deutéronome, V–XI", *RB* 85:5–49
1994 "Deut 34, Dtr History and the Pentateuch", *Studies* 47–61
Gehman, H.S.
1975 "The Oath in the Old Testament: Its Vocabulary, Idiom, and Syntax; Its Semantics and Theology in the Massoretic Text and the Septuagint", *Grace Upon Grace: Essays in Honor of Lester J. Kuyper* (ed. J.I. Cook; Eerdmans)
Geller, S.A.
1994 "Fiery Wisdom: Logos and Lexis in Deuteronomy 4", *Prooftexts* 14:103–139
Gemser, B.
1952 "*Be'ēber Hajjardēn*: In Jordan's Hinterland", *VT* 2:349–355
1953 "The Importance of the Motive Clauses in Old Testament Law", VTSup 1:50–66
Gerstenberger, E.
1965 "Covenant and Commandment", *JBL* 84:38–51
Giles, T.
1991 "Knowledge as a Boundary in the Organization of Experience: Deut 8:3, 16", *IBS* 13:155–169
Ginsberg, H.L.
1963 "'Roots Below and Fruits Above' and Related Matters", *Hebrew and Semitic Studies: Presented to G.R. Driver on His 70th Birthday* (ed. D.W. Thomas, W.D. McHardy; Clarendon Press) 72–76
Gold, J.
1982 "Deuteronomy and the Word: the Beginning and the End", *The Biblical Mosaic: Changing Perspectives* (SBL Semeia Studies; ed. R. Polzin, E. Rothman; Fortress Press/Scholars Press) 45–59
Goldingay, J.E.
1972 "That You May Know That Yahweh is God: A Study in the Relationship between Theology and Historical Truth in the Old Testament", *TynBull* 23:58–93

1985 "Divine Ideals, Human Stubbornness and Scriptural Inerrancy", *Transformation* 24:1–4
1987 *Theological Diversity and the Authority of the Old Testament* (Eerdmans)
Gordon, R.P.
1974 "Deuteronomy and the Deuteronomistic School: A Review of M. Weinfeld", *TynBull* 25:113–120
Gottwald, N.K.
1964 "'Holy War' in Deuteronomy: Analysis and Critique", *RevExp* 61:296–310
van Goudoever, J.
1985 "The Liturgical Significance of the Date in Dt 1,3", *Das Deut* 145–148
Gowan, D.E.
1981 "Reflections on the Motive Clauses in Old Testament Law", *Intergerini Parietis Septum (Eph 2:14): Essays Presented to Markus Barth on his Sixty-Fifth Birthday* (PTMS 33; ed. D.Y. Hadidian; Pickwick Press) 111–125
Grassi, J.A.
1989 "Matthew as a Second Testament Deuteronomy", *BTB* 19:23–29
Gray, G.B.
1903 *A Critical and Exegetical Commentary on Numbers* (ICC; T&T Clark)
Greenberg, M.
1951 "Hebrew *s*$^{e}$*gulla*: Akkadian *sikiltu*", *JAOS* 71:172–174
1977–78 "Moses' Intercessory Prayer (Exod. 32:11–13, 31–32; Deut. 9:26–29)", *Ecumenical Institute Tantur Yearbook* 21–35
Greenfield, J.
1967 "Some Aspects of Treaty Terminology in the Bible", *Fourth World Congress of Jewish Studies: Papers Vol 1* (World Union of Jewish Studies) 117–119
Gunn, D.M.
1987 "Joshua and Judges", *The Literary Guide to the Bible* (ed. R. Alter, F. Kermode; Fontana) 102–121
Hagelia, H.
1994 *Numbering the Stars: A Phraseological Analysis of Genesis 15* (ContBot 39; Almqvist & Wiksell)
Hals, R.M.
1973 "Is there a Genre of Preached Law?", *SBLSPS* 1:1–12
Hamilton, J.M.
1992 *Social Justice and Deuteronomy: The Case of Deuteronomy 15* (SBL Dissertation Series 136; Scholars Press)
Hamilton, V.P.
1990 *Genesis 1–17* (NICOT; Eerdmans)
Harper, A.
1895 *The Book of Deuteronomy* (The Expositor's Bible; Hodder & Stoughton)
Hays, R.B.
1989 *Echoes of Scripture in the Letters of Paul* (Yale University Press)
Herrmann, A.
1961 "Das Steinharte Herz: zur Geschichte einer Metaphor", *JAC* 4:77–107
Herrmann, S.
1971 "Die konstructive Restauration: Das Deuteronomium als Mitte biblischer Theologie", *Probleme biblischer Theologie: FS für G. von Rad* (ed. H.W. Wolff; Kaiser)

Hillers, D.R.
1964 "A Note on Some Treaty Terminology in the Old Testament", *BASOR* 176:46–47

Hoftijzer, J.
1985 *The Function and Use of the Imperfect Forms with Nun-Paragogicum in Classical Hebrew* (SSN 21; Van Gorcum)

Holladay, W.L.
1958 *The Root שׁוּב in the Old Testament (with particular references to its usages in covenantal contexts)* (E.J. Brill)
1985 "A Proposal for Reflections in the Book of Jeremiah of the Seven-Year Recitation of the Law in Deuteronomy (Deut 31,10–13)", *Das Deut* 326–328

Honeyman, A.M.
1952 "Merismus in Biblical Hebrew", *JBL* 71:11–18

Hoppe, L.J.
1980 "The Meaning of Deuteronomy", *BTB* 10:111–117
1983 "Elders and Deuteronomy: A Proposal", *EglT* 14:259–272
1985 "Jerusalem in the Deuteronomistic History", *Das Deut* 107–110

Horst, J.
1967 "οὐς", *TDNT* (Vol 5) 543–559

Howard, D.M.
1994 "Rhetorical Criticism in Old Testament Studies", *BBR* 4:87–104

Huffmon, H.B.
1966 "The Treaty Background of Hebrew *YADA*ʿ", *BASOR* 181:31–37

Huffmon, H.B. and Parker, S.B.
1966 "A Further Note on the Treaty Background of Hebrew *YADA*ʿ", *BASOR* 184:36–38

Hugenberger, G.P.
1991 *Marriage as Covenant: A Study of Biblical Law and Ethics governing Marriage developed from the Perspective of Malachi* (Unpublished PhD thesis; CNAA)

Hughes, H.W.
1990 *Divine Purpose in Deuteronomic Polity: Theological Implications of the 'Motive' Changes expressing Purpose or Result in Chapters 12–26 of Deuteronomy* (Unpublished PhD thesis; Union Theological Seminary)

Hyatt, J.P.
1942 "Jeremiah and Deuteronomy", *JNES* 1:156–173

Irwin, W.A.
1939 "An Objective Criterion for the Dating of Deuteronomy", *AJSL* 56:337–349

Jacobs, P.F.
1974 *An Examination of the Motif 'Life as Result or Reward' in the Book of Deuteronomy* (Unpublished PhD dissertation; Union Theological Seminary)

Janzen, J.G.
1987a "On the Most Important Word in the Shema (Dt vi 4–5)", *VT* 37:280–300
1987b "The Yoke That Gives Rest", *Int* 41:256–268

Janzen, W.
1992 "Land", *ABD* (Vol 4) 143–154

Johnson, A.R.
1964 *The Vitality of the Individual in the Thought of Ancient Israel* (University of Wales Press [2nd Ed])

Johnson, R.
1990 "The Old Testament Demand for Faith and Obedience", *SWJT* 32:27–36

Jones, R.C.
1992 "Deuteronomy 10:12–22", *Int* 46:281–285
Jongeling, B.
1974 "L'expression *MY YTN* dans l'Ancien Testament", *VT* 24:32–40
Joüon, P.
1925 "Crainte et peur en hébreu biblique", *Biblica* 6:174–179
1991 *A Grammar of Biblical Hebrew* (Subsidia Biblica 14; trans. and rev. T. Muraoka; Editrice Pontificio Istituto Biblico; 2 vols)
Joyce, P.
1989 *Divine Initiative and Human Response in Ezekiel* (JSOTSup 51; JSOT Press)
Kaiser, W.C.
1973 "The Promise Theme and the Theology of Rest", *BibSac* 130:135–150
Kallai, Z.
1982 "The Wandering Traditions from Kadesh-Barnea to Canaan: A Study in Biblical Historiography", *JJS* 33:175–184
1995 "Where did Moses Speak (Deuteronomy I 1–5)?", *VT* 45:188–197
Kalland, E.S.
1992 "Deuteronomy", *EBC* (Vol 3) 3–235
Kapelrud, A.S.
1988 "The Covenant as Agreement", *SJOT* 1:30–38
Käsemann, E.
1980 *Commentary on Romans* (trans. G.W. Bromiley; SCM Press)
Kaufman, S.A.
1978–79 "The Structure of the Deuteronomic Law", *Maarav* 1:105–158
Kaunfer, A.H.
1988 "Aaron and the Golden Calf: Biblical Tradition and Midrashic Interpretation", *ConsJud* 41:87–94
Kautsch, E. (ed.)
1910 *Gesenius' Hebrew Grammar* (trans. A.E. Cowley; Clarendon Press [2nd Ed])
Kearney, P.J.
1973 "The Role of the Gibeonite in the Deuteronomic History", *CBQ* 35:1–19
Keil, C.F. and Delitzsch, F.
1981 *Commentary on the Old Tesament in Ten Volumes: Volume 1: The Pentateuch (Three Volumes in One)* (trans. J. Martin; Eerdmans)
Kessler, M.
1978 "Inclusio in the Hebrew Bible", *Semitics* 6:44–49
Kitchen, K.A.
1970 "Ancient Orient, 'Deuteronomism' and the Old Testament", *New Perspectives on the Old Testament* (ed. J.B. Payne; Word) 1–24
Kittel, G.
1964 "ἀκουω", *TDNT* (Vol 1) 216–225
Kleinig, J.W.
1992 "The Attentive Heart: Meditation in the Old Testament", *RTR* 51:50–63
Kline, M.G.
1963 *The Treaty of the Great King: The Covenant Structure of Deuteronomy* (Eerdmans)
1968 *By Oath Assigned: A Reinterpretation of the Covenant Signs of Circumcision and Baptism* (Eerdmans)
1991 "Gospel Until the Law: Romans 5:13–14 and the Old Covenant", *JETS* 34:433–446

Knapp, D.

1987 *Deuteronomium 4: Literarische Analyse und theologische Interpretation* (GTA 35; Vandenhoeck & Ruprecht)

Koch, K.

1983 "Is there a Doctrine of Retribution in the Old Testament?", *Theodicy in the Old Testament* (Issues in Religion and Theology 4; ed. J.L. Crenshaw; trans. T.H. Trapp; Fortress Press/SPCK) 57–87

Köckert, M.

1985 "Das Nahe Wort: Zum entscheidenden Wandel des Gesetzesverständnisses im Alten Testament", *ThPh* 60:496–519

Koehler, L. and Baumgartner, W.

1958 *Lexicon in Veteris Testamenti Libros* (E.J. Brill)

Köhler, L.

1956 *Hebrew Man* (trans. P.R. Ackroyd; SCM Press)

König, E.

1917 *Deuteronomium* (KAT 3; A. Deichert)

Kooy, V.H.

1975 "The Fear and Love of God in Deuteronomy", *Grace Upon Grace: Essays in Honor of Lester J. Kuyper* (ed. J.I. Cook; Eerdmans) 106–116

Kopf, L.

1959 "Arabische Etymologien und Parallelen zum Bibelwörterbuch", *VT* 9:247–287

Kreuzer, S.

1987 "Homiletik und Rhetorik am Beispiel der Predigt des Deuteronomiums", *DP* 87:369–373

Kutsch, E.

1973 *Verheißung und Gesetz: Untersuchungen zum sogenannten »Bund« im Alten Testament* (BZAW 131; W. de Gruyter)

Kuyper, L.J.

1952 "The Book of Deuteronomy", *Int* 6:321–340

Labuschagne, C.J.

1966 *The Incomparability of Yahweh in the Old Testament* (POS 5; E.J. Brill)

1985 "Divine Speech in Deuteronomy", *Das Deut* 111–126

1987 *Deuteronomium IA* (De Prediking van het Oude Testament; Callenbach)

Lambdin, T.O.

1971 *Introduction to Biblical Hebrew* (Dartman, Longman and Todd)

Langlamet, F.

1969 *Gilgal et les récits de la traversé du Jourdain (Jos. 3–4)* (Cahiers de la Revue Biblique 11; J. Gabalda)

Le Déaut, R.

1981 "Le theme de la circoncision du coeur: (Dt XXX 6; Jer IV 4) dans les versions anciennes (LXX et Targum) et a Qumran", VTSup 32:178–205

Leenhardt, F.J.

1961 *The Epistle to the Romans* (trans. H. Knight; Lutterworth)

van Leeuwen, R.C.

1984 "On the Structure and Sense of Deuteronomy 8", *Proceedings: Eastern Great Lakes and Midwest Biblical Societies* 4:237–249

1985 "What Comes Out of God's Mouth: Theological Wordplay in Deuteronomy 8", *CBQ* 47:55–57

Lenchak, T.A.
1993 *"Choose Life!": A Rhetorical-Critical Investigation of Deuteronomy 28,69–30,20* (AnBib 129; Editrice Pontificio Istituto Biblico)

Levenson, J.D.
1975 "Who Inserted the Book of the Torah?", *HTR* 68:203–233
1980 "The Theologies of Commandment in Biblical Israel", *HTR* 73:17–33
1985 *Sinai and Zion: An Entry into the Jewish Bible* (Harper)
1993 *The Hebrew Bible, The Old Testament and Historical Criticism: Jews and Christians in Biblical Studies* (Westminster/John Knox Press)

Levine, B.A.
1993 *Numbers 1–20* (AB 4; Doubleday)

Lewy, I.
1959 "The Story of the Golden Calf Reanalyzed", *VT* 9:318–322
1962 "The Puzzle of Deut XXVII: Blessings Announced but Curses Noted", *VT* 12:207–211

L'Hour, J.
1967 *Die Ethik der Bundestradition im Alten Testament* (SBS 14; Verlag Katholisches Bibelwerk)

Licht, J.
1986 *Storytelling in the Bible* (Magnes Press [2nd Ed])

Lindars, B.
1968 "Torah in Deuteronomy", *Words and Meanings: Essays Presented to D.W. Thomas* (ed. P.R. Ackroyd, B. Lindars; CUP) 117–136

Lisowsky, G.
1981 *Konkordanz zum Hebräischen Alten Testament* (Deutsche Bibelgesellschaft [2nd ed])

Loewenstamm, S.E.
1968–69 "The Formula בעת ההיא in Deuteronomy" (Hebrew), *Tarbiz* 38:99–104

Lohfink, N.
1960 "Darstellungskunst und Theologie im Dtn 1:6–3:29", *Biblica* 41:105–134
1962 "Der Bundesschluß im Land Moab: Redaktionsgeschichtliches zu Dt 28,69–32,47", *BZ* (new series) 6:32–56
1963a *Das Hauptgebot: Eine Untersuchung literarischer Einleitungsfragen zu Dtn 5–11* (AnBib 20; Biblical Institute)
1963b "Hate and Love in Osee 9.15", *CBQ* 25:417
1964 "Verkündigung des Hauptgebots in der jüngsten Schicht des Deuteronomiums (Dt 4,1–40)", *BibLeb* 5:247–256
1965 *Höre Israel! Auslegung von Texten aus dem Buch Deuteronomium* (Die Welt der Bibel 18; Patmos)
1968 "Review of J.G. Plöger: *Literarkritische, formgeschichtliche und stilkritische Untersuchungen zum Deuteronomium*", *Biblica* 49:110–115
1976 "Deuteronomy", *IDB* (Supp Vol; Abingdon) 229–232
1981 "Kerygmata des deuteronomistichen Geschichtswerks", *Die Botschaft und die Boten: FS für H.W. Wolff zum 70. Geburtstag* (ed. J. Jeremias, L. Perlitt; Neukirchener Verlag) 87–100
1982a "Pluralism", *Great Themes from the Old Testament* (trans. R. Wallis; T&T Clark) 17–37

1982b "Sovereignty", *Great Themes from the Old Testament* (trans. R. Wallis; T&T Clark) 39–53

1982c "Die Gotteswortverschachtelung im Jer 30–31", *Künder des Wortes: Beiträge zur Theologie der Propheten. FS für Josef Schreiner zum 60. Geburtstag* (ed. L. Ruppert, P. Weimar, E. Zenger; Echter Verlag) 105–119

1983 "Die Bedeutungen von hebr. ירשׁ qal und hif", *BZ* (new series) 27:14–33

1989 "Zum 'Numeruswechsel' in Dtn 3,21f", *BN* 49:39–52

1990 "יָרַשׁ; יְרֵשָׁה; יְרֻשָּׁה; מוֹרָשׁ; מוֹרָשָׁה", *TDOT* (Vol 6) 368–396

1991a "Gott im Buch Deuteronomium", *Studien zum Deu0teronomium und zur deuteronomistischen Literatur II* (SBAB 12; Verlag Katholisches Bibelwerk) 25–53

1991b *The Covenant Never Revoked: Biblical Reflections on Christian–Jewish Dialogue* (trans. J.J. Scullion; Paulist Press)

1992a "Dtn 2,69 – Überschrift oder Kolophon?", *BN* 64:40–52

1992b "Deuteronomy 6:24: לְחַיֹּתֵנוּ 'To Maintain Us'", *"Sha'arei Talmon": Studies in the Bible, Qumran, and the Ancient Near East Presented to Shemaryahu Talmon* (ed. M. Fishbane, E. Tov, W.W. Fields; Eisenbrauns) 111–119

1993 "Recent Discussion on 2 Kings 22–23: The State of the Question", *A Song of Power and the Power of Song: Essays on the Book of Deuteronomy* (SBTS 3; ed. D.L. Christensen; trans. L.M. Maloney; Eisenbrauns) 36–61

1994a "The Problem of the Individual and Community in Deuteronomy 1:6–3:29", *Theology of the Pentateuch: Themes of the Priestly Narrative and Deuteronomy* (trans. L.M. Maloney; T&T Clark) 227–233

1994b "The Deuteronomistic Picture of the Transfer of Authority from Moses to Joshua: A Contribution to an Old Testament Theology of Office", *Theology of the Pentateuch: Themes of the Priestly Narrative and Deuteronomy* (trans. L.M. Maloney; T&T Clark) 234–247

1994c "The Decalogue in Deuteronomy 5", *Theology of the Pentateuch: Themes of the Priestly Narrative and Deuteronomy* (trans. L.M. Maloney; T&T Clark) 248–264

1994d "The 'Small Credo' of Deuteronomy 26:5–9", *Theology of the Pentateuch: Themes of the Priestly Narrative and Deuteronomy* (trans. L.M. Maloney; T&T Clark) 265–289

1995 *Geschichtstypologie in Deuteronomium 1–3* (Unpublished paper presented at XVth Congress of IOSOT; Cambridge, July 1995)

Long, B.O.

1971 "The Question and Answer Schemata in the Prophets", *JBL* 90:129–139

Lund, N.A.

1992 *Chiasmus in the New Testament: A Study in the Form and Function of Chiastic Structures* (Hendrickson; reprint of 1942 edition with a preface by D.M. Scholer, K.R. Snodgrass)

Lundbom, J.R.

1975 *Jeremiah: A Study in Ancient Hebrew Rhetoric* (SBL Dissertation Series 18; Scholars Press)

1976 "The Lawbook of the Josianic Reform", *CBQ* 38:293–302

Lust, J.

1992 "Review of M. Weinfeld: *Deuteronomy 1–11*", *EThL* 68:410–411

Luther, M.

1960 *Lectures on Deuteronomy* (Luther's Works Vol 9; ed. J. Pelikan; trans. R.R. Caemmerer; Concordia)

Lyonnet, S.
1968 "«La circoncision du coeur, celle qui relève de l'Esprit et non de la lettre» (Rom 2:29)", *L'Évangile, hier et aujourd'hui: Mélanges offerts au Professeur F.-J. Leenhardt* (Editions Labor et Fides) 87–97
Lyonnet, S. and Sabourin, L.
1970 *Sin, Redemption, and Sacrifice: A Biblical and Patristic Study* (AnBib 48; Biblical Institute Press)
MacKenzie, R.A.F.
1957 "The Messianism of Deuteronomy", *CBQ* 19:299–305
Malfroy, J.
1965 "Sagesse et loi dans le Deutéronome", *VT* 15:49–65
Mann, T.W.
1979 "Theological Reflections on the Denial of Moses", *JBL* 98:481–494
Martens, E.A.
1981 *God's Design: A Focus on Old Testament Theology* (Baker Book House)
1992 "Embracing the Law: A Biblical Perspective", *BBR* 2:1–28
Martin, B.L.
1989 *Christ and the Law in Paul* (*NTSup* 62; E.J. Brill)
Martin-Achard, R.
1960 "La signification théologique de l'élection d'Israël", *TZ* 16:331–341
1962 "La nouvelle alliance selon Jérémie", *RTP* (2nd series) 12:81–92
1974 "Quelques remarques sur la nouvelle alliance chez Jérémie (Jérémie 31,31–34)", *Questions disputées d'Ancien Testament: Méthode et Théologie* (BEThL 33; ed. C. Brekelmans; Leuven University Press) 141–164
Maxwell, J.C.
1987 *Deuteronomy* (TCC 5; Word)
Mayes, A.D.H.
1973 "The Nature of Sin and its Origin in the Old Testament", *ITQ* 40:250–263
1979 *Deuteronomy* (NCBC; Marshall, Morgan and Scott)
1980 "Exposition of Deuteronomy 4:25–31", *IBS* 2:67–85
1981a "Deuteronomy: Law of Moses or Law of God?", *PIBA* 5:36–54
1981b "Deuteronomy 4 and the Literary Criticism of Deuteronomy", *JBL* 100:23–51
1983 *The Story of Israel between Settlement and Exile: A Redactional Study of the Deuteronomistic History* (SCM Press)
1985 "Deuteronomy 29, Joshua 9, and the Place of the Gibeonites in Israel", *Das Deut* 321–325
1993 "On Describing the Purpose of Deuteronomy", *JSOT* 58:13–33
1994 "Deuteronomy 14 and the Deuteronomic World View", *Studies* 165–181
McBride, S.D.
1973 "The Yoke of the Kingdom: An Exposition of Dt 6:4–5", *Int* 27:273–306
1987 "Polity of the Covenant People: the Book of Deuteronomy", *Int* 41:229–244
1990 "Transcendent Authority: The Role of Moses in Old Testament Traditions", *Int* 44:229–239
McCarthy, D.J.
1965 "Notes on the Love of God in Deuteronomy and the Father–Son Relationship", *CBQ* 27:144–147
1972 *Old Testament Covenant: A Survey of Current Opinions* (Blackwell)

1973 “Review of M. Weinfeld: *Deuteronomy and the Deuteronomic School*”, *Biblica* 54:448–452
1974 “The Wrath of Yahweh and the Structural Unity of the Deuteronomistic History”, *Essays in Old Testament Ethics: J. Philip Hyatt, In Memoriam* (ed. J.L. Crenshaw, J.T. Willis; KTAV Publishing) 99–110
1981 *Treaty and Covenant: A Study in Form in the Ancient Oriental Documents and in the Old Testament* (AnBib 21A; Biblical Institute Press)

McComiskey, T.E.
1985 *The Covenants of Promise: A Theology of the Old Testament Covenants* (IVP)

McConville, J.G.
1979 “God’s ‘Name’ and God’s ‘Glory’”, *TynBull* 30:149–163
1983 “The Pentateuch Today”, *Themelios* 8:5–11
1984 *Law and Theology in Deuteronomy* (JSOTSup 33; JSOT Press)
1989 “Narrative and Meaning in the Book of Kings”, *Biblica* 70:31–49
1992 “1 Kings VIII 46–53 and the Deuteronomic Hope”, *VT* 42:67–79
1993a *Judgment and Promise: An Interpretation of the Book of Jeremiah* (Apollo/Eisenbrauns)
1993b *Grace in the End: A Study in Deuteronomic Theology* (SOTBT; Paternoster)
1994 “Deuteronomy”, *NBC* 198–232

McConville, J.G. and Millar, J.G.
1994 *Time and Place in Deuteronomy* (JSOTSup 179; Sheffield Academic Press)

McCurley, F.R.
1974 “The Home of Deuteronomy: A Methodological Analysis of the Northern Theory”, *A Light Unto My Path: Old Testament Studies in Honour of Jacob M. Myers* (ed. H.N. Bream, R.D. Heim, C.A. Moore; Temple University Press) 295–317

McEvenue, S.E.
1971 *The Narrative Style of the Priestly Writer* (AnBib 50; Biblical Institute Press)
1990 *Interpreting the Pentateuch* (Old Testament Studies; Liturgical Press)

McKay, J.W.
1972 “Man’s Love for God in Deuteronomy and the Father/Teacher–Son/Pupil Relationship”, *VT* 22:426–435

McKenzie, J.L.
1967 “The Historical Prologue of Deuteronomy”, *Fourth World Congress of Jewish Studies I* (World Union of Jewish Studies) 95–101

Mendecki, N.
1985 “Dtn 30:3–4 – nachexilisch?”, *BZ* 29:267–271

de Menezes, R.
1986 “The Pentateuchal Theology of the Land”, *BibBh* 12:5–28

Merrill, E.H.
1994 *Deuteronomy* (NAC; Broadman & Holman)

van der Merwe, C.H.J.
1992 “Is there any Difference between ירא מפני, ירא מן and ירא את?”, *JNSL* 18:177–183
1993 “Old Hebrew Particles and the Interpretation of Old Testament Texts”, *JSOT* 60:27–44

Meyers, C.L. and E.M.
1987 *Haggai, Zechariah 1–8* (AB 25B; Doubleday)

Michaelis, W.
1967 "ὁραω", *TDNT* (Vol 5) 315–382
Milgrom, J.
1973 "The Alleged 'demythologization and secularization' in Deuteronomy", *IEJ* 23:156–161
1976 "Profane Slaughter and a Formulaic Key to the Composition of Deuteronomy", *HUCA* 47:1–17
Millar, J.G.
1995 *The Ethics of Deuteronomy: An Exegetical and Theological Study of the Book of Deuteronomy* (Unpublished DPhil thesis; Oxford University)
Millard, A.R.
1966 "For He is Good", *TynBull* 17:115–117
Miller, P.D.
1965 "Fire in the Mythology of Canaan and Israel", *CBQ* 27:256–261
1969 "The Gift of God: The Deuteronomic Theology of the Land", *Int* 23:451–465
1970 "Apotropaic Imagery in Proverbs 6:20–22", *JNES* 29:129–130
1985 "The Human Sabbath: A Study in Deuteronomic Theology", *PTSB* 6:81–98
1987 "'Moses my Servant': The Deuteronomic Portrait of Moses", *Int* 41:245–255
1988 "The Many Faces of Moses: A Deuteronomic Portrait", *BibRev* 4:30–35
1990 *Deuteronomy* (Interpretation; John Knox Press)
1994 *They Cried to the Lord: The Form and Theology of Biblical Prayer* (Fortress Press)
Minette de Tillesse, G.
1962 "Sections 'tu' et sections 'vous' dans le Deutéronome", *VT* 12:29–87
Mitchell, H.G.
1899 "The Use of the Second Person in Deuteronomy", *JBL* 18:61–109
Mittmann, S.
1975 *Deuteronomium 1:1–6:3. Literarkritisch und traditionsgeschichtlich untersucht* (BZAW 139; W. de Gruyter)
Moberly, R.W.L.
1983 *At the Mountain of God: Story and Theology in Exodus 32–34* (JSOTSup 22; JSOT Press)
1990 "'Yahweh is One': The Translation of the Shema", *Studies in the Pentateuch* (VTSup 41; ed. J.A. Emerton; E.J. Brill) 209–215
1992 *The Old Testament of the Old Testament: Patriarchal Narratives and Mosaic Yahwism* (OBT; Fortress Press)
Moenikes, A.
1992 "Zur Redaktionsgeschichte des sogenannten Deuteronomistischen Geschichtswerks", *ZAW* 104:333–348
Moore, R.D.
1992 "Canon and Charisma in the Book of Deuteronomy", *JPT* 1:75–92
Moran, W.L.
1963a "The End of the Unholy War and the Anti-Exodus", *Biblica* 44:333–342
1963b "The Ancient Near Eastern Background of the Love of God in Deuteronomy", *CBQ* 25:77–87
1963c "A Note on the Treaty Terminology of the Sefîre Stelas", *JNES* 22:173–176
1969 "Deuteronomy", *A New Catholic Commentary on Holy Scripture* (ed. R.C. Fuller; Nelson) 256–276

Morris, L.L.
1988 *The Epistle to the Romans* (Eerdmans/IVP)
Most, W.
1967 "A Biblical Theology of Redemption in a Covenant Framework", *CBQ* 29:1–19
Muilenburg, J.
1953 "A Study in Hebrew Rhetoric: Repetition and Style", VTSup 1:97–111
1959 "The Form and Structure of the Covenantal Formulations", *VT* 9:347–365
1961 "The Linguistic and Rhetorical Usages of the Particle כִּי in the Old Testament", *HUCA* 32:135–160
1968 "The Intercession of the Covenant Mediator (Exodus 33: 1a, 12–17)", *Words and Meanings: Essays presented to D.W. Thomas* (ed. P.R. Ackroyd, B. Lindars; CUP) 159–181
Munchenberg, R.
1986 *Deuteronomy* (ChiRho Commentary; Lutheran Publishing House)
Muraoka, T.
1985 *Emphatic Words and Structures in Biblical Hebrew* (E.J. Brill/Magnes Press)
Murphy, R.E.
1973 "Deuteronomy – A Document of Revival", *Concilium* 9:26–36
Murray, J.
1965 *The Epistle to the Romans, Chapters 9–16* (NICNT; Eerdmans)
Myers, J.M.
1961 "The Requisites for Response: On the Theology of Deuteronomy", *Int* 15:14–31
Naylor, P.J.
1980 *The Language of Covenant: A Structural Analysis of the Semantic Field of* ברית *in Biblical Hebrew, with Particular Reference to the Book of Genesis* (Unpublished DPhil thesis; Oxford University)
Nelson, R.D.
1981 *The Double Redaction of the Deuteronomistic History* (JSOTSup 18; JSOT Press)
Niccacci, A.
1990 *The Syntax of the Verb in Classical Hebrew Prose* (trans. W.G.E. Watson; JSOTSup 86; JSOT Press)
Nicholson, E.W.
1967 *Deuteronomy and Tradition* (Blackwell)
1970 *Preaching to the Exiles: A Study of the Prose Tradition in the Book of Jeremiah* (Blackwell)
1977 "The Decalogue as the Direct Address of God", *VT* 27:422–433
1986a *God and His People: Covenant and Theology in the Old Testament* (Clarendon Press)
1986b "Covenant in a Century of Study since Wellhausen", *Crises and Perspectives* (*OTS* 24; E.J. Brill) 54–69
1991 "Deuteronomy's Vision of Israel", *Storia e tradizioni di Israele. Scritti in onore di J. Alberto Soggin* (ed. D. Garrone, F. Israel; Paideia Editrice) 191–203
Niehaus, J.J.
1992 "The Central Sanctuary: Where and When?", *TynBull* 43:3–30
Nielsen, E.
1995 *Deuteronomium* (HAT I/6; J.C.B. Mohr [Paul Siebeck])

Noth, M.

1966 "For All who Rely on Works of the Law are Under a Curse", *The Laws in the Pentateuch and Other Essays* (trans. D.R. Ap-Thomas; Oliver & Boyd) 118–131

1981 *The Deuteronomistic History* (JSOTSup 15; JSOT Press)

O'Connell, R.H.

1990 "Deuteronomy VIII 1–20: Asymetrical Concentricity and the Rhetoric of Providence", *VT* 40:437–452

1992a "Deuteronomy VII 1–26: Asymetrical Concentricity and the Rhetoric of Conquest", *VT* 42:248–265

1992b "Deuteronomy IX 7–X 7, 10–11: Panelled Structure, Double Rehearsal and the Rhetoric of Covenant Rebuke", *VT* 42:492–509

Ogushi, M.

1992 "Isr nur das Herz die Mitte des Menschen?", *Was ist der Mensch? Beiträge zur Anthropologie des Alten Testaments* (ed. F. Crüsemann, C. Hardmeier, R. Kessler; Chr. Kaiser Verlag) 42–47

Okeke, J.

1983 *The Concept of* LBB/LB *'Heart' in Jer 31:33: A Case Study in the Message and Theology of the Jeremiah Tradition, Compared with the Occurrences of the Same Word in Deut 10:12–18* (Unpublished dissertation; Lutheran School of Theology, Chicago)

Olivier, H.

1988 "A Land Flowing with Milk and Honey: Some Observations on the Modes of Existence in Ancient Israel", *NGTT* 29:2–13

Olson, D.T.

1985 *The Death of the Old and the Birth of the New: The Framework of the Book of Numbers and the Pentateuch* (BJS 71; Scholars Press)

1994 *Deuteronomy and the Death of Moses* (OBT; Fortress Press)

Ormann, G.

1938 "Die Stilmittel im Deuteronomium", *FS für Leo Baeck* (Schocken/Jüdischer Buchverlag) 39–53

Östborn, G.

1945 *Tora in the Old Testament: A Semantic Study* (Håkan Ohlssons Boktryckeri)

Ottoson, M.

1988 "Eden and the Land of Promise", *IOSOT Congress Volume: Jerusalem, 1986* (VTSup 40; ed. J.A. Emerton; E.J. Brill) 177–188

Owens, H.J.

1964 "Law and Love in Dt", *RevExp* 61:274–283

Pálfy, M.

1971 "Allgemein-menschliche Beziehungen der Frucht im Alten Testament", *Schalom: Studien zu Glaube und Geschichte Israels. FS für A. Jepsen zum 70. Geburtstag* (Arbeiten zur Theologie 1; ed. K.-H. Bernhardt; Calwer) 23–27

Payne, D.F.

1985 *Deuteronomy* (DSB; St Andrew Press/Westminster Press)

Peckham, B.

1975 "The Composition of Deuteronomy 9:1–10:11", *Word and Spirit: Essays in Honor of D.M. Stanley on his 60th Birthday* (ed. J. Plevnik; Regis College Press) 3–59

1983 “The Composition of Deuteronomy 5–11”, *The Word of the Lord Shall Go Forth: Essays in Honor of David N. Freedman in Celebration of His Sixtieth Birthday* (ASOR Special Volume Series 1; ed. C.L. Meyers, M. O’Connor; Eisenbrauns) 217–240

1985 *The Composition of the Deuteronomistic History* (HSM 35; Scholars Press)

Perlitt, L.

1981 “Wovon der Mensch lebt (Dtn 8,3b)”, *Die Botschaft und die Boten: FS für H.W. Wolff zum 70. Geburtstag* (ed. J. Jeremias, L. Perlitt; Neukirchener Verlag) 403–426

1985 “Deuteronomium 1–3 im Streit der exegetischen Methoden”, *Das Deut* 149–163

1990a “‘Evangelium’ und Gesetz im Deuteronomium”, *The Law in the Bible and its Environment* (PFES 51; ed. T. Veijola; Vandenhoeck & Ruprecht) 23–38

1990b “Hoc libro maxime fides docetur: Deuteronomium 1,19–46 bei Martin Luther und Johann Gerhard”, *NZSThR* 32:105–112

Petuchowski, J.J.

1958 “Not By Bread Alone”, *Judaism* 7:229–234

Pfeiffer, R.H.

1955 “The Fear of God”, *IEJ* 5:41–48

Phillips, A.

1973 *Deuteronomy* (CBC; CUP)

1983 “The Decalogue: Ancient Israel’s Criminal Law”, *JJS* 34:1–20

Plöger, J.G.

1967 *Literarkritische, formgeschichtliche und stilkritische Untersuchungen zum Deuteronomium* (BBB 26; Hanslein)

Polzin, R.

1980 *Moses and the Deuteronomist: A Literary Study of the Deuteronomic History* (Seabury Press)

1981 “Reporting Speech in the Book of Deuteronomy: Towards a Compositional Analysis of the Deuteronomic History”, *Traditions in Transformation: Turning Points in Biblical Faith: FS für F.M. Cross* (ed. B. Halpern, J.D. Levenson; Eisenbrauns) 193–211

1987 “Deuteronomy”, *The Literary Guide to the Bible* (ed. R. Alter, F. Kermode; Fontana) 92–101

Porúbcan, S.

1963 *Sin in the Old Testament: A Soteriological Study* (Aloisiana 3; Slovak Institute)

Potter, H.D.

1983 “The New Covenant in Jeremiah 31:31–34”, *VT* 33:347–357

Preuß, H.D.

1977 “אָתָה, בּוֹא”, *TDOT* (Vol 2 [Rev Ed]) 20–49

1982 *Deuteronomium* (Erträge der Forschung 164; Wissenschaftliche Buchgesellschaft)

1993 “Zum deuteronomistischen Geschichtswerk”, *TR* 58:229–264

Rabin, C.

1982 “Discourse Analysis and the Dating of Deuteronomy”, *Interpreting the Hebrew Bible: Essays in Honour of E.I.J. Rosenthal* (UCOP 32; ed. J.A. Emerton, S.C. Reif; CUP) 171–177

von Rad, G.

1953a “Deuteronomy and the Holy War”, *Studies in Deuteronomy* (SBT 9; trans. D. Stalker; SCM Press) 45–59

1953b "The Deuteronomistic Theology of the History in the Books of Kings", *Studies in Deuteronomy* (SBT 9; trans. D. Stalker; SCM Press) 74–91

1960 *Moses* (WCB (2nd series) 32; Lutterworth Press)

1961 "Ancient Word and Living Word: The Preaching of Deuteronomy and our Preaching" (trans. L. Gaston), *Int* 15:3–13

1962a *Old Testament Theology* (trans. D.M.G. Stalker; SCM Press; Vol 1)

1962b "Deuteronomy", *IDB* (Vol 1) 831–838

1965 *Old Testament Theology* (trans. D.M.G. Stalker; SCM Press; Vol 2)

1966a "The Form-Critical Problem of the Hexateuch", *The Problem of the Hexateuch and Other Essays* (trans. E.W.T. Dicken; Oliver & Boyd) 1–78

1966b "The Promised Land and Yahweh's Land in the Hexateuch", *The Problem of the Hexateuch and Other Essays* (trans. E.W.T. Dicken; Oliver & Boyd) 79–93

1966c "There Remains Still a Rest for the People of God: An Investigation of a Biblical Conception", *The Problem of the Hexateuch and Other Essays* (trans. E.W.T. Dicken; Oliver & Boyd) 94–102

1966d "Faith Reckoned as Righteousness", *The Problem of the Hexateuch and Other Essays* (trans. E.W.T. Dicken; Oliver & Boyd) 125–130

1966e *Deuteronomy* (OTL; SCM Press)

Ranck, T.E.

1969 *The Relationship between the So-Called Paranetic Passages (chapters 5–11) and the Legal Corpus (chapters 12–26) of the Book of Deuteronomy* (Unpublished PhD dissertation; Drew University)

Reardon, P.H.

1975 "Deuteronomy's Radical Covenant Demands", *Bible Today* 77:294–300

de Regt, L.J.

1988 *A Parametric Model for Syntactic Studies of a Textual Corpus, Demonstrated on the Hebrew of Deuteronomy 1–30* (SSN 24; Van Gorcum)

1991 "Word Order in Different Clause Types in Deuteronomy 1–30", *Studies in Hebrew and Aramaic Syntax: Presented to Professor J. Hoftijzer on the Occasion of his Sixty-Fifth Birthday* (SSLL 17; ed. K. Jongeling, H.L. Murre-van den Berg, L. Van Rompay; E.J. Brill) 152–172

Rendtorff, R.

1981 "Die Erwählung Israels als Thema der deuteronomischen Theologie", *Die Botschaft und die Boten: FS für H.W. Wolff zum 70. Geburtstag* (ed. J. Jeremias, L. Perlitt; Neukirchener Verlag) 75–86

1989 "'Covenant' as Structuring Concept in Genesis and Exodus", *JBL* 108:385–393

1993a "Between Historical Criticism and Holistic Interpretation: New Trends in Old Testament Exegesis", *Canon and Theology: Overtures to an Old Testament Theology* (OBT; ed. and tans. M. Kohl; Augsburg Fortress Press) 25–30

1993b "The Paradigm is Changing: Hopes – and Fears", *BI* 1:34–53

Rennes, J.

1967 *Le Deutéronome* (Editions Labor et Fides)

Ridderbos, J.

1984 *Deuteronomy* (BSC; trans. E.M. van der Maas; Zondervan)

Ringgren, H.

1980 "חיה, חַי, חַיִּים, חַיָּה, מִחְיָה", *TDOT* (Vol 4) 324–344

Roberge, M.
1964 "Théologie de l'alliance sinaïtique dans le Deutéronome", *RUO* 34:101–119, 164–199
Robinson, R.B.
1988 *Roman Catholic Exegesis Since Divino Afflante Spiritu: Hermeneutical Implications* (SBLDS 111; Scholars Press)
Roehrs, W.R.
1954 "Covenant and Justification in the O.T.", *CTM* 35:583–602
Rofé, A.
1985a "The Covenant in the Land of Moab (Deuteronomy 28:69–30:20): Historico-Literary, Comparative, and Formcritical Considerations", *Das Deut* 310–320
1985b "The Monotheistic Argumentation in Deut iv 32–40: Contents, Composition and Text", *VT* 35:434–445
1988 "The Arrangement of the Laws in Deut", *EThL* 64:265–288
1991 "Ephraimite versus Deuteronomistic History", *Storia e tradizioni di Israele. Scritti in onore di J. Alberto Soggin* (ed. D. Garrone, F. Israel; Paideia Editrice) 221–235
Römer, T.
1994 "The Book of Deuteronomy", *The History of Israel's Traditions: The Heritage of Martin Noth* (JSOTSup 182; ed. S.L. McKenzie, M.P. Graham: Sheffield Academic Press) 178–212
van Rooy, H.F.
1988a "Deuteronomy 28,69 – Superscript or Subscript?", *JNSL* 14:215–222
1988b "Verbond en vergewing: Deuteronomium 29 en 30 en die deuteronomistiese geskiedwerk", *HTS* 44:864–882
Rose, M.
1981 *Deuteronomist und Jahwist: Untersuchungen zu den Berührungspunkten beider Literaturwerke* (ATANT 67; Theologischer Verlag)
1994 *5. Mose Teilband 2: 5. Mose 1–11 und 26–34. Rahmenstücke zum Gesetzkorpus* (ZB 5.2; Theologischer Verlag)
Rost, L.
1965 "Die Bezeichnungen für Land und Volk im AT", *Das Kleine Credo und andere Studien zum Alten Testament* (Quelle & Meyer) 76–101
Roth, W.
1976 "Deuteronomic Rest Theology: A Redaction-Critical Study", *BibRes* 21:5–14
Rowley, H.H.
1963 "The Prophet Jeremiah and the Book of Deuteronomy", *From Moses to Qumran: Studies in the Old Testament* (Lutterworth Press) 187–208
Sailhamer, J.H.
1987 "The Canonical Approach to the OT: Its Effect on Understanding Prophecy", *JETS* 30:307–315
1991 "The Mosaic Law and the Theology of the Pentateuch", *WTJ* 53:241–261
Sanday, W. and Headlam, A.C.
1902 *A Critical and Exegetical Commentary on Paul's Letter to the Romans* (ICC; T&T Clark [5th Ed])
Sasson, J.M.
1973 "The Worship of the Golden Calf", *Orient and Occident: Essays Presented to C.H. Gordon on the Occasion of his Sixty-Fifth Birthday* (AOAT 22; ed. H.A. Hoffner; Kevelaer, Butzon & Bercker) 151–159

Sauer, A. von R.
1951 "The Concept of Sin in the Old Testament", *CTM* 22:705–718
Scharbert, J.
1977 "אֱלֹהַּ", *TDOT* (Vol 1 [Rev Ed]) 261–266
Schedl, C.
1986 "Prosa und Dichtung in der Bibel: Logotechnische Analyse von Dtn 1,9–18", *ZAW* 98:271–275
Schenker, A.
1980 "Umwiderrufliche Umkehr und neuer Bund: Vergleich zwischen Dt 4:25–31; 30:1–14; Jer 31:31–34", *FZPhTh* 27:93–106
Schmid, H.H.
1967 "Das Verständnis der Geschichte im Deuteronomium", *ZTK* 64:1–15
Schmidt, W.H.
1989 "Werk Gottes und Tun des Menschen: Ansätze zur Unterscheidung von »Gestez und Evangelium« im Alten Testament", *JBTh* 4:11–28
1990 "»Jahwe und...«: Anmerkungen zur sog. Monotheismus Debatte", *Die hebräische Bibel und ihre zweifache Nachgeschichte. FS für Rolf Rendtorff zum 65. Geburtstag* (ed. E. Blum, C. Macholz, E. Stegemann; Neukirchener Verlag) 435–447
Schneider, B.
1953 "The Meaning of St Paul's Antithesis 'The Letter and the Spirit'", *CBQ* 15:163–207
Schneider, D.
1982 *Das fünfte Buch Moses* (Wuppertaler Studienbibel; R. Brockhaus Verlag)
Schoors, A.
1981 "The Particle כִּי", *OTS* 21:240–276
Schult, H.
1979 "שׁמע", *THAT* (Vol 2) 974–982
Schultz, S.J.
1971 *Deuteronomy: The Gospel of Love* (Moody Press)
Seebass, H.
1977a "Landverheissungen an die Väter", *EvT* 37:210–229
1977b "בָּחַר", *TDOT* (Vol 2 [Rev Ed]) 73–87
Seifrid, M.A.
1985 "Paul's Approach to the Old Testament", *TJ* (new series) 6:3–37
Seim, J.
1990 "Höre Israel", *EvT* 50:567–574
Seitz, G.
1971 *Redaktionsgeschichtliche Studien zum Deuteronomium* (BWANT 93; Kohlhammer)
Selman, M.
1990 "Preaching Old Testament Law", *Evangel* 8.4:15–20
Shafer, B.E.
1977 "The Root *bhr* and the Pre-Exilic Concepts of Chosenness in the Hebrew Bible", *ZAW* 89:20–42
Sklba, R.J.
1981 "The Call to New Beginnings: A Biblical Theology of Conversion", *BTB* 11:67–73
Skweres, D.E.
1979 *Die Rückverweise im Buch Deuteronomium* (AnBib 79; Biblical Institute Press)

Smend, R.

1967 "Zur Geschichte von האמין", *Hebräische Wortforschung: FS zum 80. Geburtstag von W. Baumgartner* (VTSup 16; ed. B. Hartmann, E. Jenni, E.Y. Kutscher, V. Magg, I.L. Seeligman, R. Smend; E.J. Brill) 284–290

1971 "Das Gesetz und die Völker. Ein Beitrag zur deuteronomistischen Redaktionsgeschichte", *Probleme biblischer Theologie: FS für G. von Rad* (ed. H.W. Wolff; Chr. Kaiser Verlag) 494–509

1978 *Die Entstehung des Alten Testaments* (Theologische Wissenschaft 1; Kohlhammer)

Smith, B.

1993 *The One and Only* (St Matthias Press)

Smith, C.

1951 *The Biblical Doctrine of Man* (Epworth Press)

Smith, G.A.

1918 *The Book of Deuteronomy* (CBSC; CUP)

Soisalon-Soisinen, I.

1972 "Der Infinitivus constructus mit ל im Hebräischen", *VT* 22:82–90

Song, T.G.

1992 *Sinai Covenant and Moab Covenant: An Exegetical Study of the Covenants in Exodus 19:1–24:11 and Deuteronomy 4:45–28:69* (Unpublished PhD thesis; CNAA)

Sonsino, R.

1980 *Motive Clauses in Hebrew Law: Biblical Forms & NE Parallels* (SBLDS; Scholars Press)

Speiser, E.A.

1969 *Genesis* (AB 1; Doubleday)

Sprinkle, J.M.

1989 "Literary Approaches to the OT: A Survey of Recent Scholarship", *JETS* 32:299–310

Stahl, R.

1983 "Summary of *Aspekte der Geschichte deuteronomistischer Theologie: Zur Traditionsgeschichte der Terminologie und zur Redaktionsgeschichte der Redekompositionen*", *TLZ* 108:74–75

Stek, J.H.

1994 "Covenant Overload in Reformed Theology", *CTJ* 29:12–41

Steuernagel, C.

1900 *Übersetzung und Erklärung der Bücher Deuteronomium und Josua und allgemeine Einleitung in den Hexateuch* (HKAT; Vandenhoeck & Ruprecht)

Stolz, F.

1978 "לֵב", *THAT* (Vol 1) 861–867

Suggs, M.J.

1967 "The Word is Near You: Romans 10:6–10 within the Purpose of the Letter", *Christian History and Interpretation: Studies Presented to John Knox* (ed. W. Farmer, C.F.D. Moule, R.R. Niebuhr; CUP) 289–312

Sumner, W.A.

1968 "Israel's Encounters with Edom, Moab, Ammon, Sihon and Og According to the Deuteronomist", *VT* 18:216–228

Swanepoel, M.G.

1992 "The Important Function of Deuteronomy in the Old Testament", *OTE* 5:375–388

Swetnam, J.
1965 "Some Observations on the background of צדיק in Jeremias 23:5a", *Biblica* 46:29–40
1974 "Why was Jeremiah's Covenant New?", VTSup 26:111–115
Talmon, S.
1966 "The 'Desert Motif' in the Bible and in the Qumran Literature", *Biblical Motifs: Origins and Transformations* (Studies and Texts III; ed. A. Altmann; HUP) 31–63
Tate, M.E.
1964 "The Deuteronomic Philosophy of History", *RevExp* 61:311–319
Taylor, A.B.
1960 "Decisions in the Desert: The Temptation of Jesus in the Light of Deuteronomy", *Int* 14:300–309
Thomas, D.W.
1939 "The Root אָהֵב 'Love' in Hebrew", *ZAW* 16:57–64
Thompson, J.A.
1974 *Deuteronomy* (TOTC; IVP)
Tiffany, F.C.
1978 *Parenesis and Deuteronomy 5–11: A Form-Critical Study* (Unpublished dissertation; Claremont School of Theology)
Toombs, L.E.
1965 "Love and Justice in Deuteronomy: A Third Approach to the Law", *Int* 19:389–411
van der Toorn, K.
1985 *Sin and Sanction in Israel and Mesopotamia: A Comparative Study* (SSN 22; Van Gorcum)
Tsevat, M.
1963 "Studies in the Book of Samuel", *HUCA* 34:71–82
Tunyogi, A.
1962 "The Rebellions of Israel", *JBL* 81:385–390
Van Seters, J.
1972a "The Conquest of Sihon's Kingdom: A Literary Examination", *JBL* 91:182–197
1972b "Confessional Reformulation in the Exilic Period", *VT* 22:448–459
1994 *The Life of Moses: The Yahwist as Historian in Exodus–Numbers* (Westminster/John Knox Press)
Vanoni, G.
1981 "Der Geist und der Buchstabe: Überlegungen zum Verhältnis der Testamente und Beobachtungen zu Dtn 30,1–10", *BN* 14:65–98
Veijola, T.
1988 "Principal Observations on the Basic Story in Deuteronomy 1–3", *Wünschet Jerusalem Frieden: IOSOT Congress Jerusalem 1986* (BEATAJ 13; ed. M. Augustin, K.-D. Schunck; Peter Lang) 249–259
1995 "'Der Mensch lebt nicht vom Brot allein': Zur literarischen Schichtung und theologischen Aussage von Deuteronomium 8", *Bundesdokument und Gesetz: Studien zum Deuteronomium* (HBS 4; ed. G. Braulik; Herder) 143–158
Vermeylen, J.
1985a "Les sections narratives de Deut 5–11 et leur relation à Ex 19–34", *Das Deut* 174–207
1985b "L'affaire du veau d'or (Ex 32–34): une clé pour la »question deutéronomiste«", *ZAW* 97:1–23

Vervenne, M.
1994 "The Question of 'Deuteronomic' Elements in Genesis to Numbers", *Studies* 243–268
von Waldow, H.E.
1974 "Israel and Her Land: Some Theological Considerations", *A Light Unto My Path: Old Testament Studies in Honour of Jacob M. Myers* (ed. H.N. Bream, R.D. Heim, C.A. Moore; Temple University Press) 493–508
Wall, R.W.
1987 "The Finger of God: Dt 9:10 and Lk 11:20", *NTS* 33:144–150
Wallis, G.
1988 "Alttestamentliche Voraussetzungen einer biblischen Theologie, geprüft am Glaubensbegriff", *TLZ* 113:1–12
Walsh, J.T.
1977 "From Egypt to Moab: A Source Critical Analysis of the Wilderness Itinerary", *CBQ* 39:20–33
Waltke, B.M. and O'Connor, M.
1990 *An Introduction to Biblical Hebrew Syntax* (Eisenbrauns)
Walton, J.H.
1987 "Deuteronomy: An Exposition of the Spirit of the Law", *GTJ* 8:213–225
Wanke, G.
1979 "נַחֲלָה", *THAT* (Vol 2) 55–59
Waterhouse, S.D.
1963 "A Land Flowing with Milk and Honey", *AUSS* 1:152–166
Watson, W.G.
1989 "The Unnoticed Word Pair eyes/heart", *ZAW* 101:398–408
Watts, J.D.W.
1970 "Deuteronomy", *Leviticus–Ruth* (BBC 2; Broadman Press) 175–296
1977 "The Deuteronomic Theology", *RevExp* 74:321–336
Weinfeld, M.
1965 "Traces of Assyrian Treaty Formulae in Deuteronomy", *Biblica* 46:417–427
1967 "Deuteronomy: The Present State of Inquiry", *JBL* 86:249–262
1970 "The Covenant of Grant in the Old Testament and in the Ancient Near East", *JAOS* 90:184–203
1972 *Deuteronomy and the Deuteronomic School* (Clarendon Press)
1973 "On 'Demythologization and Secularization' in Deuteronomy", *IEJ* 23:230–233
1975 "*Bᵉrît* – Covenant vs. Obligation", *Biblica* 56:120–128
1976 "Jeremiah and the Spiritual Metamorphosis of Israel", *ZAW* 88:17–56
1985 "The Emergence of the Deuteronomic Movement: The Historical Antecedents", *Das Deut* 76–98
1991 *Deuteronomy 1–11* (AB 5; Doubleday)
1993 *The Promise of the Land: The Inheritance of the Land of Canaan by the Israelites* (The Taubman Lectures in Jewish Studies; University of California Press)
Welch, A.C.
1932 *Deuteronomy: The Framework to the Code* (OUP)
Wenham, G.J.
1970 *The Structure and Date of Deuteronomy* (Unpublished PhD thesis; University of London)
1971a "Deuteronomy and the Central Sanctuary", *TynBull* 22:103–118

1971b "The Deuteronomic Theology of the Book of Joshua", *JBL* 90:140–148
1976 *Faith in the Old Testament* (TSF)
1978 "Grace and Law in the Old Testament", *Law, Morality and the Bible* (ed. B.N. Kaye, G.J. Wenham; IVP) 3–23
1981 *Numbers* (TOTC; IVP)
1986 "Sanctuary Symbolism in the Garden of Eden Story", *Proceedings of the Ninth World Congress of Jewish Studies. Division A: The Period of the Bible* (World Union of Jewish Studies) 19–25
1987 *Genesis 1–15* (WBC; Word)
1990 "Original Sin in Genesis 1–11", *Churchman* 104:309–328
1991 "Method in Pentateuchal Criticism", *VT* 41:84–109

Werblowsky, R.J.Z.
1973 "Tora als Gnade", *Kairos* (new series) 15:156–163

Westbrook, R.
1995 "Riddles in Deuteronomic Law", *Bundesdokument und Gesetz: Studien zum Deuteronomium* (HBS 4; ed. G. Braulik; Herder) 159–174

Westermann, C.
1963 "The Way of the Promise through the Old Testament", *The Old Testament and the Christian Faith* (The Preacher's Library; ed. B.W. Anderson; Harper & Row) 200–224
1980 *The Promises to the Fathers: Studies on the Patriarchal Narratives* (trans. D.E. Green; Fortress Press)
1985 *Genesis 12–36: A Commentary* (trans. J.J. Scullion; Augsburg)
1994 "Mahnung, Warnung und Geschichte. Die Paränese Deuteronomium 1–11", *Nachdenken über Israel, Bibel und Theologie. FS für K.-D. Schunck zu seinem 65. Geburtstag* (BEATAJ 37; ed. H.M. Niemann, M. Augustin, W.H. Schmidt; Peter Lang) 51–67

Whitley, C.F.
1963 "Covenant and Commandment in Israel", *JNES* 22:37–48

Whybray, R.N.
1995 *Introduction to the Pentateuch* (Eerdmans)

Wiener, H.M.
1926 "The Arrangement of Deuteronomy 12–26", *JPOS* 6:185–195

Wiéner, C.
1957 *Recherches sur l'amour pour Dieu dans l'Ancien Testament: Étude d'une racine* (Letouzey et Ané)

Wijngaards, J.N.M.
1969 *The Dramatization of Salvific History in the Deuteronomic Schools* (*OTS* 16; E.J. Brill)

Williams, R.J.
1976 *Hebrew Syntax: An Outline* (University of Toronto Press [2nd Ed])

Willis, J.T.
1973 "Man Does Not Live by Bread Alone", *RestQ* 16:141–149

Willoughby, B.E.
1977 "A Heartfelt Love: An Exegesis of Deuteronomy 6:4–10", *RestQ* 20:73–87

Wittenberg, G.H.
1991 "The Significance of Land in the Old Testament", *JTSA* 77:58–61

Wolff, H.W.
1951 "Das Thema 'Umkehr' in der alttestamentlichen Prophetie", *ZTK* 48:129–148
1961 "Das Kerygma des deuteronomistischen Geschichtswerks", *ZAW* 73:171–186
1974a *Anthropology of the Old Testament* (trans. M. Kohl; SCM Press)
1974b "Problems between the Generations in the Old Testament", *Essays in Old Testament Ethics: J. Philip Hyatt, In Memoriam* (ed. J.L. Crenshaw, J.T. Willis; KTAV Publishing) 77–95
1982 "The Kerygma of the Deuteronomic Historical Work", *The Vitality of Old Testament Traditions* (W. Brueggemann, H.W. Wolff; John Knox Press [2nd Ed]) 83–100

Wright, C.J.H.
1990 *God's People in God's Land: Family, Land, and Property in the Old Testament* (Eerdmans/Paternoster)
1992 "Ethical Decisions in the Old Testament", *EJT* 1:123–140
1994 "Deuteronomic Depression", *Themelios* 19:3–4

Wright, G.E.
1953 "Deuteronomy", *IB* (Vol 2) 309–537

Wright, N.T.
1991 *The Climax of the Covenant: Christ and the Law in Pauline Theology* (T&T Clark)

Youngblood, R.
1978 "New Look at Three Old Testament Roots for 'Sin'", *Biblical and Near Eastern Studies: Essays in Honor of W.S. LaSor* (ed. G.A. Tuttle; Eerdmans) 201–205

Zimmerli, W.
1960 "Sinaibund und Abrahambund: Ein Beitrag zum Verständnis der Priesterschrift", *TZ* 16 (Festgabe für W. Eichrodt) 268–280
1971 *Man and His Hope in the Old Testament* (SBT (2nd series) 20; SCM Press)
1978 *Old Testament Theology in Outline* (trans. D.E. Green; T&T Clark)

Zobel, K.
1992 *Prophetie und Deuteronomium: Die Rezeption prophetischer Theologie durch das Deuteronomium* (BZAW 199; W. de Gruyter)

# Author Index

Aberbach, M., 89
Ackroyd, P.R., 9, 164
Aejmelaeus, A., 154, 155, 156
Aho, G., 191
Alexander, T.D., 1, 28, 31, 55, 98, 102, 169
Amsler, S., 27, 119, 160, 187
Anbar, M., 31, 32, 33, 75
Andersen, F.I., 58, 59, 60, 64, 161

Badenas, R., 194, 196
Baker, D.W., 109
Balentine, S.E., 94, 95, 97, 98
Baltzer, K., 13, 55, 103, 109, 162, 204
Bamberger, B.J., 160, 162
Barrett, C.K., 194, 195
Barth, K., 194
Bartholomew, C.G., 111
Bartlett, J.R., 42, 43, 44
Bee, R.E., 108
Begg, C.T., 9, 10, 87, 88, 108, 109, 117, 118, 119, 126, 179, 180
Berg, W., 74, 77
Bertholet, A., 21, 31, 33, 49, 59, 65, 66, 67, 71, 80, 101, 111, 121, 135, 139, 199, 210
Black, M., 196
Blair, E.P., 21, 60, 65, 99, 105, 136, 151, 152, 183, 187, 201
Blank, S.H., 150
Blau, J., 119
Blenkinsopp, J., 21, 103, 119, 199
Böhmer, S., 131, 181
Boissonard, R., 34
Boorer, S., 7, 9, 10, 20, 78, 86, 88, 89, 90, 92, 93, 94, 95, 97, 99, 101
Braulik, G., 2, 5, 8, 14, 15, 18, 19, 20, 21, 23, 25, 31, 32, 33, 34, 36, 38, 39, 40, 42, 43, 44, 45, 48, 50, 51, 58, 59, 61, 65, 66, 70, 71, 72, 73, 74, 75, 76, 77, 79, 80, 81, 82, 84, 85, 87, 88, 89, 90, 91, 92, 94, 95, 96, 97, 98, 100, 101, 102, 103, 105, 109, 111, 113, 115, 118, 119, 126, 127, 130, 131, 132, 134, 138, 139, 141, 142, 145, 149, 150, 151, 152, 154, 156, 165, 167, 168, 169, 170, 171, 175, 176, 177, 178, 179, 181, 183, 184, 185, 186, 187, 189, 195, 199, 200, 201, 205, 210, 213, 219
Brekelmans, C., 161
Brettler, M.Z., 213
Brichto, H.C., 96, 132
Bright, J., 126
Brongers, H.A., 103
Brown, R., 33, 39, 105, 111, 183
Bruce, F.F., 194, 196
Brueggemann, W., 9, 26, 27, 29, 33, 34, 72, 76, 91, 92, 93, 96, 98, 99, 103, 110, 135, 136, 170, 171, 177, 199, 204, 210, 217
Brunner, H., 68
Budd, P.J., 88
Buis, P., 13, 14, 15, 18, 21, 23, 24, 25, 38, 43, 46, 65, 74, 78, 83, 86, 89, 94, 98, 100, 101, 104, 108, 111, 112, 153, 167, 170, 171, 181, 187, 188, 189, 192, 199, 201, 205
Burden, T.L., 19, 21, 24, 30, 33, 60, 65, 66, 67, 92, 98, 119

Cairns, I., 15, 16, 18, 20, 21, 22, 24, 26, 29, 35, 39, 41, 42, 43, 44, 50, 66, 67, 81, 86, 87, 88, 90, 91, 94, 95, 99, 100, 101, 103, 105, 115, 119, 132, 134, 136, 137, 138, 139, 153, 179, 187, 188, 189, 190, 191, 193, 195, 201, 202, 208
Calvin, J., 195, 196, 197
Campbell, A.F., 7, 9
Campbell, W.S., 194
Carpenter, E.E., 13, 17, 22, 29, 59, 74
Carroll, R.P., 68
Cazelles, H., 10, 40, 63, 69, 174, 181
Childs, B.S., 26, 28, 117, 199, 204
Cholewinski, A., 111, 113, 114, 138, 181
Christensen, D.L., 13, 14, 17, 20, 22, 32, 37, 38, 39, 40, 43, 46, 50, 59, 61, 70, 74, 76, 78, 80, 83, 85, 88, 89, 90, 94, 98, 99, 100, 101, 102, 103, 123, 151, 163, 169, 176, 179, 190
Claassen, W.T., 156, 185, 186
Clark, W.M., 29, 211
Clements, R.E., 5, 8, 15, 16, 31, 161, 164, 174, 175
Clifford, R., 34, 41, 42, 45, 46, 58, 63, 66, 67, 74, 101, 112, 122, 139, 164, 199, 201, 210, 213
Clines, D.J.A., 31, 33
Coats, G.W., 15, 41, 43
Collier, G.D., 9
Coppens, J., 181
Couroyer, B., 82, 168, 188, 189, 190
Craigie, P.C., 12, 13, 16, 18, 20, 21, 32, 33, 35, 38, 39, 42, 43, 44, 46, 58, 73, 76, 78, 83, 84, 88, 90, 94, 100, 101, 103, 104, 105, 111, 112, 115, 116, 120, 132, 136, 138, 139, 144, 147, 152, 153, 154, 155, 158, 170, 179, 182, 183, 184, 190, 193, 201, 202, 208
Cranfield, C.E.B., 193, 194, 195, 196, 197
Crenshaw, J.L., 98
Cross, F.M., 9, 10, 105, 179
Cunliffe-Jones, H., 42, 65, 68, 74, 105, 112, 135, 139, 161, 182, 183, 194, 195, 197, 199
Curtis, A.H.W., 204

Daube, D., 19, 24, 36, 94, 108
Davies, G.I., 14, 16
Davies, G.N., 194, 196, 197
Davis, D.R., 95
Delitzsch, F., 68, 83, 89, 90, 100, 103, 104, 105
Derrett, J.D.M., 201
Deurloo, K.A., 26, 27, 43, 115
DeVries, S.J., 115, 118, 185, 199, 200, 203, 204
Dhorme, P., 69, 121, 124, 158
Diepold, P., 31, 32, 43, 44, 148, 154, 175, 176, 192
Dillmann, A., 8, 13, 21, 26, 29, 32, 33, 42, 44, 45, 46, 68, 69, 71, 75, 78, 83, 91, 94, 101, 105, 137, 139, 177
Driver, S.R., 13, 15, 18, 21, 24, 28, 29, 30, 32, 33, 35, 38, 39, 42, 43, 45, 46, 48, 49, 50, 67, 68, 71, 73, 74, 75, 79, 83, 87, 88, 89, 94, 98, 99, 100, 101, 104, 105, 108, 111, 120, 121, 125, 131, 132, 133, 134, 135, 136, 137, 138, 139, 143, 144, 146, 147, 150, 152, 153, 154, 158, 161, 167, 168, 172, 177, 179, 182, 185, 187, 189, 190, 191, 199, 200, 201, 205, 207, 208, 210
Dumbrell, W.J., 133
Dunn, J.D.G., 194, 195, 196, 197
Durham, J.I., 204

Eichrodt, W., 69, 157, 161, 175
Emerton, J.A., 69
Even-Shoshan, A., 113, 118, 170, 171
Eybers, I.H., 33

Fensham, F.C., 174
Flückiger, F., 194
Fox, M.V., 170
Frankena, R., 114
Freedman, D.N., 161, 164, 174
Fretheim, T.E., 6, 8, 9, 207
Friedman, R.E., 9, 182, 183, 187

Gammie, J.G., 27, 77
García López, F., 10, 56, 60, 64, 67, 68, 72, 78, 80, 81, 83
Geller, S.A., 27
Gemser, B., 14
Giles, T., 75, 76, 122
Ginsberg, H.L., 136

Goldingay, J.E., 81, 82, 107, 108, 149, 153
Gottwald, N.K., 80
van Goudoever, J., 26
Gowan, D.E., 108
Grassi, J.A., 199
Greenberg, M., 94, 95, 96, 97
Gunn, D.M., 204

Hagelia, H., 16, 31, 32, 33, 35, 49, 79, 81, 92, 95, 119, 132, 173
Hals, R.M., 107, 139, 193
Hamilton, V.P., 136
Harper, A., 81
Hays, R.B., 194, 196
Headlam, A.C., 194, 196
Hillers, D.R., 170
Hoftijzer, J., 75
Holladay, W.L., 1, 145, 146, 147
Honeyman, A.M., 136
Hoppe, L.J., 1, 181
Horst, J., 27
Huffmon, H.B., 91, 122
Hugenberger, G.P., 132, 169, 174

Jacobs, P.F., 15, 27, 28, 29, 52, 59, 61, 62, 63, 67, 68, 102, 103, 104, 152, 153, 165, 166, 171, 173, 177, 180, 198, 199, 201, 202, 207, 208, 210, 211, 212, 213
Janzen, J.G., 22, 30, 91, 98, 128, 172, 173
Jones, R.C., 162
Joüon, P., 35, 154, 155, 162, 186, 211
Joyce, P., 138, 148, 158, 164, 178, 215

Kaiser, W.C., 44
Kallai, Z., 14, 43
Kalland, E.S., 15, 21, 23, 24, 30, 32, 33, 35, 39, 42, 43, 45, 71, 82, 83, 87, 88, 90, 95, 97, 99, 100, 103, 105, 132, 135, 136, 137, 138, 139, 149, 152, 179, 184, 188, 189, 191, 193, 194, 199, 205, 207
Käsemann, E., 194, 196
Kaufman, S.A., 8
Kaunfer, A.H., 89
Kearney, P.J., 115, 117, 119, 120, 121, 137, 139, 140
Keil, C.F., 68, 83, 89, 90, 100, 103, 104, 105
Kessler, M., 16
Kittel, G., 27
Kline, M.G., 12, 16, 24, 30, 32, 33, 34, 43, 49, 71, 87, 91, 99, 105, 111, 120, 132, 133, 169, 173, 177, 178, 181, 183, 191, 194, 213
Knapp, D., 108, 109, 113, 115, 117, 132
Koch, K., 27, 135, 136, 207
Köckert, M., 10, 143, 152, 156, 157, 160, 162, 178, 181, 182, 185, 188, 208
König, E., 13, 32, 33, 38, 39, 72, 74, 88, 90, 100, 102, 111, 120, 121, 132, 136, 188, 189, 201, 208
Kooy, V.H., 161, 162
Kopf, L., 135
Kutsch, E., 31, 77, 111, 113, 131

L'Hour, J., 59, 61, 73, 74, 80, 81, 103, 160, 161, 175, 176, 177, 208, 209, 210
Labuschagne, C.J., 26, 46, 139
Lambdin, T.O., 154, 155, 156
Langlamet, F., 41
Le Déaut, R., 163, 164, 166, 169, 181
Leclerq, J., 13, 14, 15, 18, 21, 23, 24, 25, 38, 43, 46, 65, 74, 78, 83, 86, 89, 94, 98, 100, 101, 104, 108, 111, 112, 153, 167, 187, 188, 189, 192, 199, 201, 205
Leenhardt, F.J., 197
van Leeuwen, R.C., 61, 63, 64, 67, 68
Lenchak, T.A., 3, 10, 18, 27, 108, 109, 110, 111, 112, 113, 115, 117, 118, 119, 120, 121, 124, 126, 130, 131, 133, 135, 136, 137, 138, 139, 140, 143, 144, 145, 171, 179, 180, 185, 187, 192, 193, 198, 200, 201, 202, 203
Levenson, J.D., 8, 9, 139, 144, 145, 164, 173, 179, 180, 205
Lewy, I., 89
Licht, J., 4
Lisowsky, G., 35, 69, 124, 126, 147, 156, 160, 191, 201, 207
Loewenstamm, S.E., 33
Lohfink, N., 2, 5, 7, 8, 9, 10, 13, 15, 16, 18, 19, 20, 21, 22, 23, 24, 25, 27, 28, 29, 31, 32, 36, 38, 40, 41, 45, 50, 56, 57, 58, 59, 60, 61, 63, 65, 66, 67, 68, 69, 71, 74, 75, 77, 78, 79, 80, 83, 85, 86, 89, 90, 92, 93, 102, 103, 104, 105,

109, 110, 111, 112, 114, 117, 118, 119, 122, 131, 132, 134, 135, 136, 138, 139, 143, 151, 152, 155, 159, 160, 161, 167, 172, 173, 175, 181, 182, 185, 198, 199, 200, 203, 204, 208, 217, 219
Lund, N.A., 59, 60, 62, 143
Lundbom, J.R., 18, 112
Luther, M., 21, 22, 23, 39, 67, 81, 112, 175, 191, 192
Lyonnet, S., 160, 181

MacKenzie, R.A.F., 178
Malfroy, J., 161
Mann, T.W., 21, 23, 24, 50
Martens, E.A., 174, 194, 207
Martin, B.L., 194, 195
Martin-Achard, R., 105, 181
Maxwell, J.C., 33, 42, 46, 49, 90, 97, 100, 105, 116, 135, 139
Mayes, A.D.H., 1, 7, 8, 9, 10, 13, 14, 15, 18, 19, 20, 21, 22, 23, 32, 33, 34, 38, 39, 40, 43, 45, 46, 50, 57, 59, 60, 61, 65, 66, 68, 69, 71, 72, 74, 75, 76, 78, 79, 81, 86, 88, 89, 91, 98, 99, 101, 102, 104, 109, 110, 111, 117, 118, 119, 120, 121, 122, 131, 132, 133, 134, 137, 138, 139, 141, 145, 146, 147, 152, 153, 172, 177, 179, 180, 183, 184, 187, 189, 190, 192, 198, 199, 200, 201, 202, 203, 210
McBride, S.D., 160, 161
McCarthy, D.J., 3, 13, 50, 55, 63, 69, 102, 104, 109, 111, 122, 139, 152, 153, 161, 183, 204
McComiskey, T.E., 30, 174, 194, 195, 207
McConville, J.G., 9, 13, 14, 16, 19, 21, 22, 24, 25, 26, 28, 30, 33, 34, 42, 46, 48, 50, 51, 74, 79, 81, 82, 84, 85, 101, 104, 105, 107, 115, 118, 132, 147, 150, 152, 153, 157, 164, 165, 170, 171, 181, 182, 185, 192, 193, 194, 196, 197, 198, 199, 200, 202, 203, 205, 208, 210, 214
McCurley, F.R., 161
McEvenue, S.E., 19, 39, 75, 88, 94, 111, 153
McKay, J.W., 161
McKenzie, J.L., 14, 15, 17, 20, 21, 24, 28, 30, 36, 41, 43, 52
de Menezes, R., 45
Merrill, E.H., 13, 14, 16, 21, 22, 24, 29, 32, 35, 43, 45, 65, 75, 76, 78, 79, 82, 83, 85, 86, 87, 88, 89, 91, 99, 100, 103, 105, 111, 120, 132, 133, 136, 139, 150, 154, 155, 160, 161, 162, 178, 182, 195, 201, 211
Meyers, C.L. and E.M., 144
Milgrom, J., 15
Millar, J.G., 14, 16, 21, 24, 25, 26, 28, 30, 33, 36, 46, 48, 50, 66, 72, 73, 74, 79, 85, 89, 95, 101, 104, 107, 115, 116, 118, 132, 190, 198, 199, 200, 202, 203, 206, 214
Millard, A.R., 170
Miller, P.D., 14, 15, 17, 18, 20, 23, 24, 30, 32, 39, 40, 41, 44, 49, 50, 52, 65, 66, 67, 70, 77, 80, 82, 83, 84, 85, 88, 95, 96, 98, 105, 112, 115, 119, 120, 122, 125, 129, 131, 134, 136, 139, 154, 167, 177, 178, 183, 187, 190, 193, 198, 199, 200, 202, 203
Minette de Tillesse, G., 10, 30, 48, 94, 96, 104
Mitchell, H.G., 10, 108, 111, 119
Mittmann, S., 10, 12, 13, 14, 15, 17, 19, 21, 30, 32, 33, 50
Moberly, R.W.L., 3, 4, 5, 27, 72, 74, 82, 88, 96, 99
Moenikes, A., 9
Moore, R.D., 187
Moran, W.L., 22, 23, 43, 45, 58, 61, 71, 76, 161, 162, 170, 211
Morris, L.L., 194, 197
Muilenburg, J., 204
Munchenberg, R., 19, 21, 24, 112, 137, 170
Muraoka, T., 45, 48, 102
Murphy, R.E., 26, 199, 202
Murray, J., 194, 195, 197
Myers, J.M., 8, 160

Naylor, P.J., 75, 91, 132
Nelson, R.D., 9, 10
Niccacci, A., 89, 103
Nicholson, E.W., 1, 9, 108, 111, 161, 181
Niehaus, J.J., 16

Nielsen, E., 10, 13, 22, 24, 36, 60, 65, 67, 80, 82, 83, 87, 89, 91, 108, 111, 113, 115, 131, 136, 137, 139, 188, 201
Noth, M., 4, 7, 8, 9, 10, 14, 16, 27, 28, 34, 153, 203

O'Connell, R.H., 60, 61, 62, 78, 85, 93, 94
Ogushi, M., 125
Okeke, J., 162, 181
Olson, D.T., 15, 16, 24, 25, 28, 50, 64, 74, 77, 81, 86, 87, 88, 90, 94, 97, 98, 104, 111, 114, 148, 153, 203
Ottoson, M., 32

Parker, S.B., 122
Payne, D.F., 120, 136, 137, 138, 139, 144, 183, 189, 190, 195
Peckham, B., 5, 9, 24, 56, 65, 73, 77, 78, 79, 80, 81, 83, 84, 85, 86, 89, 90, 91, 92, 93, 94, 95, 99, 100, 101, 105
Perlitt, L., 11, 12, 14, 15, 23, 25, 36, 41, 60, 67, 68, 71, 81, 175, 205, 208
Phillips, A., 16, 24, 32, 42, 86, 100, 113
Plöger, J.G., 10, 18, 19, 26, 29, 31, 32, 40, 52, 61, 79, 83, 96, 175
Polzin, R., 11, 46, 51, 82, 84, 120, 144, 145, 170, 200, 203, 206
Potter, H.D., 181
Preuß, H.D., 7, 8, 10, 14, 18, 19, 21, 23, 30, 31, 32, 36, 55, 56, 59, 77, 78, 81, 108, 109, 110, 111, 112, 113, 116, 119, 134, 199

von Rad, G., 1, 8, 9, 13, 19, 24, 26, 27, 31, 32, 43, 55, 65, 67, 68, 74, 75, 76, 78, 81, 82, 90, 95, 98, 100, 101, 103, 104, 105, 110, 111, 118, 119, 120, 132, 134, 138, 139, 152, 154, 157, 161, 173, 179, 181, 182, 184, 188, 189, 190, 191, 193, 199, 202, 203, 206
Ranck, T.E., 75, 77, 104
de Regt, L.J., 10, 99, 186, 201
Rendtorff, R., 3, 74, 82, 105
Rennes, J., 1, 14, 27, 28, 31, 35, 57, 96, 101, 102, 111, 120, 122, 136, 139, 160, 161, 201, 206, 211
Ridderbos, J., 16, 19, 24, 26, 33, 42, 49, 79, 81, 91, 97, 100, 101, 103, 105, 108, 111, 112, 135, 136, 138, 139, 153, 154, 162, 163, 179, 183, 186, 188, 189, 191, 192, 210
Roberge, M., 64, 104, 174
Robinson, R.B., 109, 111, 143, 199
Roehrs, W.R., 81, 84
Rofé, A., 8, 108, 109, 111, 115, 137, 138, 139, 145, 146, 153, 182, 198
Römer, T., 7, 8, 9, 10, 31, 32, 105
van Rooy, H.F., 111, 144, 179
Rose, M., 14, 15, 18, 19, 21, 23, 25, 29, 32, 33, 35, 39, 43, 59, 65, 68, 77, 87, 88, 89, 90, 91, 96, 98, 101, 103, 105, 133, 136, 167, 171
Roth, W., 43
Rowley, H.H., 181

Sailhamer, J.H., 25, 47
Sanday, W., 194, 196
Sauer, A. von R., 128
Scharbert, J., 132
Schenker, A., 143, 149, 150, 151, 152, 173, 174, 177, 179, 181, 182, 185, 187, 188, 189
Schmid, H.H., 4, 161, 167, 173
Schmidt, W.H., 177
Schneider, B., 194
Schneider, D., 13, 14, 16, 20, 21, 22, 24, 31, 32, 38, 39, 43, 44, 45, 46, 47, 51, 52, 53, 66, 73, 74, 84, 87, 88, 91, 96, 100, 103, 182, 188, 199, 210, 213, 214
Schoors, A., 154, 155
Schult, H., 126, 127
Seebass, H., 105, 170, 209, 213
Seifrid, M.A., 194, 195, 196, 197
Seitz, G., 8, 10, 14, 56, 60, 78, 79, 96, 100, 111, 112
Selman, M., 3, 194, 198, 207, 211
Shafer, B.E., 105
Sklba, R.J., 148, 183, 193
Skweres, D.E., 18, 29, 31, 32, 33, 35, 36, 40, 45, 73, 75, 79, 88, 94, 99, 131, 150, 153
Smend, R., 9, 10, 15
Smith, B., 27
Smith, G.A., 139
Smolar, L., 89
Soisalon-Soisinen, I., 162, 211

Song, T.G., 111, 112
Speiser, E.A., 136
Stahl, R., 9
Stek, J.H., 116, 157, 174
Steuernagel, C., 18, 21, 31, 32, 33, 59, 80, 100, 108, 111, 119, 133, 139, 178, 185, 199
Suggs, M.J., 194, 195, 196
Sumner, W.A., 39, 40, 45, 46
Swanepoel, M.G., 113, 114
Swetnam, J., 181

Thomas, D.W., 161
Thompson, J.A., 16, 18, 21, 22, 23, 31, 32, 35, 36, 39, 42, 43, 45, 66, 71, 77, 83, 88, 89, 99, 100, 103, 105, 111, 120, 121, 132, 134, 136, 138, 152, 167, 183, 184, 187, 190, 191, 193, 194, 195, 201, 207, 210
Tiffany, F.C., 55, 61, 70, 77, 79, 80, 81, 199
Toombs, L.E., 157, 160, 193
van der Toorn, K., 136
Tsevat, M., 174
Tunyogi, A., 6, 25, 28

Van Seters, J., 15, 18, 19, 20, 27, 31, 35, 41, 46, 78, 87, 89, 91, 96, 97, 99, 169
Vanoni, G., 141, 142, 143, 144, 145, 148, 149, 151, 152, 153, 155, 156, 157, 162, 165, 166, 167, 171, 172, 177, 178, 181, 182, 183, 211, 219
Veijola, T., 8, 10, 11, 32, 33, 59, 60, 67, 68
Vermeylen, J., 2, 28, 56, 87, 88
Vervenne, M., 92
Vouga, F., 34

von Waldow, H.E., 31

Waltke, B.M., 75, 154, 155, 156
Walton, J.H., 8
Watson, W.G., 121, 126, 130
Watts, J.D.W., 13, 18, 20, 35, 40, 58, 67, 71, 72, 81, 82, 85, 86, 100, 103, 105, 170, 177, 181, 184, 192, 200
Weinfeld, M., 12, 15, 18, 21, 22, 23, 26, 28, 32, 33, 34, 35, 38, 39, 41, 42, 43, 44, 45, 46, 48, 49, 58, 59, 61, 65, 66, 67, 68, 69, 71, 72, 73, 74, 75, 76, 77, 79, 80, 81, 83, 85, 86, 87, 89, 90, 91, 92, 94, 95, 96, 97, 99, 100, 102, 103, 104, 105, 115, 119, 122, 123, 124, 125, 126, 127, 128, 129, 132, 135, 138, 139, 158, 163, 164, 168, 169, 170, 173, 174, 179, 180, 181, 184, 190, 191, 193, 195, 201, 205, 207
Welch, A.C., 55, 75, 115
Wenham, G.J., 12, 15, 29, 102, 104, 109, 114, 135, 164, 173, 198, 202, 203
Werblowsky, R.J.Z., 175
Westbrook, R., 8
Westermann, C., 59, 60, 62, 105, 110
Whybray, R.N., 26, 32
Wiéner, C., 160, 161, 162, 164
Williams, R.J., 155
Willis, J.T., 68
Willoughby, B.E., 160, 162
Wolff, H.W., 9, 10, 67, 77, 108, 145, 148, 149, 150, 151, 152, 153, 158, 171, 179, 204
Wright, C.J.H., 161, 173
Wright, G.E., 108, 110, 112, 139, 163
Wright, N.T., 196

Youngblood, R., 89

Zimmerli, W., 4, 9, 61, 74, 167, 175
Zobel, K., 160, 161, 162, 199, 211

# Scripture Index

References in this study follow the Hebrew versification. For verses in Deuteronomy, the following variations apply:

| Hebrew | = | English |
|---|---|---|
| 13:1–19 | | 12:32; 13:1–18 |
| 23:1–26 | | 22:30; 23:1–25 |
| 28:69; 29:1–28 | | 29:1–29 |

Page numbers listed in bold mark the start of focused discussion on that verse(s).


**Genesis**
1–11 *104*
1 *29, 172*
1:22 *172*
1:28 *172*
2 *29, 74*
2:15–17 *29*
2:17 *29*
3 *29, 74*
3:5 *19*
3:8 *77*
3:10 *77*
3:17 *77*
4:7 *135*
6:5 *74, 82*
6:8 *82*
6:18 *133*
8:17 *172*
8:21 *74, 82*
9:1 *172*
9:7 *172*
9:9 *133*
9:11 *133*
9:12–17 *39*
12:2–3 *31, 33*
12:2 *33*
13:16 *33*
15 *132, 170*
15:2 *49, 95*
15:5–6 *105*
15:5 *33, 172*
15:6 *34, 81*
15:7 *79, 131*
15:8 *49, 95*
15:14 *173*
15:16 *43, 79*
15:17 *133*
15:18 *31, 32, 79*
16:13 *128*
17 *39, 105, 133*
17:2–6 *33*
17:2 *172*
17:7 *131*
17:8 *31*
17:9–14 *39*
17:9–12 *169*
17:14 *169*
17:19 *133*
17:20 *172*
17:21 *133*
18:14 *191*
19:21 *131*
19:24–29 *138*
22 *31, 72*
22:16 *31*
22:17 *33, 73, 172*
24:7 *31*
26:3–4 *33*
26:3 *31*
26:4 *33, 73, 172*
26:24 *33, 73, 172*
27:40 *67*
28:3 *172*
28:14 *33*
35:11 *33, 172*
46:3 *33*
47:27 *172*
48:4 *172*
50:24 *31*

**Exodus**
1:7 *172*
1:10 *172*
1:12 *172*
1:20 *172*

6:4 *133*
6:12 *105*
6:30 *105*
7:3 *42*
10:27 *42*
13:21 *23*
14:13 *23*
14:31 *22, 23*
15:14–16 *39*
15:14 *43*
15:16 *43*
16:3–4 *66*
16:4 *65*
17:4–7 *98*
19–34 *56*
19 *90, 204*
19:3–9 *202*
19:3–8 *204, 205*
19:5–6 *131*
19:8 *204*
20 *99*
20:20 *65, 72*
23:23–33 *109*
23:25–29 *33*
23:31 *32*
24 *202, 204*
24:1–11 *204*
24:3–8 *205*
24:3 *202, 204*
24:7 *202, 204*
24:18 *85*
32–34 *27, 82, 87, 95, 97*
32 *94, 95*
32:7 *97*
32:9–14 *95*
32:9 *82, 90, 97*
32:10 *86, 87*
32:11–14 *86*
32:11–13 *94, 95*
32:11 *96*
32:13 *33, 96, 97, 172*
32:14 *98*
32:19 *87, 89*
32:20 *87, 90*
32:21 *89*
32:30–34 *89*
32:32 *95*
32:33 *98*
33:12 *82*
33:20 *128*
34 *99*
34:1–4 *99*
34:6–7 *95*
34:9 *82*
34:10 *82*
34:28 *85, 99*
37 *99*

**Leviticus**
18:5 *194, 196*
26:9 *172*
26:41 *105*
26:42 *173*
26:45 *97*

**Numbers**
5 *88*
10:11–13 *34*
11:4–6 *66*
11:11–15 *30, 33*
13–14 *17, 39, 92*
13 *15, 28*
13:2 *15*
13:31 *46*
13:33 *46*
14 *15, 94*
14:1–25 *88*
14:2 *21*
14:3 *15, 29*
14:6 *15*
14:7–9 *20*
14:9 *22*
14:11 *21*
14:12 *27, 88*
14:13–19 *27, 95, 98*
14:16 *94*
14:20 *98*
14:23 *18*
14:26–38 *27*
14:29–31 *210*
14:29 *29*
14:30 *15*
14:31 *15, 29*
14:38 *15*
14:39–45 *22*
14:44 *23*
20:2–5 *67*
20:10–12 *23*
20:14–21 *44*
21:5 *66*
21:21–31 *41*
21:23 *42*
21:24 *43*
21:33–35 *42*
22 *100*
23:10 *33*
25:1–9 *50*
32:7–15 *43*
32:40–41 *43*
32:42 *43*
34:1–12 *43*

**Deuteronomy**
1–30 *15, 186*
1–28 *111, 132*
1–26 *132*
1–11 *16, 157*
1–4 *111*
1:1–4:43 *7*
1–3 *2, 3, 5, 6,* ***7****, 28, 55, 57, 58, 65, 73, 75, 82, 83, 92, 93, 94, 100, 106, 114, 137, 168, 173, 174, 176, 217, 219*
1 ***17****, 38, 40, 44, 47, 48, 50, 55, 78, 83, 88, 119, 124, 217*
1:1–6 *13*
1:1–5 *10, 13, 14, 15, 16, 25, 111*
1:1 *13, 14, 44, 111, 112*
1:2 *16, 25*
1:3 *16*
1:4 *16, 42*
1:5 *14, 44, 78*
1:6–46 *17, 18*
1:6–8 *16, 18, 19, 22, 30, 35, 40, 48*
1:6 *14*
1:7–8 *76, 101*
1:7 *26, 32, 34, 92*

1:8 *16, 19, 21, 30, 31, 32, 33, 35, 36, 73, 79, 123, 169, 200, 210*
1:9–2:1 *92*
1:9–18 *18, 33, 34*
1:9 *26, 33*
1:10–11 *33*
1:10 *33, 73, 105, 172*
1:11 *33*
1:12–18 *33*
1:16 *33*
1:17 *163*
1:18 *26, 33, 183*
1:19 *18, 20, 23, 33, 34, 40, 73*
1:19–2:1 *17*
1:19–46 *2, 8, 12, 19, 20, 28, 33, 36, 52, 211*
1:19–32 *92*
1:20–30 *18*
1:20–21 *18, 21, 22*
1:20 *35*
1:21 *17, 18, 20, 21, 29, 35, 83, 91, 123*
1:22–30 *20*
1:22 *19, 21, 91*
1:23 *15, 23*
1:24 *73*
1:25–28 *17*
1:25 *18, 19, 21, 22, 35, 73*
1:26–46 *25*
1:26–28 *17, 22*
1:26 *19, 21, 26, 29, 67, 91*
1:27–28 *19, 21, 22*
1:27 *97, 98*
1:28–30 *19*
1:28 *15, 17, 19, 20, 22, 42, 46, 83, 158, 159, 218*
1:29–32 *158*
1:29–31 *17, 18, 20, 21, 23*
1:29 *23*
1:30–33 *125*
1:30 *19, 20, 26, 41, 48, 83, 123, 124*
1:31 *19, 20, 65, 69, 91, 124*
1:32–36 *17*
1:32 *19, 21, 22, 23, 34, 47, 81, 91, 124, 125, 211*
1:33 *19, 21, 23, 124*
1:34–40 *26*
1:34–39 *87*
1:34 *19, 35, 50, 91, 137, 211*
1:35–40 *35*
1:35–36 *19*
1:35 *16, 18, 19, 22, 27, 28, 30, 31, 32, 35, 36, 45, 49, 73, 83*
1:36–39 *211*
1:36 *15, 18*
1:37–38 *24*
1:37 *11, 23, 26, 50*
1:38 *15*
1:39–46 *22, 23*
1:39 *15, 28, 29, 35, 36, 210, 211*
1:40 *40*
1:41 *23, 40, 76, 92*
1:42–43 *76*
1:42 *41, 92*
1:43 *19, 23, 67, 76, 91, 128*
1:45 *23, 126, 127*
1:46 *18*
2–3 *16, 34,* ***36***
2:1–3:20 *36*
2:1–3:11 *37*
2 *2, 34, 218*
2:1–23 *45*
2:1 *39, 40*
2:2–3:11 *40*
2:2–25 *37*
2:2–8 *38*
2:2 *38, 41, 101*
2:3–7 *39*
2:5 *11, 37, 44, 45*
2:7 *35, 37, 65, 73, 119*
2:8–9 *37*
2:8 *37, 39*
2:9–13 *38, 39*
2:9–12 *37*
2:9 *11, 37, 41, 45*
2:10–12 *46*
2:10 *40, 46, 83*
2:12 *37, 40, 41, 45, 46*
2:13–15 *37*
2:13–14 *37, 43*
2:13 *39*
2:14–33 *38*
2:14–16 *22, 28, 37, 45*
2:15 *45*
2:17 *41*
2:18–20 *39*
2:18 *39, 83*
2:19 *11, 37, 45*
2:20–23 *37, 46*
2:20–22 *41*
2:20–21 *42*
2:21–22 *11*
2:21 *46, 83*
2:22 *118*
2:24–31 *39*
2:24–25 *37, 38, 43*
2:24 *38, 39, 40, 41, 43, 123*
2:25 *39, 41, 43*
2:26–3:11 *37*
2:26–30 *38*
2:26 *38*
2:28–29 *41*
2:29 *40, 44*
2:30 *39, 42, 158, 159, 163*
2:31 *38, 39, 41, 43, 123*
2:32–37 *39*
2:32 *38*
2:33 *39, 41*
2:34–37 *38*
2:34–36 *42*
2:34 *34, 39, 42, 43*
2:36 *39, 41, 42*
2:37–3:2 *38*
2:37 *41*
3 *2, 34, 218*
3:1–3 *38*
3:1 *39*
3:2 *39, 41, 42*
3:3–11 *39*

3:3–10 *42*
3:3–7 *37*
3:3 *39, 42*
3:4 *34, 42*
3:5 *42, 46*
3:6 *39, 41*
3:7 *39*
3:8–11 *37*
3:8–10 *42*
3:8 *34, 44*
3:10 *43*
3:11 *38, 40, 46*
3:12–17 *43*
3:12 *33*
3:14 *43, 118*
3:16–17 *43*
3:17 *44*
3:18–29 *48*
3:18 *33, 44*
3:20 *43, 44, 45*
3:21–29 ***48***
3:21–22 *48*
3:21 *33, 41*
3:23–28 *24, 50*
3:23–27 *50*
3:23–25 *49*
3:23 *33*
3:24 *94, 96*
3:25–27 *44*
3:25 *18, 44, 83*
3:26–29 *50*
3:26 *11, 26, 41, 127, 137*
3:27 *44, 123, 124*
3:28 *49, 50*
4–30 *13, 14, 17*
4–28 *142*
4–11 *28, 72*
4 *8, 10, 15, 16, 27, 55, 68, 109, 113, 114, 126, 128, 179, 180*
4:1–4 *108*
4:1 *79, 103, 114, 127, 128, 143, 166, 194*
4:2–5 *124*
4:3 *123, 129*
4:5–8 *98, 176*
4:5 *115, 123, 200*
4:6 *127*
4:7–8 *31*
4:7 *187*
4:8 *114, 180*
4:9–14 *108, 113*
4:9 *69, 70, 72, 121, 123, 125, 129, 158, 159, 166*
4:10 *70, 127*
4:11–13 *93*
4:11 *68, 69*
4:12 *127*
4:14 *34, 115*
4:15–16 *108*
4:19–28 *108*
4:21–22 *11*
4:21 *18, 50*
4:22 *18*
4:23 *72*
4:25 *155, 179*
4:25–28 *1*
4:26 *76, 199, 201*
4:28 *67*
4:29–35 *109*
4:29–31 *150, 172, 179*
4:29 *109, 150, 157, 158*
4:30–31 *148*
4:30 *126, 127, 145, 149, 150, 151, 176*
4:31 *16, 31, 72, 75, 131, 150, 172*
4:32–40 *124*
4:32 *67*
4:33 *127, 128, 166*
4:34–36 *124*
4:34 *123, 124*
4:35–40 *65*
4:35 *69, 70, 121, 124, 129*
4:36 *69, 124, 127, 128, 129*
4:37–39 *105*
4:37 *75, 131, 160, 172, 201, 210*
4:38 *156*
4:39 *69, 121, 124*
4:40 *124, 171*
4:41–5:1 *111*
4:42 *166*
4:44 *111, 112*
5–26 *113, 115*
5–11 *3, 8,* **55**, *57, 77*
5 *103, 115, 126*
5:1–5 *113*
5:1 *79, 126, 127, 128*
5:2–23 *93*
5:3 *115*
5:5 *34*
5:10 *162*
5:15 *72*
5:16 *171*
5:20 *127*
5:21–26 *124*
5:21 *124, 127, 166*
5:22 *127*
5:23 *127, 166*
5:24 *67, 127*
5:25 *103, 127*
5:26 *124, 158, 168, 171*
5:28 *184*
5:29–6:17 *103*
5:29 *71, 72*
5:30 *143, 166*
5:33 *79*
6–11 *67*
6 *103, 189*
6:1 *184*
6:2 *71, 166*
6:3 *73, 74, 127, 128, 171, 172, 173*
6:4–9:7 *56*
6:4–5 *79, 80*
6:4 *160*
6:5–9 *189, 190*
6:5 *80, 157, 158, 160, 161, 162, 189*
6:6–7 *189*
6:6 *159, 183, 189, 190*
6:7–9 *189, 190*
6:8–9 *190*
6:8 *190*
6:9 *190*
6:10–15 *74*
6:10–11 *74*
6:10 *31, 32, 154, 156*
6:12 *72*
6:15 *50*

6:16 *66*
6:17–19 *71*
6:18–25 *81*
6:18 *16, 18, 29, 31, 171, 176*
6:20–24 *29, 68*
6:22 *123*
6:23 *16, 31, 156*
6:24 *166, 171, 194*
6:25 *81, 184*
7–9 *10, 77*
7 *73*
7:1 *155, 156*
7:4 *50*
7:6–11 *105*
7:6 *201*
7:7–11 *65*
7:7–8 *81*
7:7 *201*
7:8 *16, 31, 75, 79, 95, 131, 160, 172*
7:9 *69, 70, 91, 121, 162*
7:11–12 *71*
7:12–8:18 *59*
7:12 *16, 31, 75, 76, 79, 131, 172*
7:13 *16, 31, 73, 160, 171, 172*
7:17 *71, 77, 80, 158*
7:18 *72*
7:19 *123, 124*
7:24 *137*
7:26 *59*
8–10 *2, 3, 5, 6, 14, 24,* **55**, *114, 137, 168, 173, 174, 218, 219*
8 **57**, *68, 80, 81, 88, 104, 119, 218*
8:1–9:8 *57*
8:1–9:7 *104*
8:1–20 *92*
8:1–6 *60*
8:1–5 *218*
8:1–3 *166*
8:1 *16, 31, 58, 59, 60, 61, 62, 63, 64, 71, 73, 76, 104, 143, 166, 172, 176, 184*
8:2–19 *59*
8:2–6 *62,* ***64****, 65, 66, 67, 69, 70, 81, 121*
8:2–5 *60, 62, 119*
8:2–4 *65, 69*
8:2–3 *58, 63*
8:2 *58, 59, 60, 61, 64, 65, 66, 67, 68, 69, 70, 71, 72, 77, 78, 104, 119, 121, 159*
8:3 *63, 64, 65, 66, 67, 68, 69, 71, 75, 78, 117, 119, 120, 121, 166, 188, 208, 218*
8:4 *65, 67, 119*
8:5–9 *61*
8:5–7 *58*
8:5–6 *67*
8:5 *35, 60, 61, 62, 65, 66, 68, 69, 70, 72, 80, 100, 119, 121, 159*
8:6–11 *60, 61*
8:6 *60, 61, 63, 64, 65, 67, 69, 70, 71, 72, 104*
8:7–18 *59*
8:7–17 *72*
8:7–11 *60*
8:7–10 *59, 61, 62, 63, 74, 75*
8:7–9 *61*
8:7 *61, 73, 100, 156*
8:8 *61*
8:9 *61, 73*
8:10 *18, 58, 61, 63, 73, 74, 83*
8:11–18 *59, 62*
8:11–17 *59*
8:11–16 *58*
8:11 *58, 59, 60, 61, 62, 63, 64, 71, 72, 104, 218*
8:12–18 *62*
8:12–17 *75*
8:12–14 *58, 60, 61, 62*
8:12–13 *74, 75*
8:12 *58, 59, 60, 61, 63, 64*
8:13 *73*
8:14–18 *70*
8:14–16 *58, 59, 60, 63, 64, 66, 71, 75*
8:14 *58, 60, 61, 63, 68, 70, 71, 72, 90, 158, 159*
8:15–16 *58, 60*
8:15 *63, 65, 68, 73, 119*
8:16 *65, 66, 69, 75, 171*
8:17–18 *58, 60, 63, 76, 105*
8:17 *59, 60, 62, 63, 68, 70, 71, 72, 75, 77, 80, 135, 158, 196*
8:18–20 *60, 62*
8:18 *16, 31, 58, 59, 60, 61, 63, 64, 68, 71, 72, 73, 75, 77, 78, 79, 131, 132, 133*
8:19–20 *59, 62, 76, 77, 88, 92*
8:19 *58, 60, 63, 64, 72, 199*
8:20 *63, 76, 77, 92, 126*
9:1–10:11 *2, 82*
9 *55, 65, 77,* **78**, *80, 119, 218*
9:1–7 *78, 101*
9:1–6 *22, 77,* **78**, *84, 96*
9:1–3 *83*
9:1–2 *83*
9:1 *44, 77, 79, 83, 127, 128*
9:2 *82, 83*
9:3 *69, 70, 79, 80, 81, 83, 85, 121*
9:4–7 *81*
9:4–6 *78, 79, 81, 82, 84*
9:4–5 *80, 84, 173*
9:4 *71, 77, 79, 80, 83, 156, 158, 196, 197*
9:5 *16, 31, 32, 75, 77, 79, 80, 81, 83, 96, 97, 132, 133*
9:6–7 *95, 168*
9:6 *18, 69, 70, 79, 80, 81, 83, 86, 89, 105, 121, 163, 171, 180*

9:7–10:11 *55, 78, 93, 104*
9:7–24 *24,* ***84****, 93*
9:7–22 *137*
9:7–8 *85, 91, 93*
9:7 *35, 72, 77, 85, 86, 87, 88, 90, 91, 92, 122*
9:8–29 *85*
9:8–21 *85, 86, 93*
9:8 *35, 50, 87, 88, 89, 91*
9:9–10:11 *104*
9:9–29 *101*
9:9–19 *57*
9:9 *85, 90, 92, 99, 101*
9:10 *78, 85, 90, 99*
9:11 *78, 85, 90, 99*
9:12–14 *90*
9:12–13 *97*
9:12 *78, 90, 97*
9:13–14 *78*
9:13 *90, 105, 163*
9:14 *86, 87, 88, 97, 101*
9:15–17 *90*
9:15 *85, 87, 90, 99*
9:16 *88, 89, 90*
9:17–20 *90*
9:17 *91, 99, 123*
9:18–20 *89*
9:18 *78, 85, 86, 89, 90, 94, 98, 101*
9:19–20 *92*
9:19 *35, 50, 87, 90, 91, 101*
9:20 *33, 50, 78, 87, 90, 92, 100*
9:21 *57, 85, 87, 89, 90*
9:22–24 *57, 78, 85, 86, 88, 90, 92, 93, 100*
9:22 *35, 87, 91*
9:23–24 *101*
9:23 *76, 91, 92, 126, 168*
9:24 *91, 121, 122*
9:25–10:11 *84, 85, 87,* ***93***
9:25–10:7 *93*
9:25–29 *57, 84, 86, 87, 93,* ***94***
9:25 *78, 85, 87, 93, 94, 101*
9:26–29 *27, 78, 86, 101*
9:26 *49, 94, 95, 97, 100*
9:27–29 *94*
9:27 *72, 78, 82, 89, 95, 96, 97, 105*
9:28 *22, 94, 97, 98, 156*
9:29 *94, 95, 97, 100*
10 *2, 107*
10:1–11 *85, 93,* ***98***
10:1–9 *101*
10:1–5 *57, 98, 99, 100, 101*
10:1 *33, 78, 92, 99*
10:2 *99*
10:3 *99*
10:4 *85, 90, 99*
10:5 *78, 100*
10:6–7 *78, 100*
10:6 *90*
10:7 *90*
10:8–9 *100*
10:8 *33, 78, 92, 118*
10:10–18 *57*
10:10–11 *93, 98, 101*
10:10 *78, 85, 93, 97, 101, 127*
10:11 *16, 31, 84, 101*
10:12–11:32 *102, 103*
10:12–11:25 *56*
10:12–22 *93,* ***101****, 114, 174, 219*
10:12–13 *102, 103, 160*
10:12 *102, 104, 157, 158, 160, 162*
10:13 *102, 104, 160, 171*
10:14–16 *102*
10:14–15 *102, 105*
10:14 *102, 105*
10:15 *102, 104, 105, 160, 169, 172, 201, 210*
10:16 *79, 80, 84, 101, 102, 104, 105, 106, 159, 163, 164, 165, 168, 169, 190, 206, 218, 219*
10:17–19 *102*
10:17–18 *102*
10:18 *102*
10:19 *98, 102*
10:20–22 *57, 102*
10:20 *102*
10:21–22 *102*
10:21 *123, 124*
10:22 *33, 103, 104, 105*
11:1 *160, 162*
11:2–8 *70*
11:2 *69, 70, 121*
11:4 *118*
11:7 *123, 124*
11:8 *70, 124, 176, 184*
11:9 *16, 31, 74, 210*
11:10–12 *102*
11:13 *127, 129, 157, 158, 160, 161, 162, 176*
11:16 *158, 159*
11:17 *18, 50*
11:18–20 *189*
11:18–19 *159*
11:18 *125, 159, 183*
11:21 *16, 31, 73, 213*
11:22 *160, 161, 162, 176, 184*
11:24 *32*
11:26–32 *152*
11:26–27 *207*
11:26 *123, 124, 200*
11:27 *127*
11:28 *122, 127*
11:29 *154, 156*
11:31 *44*
11:32 *124*
12–26 *3, 57*
12:1–25:16 *8*
12 *16*
12:5 *201*
12:10 *43*
12:11 *201*
12:14 *201*
12:18 *201*
12:20 *155*
12:21 *201*
12:25 *171*
12:26 *201*
12:28 *29, 171*
12:29 *155*
12:30 *120*
13 *107, 135*

13:1–2 *108*
13:3 *122*
13:4 *65, 69, 121, 127, 129, 157, 158, 159, 160, 162*
13:5 *76, 92, 126*
13:6–7 *108*
13:6 *95*
13:7 *122*
13:12–13 *108*
13:14 *122*
13:18 *16, 31, 73, 172*
13:19 *126*
14:1 *35*
14:2 *201*
14:23 *201*
14:24 *201*
14:25 *201*
15:1–11 *107*
15:5 *126, 184*
15:7–10 *158*
15:7 *158*
15:9 *125, 126, 159*
15:15 *72, 95*
15:16 *154*
15:17 *126*
15:18 *163*
15:20 *201*
16:2 *201*
16:3 *72, 166*
16:6 *201*
16:7 *201*
16:11 *201*
16:12 *72*
16:15 *201*
16:16 *201*
16:19 *125*
16:20 *143, 166*
17:8 *191, 201*
17:10 *201*
17:12 *127*
17:14 *155*
17:15 *201*
17:17 *158, 159*
17:19–20 *159*
17:19 *166*
18:5 *201*
18:6 *201*
18:9 *155*
18:19 *127*
18:21 *69, 121, 158*
19 *107*
19:1 *155*
19:4 *166*
19:5 *166*
19:8 *16, 31*
19:9 *160, 161, 162, 184*
19:10 *136*
20:1 *155*
20:3 *22, 127, 128, 129, 158*
20:8 *22, 158, 159*
20:10 *155*
20:16 *166*
20:18 *207*
20:19 *67, 155*
21:1 *136*
21:5 *201*
21:8 *95*
21:10 *147, 155*
21:11 *147*
21:13 *147*
21:20 *126, 127*
22 *107*
22:4 *132*
22:7 *171*
23:3 *40*
23:6 *127, 160, 172*
23:7 *170*
23:17 *201*
24:9 *72*
24:18 *72, 95*
24:19 *72*
24:22 *72*
25:1 *80*
25:7 *132*
25:17 *72*
25:19 *43, 72, 137*
26 *16, 28*
26:1 *154*
26:2 *201*
26:3 *16, 31, 200*
26:9 *74, 156*
26:10 *103*
26:12 *155*
26:13 *72, 184*
26:14 *76, 126*
26:15 *16, 31, 74*
26:16 *157, 158, 159, 183*
26:17 *76, 126, 200*
26:18 *200*
27–28 *111*
27 *1, 108, 153*
27:1–8 *108*
27:1 *184*
27:3 *74*
27:9 *127, 128, 200*
27:10 *126*
28 *1, 68, 108, 126, 129, 132, 138, 150, 152, 153, 176, 201, 219*
28:1–14 *130*
28:1 *126, 130*
28:2 *126, 130*
28:4 *171*
28:7 *130*
28:8 *130*
28:9 *79*
28:11 *16, 31, 130, 171*
28:12 *130*
28:13 *127, 130*
28:15 *126, 130*
28:18 *171*
28:24 *130*
28:25 *130*
28:28 *130, 159*
28:31 *130*
28:32 *130*
28:33 *122*
28:34 *130*
28:36 *119, 122*
28:41 *147*
28:45–69 *153*
28:45–48 *153*
28:45 *126, 130*
28:46 *210*
28:47 *130, 153*
28:48 *130*
28:52 *130*
28:53 *130*
28:55 *130*
28:59 *210*
28:62 *33, 126, 130, 172*
28:63 *146, 171, 172*

28:64 *122*
28:65 *68, 69, 125, 130, 158, 159*
28:66 *166*
28:67 *125, 130*
28:68 *111*
28:69 ***110**, 112, 113, 140*
29–34 *16*
29–32 *111*
29–30 *3, 6, 24, 55, **107**, 219*
29 *2, 4, 5, 68, 107, 140, 201, 205, 219*
29:1–24 *111*
29:1–20 *108, 183, 205*
29:1–14 *108*
29:1–8 *110, **117**, 134, 166, 167*
29:1–7 *110, 117*
29:1–5 *65, 121*
29:1–3 *117, 118, 120, 124*
29:1–2 *118, 120*
29:1 *113, 115, 117, 120, 123, 128, 131, 134*
29:2 *120, 123, 128, 131*
29:3–5 *119*
29:3 *20, 68, 69, 70, 76, 110, 117, 118, 119, 120, 121, 122, 123, 125, 126, 128, 129, 130, 131, 133, 134, 140, 145, 158, 159, 162, 167, 168, 188, 219*
29:4–6 *118, 120*
29:4–5 *118, 119*
29:4 *65, 117, 119*
29:5 *65, 70, 117, 119, 120, 121, 122, 131, 133*
29:6–8 *118*
29:6 *118*
29:8–14 *110*
29:8 *111, 113, 117, 124, 130, 140*
29:9–28 ***131**, 140*
29:9–14 *113, 114, **131**, 134, 140*
29:9 *109, 110, 115, 117, 131, 132, 133*
29:10 *131*
29:11 *110, 111, 113, 115, 131, 132*
29:12 *16, 31, 32, 110, 115, 131, 132, 133*
29:13–14 *115*
29:13 *111, 113, 131, 132*
29:14 *109, 110, 115, 131, 133*
29:15–28 *140*
29:15–27 *1, 2, 107, 108, 205*
29:15–20 ***133***
29:15–18 *110*
29:15 *117, 134*
29:16 *124*
29:17–27 *145*
29:17–20 *109*
29:17–18 *134, 163*
29:17 *110, 134, 136, 137, 138, 158, 159, 205*
29:18–20 *134*
29:18 *68, 129, 134, 135, 137, 138, 140, 158, 159*
29:19–20 *139*
29:19 *50, 135, 137*
29:20–27 *153*
29:20 *108, 111, 113, 132, 137, 138, 140*
29:21–30:20 *164*
29:21–30:10 *109, 183*
29:21–28 *151*
29:21–27 *108, **137**, 139, 152*
29:21 *108, 138*
29:22 *87, 138*
29:23 *50, 138*
29:24 *111, 113*
29:25–28 *98*
29:25 *122, 205*
29:26–27 *138*
29:26 *50, 150, 152*
29:27 *35, 50, 87, 137*
29:28 *130, **139**, 151, 152, 182, 183, 192, 193, 220*
30 *2, 4, 5, 13, 15, 16, 68, 107, 126, 166, 180, 181, 184, 189, 195, 196, 197, 198, 220*
30:1–14 *152, 165, 186, 188, 189, 202, 205, 209, 212, 213, 214, 220*
30:1–10 *2, 10, 16, 108, 110, 138, **140**, 182, 183, 184, 185, 186, 187, 188, 190, 193, 195, 198, 200, 206, 207, 210, 212, 213, 219, 220*
30:1–6 *155*
30:1–3 *144, 156*
30:1–2 *150, 155, 165*
30:1 *140, 141, 142, 143, 145, 147, 148, 150, 151, 152, 153, 154, 155, 156, 157, 159, 160, 162, 173, 176, 183, 198, 205, 212, 219*
30:2–3 *148*
30:2 *110, 126, 129, 141, 142, 143, 145, 146, 147, 148, 149, 150, 151, 152, 154, 156, 157, 158, 159, 160, 162, 183, 184, 185, 199, 205, 212*
30:3–7 *143*
30:3–5 *153, 165*
30:3 *141, 142, 145, 146, 147, 148, 149, 172*
30:4 *141, 142, 148, 149, 183*
30:5 *141, 142, 143, 149, 156, 157, 170, 171, 172, 212*
30:6–9 *210*

30:6–8 *144, 150, 157, 162, 165, 168, 178, 219*
30:6 *84, 105, 106, 114, 130, 141, 142, 143, 144, 148, 157, 158, 159, 160, 161, 162, 163, 164, 165, 166, 167, 168, 169, 171, 172, 173, 177, 178, 181, 183, 185, 187, 188, 189, 190, 192, 196, 198, 200, 205, 206, 209, 210, 211, 212, 219, 220, 221*
30:7 *108, 141, 142, 143, 165, 166, 177*
30:8 *110, 126, 130, 140, 141, 142, 143, 144, 145, 146, 148, 149, 152, 157, 159, 161, 165, 166, 167, 177, 178, 183, 184, 185, 186, 190, 199, 212*
30:9–11 *185*
30:9–10 *155, 219, 220*
30:9 *141, 142, 145, 146, 147, 148, 154, 155, 156, 165, 166, 170, 171, 186, 190, 210*
30:10–11 *186*
30:10 *108, 126, 129, 140, 142, 145, 146, 148, 149, 152, 154, 155, 156, 157, 158, 159, 160, 162, 165, 183, 184, 185, 186, 205, 212*
30:11–20 *108, 110, 183, 185*
30:11–14 *3, 4, 108, 110, 125, 139, 140, 145, 151,* **182**, *200, 204, 205, 206, 214, 220*
30:11 *108, 110, 156, 182, 183, 184, 185, 186, 187, 189, 191, 192, 196, 199, 220*
30:12–13 *195*
30:12 *130, 140, 183, 184, 188, 192, 193*
30:13 *130, 140, 183, 184, 188, 192, 193*
30:14 *130, 139, 140, 159, 183, 184, 186, 187, 188, 189, 190, 192, 193, 196, 197, 198, 205, 214*
30:15–20 *3, 4, 15, 29, 119, 145, 151, 166, 182,* **198**
30:15–19 *29*
30:15 *68, 123, 124, 166, 199, 200, 207, 208, 210, 211*
30:16 *73, 110, 143, 160, 161, 162, 166, 172, 199, 207, 210, 211, 212*
30:17–18 *205, 214*
30:17 *134, 158, 159, 205*
30:18 *44, 110, 172, 199, 205*
30:19–20 *212*
30:19 *29, 76, 107, 110, 116, 124, 143, 166, 179, 198, 199, 201, 207, 209, 210, 211, 212, 214*
30:20 *16, 31, 32, 126, 160, 162, 166, 207, 208, 210, 211, 212, 213, 214*
31–34 *2, 5, 13, 15, 16, 17, 40*
31 *24, 109*
31:1–2 *50*
31:1 *8, 202*
31:3 *44*
31:5 *184*
31:6 *109*
31:7 *16, 31, 50*
31:9–13 *7*
31:11 *126, 201*
31:13 *120*
31:16–29 *145*
31:16–21 *114*
31:16–17 *1*
31:17 *50*
31:19 *103*
31:20 *16, 74, 155, 156*
31:21 *16, 154, 156, 210*
31:23 *16, 31, 156*
31:27–29 *1*
31:27 *163*
31:28 *126, 179*
31:29 *114*
31:30 *126*
32 *109, 120*
32:1–43 *1*
32:1 *201*
32:4 *91*
32:7 *72*
32:8 *45, 67*
32:9 *45*
32:17 *122*
32:18 *72*
32:20 *91*
32:36 *155*
32:39 *166, 208*
32:42 *147*
32:44 *126*
32:46 *76, 159*
32:47 *68, 166, 207*
32:49 *123*
32:51–52 *23*
33:1 *111, 112*
33:6 *166*
33:13–14 *74*
33:16 *74*
33:28 *74*
34 *24, 50*
34:1–8 *50*
34:1–4 *43*
34:1 *124*
34:4 *16, 32, 124, 169, 210*
34:6 *118*
34:10 *122*
34:12 *13*

**Joshua**
1 *203*
1:4 *32*
2:9–11 *43*
2:11 *22*
4:24 *43*
5:1 *22, 43*
7 *137*
7:7 *49*
7:9 *98*
13 *43*
13:1 *203*
14 *8*
15:63 *203*
16:10 *203*
23 *109*
23:16 *203*
24 *202, 204, 208*
24:16–18 *202*
24:19–20 *203*
24:21 *202*
24:24 *202*

**Judges**
5:4 *44*
6:22 *49*
11:17 *40*
15:18–19 *98*
16:28–30 *98*
16:28 *49*

**1 Samuel**
12:20–25 *109*

**2 Samuel**
1:26 *191*
7:18–29 *49, 98*
13:2 *191*
17:14 *98*

**1 Kings**
2:26 *49*
3:9 *129*
8:46–53 *170*
8:53 *49*
18:36–38 *98*

**2 Kings**
23:25–27 *9*

**2 Chronicles**
6:42 *96*

**Nehemiah**
1:9 *147*
4:6–22 *98*
9:21 *65*

**Psalms**
9:2 *191*
25:7 *96*
26:7 *191*
40:6 *191*
78 *65*
106 *65*
132:1 *96*
136:23 *96*
139:6 *191*

**Proverbs**
6:17 *125*
10:10 *125*
21:4 *125*
27:20 *125*
30:17 *125*
30:18 *191*

**Ecclesiastes**
2:10 *125*

**Isaiah**
6:10 *121, 131*
7 *22*
19:14 *119*
29:9–10 *119*
32:3 *131*
51:3 *74*
53 *24*

**Jeremiah**
1:17–19 *121*
2:2 *65, 96*
4:4 *105*
5:21 *121*
6:10 *105*
9:25 *105*
23:3 *147*
30–33 *150*
31 *144, 181*
31:31–34 *170*
31:31–33 *188*
31:33 *125*
32:17 *191, 192*
32:27 *192*

**Ezekiel**
3:4–11 *121*
11:19–20 *164*
18 *164*
20 *65*
28:13–14 *74*
28:15–17 *74*
33:19 *67*
36 *144, 164*
36:24–31 *144*
36:26–27 *164*
36:35 *74*
40:4 *121*
44:5 *121*
44:7 *105*
44:9 *105*

**Daniel**
8:24 *191*
11:4 *113*
11:36 *191*

**Hosea**
6:7 *74*
9:10 *65*

**Joel**
2:3 *74*

**Jonah**
1:14–15 *98*

**Zephaniah**
3:20 *147*

**Zechariah**
8:6 *192*

**Matthew**
4:4 *68*

**Mark**
3:1–6 *201*

**Romans**
2:15 *195*
2:25–29 *178, 195*
2:29 *196*
3:3–4 *6, 215*
3:9 *81*
5:6–8 *84*
6:17 *195*
10 ***194***, *220*
10:3 *196*
10:4 *198*
10:5–13 *195*
10:5–7 *194*
10:5 *194*
10:6–8 *195*
10:6–7 *195*
10:6 *194, 195, 196*
10:7 *196*
10:8 *176*
10:9 *197*
10:10 *197*
10:16 *176*

**Galatians**
3:19–25 *177*

**Colossians**
2:11–14 *178, 195*
2:11 *221*

**Hebrews**
12:15 *136*

# Paternoster Biblical Monographs

*(All titles uniform with this volume)*

Joseph Abraham

**Eve: Accused or Acquitted?**

*A Reconsideration of Feminist Readings of the Creation Narrative Texts in Genesis 1–3*

Two contrary views dominate contemporary feminist biblical scholarship. One finds in the Bible an unequivocal equality between the sexes from the very creation of humanity, whilst the other sees the biblical text as irredeemably patriarchal and androcentric. Dr. Abraham enters into dialogue with both camps as well as introducing his own method of approach. An invaluable tool for anyone who is interested in this contemporary debate.

*2002 / ISBN 0-85364-971-5 / xxiv + 272pp*

Paul Barker

**The Triumph of Grace in Deuteronomy**

This book is a textual and theological analysis of the interaction between the sin and faithlessness of Israel and the grace of Yahweh in response, looking especially at Deuteronomy chapters 1–3, 8–10 and 29–30. The author argues that the grace of Yahweh is determinative for the ongoing relationship between Yahweh and Israel and that Deuteronomy anticipates and fully expects Israel to be faithless.

*2004 / ISBN 1-84227-226-8 / xxii + 270pp*

Jonathan F. Bayes

**The Weakness of the Law**

*God's Law and the Christian in New Testament Perspective*

A study of the four New Testament books which refer to the law as weak (Acts, Romans, Galatians, Hebrews) leads to a defence of the third use in the Reformed debate about the law in the life of the believer.

*2000 / ISBN 0-85364-957-X / xii + 244pp*

Mark Bonnington

**The Antioch Episode of Galatians 2:11-14 in Historical and Cultural Context**

The Galatians 2 'incident' in Antioch over table-fellowship suggests significant disagreement between the leading apostles. This book analyses the background to the disagreement by locating the incident within the dynamics of social interaction between Jews and Gentiles. It proposes a new way of understanding the relationship between the individuals and issues involved.

*2004 / ISBN 1-84227-050-8 / approx. 350pp*

May 2004

Mark Bredin
**Jesus, Revolutionary of Peace**
*A Nonviolent Christology in the Book of Revelation*
This book aims to demonstrate that the figure of Jesus in the Book of Revelation can best be understood as an active nonviolent revolutionary.
*2003 / ISBN 1-84227-153-9 / xviii + 262pp*

Daniel J-S Chae
**Paul as Apostle to the Gentiles**
*His Apostolic Self-awareness and its Influence on the Soteriological Argument in Romans*
Opposing 'the post-Holocaust interpretation of Romans', Daniel Chae competently demonstrates that Paul argues for the equality of Jew and Gentile in Romans. Chae's fresh exegetical interpretation is academically outstanding and spiritually encouraging.
*1997 / ISBN 0-85364-829-8 / xiv + 378pp*

Luke L. Cheung
**The Genre, Composition and Hermeneutics of the Epistle of James**
The present work examines the employment of the wisdom genre with a certain compositional structure and the interpretation of the law through the Jesus' tradition of the double love command by the author of the Epistle of James to serve his purpose in promoting perfection and warning against doubleness among the eschatologically renewed people of God in the Diaspora.
*2003 / ISBN 1-84227-062-1 / xvi + 372pp*

Andrew C. Clark
**Parallel Lives**
*The Relation of Paul to the Apostles in the Lucan Perspective*
This study of the Peter-Paul parallels in Acts argues that their purpose was to emphasize the themes of continuity in salvation history and the unity of the Jewish and Gentile missions. New light is shed on Luke's literary techniques, partly through a comparison with Plutarch.
*2001 / 1-84227-035-4 / xviii + 386pp*

May 2004

Andrew D. Clarke

**Secular and Christian Leadership in Corinth**

*A Socio-Historical and Exegetical Study of 1 Corinthians 1–6*

This volume is an investigation into the leadership structures and dynamics of first-century Roman Corinth. These are compared with the practice of leadership in the Corinthian Christian community which are reflected in 1 Corinthians 1–6, and contrasted with Paul's own principles of Christian leadership.

*2004 / ISBN 1-84227-229-2 / xii + 188pp*

Stephen Finamore

**God, Order and Chaos**

*René Girard and the Apocalypse*

Readers are often disturbed by the images of destruction in the book of Revelation and unsure why they are unleashed after the exaltation of Jesus. This book examines past approaches to these texts and uses René Girard's theories to revive some old ideas and propose some new ones.

*2004 / ISBN 1-84227-197-0 / approx. 344pp*

Scott J. Hafemann

**Suffering and Ministry in the Spirit**

*Paul's Defence of His Ministry in II Corinthians 2:14–3:3*

Shedding new light on the way Paul defended his apostleship, the author offers a careful, detailed study of 2 Corinthians 2:14–3:3 linked with other key passages throughout 1 and 2 Corinthians. Demonstrating the unity and coherence of Paul's argument in this passage, the author shows that Paul's suffering served as the vehicle for revealing God's power and glory through the Spirit.

*2000 / ISBN 0-85364-967-7 / xiv + 262pp*

Douglas S. McComiskey

**Lukan Theology in the Light of the Gospel's Literary Structure**

Luke's Gospel was purposefully written with theology embedded in its patterned literary structure. A critical analysis of this cyclical structure provides new windows into Luke's interpretation of the individual pericopes comprising the Gospel and illuminates several of his theological interests.

*2004 / ISBN 1-84227-148-2 / approx. 400pp*

Stephen Motyer

**Your Father the Devil?**

*A New Approach to John and 'The Jews'*

Who are 'the Jews' in John's Gospel? Defending John against the charge of anti-semitism, Motyer argues that, far from demonizing the Jews, the Gospel seeks to present Jesus as 'Good News for Jews' in a late first century setting.

*1997 / ISBN 0-85364-832-8 / xiv + 260pp*

Esther Ng

**Reconstructing Christian Origins?**

*The Feminist Theology of Elizabeth Schüssler Fiorenza: An Evaluation*

In a detailed evaluation, the author challenges Elizabeth Schüssler Fiorenza's reconstruction of early Christian origins and her underlying presuppositions. The author also presents her own views on women's roles both then and now.

*2002 / ISBN 1-84227-055-9 / xxiv + 468pp*

Robin Parry

**Old Testament Story and Christian Ethics**

*The Rape of Dinah as a Case Study*

What is the role of story in ethics and, more particularly, what is the role of Old Testament story in Christian ethics? This book, drawing on the work of contemporary philosophers, argues that narrative is crucial in the ethical shaping of people and, drawing on the work of contemporary Old Testament scholars, that story plays a key role in Old Testament ethics. Parry then argues that when situated in canonical context Old Testament stories can be reappropriated by Christian readers in their own ethical formation. The shocking story of the rape of Dinah and the massacre of the Shechemites provides a fascinating case study for exploring the parameters within which Christian ethical appropriations of Old Testament stories can live.

*2004 / ISBN 1-84227-210-1 / approx. 350pp*

David Powys

**'Hell': A Hard Look at a Hard Question**

*The Fate of the Unrighteous in New Testament Thought*

This comprehensive treatment seeks to unlock the original meaning of terms and phrases long thought to support the traditional doctrine of hell. It concludes that there is an alternative – one which is more biblical, and which can positively revive the rationale for Christian mission.

*1997 / ISBN 0-85364-831-X / xxii + 478pp*

May 2004

Rosalind Selby

**The Comical Doctrine**

*Can a Gospel Convey Truth?*

This book argues that the Gospel breaks through postmodernity's critique of truth and the referential possibilities of textuality and its gift of grace. With a rigorous, philosophical challenge to modernist and postmodernist assumptions, it offers an alternative epistemology to all who would still read with faith *and* with academic credibility.

*2004 / ISBN 1-84227-212-8 approx. 350pp*

Kevin Walton

**Thou Traveller Unknown**

*The Presence and Absence of God in the Jacob Narrative*

The author offers a fresh reading of the story of Jacob in the book of Genesis through the paradox of divine presence and absence. The work also seeks to make a contribution to Pentateuchal studies by bringing together a close reading of the final text with historical critical insights, doing justice to the text's historical depth, final form and canonical status.

*2003 / ISBN 1-84227-059-1 / xvi + 238pp*

Alistair Wilson

**When Will These Things Happen?**

*A Study of Jesus as Judge in Matthew 21–25*

This study seeks to allow Matthew's carefully constructed presentation of Jesus to be given full weight in the modern evaluation of Jesus' eschatology. Careful analysis of the text of Matthew 21–25 reveals Jesus to be standing firmly in the Jewish prophetic and wisdom traditions as he proclaims and enacts imminent judgement on the Jewish authorities then boldly claims the central role in the final and universal judgement.

*2004 / ISBN 1-84227-146-6 / xvi + 292pp*

Lindsay Wilson

**Joseph Wise and Otherwise**

*The Intersection of Covenant and Wisdom in Genesis 37–50*

This book offers a careful literary reading of Genesis 37–50 that argues that the Joseph story contains both strong covenant themes and many wisdom-like elements. The connections between the two helps to explore how covenant and wisdom might intersect in an integrated biblical theology.

*2004 / ISBN 1-84227-140-7 approx. 350pp*

May 2004

Stephen I. Wright

**The Voice of Jesus**

*Studies in the Interpretation of Six Gospel Parables*

This literary study considers how the 'voice' of Jesus has been heard in different periods of parable interpretation, and how the categories of figure and trope may help us towards a sensitive reading of the parables today.

*2000 / ISBN 0-85364-975-8 / xiv + 280pp*

May 2004

## Paternoster Theological Monographs

*(All titles uniform with this volume)*

Emil Bartos

**Deification in Eastern Orthodox Theology**

*An Evaluation and Critique of the Theology of Dumitru Staniloae*

Bartos studies a fundamental yet neglected aspect of Orthodox theology: deification. By examining the doctrines of anthropology, christology, soteriology and ecclesiology as they relate to deification, he provides an important contribution to contemporary dialogue between Eastern and Western theologians.

*1999 / ISBN 0-85364-956-1 / xii + 370pp*

James Bruce

**Prophecy, Miracles, Angels *and* Heavenly Light?**

*The Eschatology, Pneumatology and Missiology of Adomnán's* Life of Columba

This book surveys approaches to the marvellous in hagiography, providing the first critique of Plummer's hypothesis of Irish saga origin. It then analyses the uniquely systematized phenomena in the *Life of Columba* from Adomnán's seventh-century theological perspective, identifying the coming of the eschatological Kingdom as the key to understanding.

*2004 / ISBN 1-84227-227-6 / approx. 400pp*

Colin J. Bulley

**The Priesthood of Some Believers**

*Developments from the General to the Special Priesthood in the Christian Literature of the First Three Centuries*

The first in-depth treatment of early Christian texts on the priesthood of all believers shows that the developing priesthood of the ordained related closely to the division between laity and clergy and had deleterious effects on the practice of the general priesthood.

*2000 / ISBN 1-84227-034-6 / xii + 336pp*

May 2004

Iain D. Campbell

**Fixing the Indemnity**

*The Life and Work of George Adam Smith*

When Old Testament scholar George Adam Smith (1856–1942) delivered the Lyman Beecher lectures at Yale University in 1899 he confidently declared that 'modern criticism has won its war against traditional theories. It only remains to fix the amount of the indemnity.' In this biography, Iain D. Campbell assesses Smith's critical approach to the Old Testament and evaluates its consequences, showing that Smith's life and work still raises questions about the relationship between biblical scholarship and evangelical faith.

*2004 / ISBN 1-84227-228-4 / approx. 276pp*

Sylvia W. Collinson

**Making Disciples**

*The Significance of Jesus' Educational Strategy for Today's Church*

This study examines the biblical practice of discipling, formulates a definition, and makes comparisons with modern models of education. A recommendation is made for greater attention to its practice today.

*2004 / ISBN 1-84227-116-4 / approx. 320pp*

Stephen M. Dunning

**The Crisis and the Quest**

*A Kierkegaardian Reading of Charles Williams*

Employing Kierkegaardian categories and analysis, this study investigates both the central crisis in Charles Williams's authorship between hermetism and Christianity (Kierkegaard's Religions A and B), and the quest to resolve this crisis, a quest that ultimately presses the bounds of orthodoxy.

*2000 / ISBN 0-85364-985-5 / xxiv + 254pp*

Keith Ferdinando

**The Triumph of Christ in African Perspective**

*A Study of Demonology and Redemption in the African Context*

The book explores the implications of the gospel for traditional African fears of occult aggression. It analyses such traditional approaches to suffering and biblical responses to fears of demonic evil, concluding with an evaluation of African beliefs from the perspective of the gospel.

*1999 / ISBN 0-85364-830-1 / xviii + 450pp*

Andrew Goddard

**Living the Word, Resisting the World**

*The Life and Thought of Jacques Ellul*

This work offers a definitive study of both the life and thought of the French Reformed thinker Jacques Ellul (1912-1994). It will prove an indispensable resource for those interested in this influential theologian and sociologist and for Christian ethics and political thought generally.

*2002 / ISBN 1-84227-053-2 / xxiv + 378pp*

Ruth Gouldbourne

**The Flesh and the Feminine**

*Gender and Theology in the Writings of Caspar Schwenckfeld*

Caspar Schwenckfeld and his movement exemplify one of the radical communities of the sixteenth century. Challenging theological and liturgical norms, they also found themselves challenging social and particularly gender assumptions. In this book, the issues of the relationship between radical theology and the understanding of gender are considered.

*2004 / ISBN 1-84227-048-6 / approx. 304pp*

Roger Hitching

**The Church and Deaf People**

*A Study of Identity, Communication and Relationships with Special Reference to the Ecclesiology of Jürgen Moltmann*

In *The Church and Deaf People* Roger Hitching sensitively examines the history and present experience of deaf people and finds similarities between aspects of sign language and Moltmann's theological method that 'open up' new ways of understanding theological concepts.

*2003 / ISBN 1-84227-222-5 / xxii + 236pp*

John G. Kelly

**One God, One People**

*The Differentiated Unity of the People of God in the Theology of Jürgen Moltmann*

The author expounds and critiques Moltmann's doctrine of God and highlights the systematic connections between it and Moltmann's influential discussion of Israel. He then proposes a fresh approach to Jewish-Christian relations building on Moltmann's work using insights from Habermas and Rawls.

*2004 / ISBN 0-85346-969-3 / approx. 350pp*

Mark F.W. Lovatt

**Confronting the Will-to-Power**

*A Reconsideration of the Theology of Reinhold Niebuhr*

*Confronting the Will-to-Power* is an analysis of the theology of Reinhold Niebuhr, arguing that his work is an attempt to identify, and provide a practical theological answer to, the existence and nature of human evil.

*2001 / ISBN 1-84227-054-0 / xviii + 216pp*

Neil B. MacDonald

**Karl Barth and the Strange New World within the Bible**

*Barth, Wittgenstein, and the Metadilemmas of the Enlightenment*

Barth's discovery of the strange new world within the Bible is examined in the context of Kant, Hume, Overbeck, and, most importantly, Wittgenstein. MacDonald covers some fundamental issues in theology today: epistemology, the final form of the text and biblical truth-claims.

*2000 / ISBN 0-85364-970-7 / xxvi + 374pp*

Gillian McCulloch

**The Deconstruction of Dualism in Theology**

*With Reference to Ecofeminist Theology and New Age Spirituality*

This book challenges eco-theological anti-dualism in Christian theology, arguing that dualism has a twofold function in Christian religious discourse. Firstly, it enables us to express the discontinuities and divisions that are part of the process of reality. Secondly, dualistic language allows us to express the mysteries of divine transcendence/immanence and the survival of the soul without collapsing into monism and materialism, both of which are problematic for Christian epistemology.

*2002 / ISBN 1-84227-044-3 / xii + 282pp*

Leslie McCurdy

**Attributes and Atonement**

*The Holy Love of God in the Theology of P.T. Forsyth*

*Attributes and Atonement* is an intriguing full-length study of P.T. Forsyth's doctrine of the cross as it relates particularly to God's holy love. It includes an unparalleled bibliography of both primary and secondary material relating to Forsyth.

*1999 / ISBN 0-85364-833-6 / xiv + 328pp*

Nozomu Miyahira

**Towards a Theology of the Concord of God**

*A Japanese Perspective on the Trinity*

This book introduces a new Japanese theology and a unique Trinitarian formula based on the Japanese intellectual climate: three betweennesses and one concord. It also presents a new interpretation of the Trinity, a co-subordinationism, which is in line with orthodox Trinitarianism; each single person of the Trinity is eternally and equally subordinate (or serviceable) to the other persons, so that they retain the mutual dynamic equality.

*2000 / ISBN 0-85364-863-8 / xiv + 256pp*

Eddy José Muskus

**The Origins and Early Development of Liberation Theology in Latin America**

*With Particular Reference to Gustavo Gutiérrez*

This work challenges the fundamental premise of Liberation Theology, 'opting for the poor', and its claim that Christ is found in them. It also argues that Liberation Theology emerged as a direct result of the failure of the Roman Catholic Church in Latin America.

*2002 / ISBN 0-85364-974-X / xiv + 296pp*

Anna Robbins

**Methods in the Madness**

*Diversity in Twentieth-Century Christian Social Ethics*

The author compares the ethical methods of Walter Rauschenbusch, Reinhold Niebuhr and others. She argues that unless Christians are clear about the ways that theology and philosophy are expressed practically they may lose the ability to discuss social ethics across contexts, let alone reach effective agreements.

*2004 / ISBN 1-84227-211-X / xvi + 320pp*

Ed Rybarczyk

**Beyond Salvation**

*Eastern Orthodoxy and Classical Pentecostalism on becoming like Christ*

At first glance eastern Orthodoxy and Classical Pentecostalism seem quite distinct. This groundbreaking study shows that they share much in common, especially as it concerns the experiential elements of following Christ. Both traditions assert that authentic Christianity transcends the wooden categories of modernism.

*2003 / ISBN 1-84227-144-X / xii + 356pp*

Signe Sandsmark

**Is World View Neutral Education Possible and Desirable?**

*A Christian Response to Liberal Arguments*

(Published jointly with The Stapleford Centre)

This book discusses reasons for belief in world view neutrality, and argues that 'neutral' education will have a hidden, but strong world view influence. It discusses the place for Christian education in the common school.

*2000 / ISBN 0-85364-973-1 / xiv + 182pp*

Hazel Sherman

**Reading Zechariah**

*The Allegorical Tradition of Biblical Interpretation through the Commentaries of Didymus the Blind and Theodore of Mopsuestia*

A close reading of the commentary on Zechariah by Didymus the Blind alongside that of Theodore of Mopsuestia suggests that popular categorising of Antiochene and Alexandrian biblical exegesis as 'historical' or 'allegorical' is inadequate and misleading.

*2004 / ISBN 1-84227-213-6 / approx. 280pp*

Andrew Sloane

**On Being a Christian in the Academy**

*Nicholas Wolterstorff and the Practice of Christian Scholarship*

An exposition and critical appraisal of Nicholas Wolterstorff's epistemology in the light of the philosophy of science, and an application of his thought to the practice of Christian scholarship.

*2003 / ISBN 1-84227-058-3 / xvi + 274pp*

Daniel Strange

**The Possibility of Salvation Among the Unevangelised**

*An Analysis of Inclusivism in Recent Evangelical Theology*

For evangelical theologians the 'fate of the unevangelised' impinges upon fundamental tenets of evangelical identity. The position known as 'inclusivism', defined by the belief that the unevangelised can be ontologically saved by Christ whilst being epistemologically unaware of him, has been defended most vigorously by the Canadian evangelical Clark H. Pinnock. Through a detailed analysis and critique of Pinnock's work, this book examines a cluster of issues surrounding the unevangelised and its implications for christology, soteriology and the doctrine of revelation.

*2002 / ISBN 1-84227-047-8 / xviii + 362pp*

G. Michael Thomas

**The Extent of the Atonement**

*A Dilemma for Reformed Theology from Calvin to the Consensus*

This is a study of the way Reformed theology addressed the question, 'Did Christ die for all, or for the elect only?', commencing with John Calvin, and including debates with Lutheranism, the Synod of Dort and the teaching of Moïse Amyraut.

*1997 / ISBN 0-85364-828-X / x + 278pp*

Mark D. Thompson

**A Sure Ground on which to Stand**

*The Relation of Authority and Interpretive Method in Luther's Approach to Scripture*

The best interpreter of Luther is Luther himself. Unfortunately many modern studies have superimposed contemporary agendas upon this sixteenth-century Reformer's writings. This fresh study examines Luther's own words to find an explanation for his robust confidence in the Scriptures, a confidence that generated the famous 'stand' at Worms in 1521.

*2004 / ISBN 1-84227-145-8 / xvi + 322pp*

Graham Tomlin

**The Power of the Cross**

*Theology and the Death of Christ in Paul, Luther and Pascal*

This book explores the theology of the cross in St Paul, Luther and Pascal. It offers new perspectives on the theology of each, and some implications for the nature of power, apologetics, theology and church life in a postmodern context.

*1999 / ISBN 0-85364-984-7 / xiv + 344pp*

Graham J. Watts

**Revelation and the Spirit**

*A Comparative Study of the Relationship between the Doctrine of Revelation and Pneumatology in the Theology of Eberhard Jüngel and of Wolfhart Pannenberg*

The relationship between revelation and pneumatology is relatively unexplored. This approach offers a fresh angle on two important twentieth century theologians and raises pneumatological questions which are theologically crucial and relevant to mission in a post modern culture.

*2004 / ISBN 1-84227-104-0 / xxii + 232pp*